the Pajama Diaries

Having it all...
and no time to do it

TJStudios
LTD

Printed by Laserwave Graphics - www.Laserwave.com

The Pajama Diaries is distributed internationally by King Features Syndicate, Inc. For information, write King Features Syndicate, Inc., 300 W. 57th Street, New York, NY 10019

ISBN: 978-0-9833272-3-3

Library of Congress Control Number: 2013945423

See www.pajamadiaries.com for the latest news, daily strips, and merchandise. You can also find the "The Pajama Diaries" page on Facebook.

If you would like your local paper to carry *The Pajama Diaries*, please contact the newspaper editor and request that they add it to their lineup.

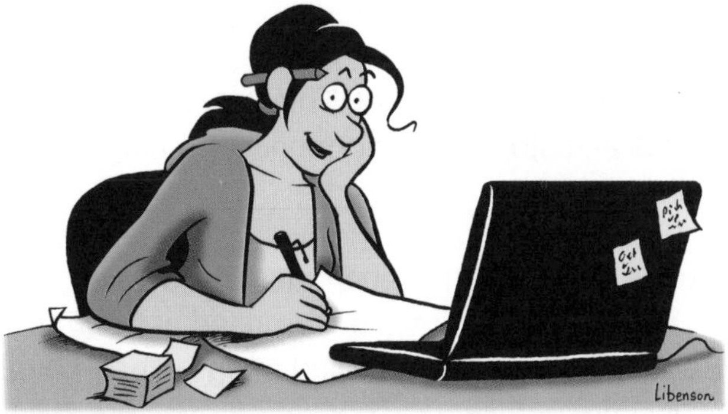
Libenson

Dedicated to my family, friends, and all my readers. This enviable job wouldn't be possible without your support.

I created *The Pajama Diaries* in 2004 as a way of connecting with other parents of young kids. We were all leading these crazy, harried lives, and this was my way of reaching out.

Back then, my kids were 1 and 3. It's been a decade, and now I have a preteen and a teenager. As the strip has evolved, the characters have aged up as well. This new reality is reflected in recent plots and story lines: hormones, training bras, boys, and Bat Mitzvahs.

The cartoon is about Jill's life and outlook. However, reflecting on the last few years of strips, I'm surprised at how affected Jill and Rob are by their kids' coming of age. Then I thought about my own preteen years. Those memories are still vivid. Nowadays, I can't remember people's names a moment after they tell me, but I can recall what I was wearing at my first 6th grade dance.

Sure, we still see Jill and Rob getting sucked into the vortex of their busy lives. We watch Jill and her friends try to balance everything. But there's a new vibe. As someone recently said, "I can tell your own kids are becoming teens...I detect a new snarkiness in Jill."

Some things are hard to hide. And if you have preteen kids of your own (or are past it and can now relish in someone else's experience), you've probably reached the same conclusion...

...humor is a great coping mechanism.

-Terri Libenson, 2013

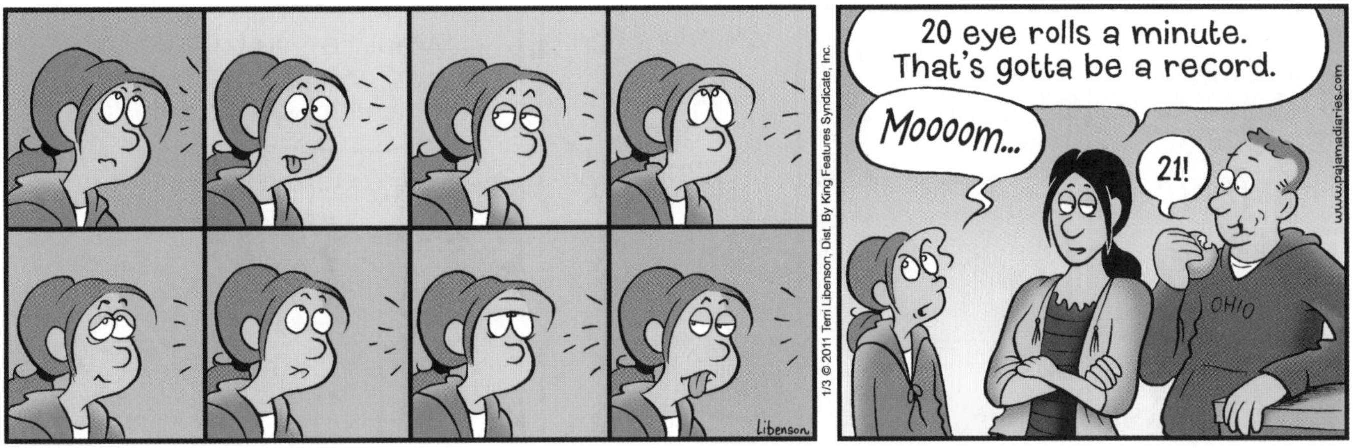
Libenson
1/3 © 2011 Terri Libenson, Dist. By King Features Syndicate, Inc.
20 eye rolls a minute. That's gotta be a record.
Moooom...
21!
OHIO
www.pajamadiaries.com

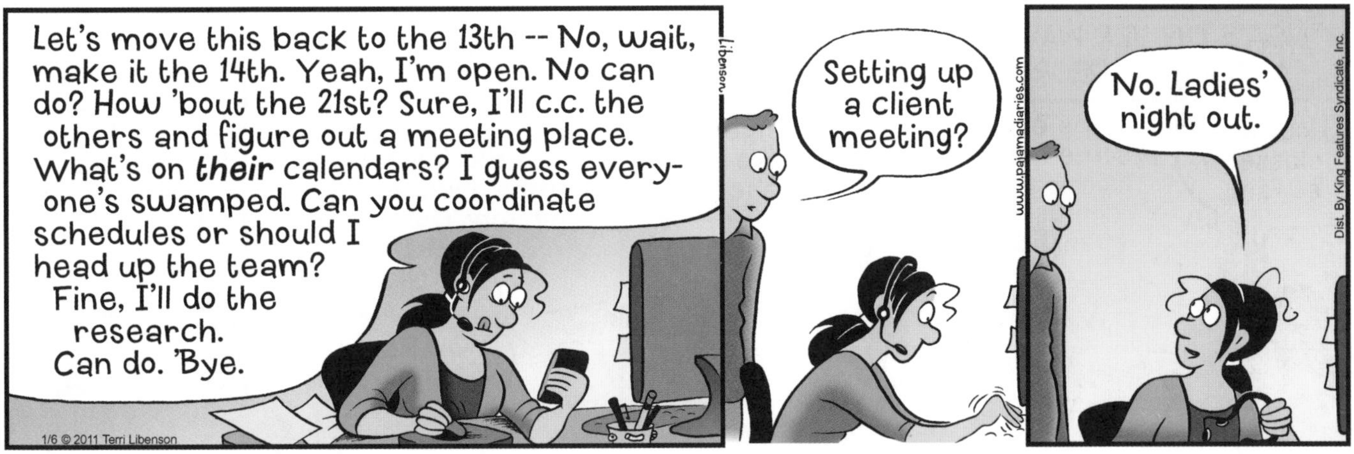
Let's move this back to the 13th -- No, wait, make it the 14th. Yeah, I'm open. No can do? How 'bout the 21st? Sure, I'll c.c. the others and figure out a meeting place. What's on *their* calendars? I guess every-one's swamped. Can you coordinate schedules or should I head up the team? Fine, I'll do the research. Can do. 'Bye.
1/6 © 2011 Terri Libenson
Libenson
Setting up a client meeting?
www.pajamadiaries.com
No. Ladies' night out.
Dist. By King Features Syndicate, Inc.

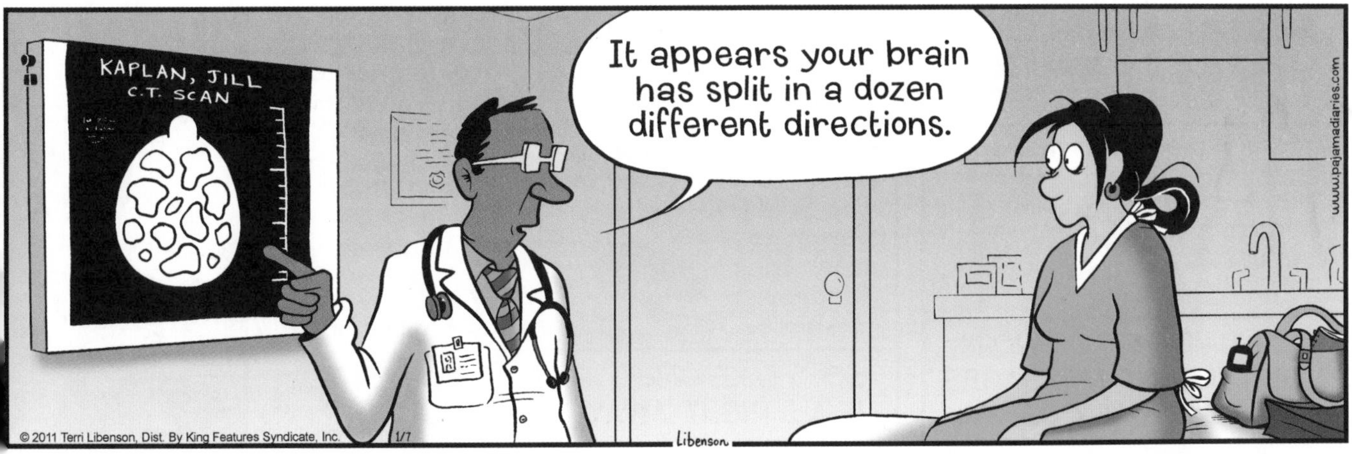
KAPLAN, JILL
C.T. SCAN
It appears your brain has split in a dozen different directions.
www.pajamadiaries.com
© 2011 Terri Libenson, Dist. By King Features Syndicate, Inc.
1/7
Libenson

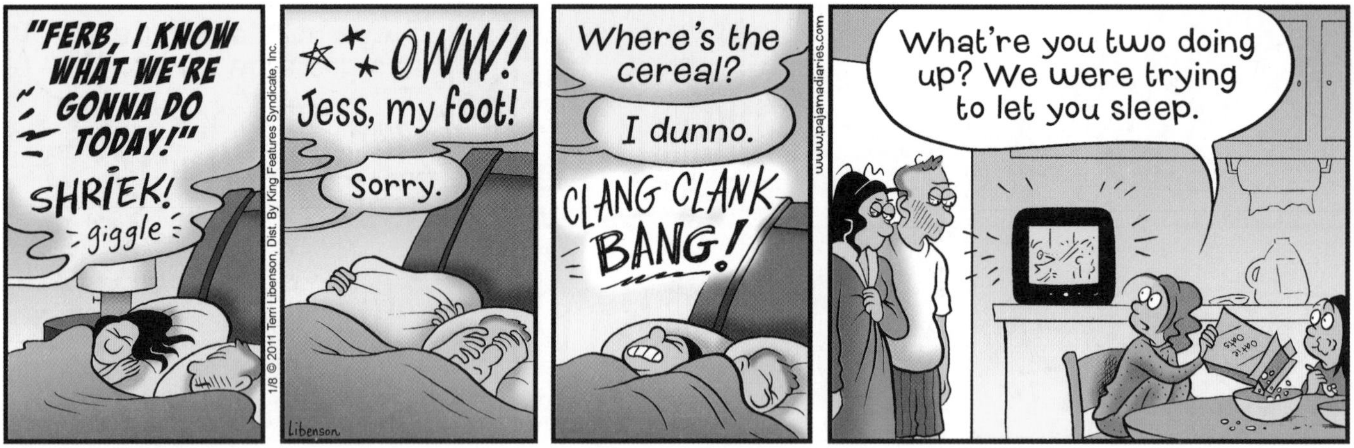
"FERB, I KNOW WHAT WE'RE GONNA DO TODAY!"
SHRIEK!
giggle
1/8 © 2011 Terri Libenson, Dist. By King Features Syndicate, Inc.
OWW! Jess, my foot!
Sorry.
Libenson
Where's the cereal?
I dunno.
CLANG CLANK BANG!
www.pajamadiaries.com
What're you two doing up? We were trying to let you sleep.
Oatie Oats

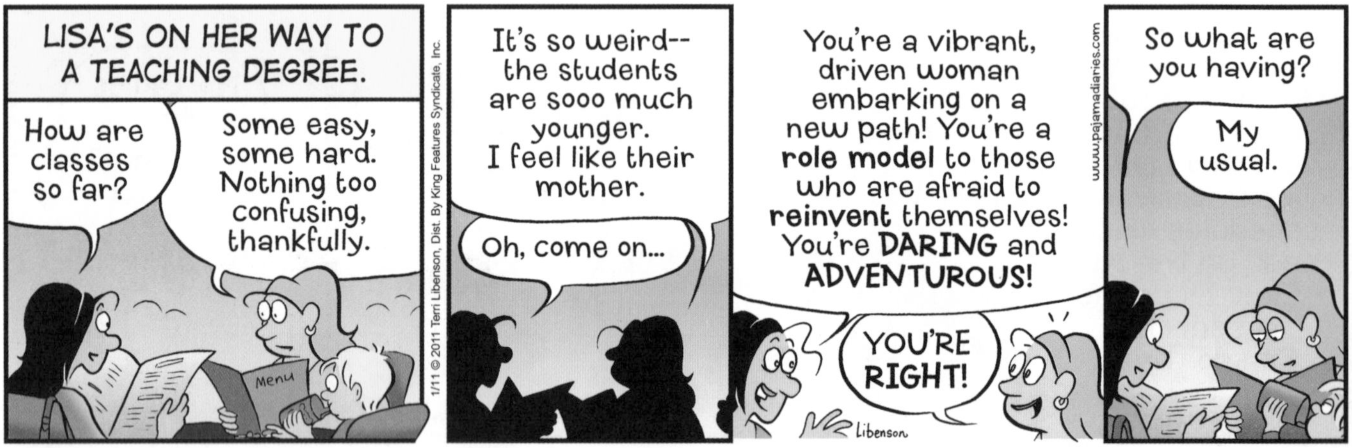
LISA'S ON HER WAY TO A TEACHING DEGREE.
How are classes so far?
Some easy, some hard. Nothing too confusing, thankfully.
Menu
1/11 © 2011 Terri Libenson, Dist. By King Features Syndicate, Inc.
It's so weird-- the students are sooo much younger. I feel like their mother.
Oh, come on...
You're a vibrant, driven woman embarking on a new path! You're a role model to those who are afraid to reinvent themselves! You're DARING and ADVENTUROUS!
YOU'RE RIGHT!
Libenson
www.pajamadiaries.com
So what are you having?
My usual.

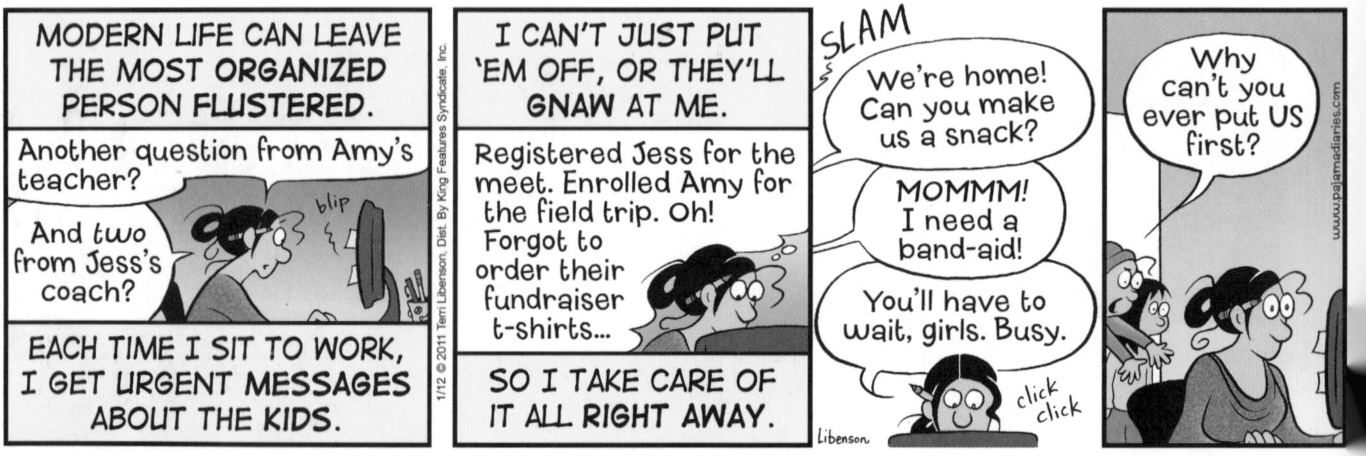
MODERN LIFE CAN LEAVE THE MOST ORGANIZED PERSON FLUSTERED.
Another question from Amy's teacher?
And two from Jess's coach?
blip
EACH TIME I SIT TO WORK, I GET URGENT MESSAGES ABOUT THE KIDS.
1/12 © 2011 Terri Libenson, Dist. By King Features Syndicate, Inc.
I CAN'T JUST PUT 'EM OFF, OR THEY'LL GNAW AT ME.
Registered Jess for the meet. Enrolled Amy for the field trip. Oh! Forgot to order their fundraiser t-shirts...
SO I TAKE CARE OF IT ALL RIGHT AWAY.
SLAM
We're home! Can you make us a snack?
MOMMM! I need a band-aid!
You'll have to wait, girls. Busy.
click click
Libenson
Why can't you ever put US first?
www.pajamadiaries.com

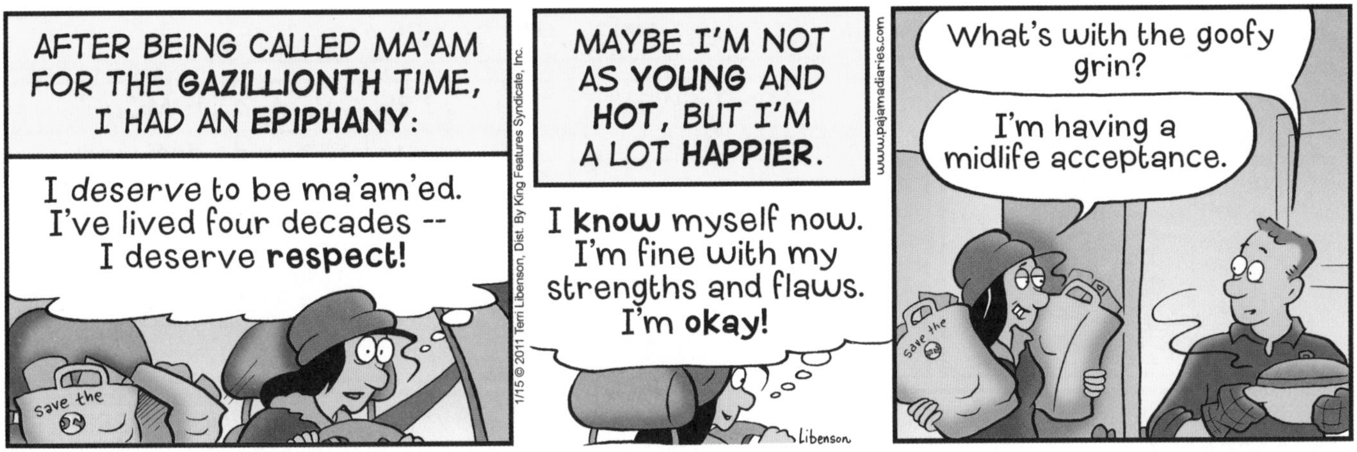
AFTER BEING CALLED MA'AM FOR THE **GAZILLIONTH** TIME, I HAD AN **EPIPHANY**:
I *deserve* to be ma'am'ed. I've lived four decades -- I deserve **respect!**
save the
1/15 © 2011 Terri Libenson, Dist. By King Features Syndicate, Inc.
MAYBE I'M NOT AS **YOUNG** AND **HOT**, BUT I'M A LOT **HAPPIER**.
I **know** myself now. I'm fine with my strengths and flaws. I'm **okay!**
Libenson
www.pajamadiaries.com
What's with the goofy grin?
I'm having a midlife acceptance.
save the

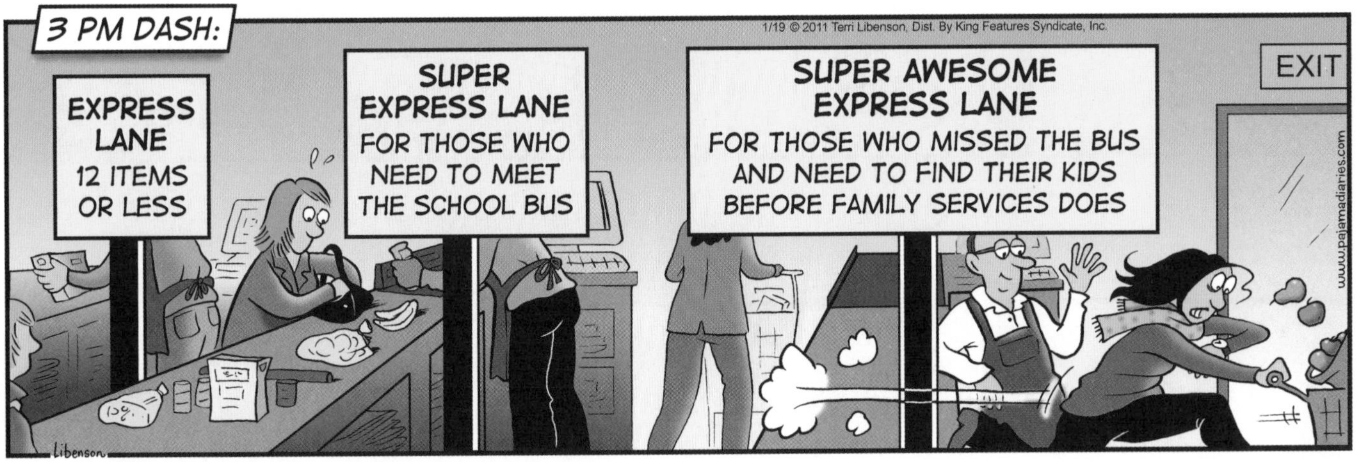
3 PM DASH:
1/19 © 2011 Terri Libenson, Dist. By King Features Syndicate, Inc.
EXPRESS LANE 12 ITEMS OR LESS
SUPER EXPRESS LANE FOR THOSE WHO NEED TO MEET THE SCHOOL BUS
SUPER AWESOME EXPRESS LANE FOR THOSE WHO MISSED THE BUS AND NEED TO FIND THEIR KIDS BEFORE FAMILY SERVICES DOES
EXIT
www.pajamadiaries.com
Libenson

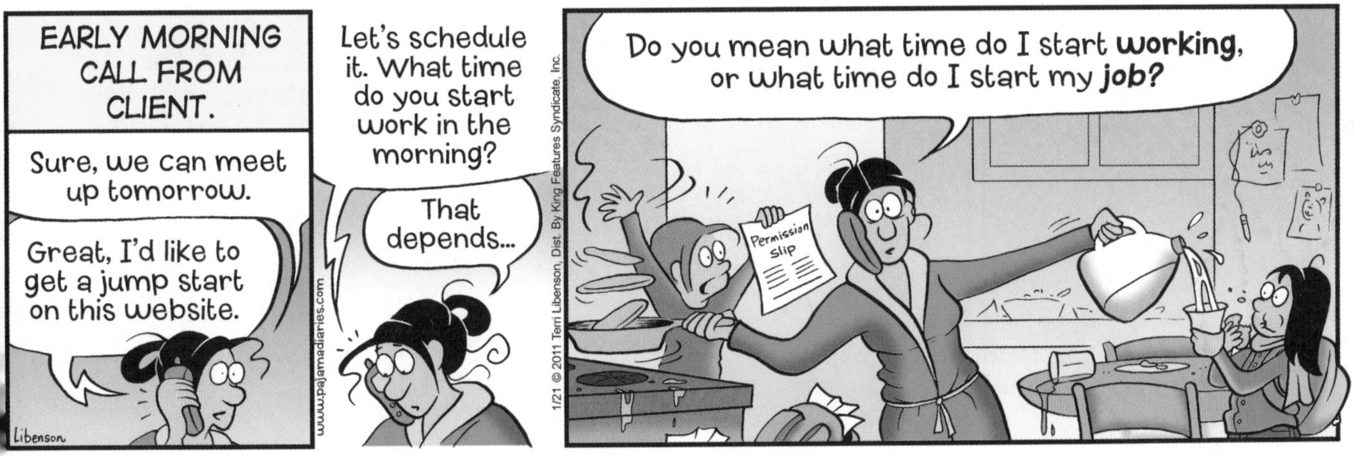
EARLY MORNING CALL FROM CLIENT.
Sure, we can meet up tomorrow.
Great, I'd like to get a jump start on this website.
Libenson
www.pajamadiaries.com
Let's schedule it. What time do you start work in the morning?
That depends...
1/21 © 2011 Terri Libenson, Dist. By King Features Syndicate, Inc.
Do you mean what time do I start **working**, or what time do I start my ***job?***
Permission slip

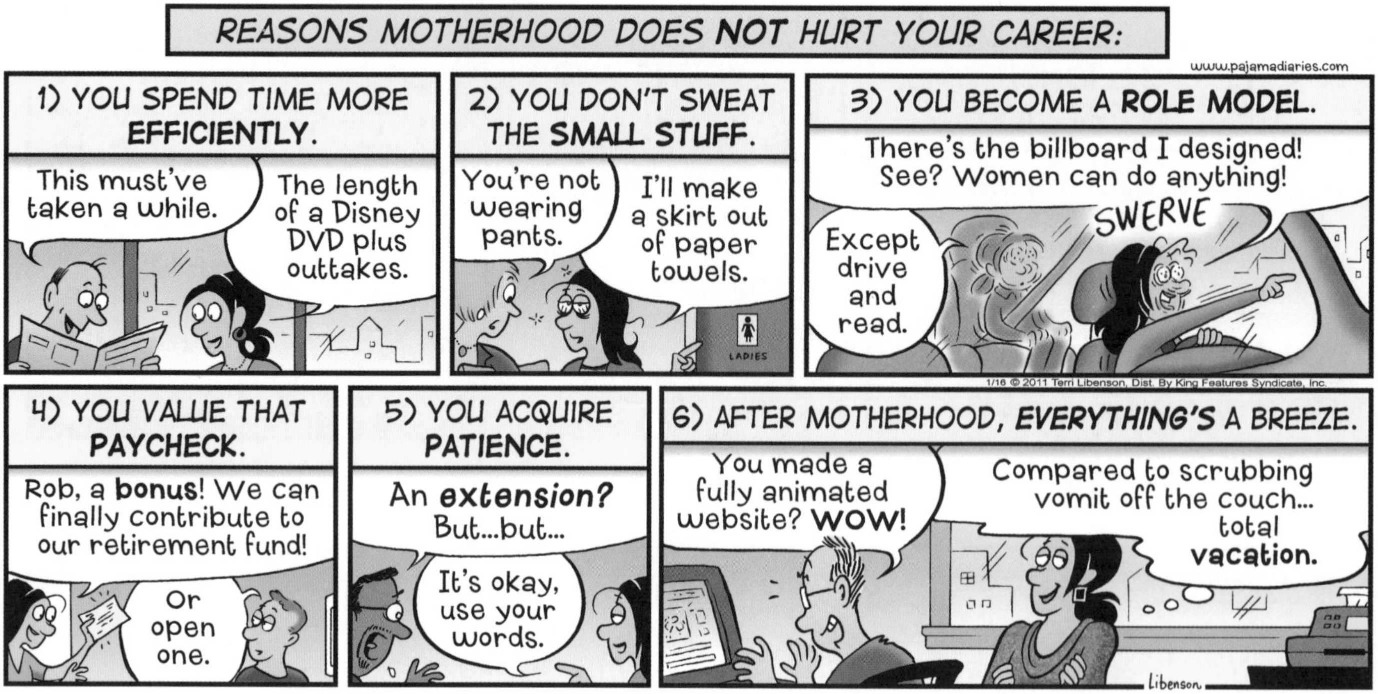
REASONS MOTHERHOOD DOES NOT HURT YOUR CAREER:
www.pajamadiaries.com
1) YOU SPEND TIME MORE EFFICIENTLY.
This must've taken a while.
The length of a Disney DVD plus outtakes.
2) YOU DON'T SWEAT THE SMALL STUFF.
You're not wearing pants.
I'll make a skirt out of paper towels.
LADIES
3) YOU BECOME A ROLE MODEL.
There's the billboard I designed! See? Women can do anything!
Except drive and read.
SWERVE
1/16 © 2011 Terri Libenson, Dist. By King Features Syndicate, Inc.
4) YOU VALUE THAT PAYCHECK.
Rob, a bonus! We can finally contribute to our retirement fund!
Or open one.
5) YOU ACQUIRE PATIENCE.
An extension? But...but...
It's okay, use your words.
6) AFTER MOTHERHOOD, EVERYTHING'S A BREEZE.
You made a fully animated website? WOW!
Compared to scrubbing vomit off the couch... total vacation.
Libenson

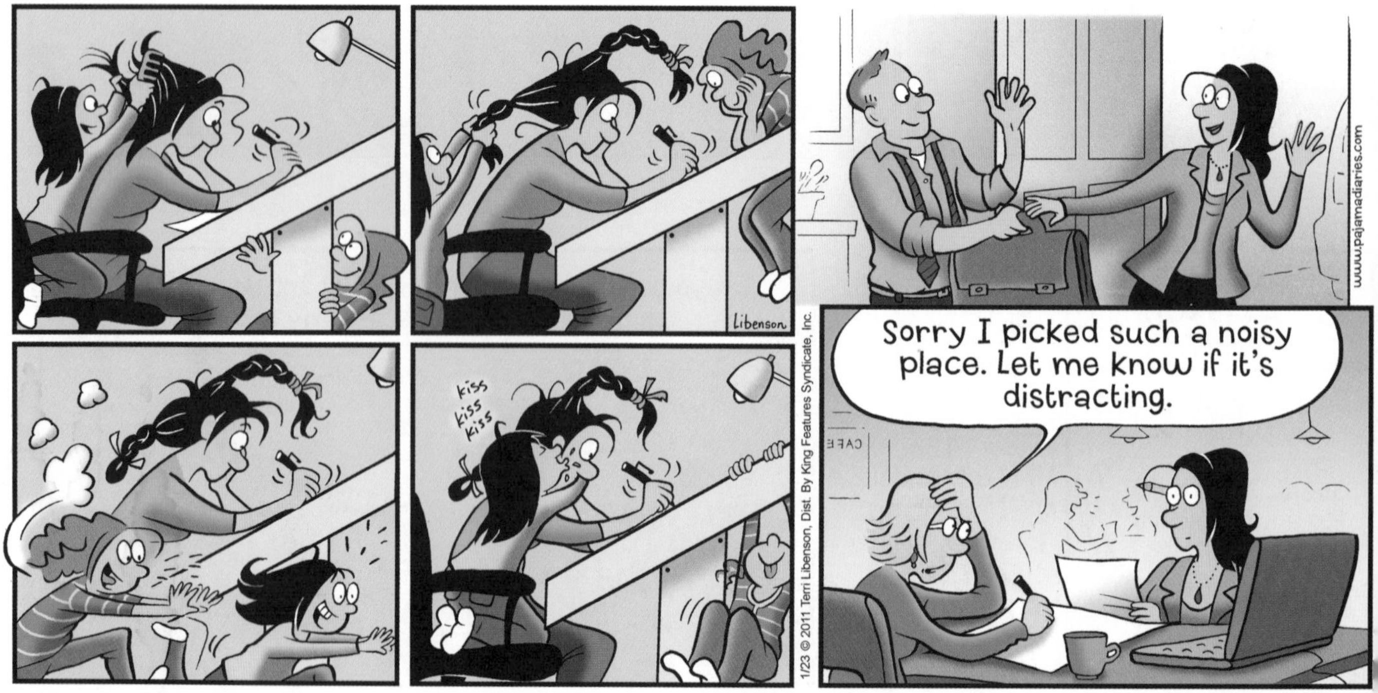
Libenson
kiss kiss kiss
1/23 © 2011 Terri Libenson, Dist. By King Features Syndicate, Inc.
www.pajamadiaries.com
Sorry I picked such a noisy place. Let me know if it's distracting.

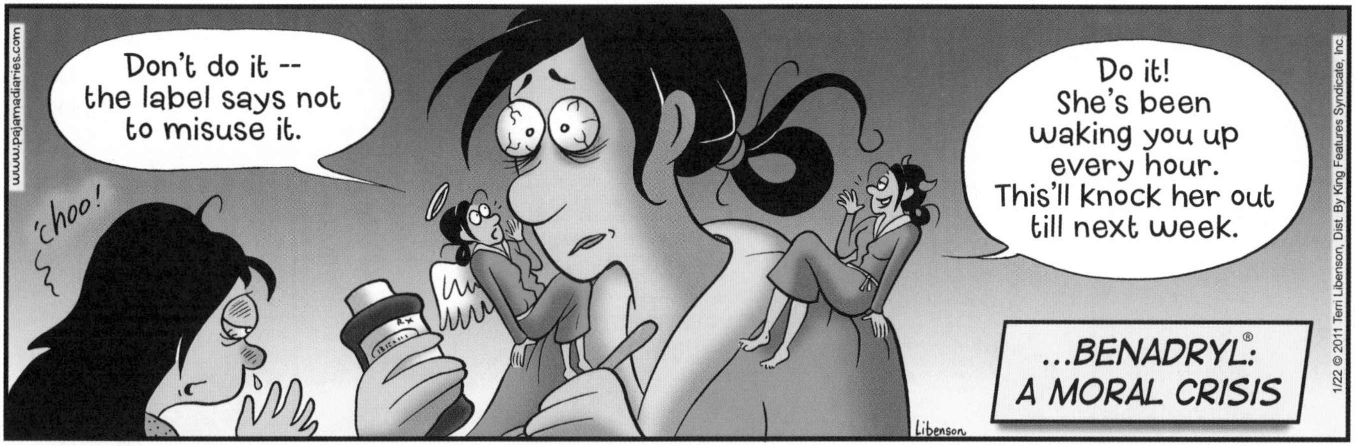
www.pajamadiaries.com
Don't do it -- the label says not to misuse it.
'choo!
Do it! She's been waking you up every hour. This'll knock her out till next week.
...BENADRYL®: A MORAL CRISIS
Libenson
1/22 © 2011 Terri Libenson, Dist. By King Features Syndicate, Inc.

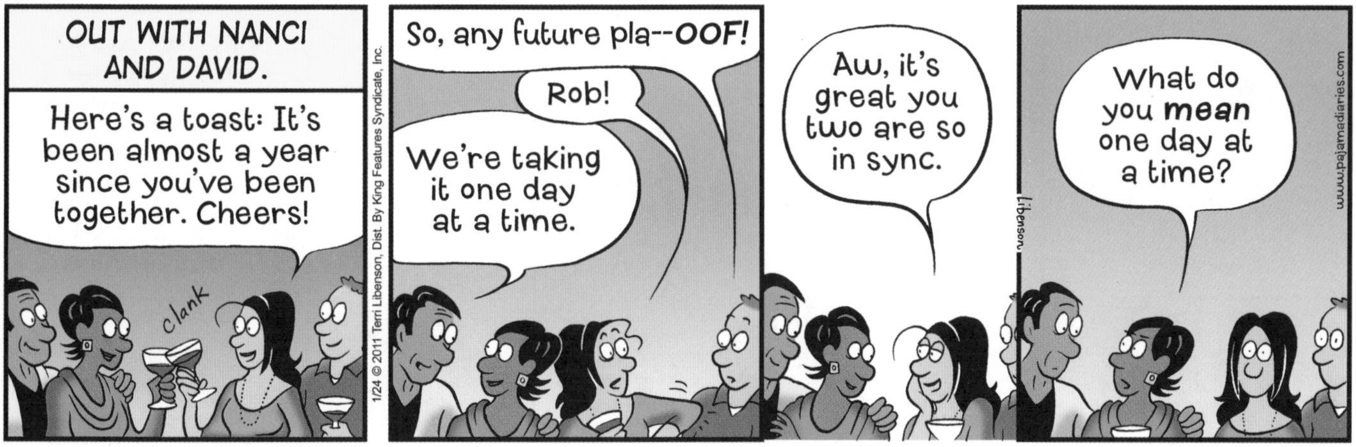
OUT WITH NANCI AND DAVID.
Here's a toast: It's been almost a year since you've been together. Cheers!
clank
1/24 © 2011 Terri Libenson, Dist. By King Features Syndicate, Inc.
So, any future pla--OOF!
Rob!
We're taking it one day at a time.
Aw, it's great you two are so in sync.
Libenson
What do you **mean** one day at a time?
www.pajamadiaries.com

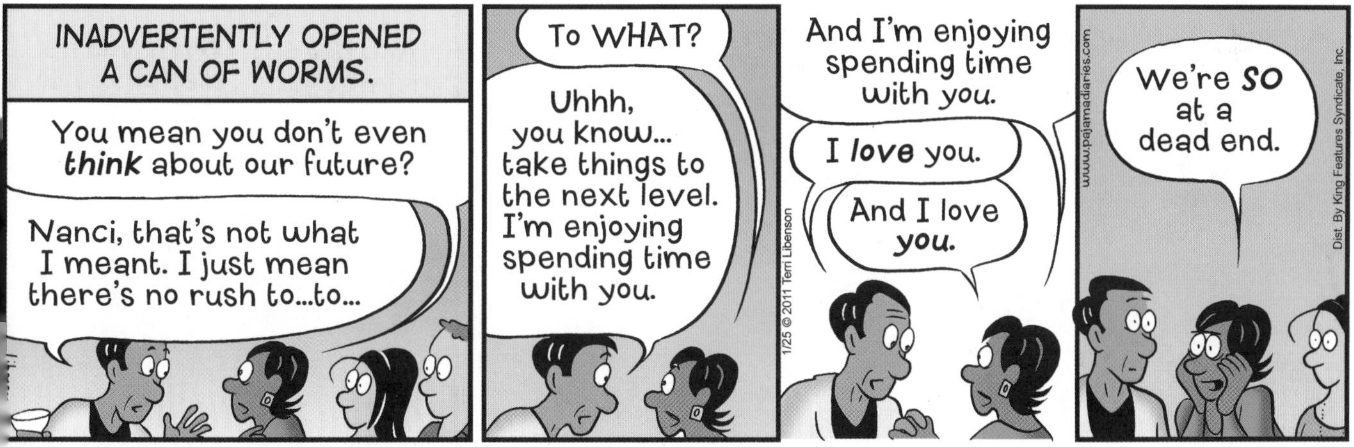
INADVERTENTLY OPENED A CAN OF WORMS.
You mean you don't even ***think*** about our future?
Nanci, that's not what I meant. I just mean there's no rush to...to...
To WHAT?
Uhhh, you know... take things to the next level. I'm enjoying spending time with you.
1/25 © 2011 Terri Libenson
And I'm enjoying spending time with you.
I ***love*** you.
And I love ***you.***
www.pajamadiaries.com
Dist. By King Features Syndicate, Inc.
We're ***SO*** at a dead end.

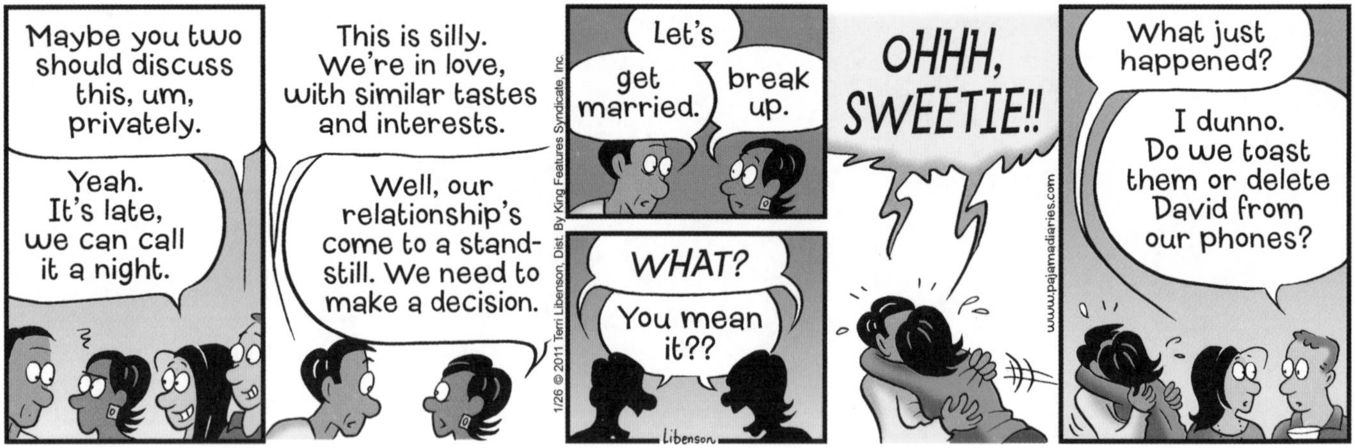
Maybe you two should discuss this, um, privately.
Yeah. It's late, we can call it a night.
This is silly. We're in love, with similar tastes and interests.
Well, our relationship's come to a stand-still. We need to make a decision.
Let's
get married.
break up.
WHAT?
You mean it??
1/26 © 2011 Terri Libenson, Dist. By King Features Syndicate, Inc.
Libenson
OHHH, SWEETIE!!
www.pajamadiaries.com
What just happened?
I dunno. Do we toast them or delete David from our phones?

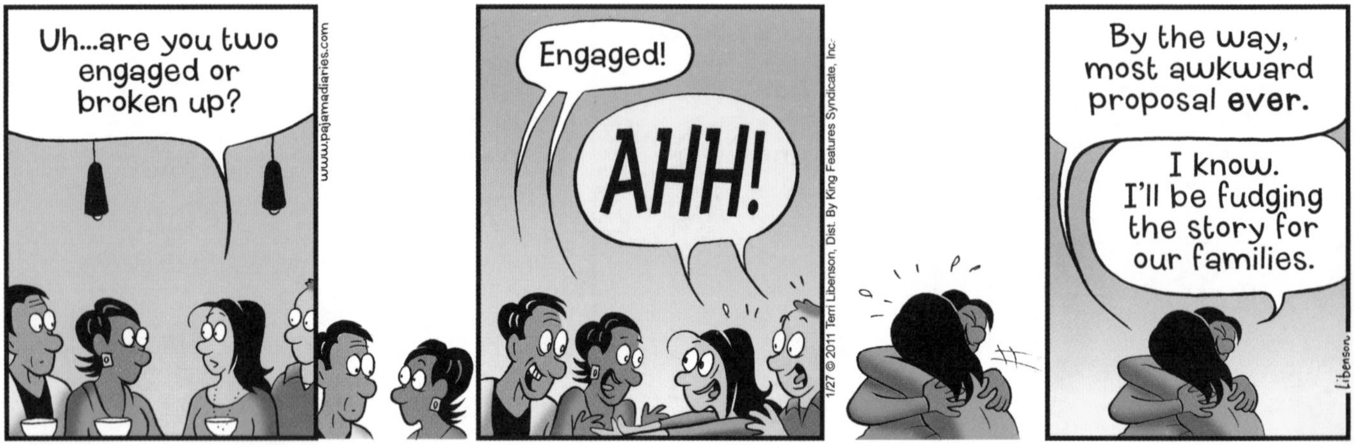
Uh...are you two engaged or broken up?
www.pajamadiaries.com
Engaged!
AHH!
1/27 © 2011 Terri Libenson, Dist. By King Features Syndicate, Inc.
By the way, most awkward proposal **ever.**
I know. I'll be fudging the story for our families.
Libenson

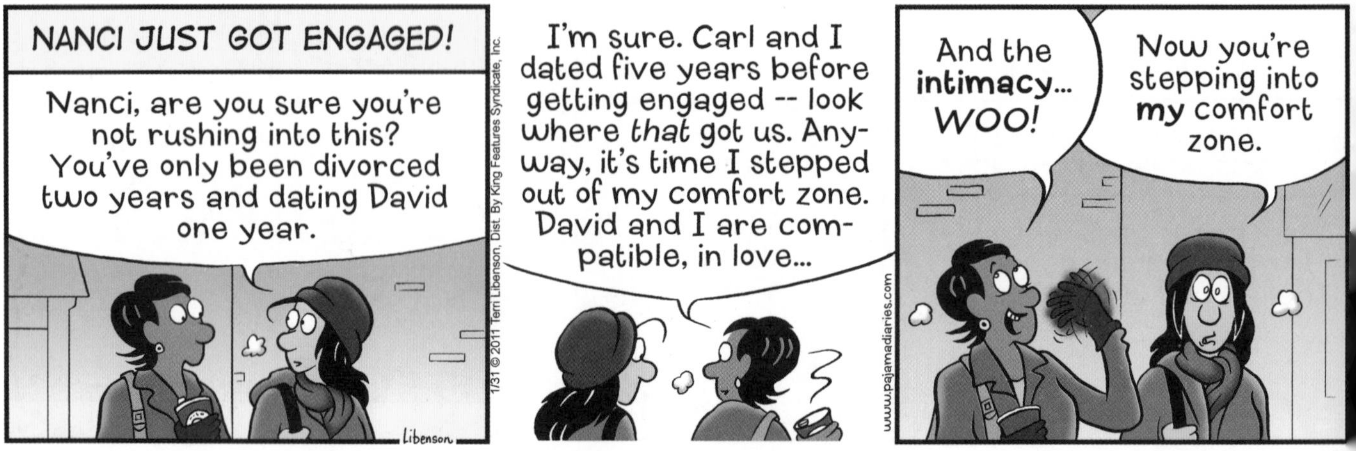
NANCI JUST GOT ENGAGED!
Nanci, are you sure you're not rushing into this? You've only been divorced two years and dating David one year.
Libenson
1/31 © 2011 Terri Libenson, Dist. By King Features Syndicate, Inc.
I'm sure. Carl and I dated five years before getting engaged -- look where *that* got us. Any-way, it's time I stepped out of my comfort zone. David and I are com-patible, in love...
www.pajamadiaries.com
And the **intimacy...** *WOO!*
Now you're stepping into **my** comfort zone.

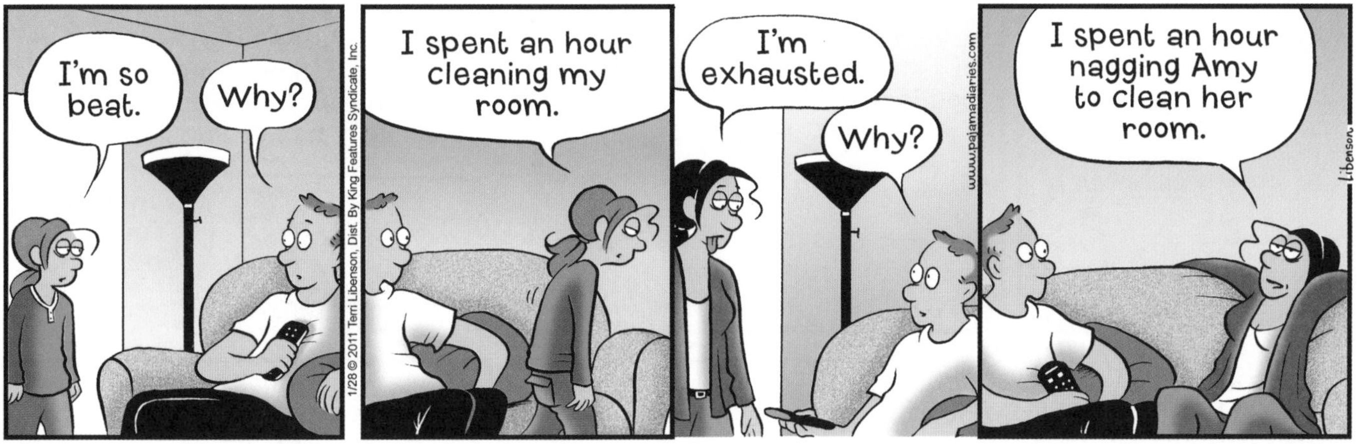
I'm so beat.
Why?
1/28 © 2011 Terri Libenson, Dist. By King Features Syndicate, Inc.
I spent an hour cleaning my room.
I'm exhausted.
Why?
www.pajamadiaries.com
I spent an hour nagging Amy to clean her room.
Libenson

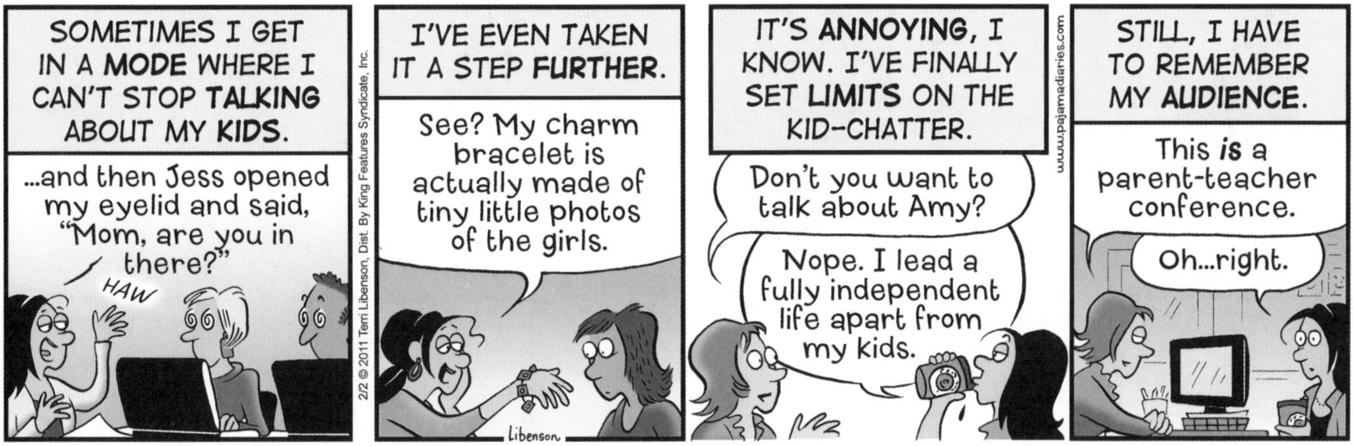
SOMETIMES I GET IN A **MODE** WHERE I CAN'T STOP **TALKING** ABOUT MY **KIDS**.
...and then Jess opened my eyelid and said, "Mom, are you in there?"
HAW
2/2 © 2011 Terri Libenson, Dist. By King Features Syndicate, Inc.
I'VE EVEN TAKEN IT A STEP **FURTHER**.
See? My charm bracelet is actually made of tiny little photos of the girls.
Libenson
IT'S **ANNOYING**, I KNOW. I'VE FINALLY SET **LIMITS** ON THE KID-CHATTER.
Don't you want to talk about Amy?
Nope. I lead a fully independent life apart from my kids.
www.pajamadiaries.com
STILL, I HAVE TO REMEMBER MY **AUDIENCE**.
This *is* a parent-teacher conference.
Oh...right.

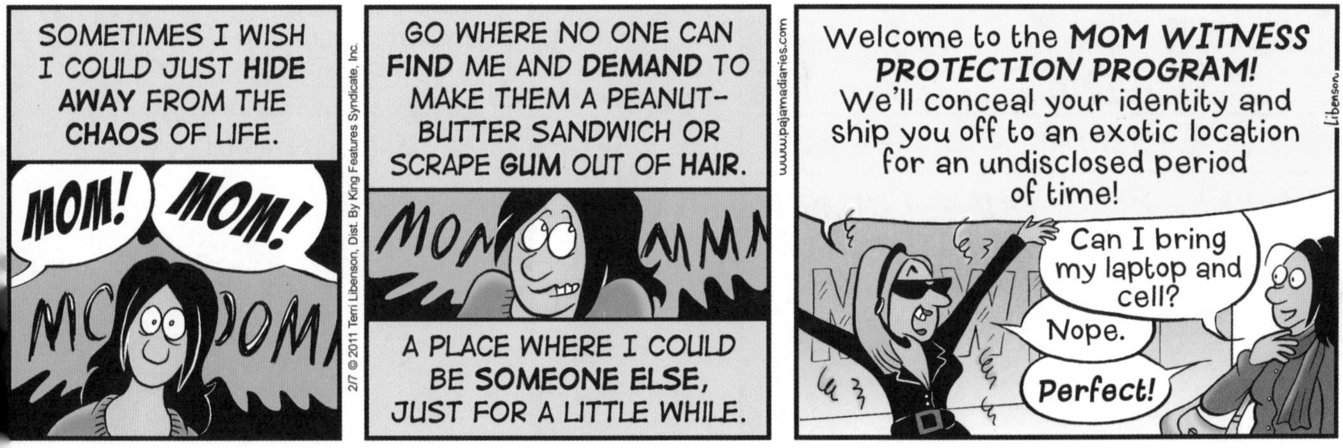
SOMETIMES I WISH I COULD JUST **HIDE AWAY** FROM THE **CHAOS** OF LIFE.
MOM!
MOM!
2/7 © 2011 Terri Libenson, Dist. By King Features Syndicate, Inc.
GO WHERE NO ONE CAN **FIND** ME AND **DEMAND** TO MAKE THEM A PEANUT-BUTTER SANDWICH OR SCRAPE **GUM** OUT OF **HAIR**.
A PLACE WHERE I COULD BE **SOMEONE ELSE**, JUST FOR A LITTLE WHILE.
www.pajamadiaries.com
Welcome to the **MOM WITNESS PROTECTION PROGRAM!** We'll conceal your identity and ship you off to an exotic location for an undisclosed period of time!
Can I bring my laptop and cell?
Nope.
Perfect!
Libenson

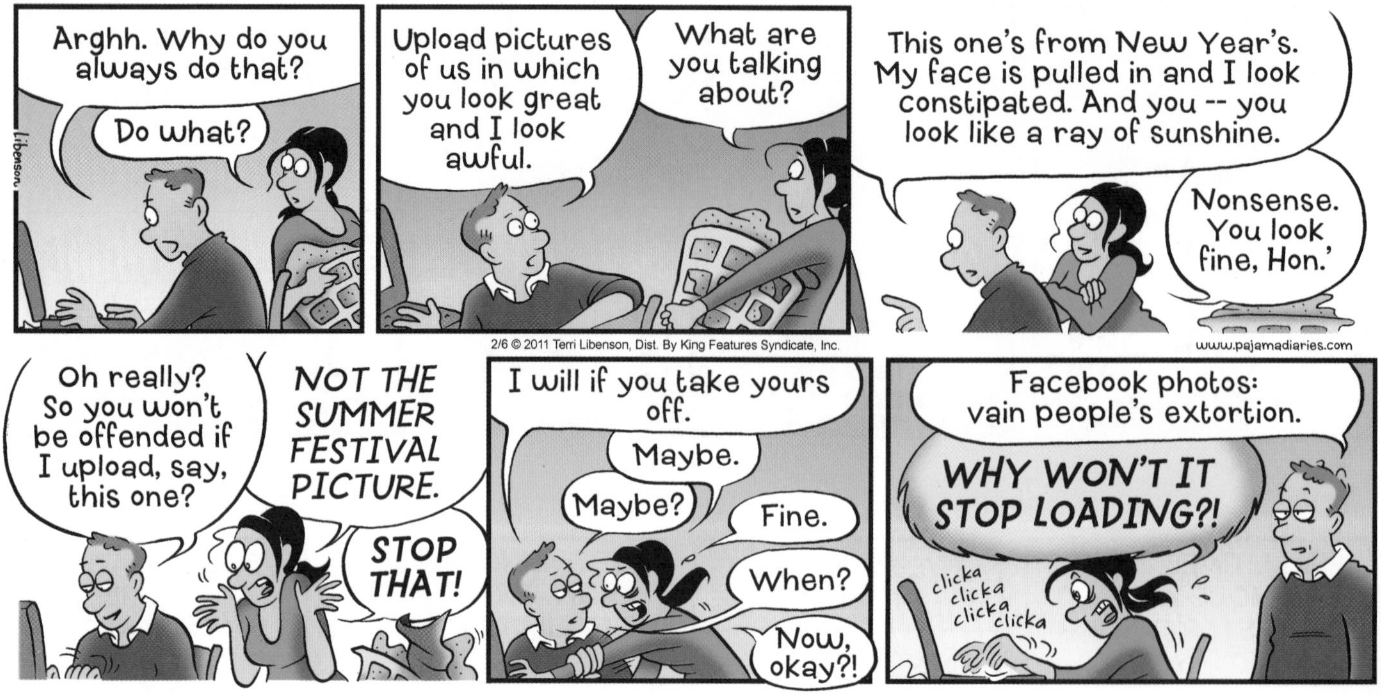
Arghh. Why do you always do that?
Do what?
Libenson
Upload pictures of us in which you look great and I look awful.
What are you talking about?
This one's from New Year's. My face is pulled in and I look constipated. And you -- you look like a ray of sunshine.
Nonsense. You look fine, Hon.'
2/6 © 2011 Terri Libenson, Dist. By King Features Syndicate, Inc.
www.pajamadiaries.com
Oh really? So you won't be offended if I upload, say, this one?
NOT THE SUMMER FESTIVAL PICTURE.
STOP THAT!
I will if you take yours off.
Maybe.
Maybe?
Fine.
When?
Now, okay?!
Facebook photos: vain people's extortion.
WHY WON'T IT STOP LOADING?!
clicka clicka clicka clicka

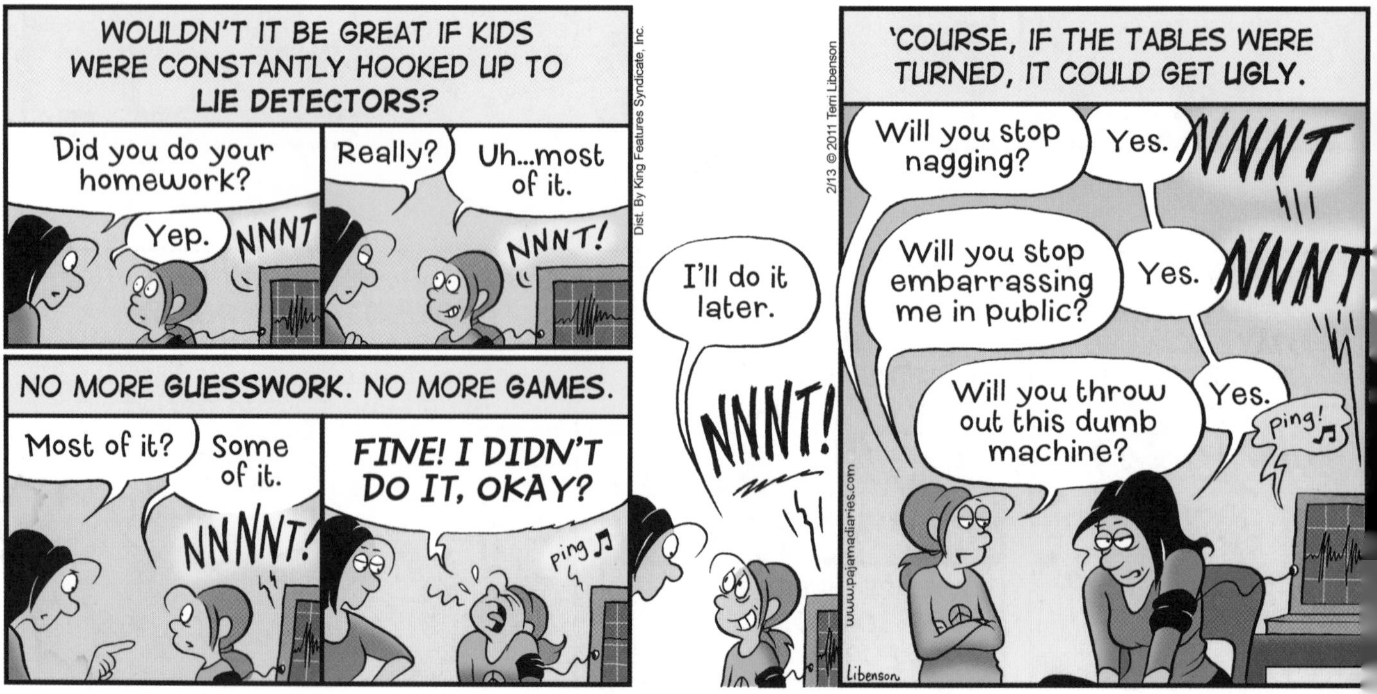
WOULDN'T IT BE GREAT IF KIDS WERE CONSTANTLY HOOKED UP TO LIE DETECTORS?
Did you do your homework?
Yep.
NNNT
Really?
Uh...most of it.
NNNT!
Dist. By King Features Syndicate, Inc.
NO MORE GUESSWORK. NO MORE GAMES.
Most of it?
Some of it.
NNNNT!
FINE! I DIDN'T DO IT, OKAY?
ping ♫
I'll do it later.
NNNT!
2/13 © 2011 Terri Libenson
'COURSE, IF THE TABLES WERE TURNED, IT COULD GET UGLY.
Will you stop nagging?
Yes.
NNNT
Will you stop embarrassing me in public?
Yes.
NNNT
Will you throw out this dumb machine?
Yes.
ping! ♫
www.pajamadiaries.com
Libenson

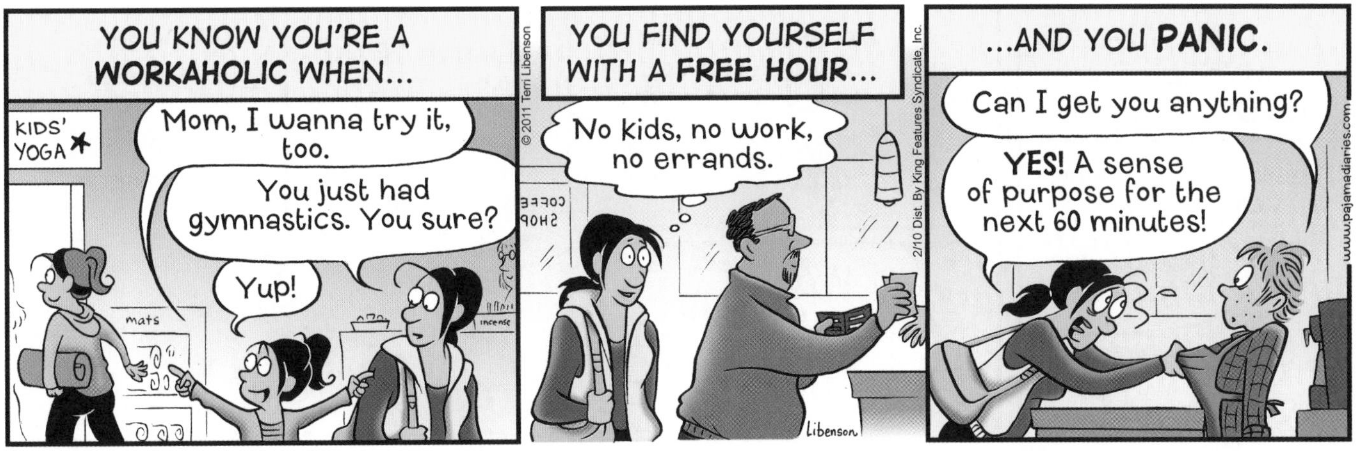
YOU KNOW YOU'RE A WORKAHOLIC WHEN...
KIDS' YOGA
Mom, I wanna try it, too.
You just had gymnastics. You sure?
Yup!
mats
incense
© 2011 Terri Libenson
YOU FIND YOURSELF WITH A FREE HOUR...
No kids, no work, no errands.
2/10 Dist. By King Features Syndicate, Inc.
Libenson
...AND YOU PANIC.
Can I get you anything?
YES! A sense of purpose for the next 60 minutes!
www.pajamadiaries.com

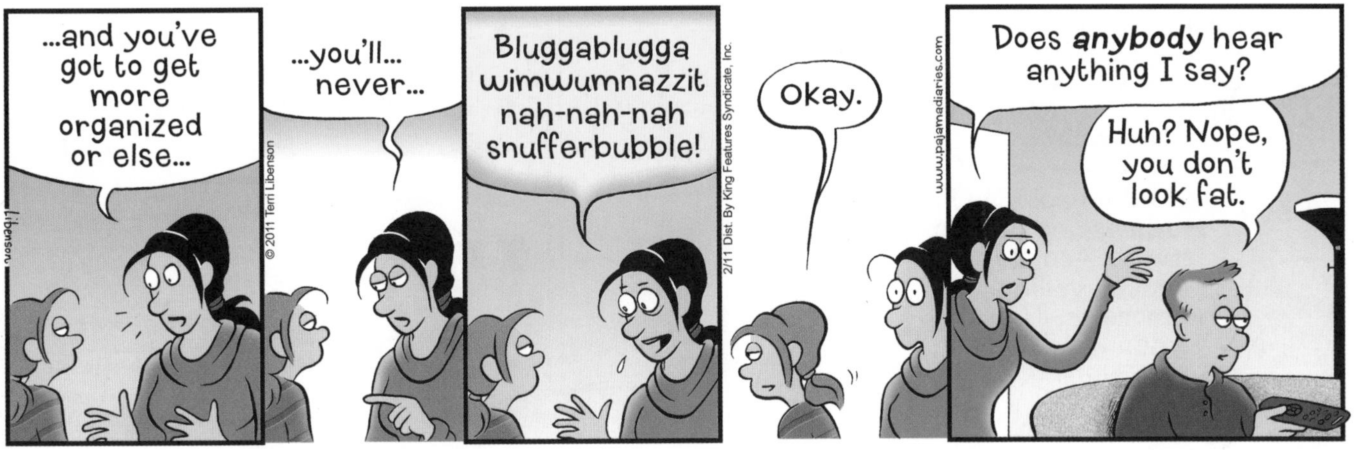
...and you've got to get more organized or else...
Libenson
© 2011 Terri Libenson
...you'll... never...
Bluggablugga wimwumnazzit nah-nah-nah snufferbubble!
2/11 Dist. By King Features Syndicate, Inc.
Okay.
www.pajamadiaries.com
Does anybody hear anything I say?
Huh? Nope, you don't look fat.

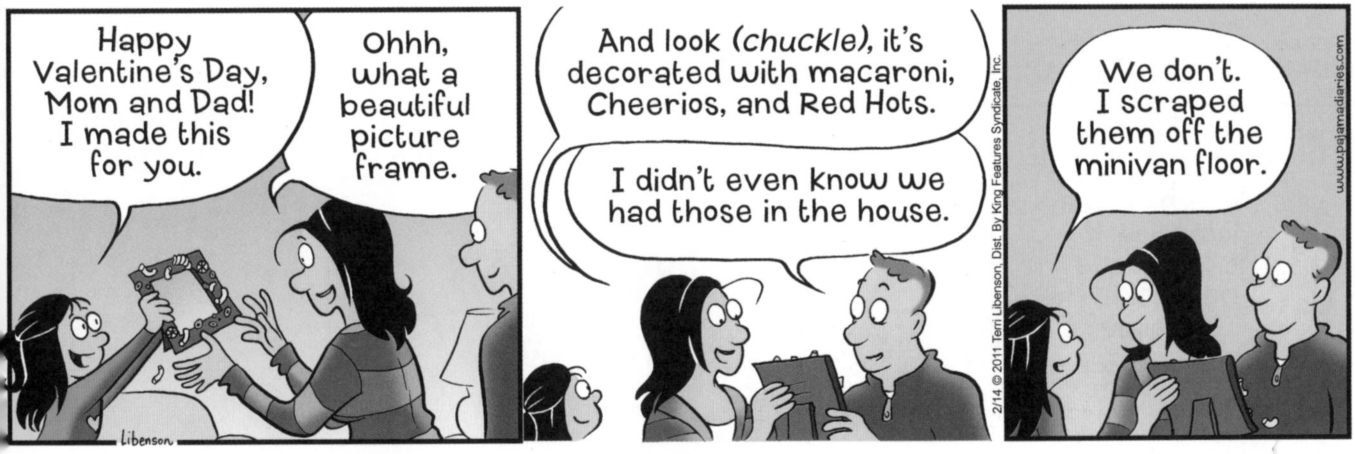
Happy Valentine's Day, Mom and Dad! I made this for you.
Ohhh, what a beautiful picture frame.
Libenson
And look (chuckle), it's decorated with macaroni, Cheerios, and Red Hots.
I didn't even know we had those in the house.
2/14 © 2011 Terri Libenson, Dist. By King Features Syndicate, Inc.
We don't. I scraped them off the minivan floor.
www.pajamadiaries.com

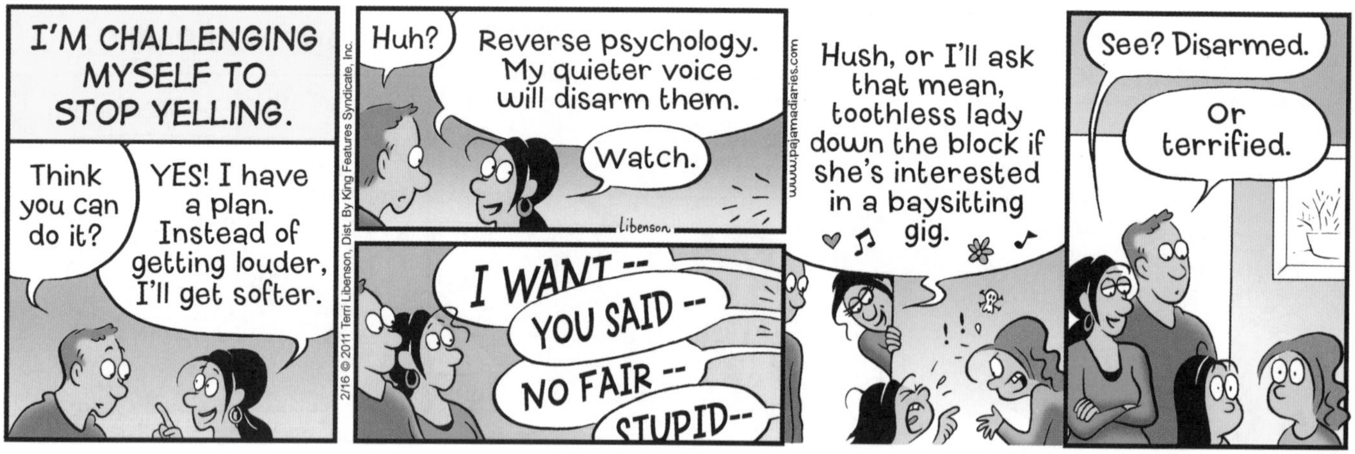
I'M CHALLENGING MYSELF TO STOP YELLING.
Think you can do it?
YES! I have a plan. Instead of getting louder, I'll get softer.
2/16 © 2011 Terri Libenson, Dist. By King Features Syndicate, Inc.
Huh?
Reverse psychology. My quieter voice will disarm them.
Watch.
Libenson
I WANT --
YOU SAID --
NO FAIR --
STUPID--
www.pajamadiaries.com
Hush, or I'll ask that mean, toothless lady down the block if she's interested in a baysitting gig.
See? Disarmed.
Or terrified.

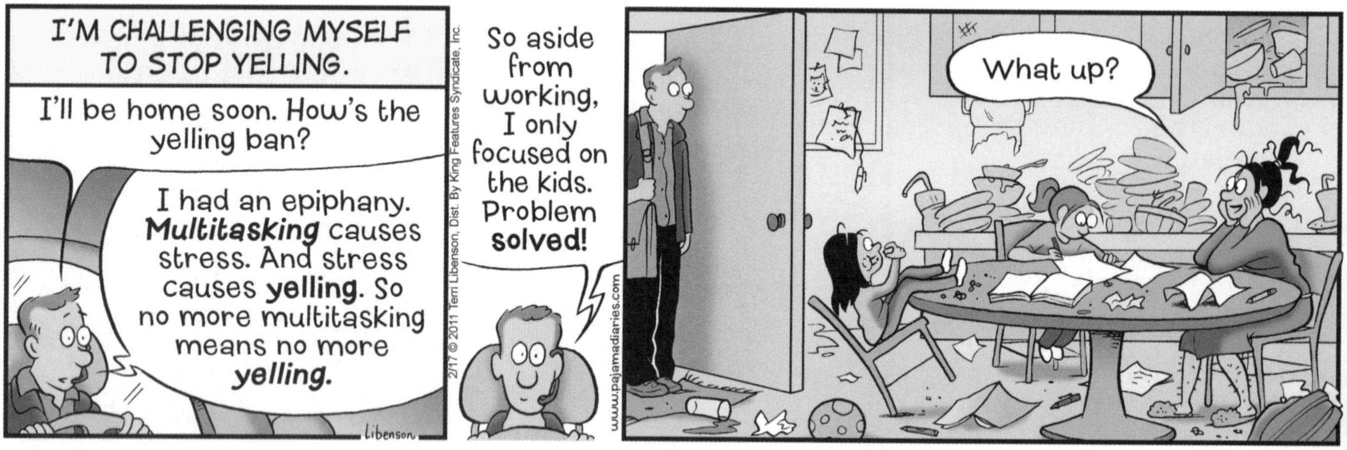
I'M CHALLENGING MYSELF TO STOP YELLING.
I'll be home soon. How's the yelling ban?
I had an epiphany. Multitasking causes stress. And stress causes yelling. So no more multitasking means no more yelling.
Libenson
2/17 © 2011 Terri Libenson, Dist. By King Features Syndicate, Inc.
So aside from working, I only focused on the kids. Problem solved!
www.pajamadiaries.com
What up?

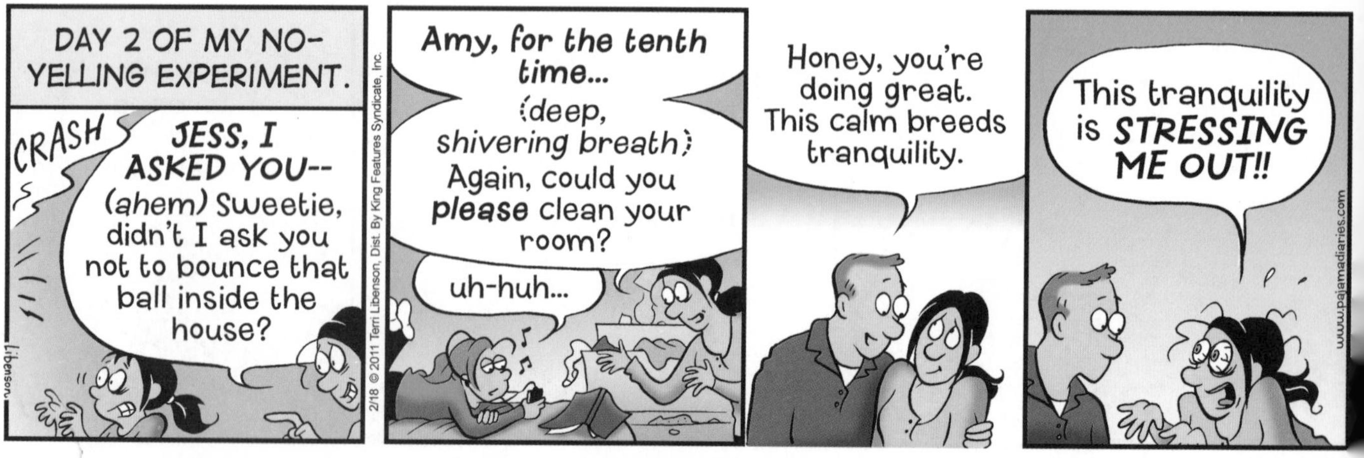
DAY 2 OF MY NO-YELLING EXPERIMENT.
CRASH
JESS, I ASKED YOU-- (ahem) Sweetie, didn't I ask you not to bounce that ball inside the house?
Libenson
2/18 © 2011 Terri Libenson, Dist. By King Features Syndicate, Inc.
Amy, for the tenth time... (deep, shivering breath) Again, could you please clean your room?
uh-huh...
Honey, you're doing great. This calm breeds tranquility.
This tranquility is STRESSING ME OUT!!
www.pajamadiaries.com

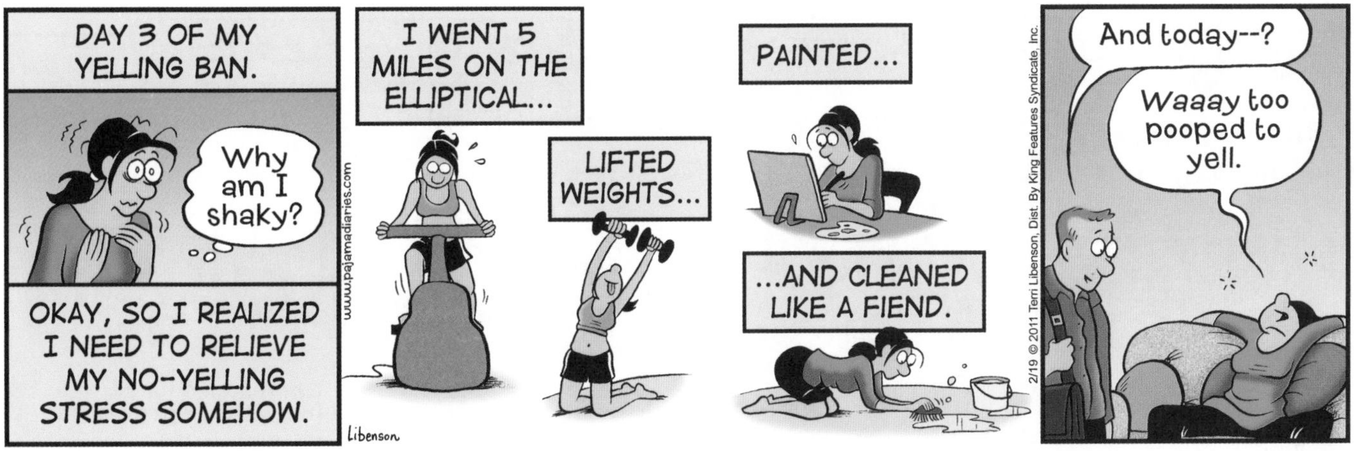
DAY 3 OF MY YELLING BAN.
Why am I shaky?
OKAY, SO I REALIZED I NEED TO RELIEVE MY NO-YELLING STRESS SOMEHOW.
www.pajamadiaries.com
Libenson
I WENT 5 MILES ON THE ELLIPTICAL...
LIFTED WEIGHTS...
PAINTED...
...AND CLEANED LIKE A FIEND.
2/19 © 2011 Terri Libenson, Dist. By King Features Syndicate, Inc.
And today--?
Waaay too pooped to yell.

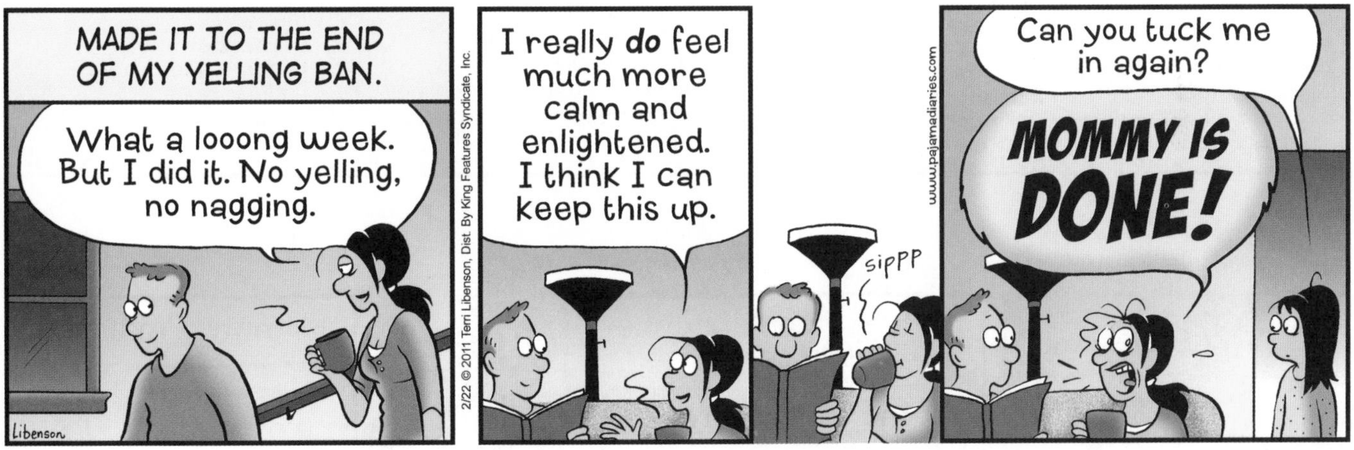
MADE IT TO THE END OF MY YELLING BAN.
What a looong week. But I did it. No yelling, no nagging.
Libenson
2/22 © 2011 Terri Libenson, Dist. By King Features Syndicate, Inc.
I really do feel much more calm and enlightened. I think I can keep this up.
sipPP
www.pajamadiaries.com
Can you tuck me in again?
MOMMY IS DONE!

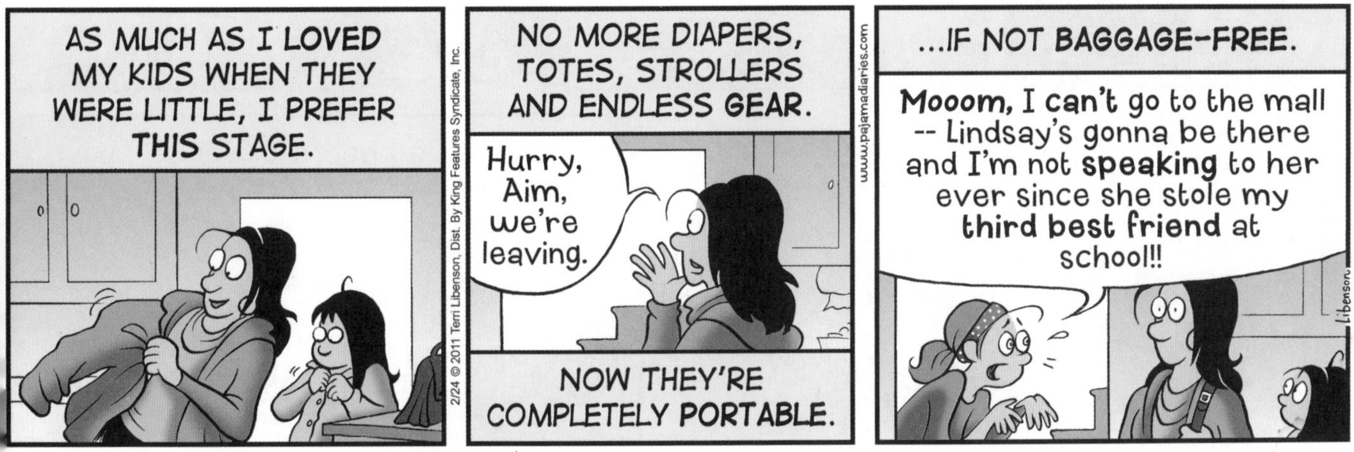
AS MUCH AS I LOVED MY KIDS WHEN THEY WERE LITTLE, I PREFER THIS STAGE.
2/24 © 2011 Terri Libenson, Dist. By King Features Syndicate, Inc.
NO MORE DIAPERS, TOTES, STROLLERS AND ENDLESS GEAR.
Hurry, Aim, we're leaving.
NOW THEY'RE COMPLETELY PORTABLE.
www.pajamadiaries.com
...IF NOT BAGGAGE-FREE.
Mooom, I can't go to the mall -- Lindsay's gonna be there and I'm not speaking to her ever since she stole my third best friend at school!!
Libenson

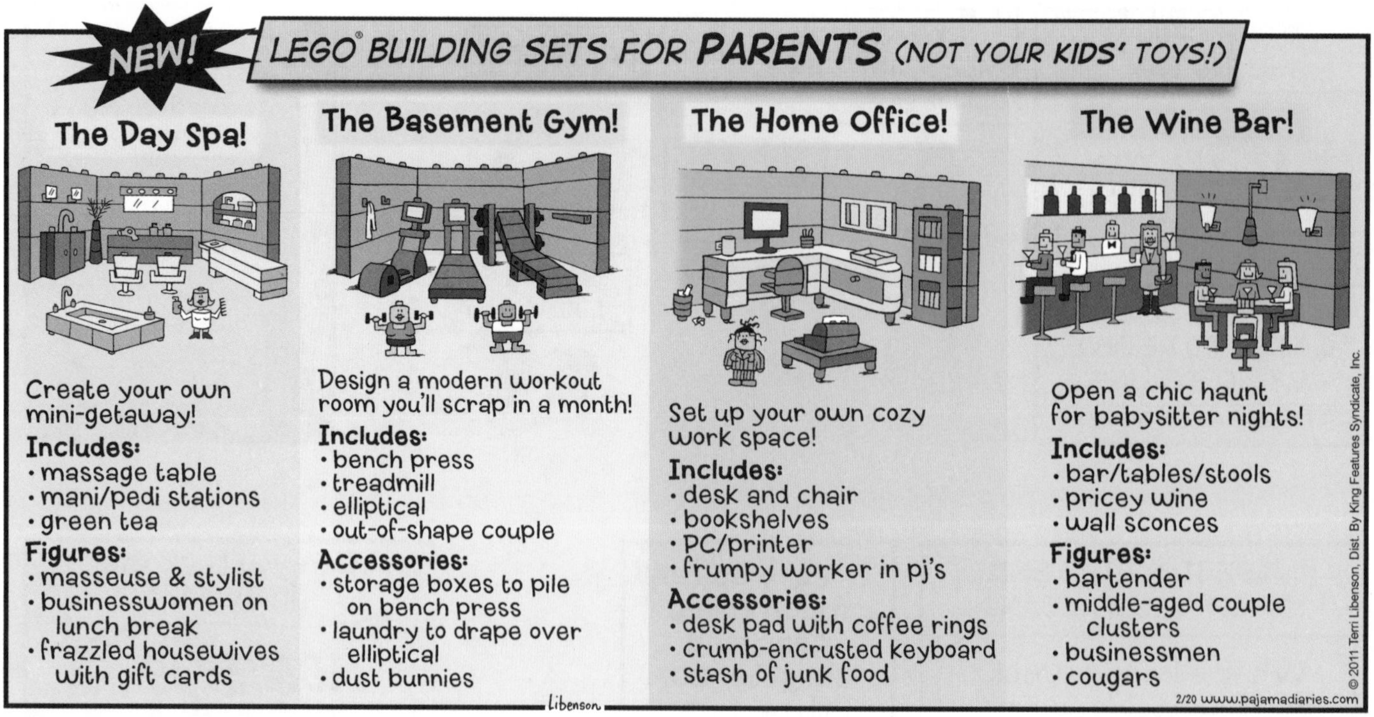
NEW!
LEGO® BUILDING SETS FOR PARENTS (NOT YOUR KIDS' TOYS!)
The Day Spa!
Create your own mini-getaway!
Includes:
• massage table
• mani/pedi stations
• green tea
Figures:
• masseuse & stylist
• businesswomen on lunch break
• frazzled housewives with gift cards
The Basement Gym!
Design a modern workout room you'll scrap in a month!
Includes:
• bench press
• treadmill
• elliptical
• out-of-shape couple
Accessories:
• storage boxes to pile on bench press
• laundry to drape over elliptical
• dust bunnies
The Home Office!
Set up your own cozy work space!
Includes:
• desk and chair
• bookshelves
• PC/printer
• frumpy worker in pj's
Accessories:
• desk pad with coffee rings
• crumb-encrusted keyboard
• stash of junk food
The Wine Bar!
Open a chic haunt for babysitter nights!
Includes:
• bar/tables/stools
• pricey wine
• wall sconces
Figures:
• bartender
• middle-aged couple clusters
• businessmen
• cougars
Libenson
© 2011 Terri Libenson, Dist. By King Features Syndicate, Inc.
2/20 www.pajamadiaries.com

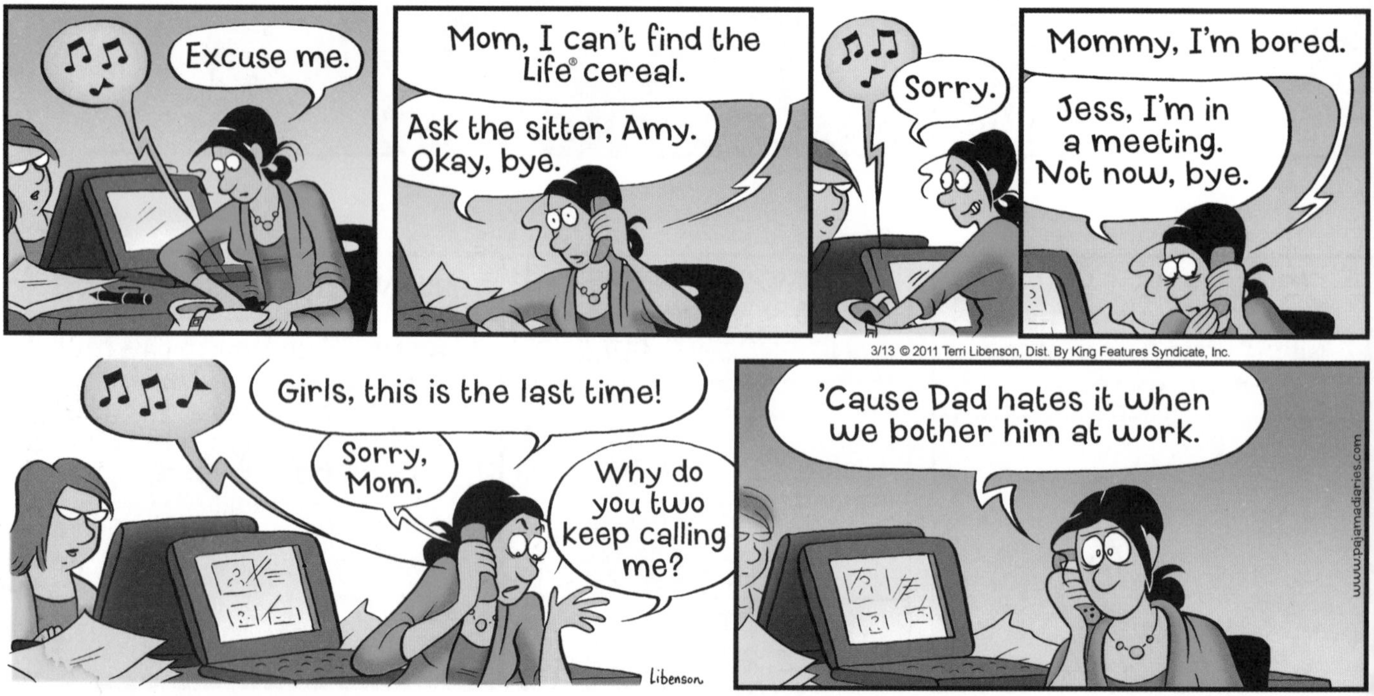
Excuse me.
Mom, I can't find the Life® cereal.
Ask the sitter, Amy. Okay, bye.
Sorry.
Mommy, I'm bored.
Jess, I'm in a meeting. Not now, bye.
3/13 © 2011 Terri Libenson, Dist. By King Features Syndicate, Inc.
Girls, this is the last time!
Sorry, Mom.
Why do you two keep calling me?
Libenson
'Cause Dad hates it when we bother him at work.
www.pajamadiaries.com

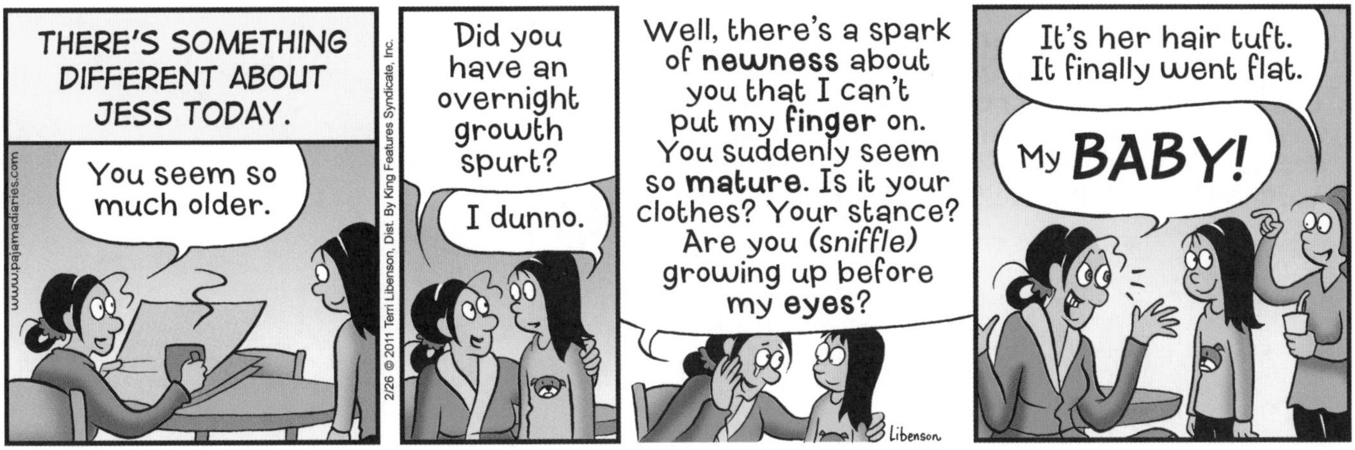
THERE'S SOMETHING DIFFERENT ABOUT JESS TODAY.
www.pajamadiaries.com
You seem so much older.
2/26 © 2011 Terri Libenson, Dist. By King Features Syndicate, Inc.
Did you have an overnight growth spurt?
I dunno.
Well, there's a spark of **newness** about you that I can't put my **finger** on. You suddenly seem so **mature**. Is it your clothes? Your stance? Are you (*sniffle*) growing up before my **eyes**?
Libenson
It's her hair tuft. It finally went flat.
My **BABY!**

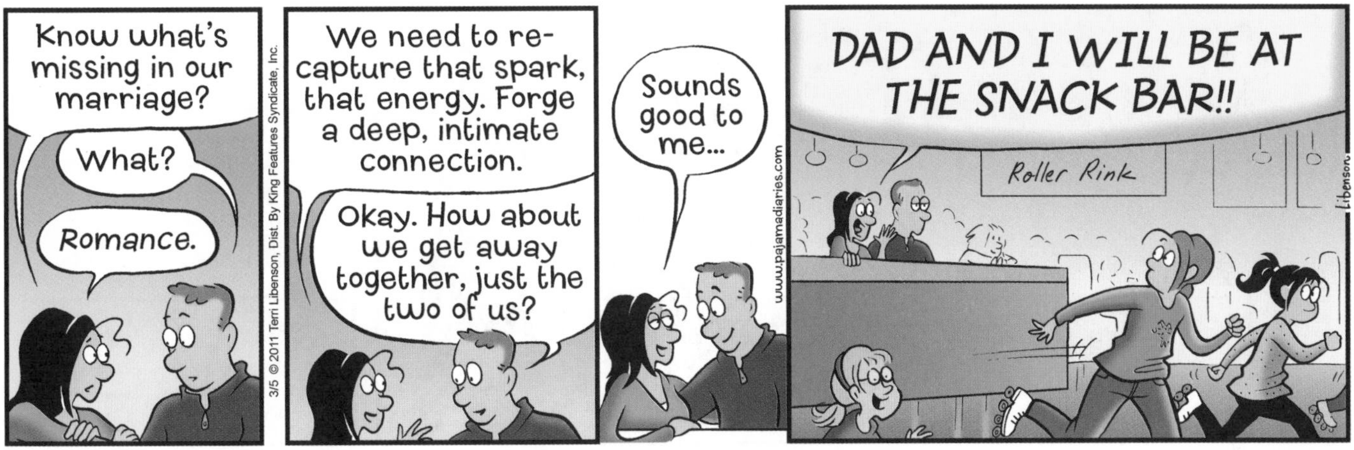
Know what's missing in our marriage?
What?
Romance.
3/5 © 2011 Terri Libenson, Dist. By King Features Syndicate, Inc.
We need to re-capture that spark, that energy. Forge a deep, intimate connection.
Okay. How about we get away together, just the two of us?
Sounds good to me...
www.pajamadiaries.com
DAD AND I WILL BE AT THE SNACK BAR!!
Roller Rink
Libenson

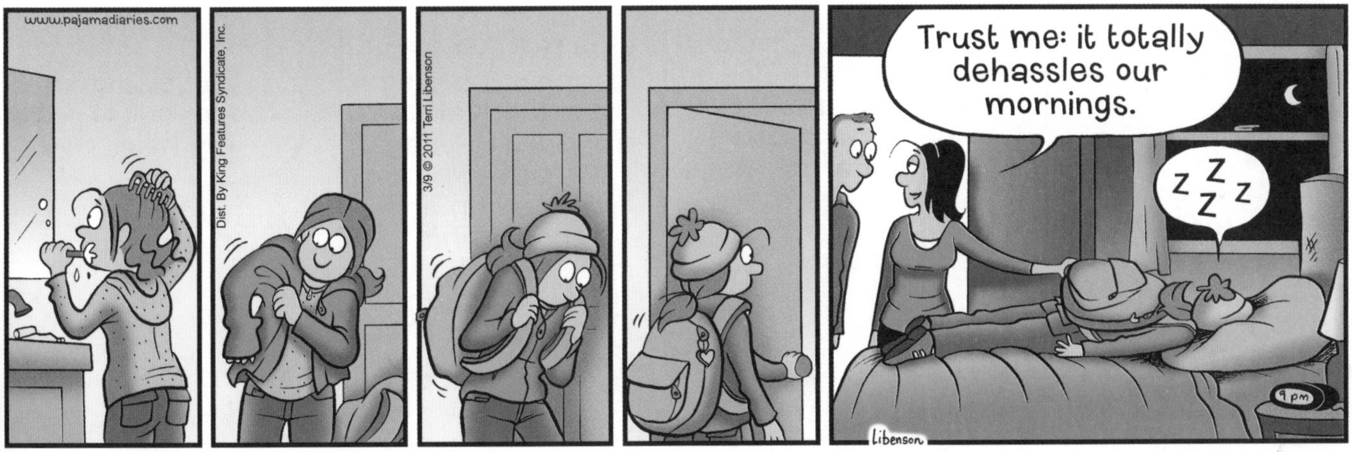
www.pajamadiaries.com
Dist. By King Features Syndicate, Inc.
3/9 © 2011 Terri Libenson
Trust me: it totally dehassles our mornings.
Z Z Z Z
9 pm
Libenson

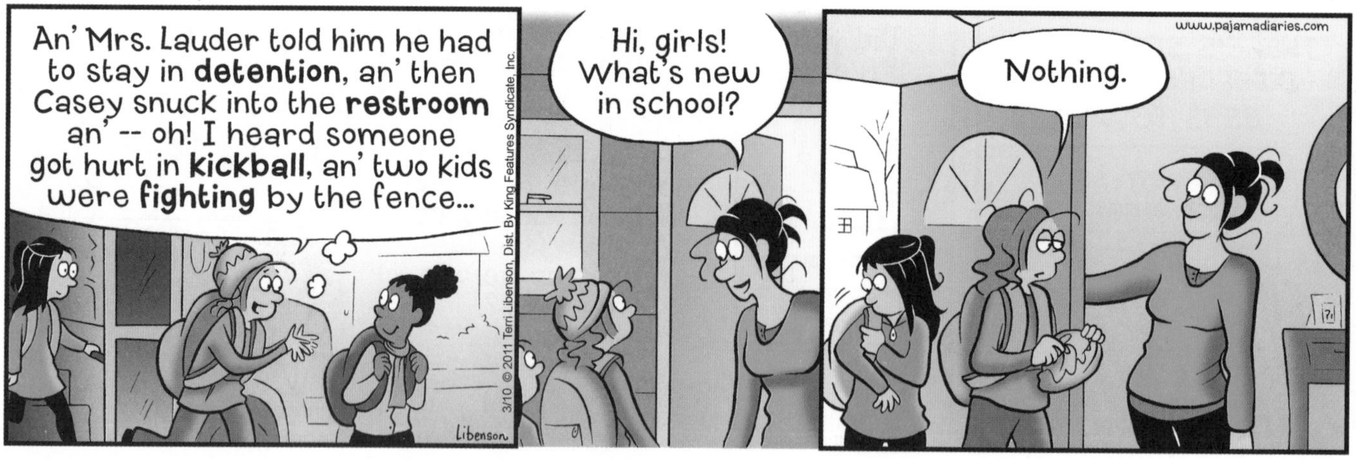
An' Mrs. Lauder told him he had to stay in **detention**, an' then Casey snuck into the **restroom** an' -- oh! I heard someone got hurt in **kickball**, an' two kids were **fighting** by the fence...
3/10 © 2011 Terri Libenson, Dist. By King Features Syndicate, Inc.
Libenson
Hi, girls! What's new in school?
www.pajamadiaries.com
Nothing.

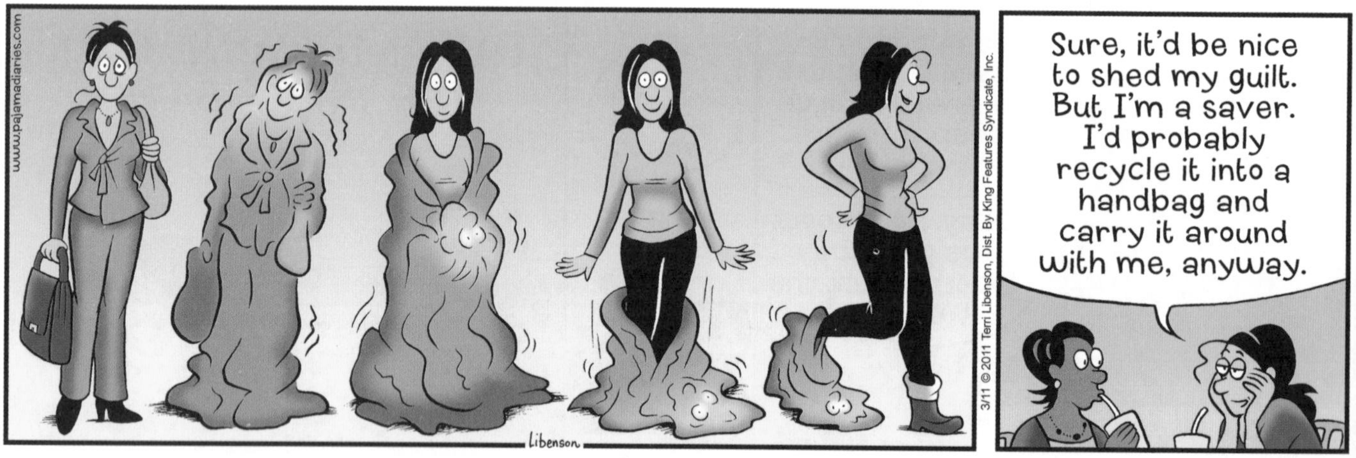
www.pajamadiaries.com
Libenson
3/11 © 2011 Terri Libenson, Dist. By King Features Syndicate, Inc.
Sure, it'd be nice to shed my guilt. But I'm a saver. I'd probably recycle it into a handbag and carry it around with me, anyway.

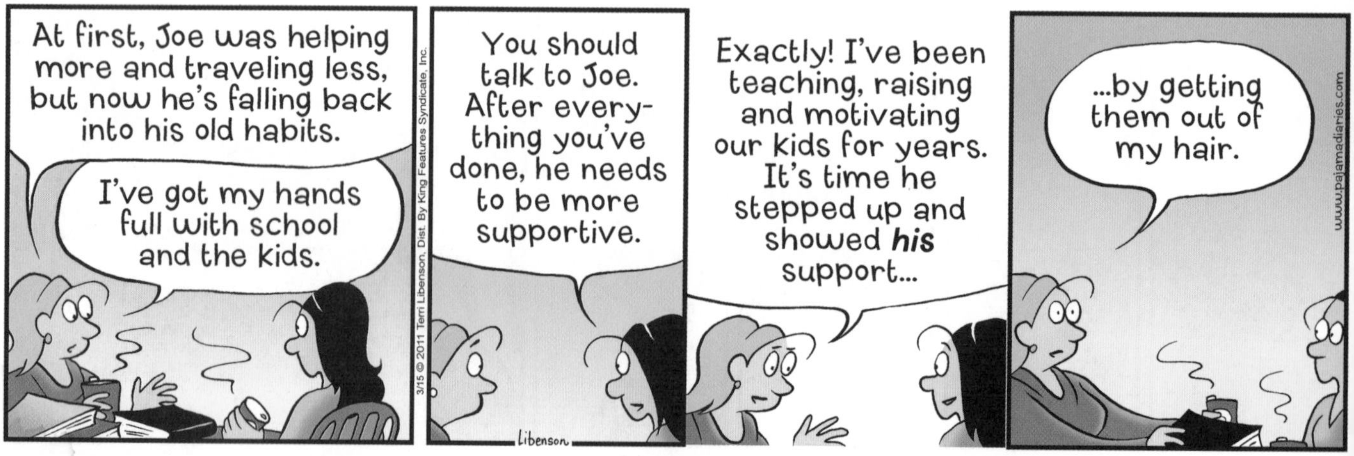
At first, Joe was helping more and traveling less, but now he's falling back into his old habits.
I've got my hands full with school and the kids.
3/15 © 2011 Terri Libenson, Dist. By King Features Syndicate, Inc.
You should talk to Joe. After everything you've done, he needs to be more supportive.
Libenson
Exactly! I've been teaching, raising and motivating our kids for years. It's time he stepped up and showed ***his*** support...
...by getting them out of my hair.
www.pajamadiaries.com

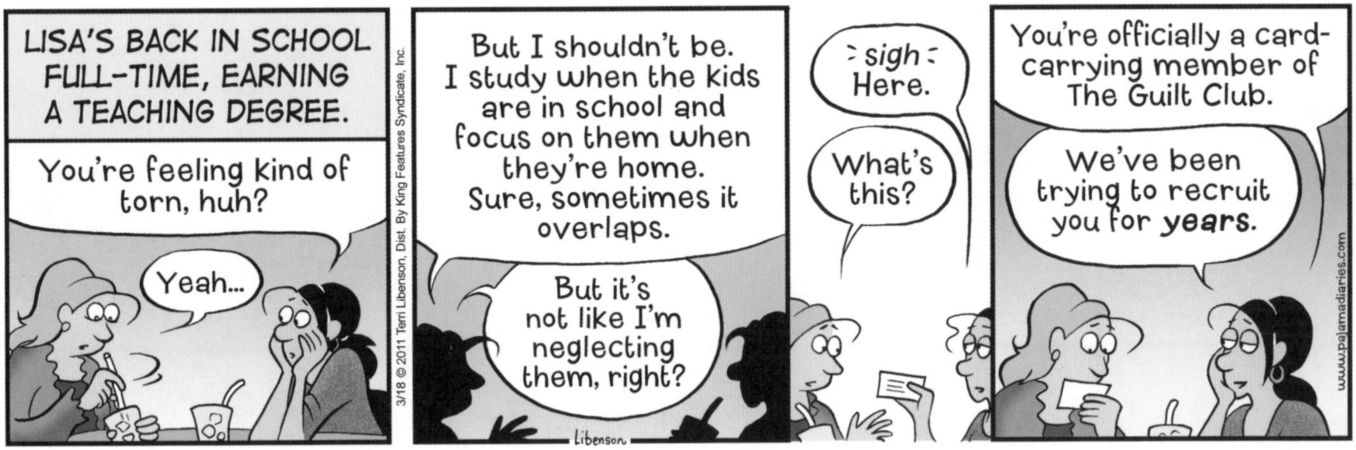
LISA'S BACK IN SCHOOL FULL-TIME, EARNING A TEACHING DEGREE.
You're feeling kind of torn, huh?
Yeah...
3/18 © 2011 Terri Libenson, Dist. By King Features Syndicate, Inc.
But I shouldn't be. I study when the kids are in school and focus on them when they're home. Sure, sometimes it overlaps.
But it's not like I'm neglecting them, right?
Libenson
What's this?
sigh Here.
You're officially a card-carrying member of The Guilt Club.
We've been trying to recruit you for **years**.
www.pajamadiaries.com

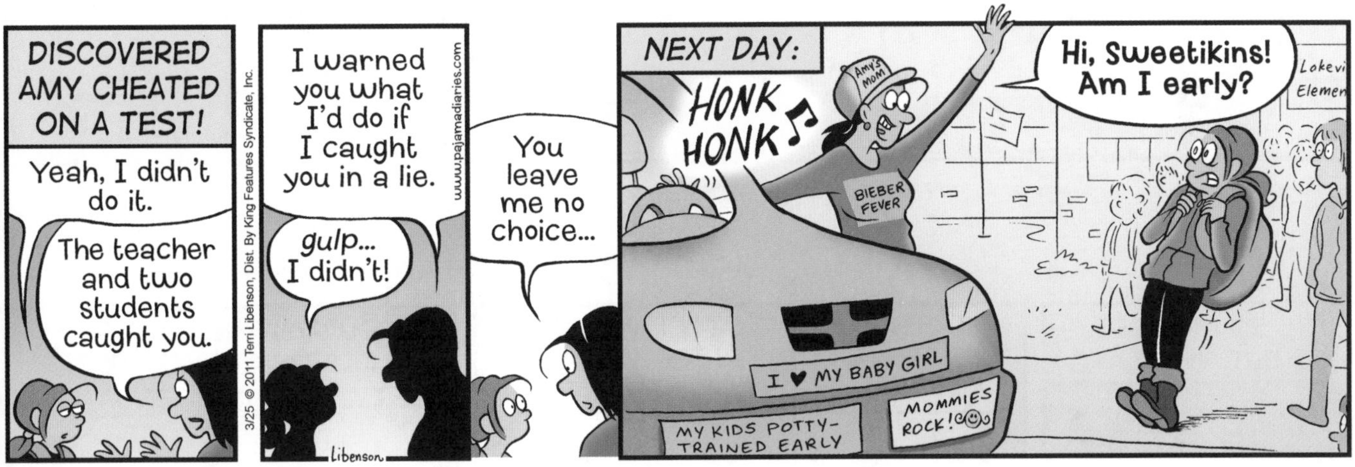
DISCOVERED AMY CHEATED ON A TEST!
Yeah, I didn't do it.
The teacher and two students caught you.
3/25 © 2011 Terri Libenson, Dist. By King Features Syndicate, Inc.
I warned you what I'd do if I caught you in a lie.
gulp... I didn't!
www.pajamadiaries.com
Libenson
You leave me no choice...
NEXT DAY:
HONK HONK
Amy's MOM
BIEBER FEVER
Hi, Sweetikins! Am I early?
I ♥ MY BABY GIRL
MY KIDS POTTY-TRAINED EARLY
MOMMIES ROCK!

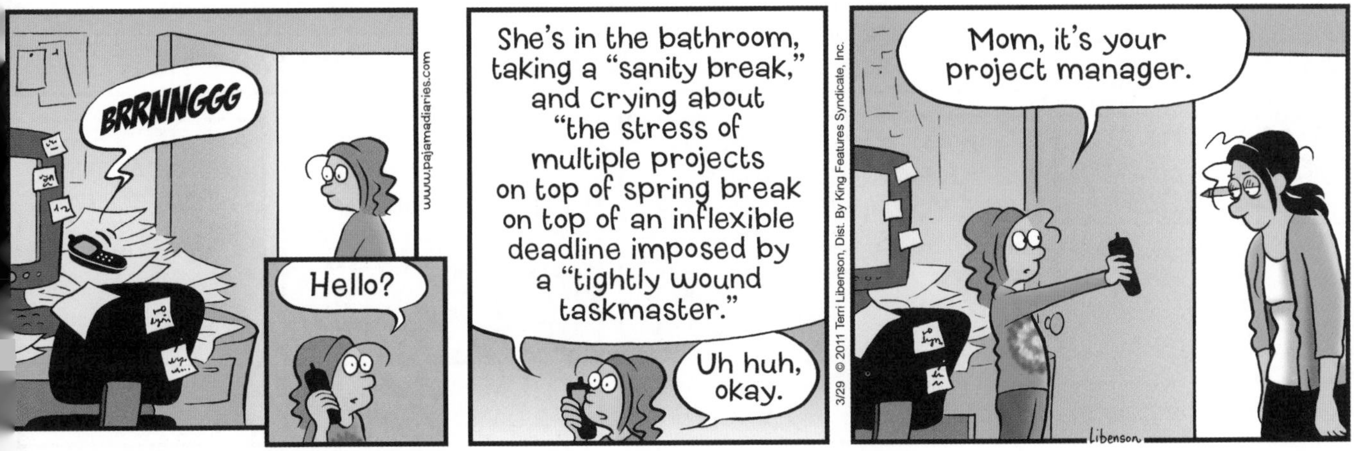
BRRNNGGG
www.pajamadiaries.com
Hello?
She's in the bathroom, taking a "sanity break," and crying about "the stress of multiple projects on top of spring break on top of an inflexible deadline imposed by a "tightly wound taskmaster."
Uh huh, okay.
3/29 © 2011 Terri Libenson, Dist. By King Features Syndicate, Inc.
Mom, it's your project manager.
Libenson

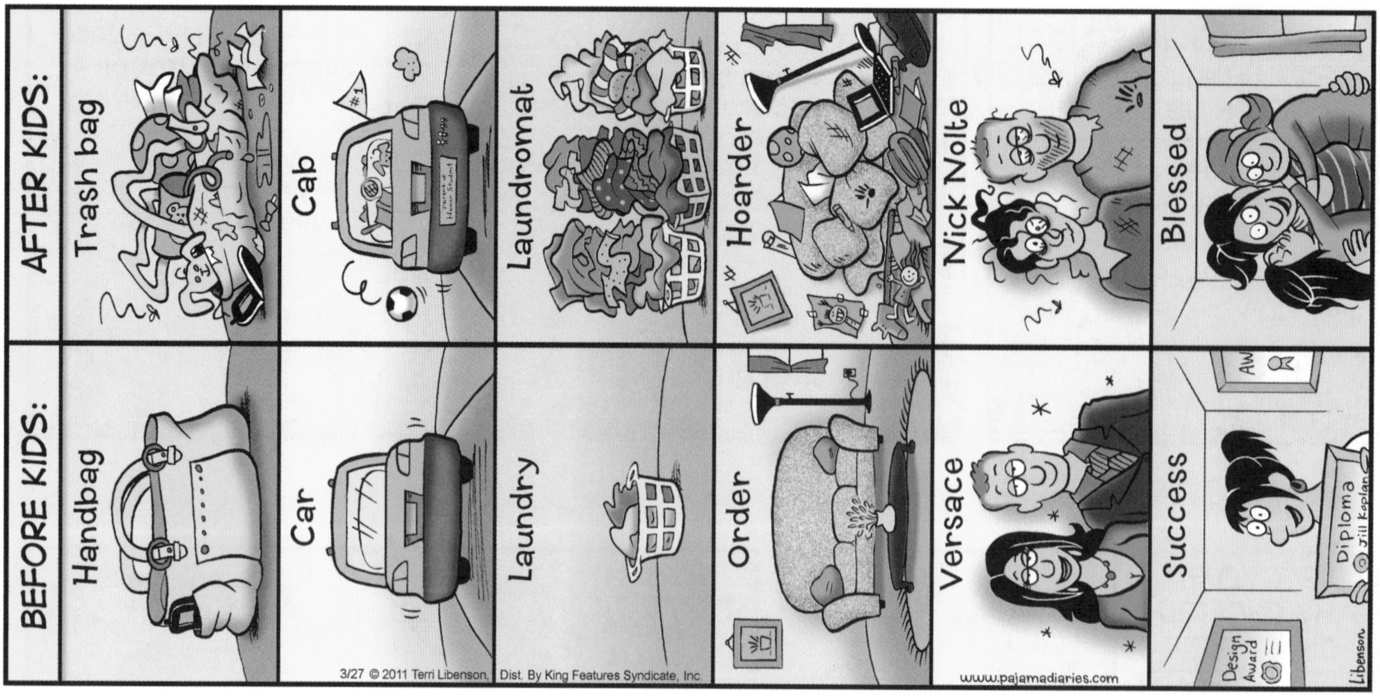
BEFORE KIDS:
AFTER KIDS:
Handbag
Trash bag
Car
Cab
#1
Laundry
Laundromat
Order
Hoarder
Versace
Nick Nolte
Success
Diploma
Jill Kaplan
Design Award
Blessed
3/27 © 2011 Terri Libenson, Dist. By King Features Syndicate, Inc.
www.pajamadiaries.com
Libenson

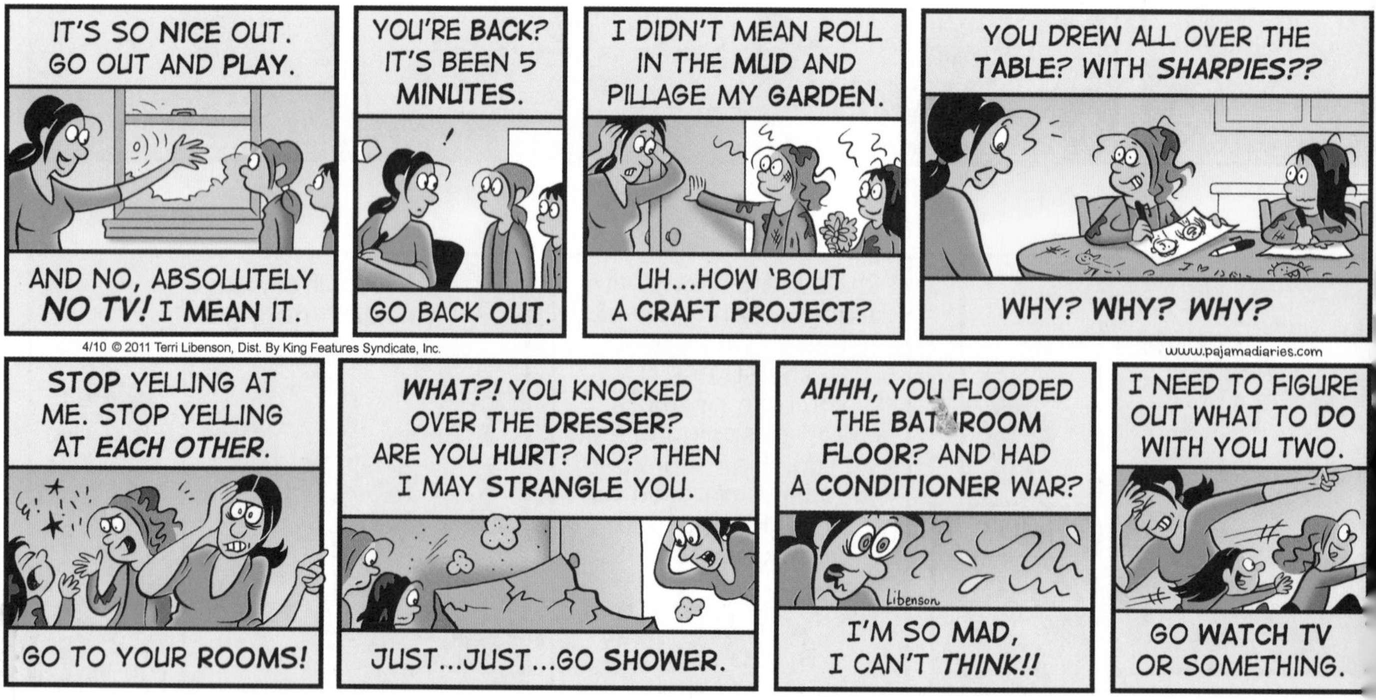
IT'S SO NICE OUT. GO OUT AND PLAY.
AND NO, ABSOLUTELY NO TV! I MEAN IT.
YOU'RE BACK? IT'S BEEN 5 MINUTES.
GO BACK OUT.
I DIDN'T MEAN ROLL IN THE MUD AND PILLAGE MY GARDEN.
UH...HOW 'BOUT A CRAFT PROJECT?
YOU DREW ALL OVER THE TABLE? WITH SHARPIES??
WHY? WHY? WHY?
4/10 © 2011 Terri Libenson, Dist. By King Features Syndicate, Inc.
www.pajamadiaries.com
STOP YELLING AT ME. STOP YELLING AT EACH OTHER.
GO TO YOUR ROOMS!
WHAT?! YOU KNOCKED OVER THE DRESSER? ARE YOU HURT? NO? THEN I MAY STRANGLE YOU.
JUST...JUST...GO SHOWER.
AHHH, YOU FLOODED THE BATHROOM FLOOR? AND HAD A CONDITIONER WAR?
Libenson
I'M SO MAD, I CAN'T THINK!!
I NEED TO FIGURE OUT WHAT TO DO WITH YOU TWO.
GO WATCH TV OR SOMETHING.

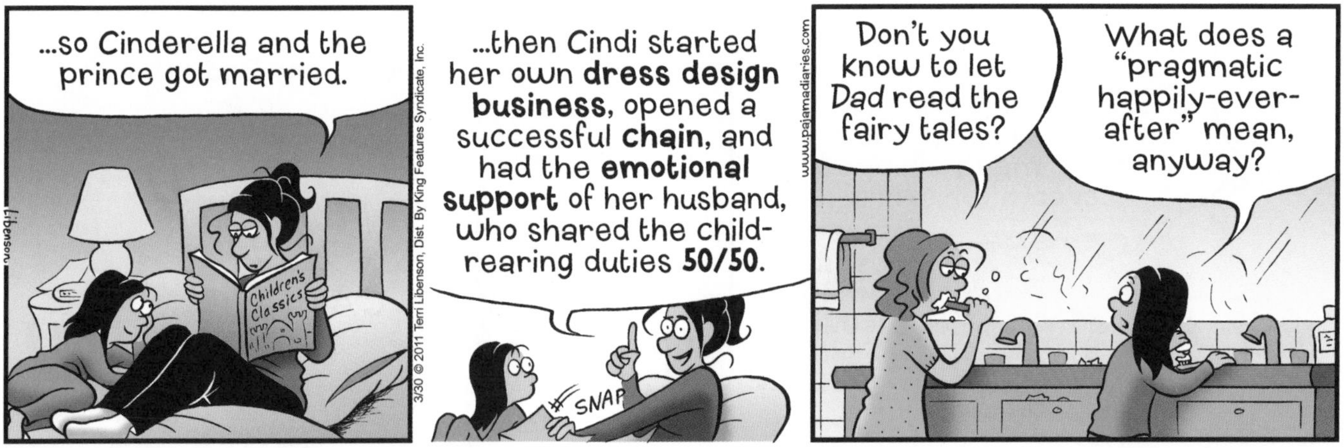
...so Cinderella and the prince got married.
Children's Classics
Libenson
3/30 © 2011 Terri Libenson, Dist. By King Features Syndicate, Inc.
...then Cindi started her own **dress design business**, opened a successful **chain**, and had the **emotional support** of her husband, who shared the child-rearing duties **50/50**.
SNAP
www.pajamadiaries.com
Don't you know to let *Dad* read the fairy tales?
What does a "pragmatic happily-ever-after" mean, anyway?

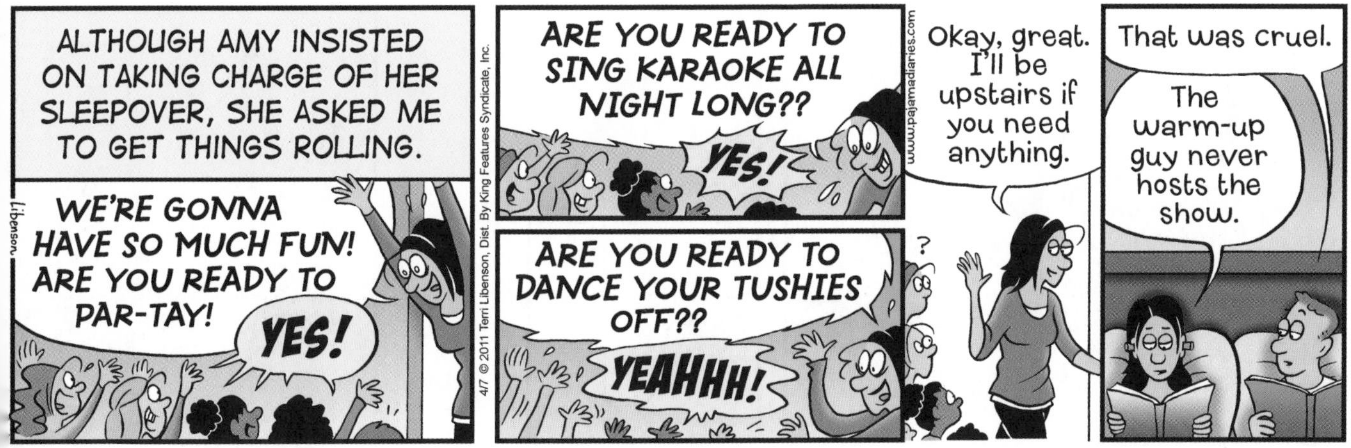
ALTHOUGH AMY INSISTED ON TAKING CHARGE OF HER SLEEPOVER, SHE ASKED ME TO GET THINGS ROLLING.
Libenson
WE'RE GONNA HAVE SO MUCH FUN! ARE YOU READY TO PAR-TAY!
YES!
4/7 © 2011 Terri Libenson, Dist. By King Features Syndicate, Inc.
ARE YOU READY TO SING KARAOKE ALL NIGHT LONG??
YES!
ARE YOU READY TO DANCE YOUR TUSHIES OFF??
YEAHHH!
www.pajamadiaries.com
Okay, great. I'll be upstairs if you need anything.
?
That was cruel.
The warm-up guy never hosts the show.

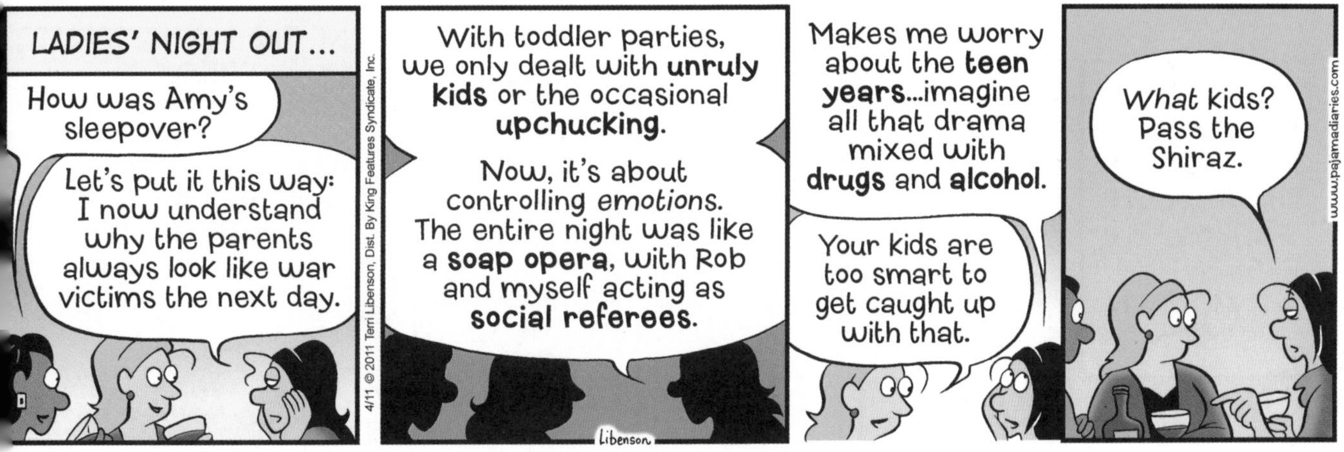
LADIES' NIGHT OUT...
How was Amy's sleepover?
Let's put it this way: I now understand why the parents always look like war victims the next day.
4/11 © 2011 Terri Libenson, Dist. By King Features Syndicate, Inc.
With toddler parties, we only dealt with **unruly kids** or the occasional **upchucking**.
Now, it's about controlling *emotions*. The entire night was like a **soap opera**, with Rob and myself acting as **social referees**.
Libenson
Makes me worry about the **teen years**...imagine all that drama mixed with **drugs** and **alcohol**.
Your kids are too smart to get caught up with that.
What kids? Pass the Shiraz.
www.pajamadiaries.com

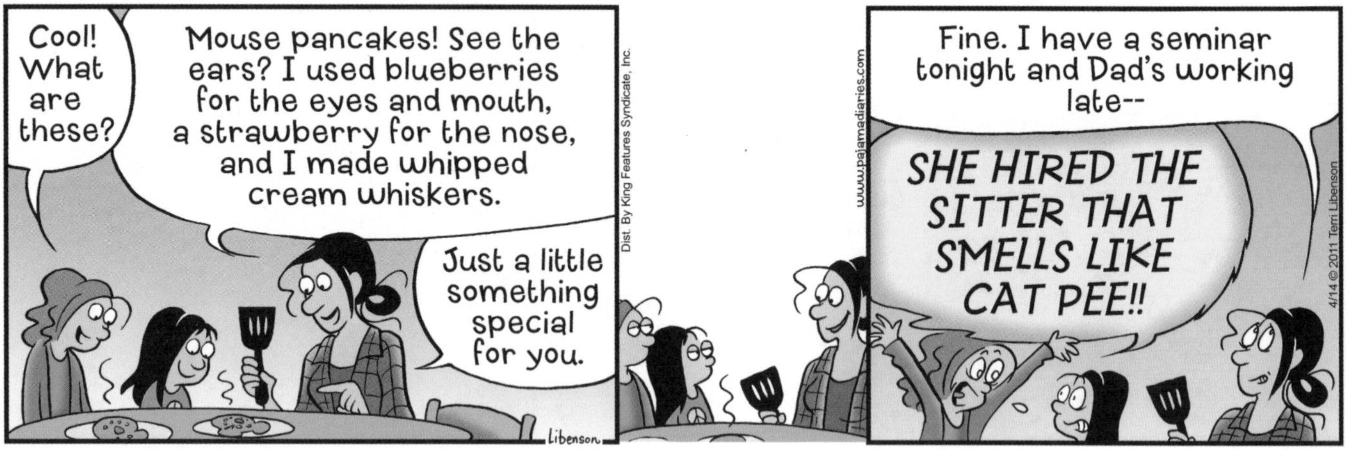
Cool! What are these?
Mouse pancakes! See the ears? I used blueberries for the eyes and mouth, a strawberry for the nose, and I made whipped cream whiskers.
Just a little something special for you.
Libenson
Dist. By King Features Syndicate, Inc.
www.pajamadiaries.com
Fine. I have a seminar tonight and Dad's working late--
SHE HIRED THE SITTER THAT SMELLS LIKE CAT PEE!!
4/14 © 2011 Terri Libenson

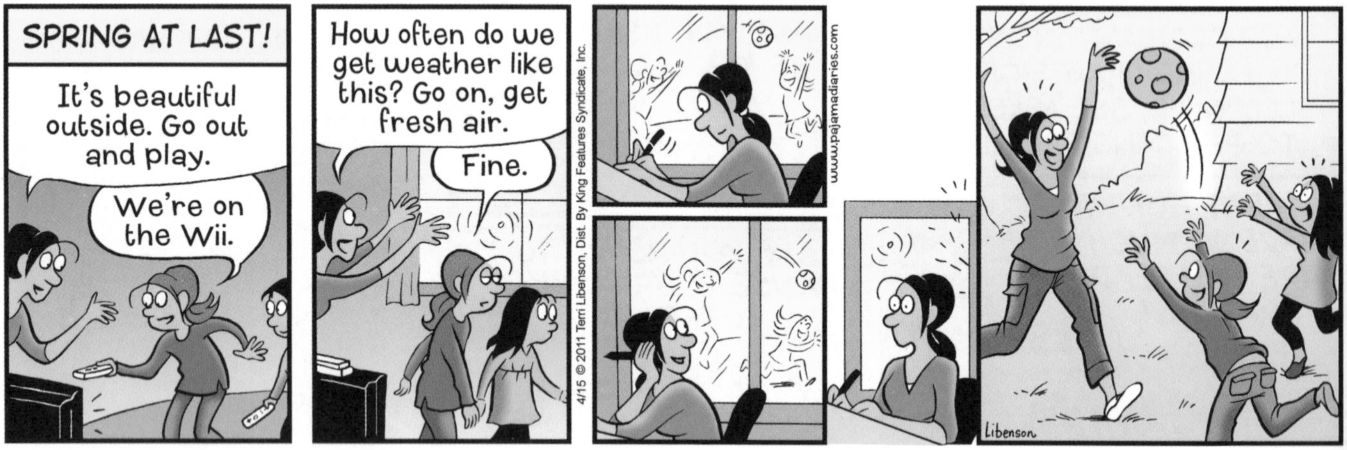
SPRING AT LAST!
It's beautiful outside. Go out and play.
We're on the Wii.
How often do we get weather like this? Go on, get fresh air.
Fine.
4/15 © 2011 Terri Libenson, Dist. By King Features Syndicate, Inc.
www.pajamadiaries.com
Libenson

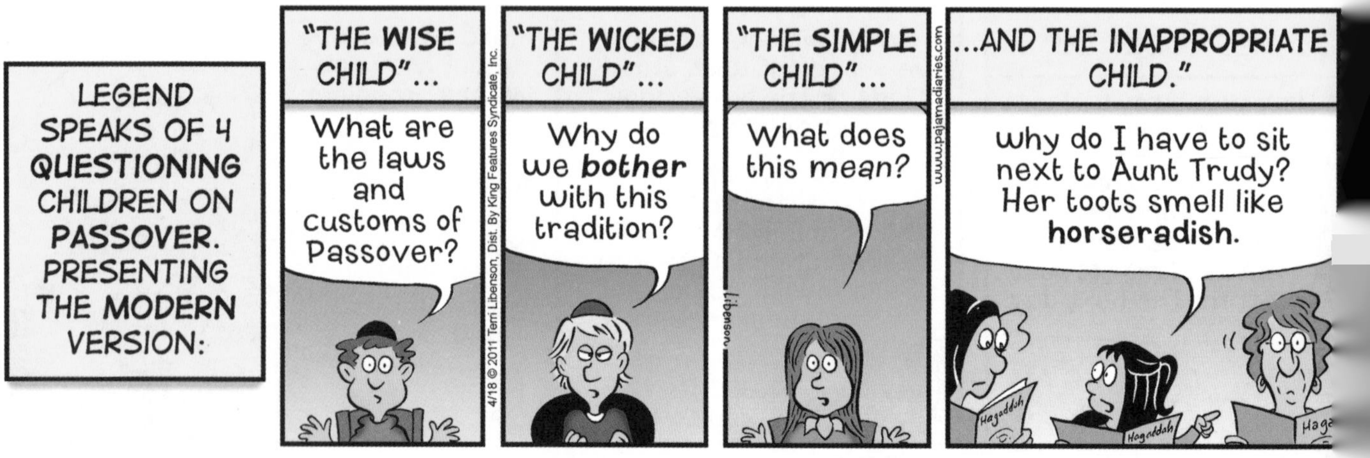
LEGEND SPEAKS OF 4 QUESTIONING CHILDREN ON PASSOVER. PRESENTING THE MODERN VERSION:
"THE WISE CHILD"...
What are the laws and customs of Passover?
4/18 © 2011 Terri Libenson, Dist. By King Features Syndicate, Inc.
"THE WICKED CHILD"...
Why do we bother with this tradition?
Libenson
"THE SIMPLE CHILD"...
What does this mean?
www.pajamadiaries.com
...AND THE INAPPROPRIATE CHILD."
Why do I have to sit next to Aunt Trudy? Her toots smell like horseradish.
Hagaddah
Hagaddah

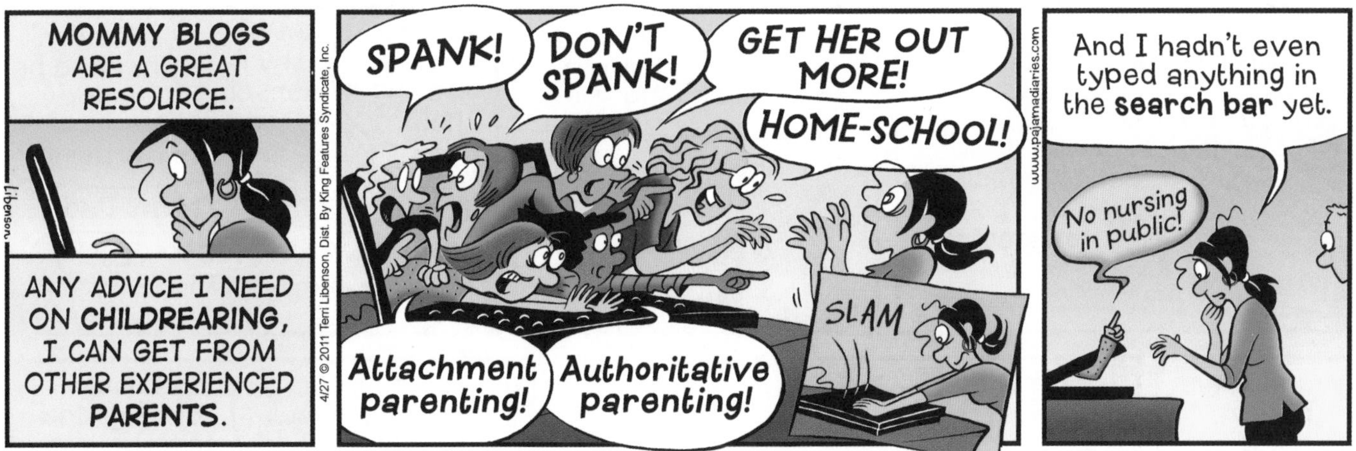
MOMMY BLOGS ARE A GREAT RESOURCE.
ANY ADVICE I NEED ON CHILDREARING, I CAN GET FROM OTHER EXPERIENCED PARENTS.
Libenson
4/27 © 2011 Terri Libenson, Dist. By King Features Syndicate, Inc.
SPANK!
DON'T SPANK!
GET HER OUT MORE!
HOME-SCHOOL!
Attachment parenting!
Authoritative parenting!
SLAM
www.pajamadiaries.com
And I hadn't even typed anything in the search bar yet.
No nursing in public!

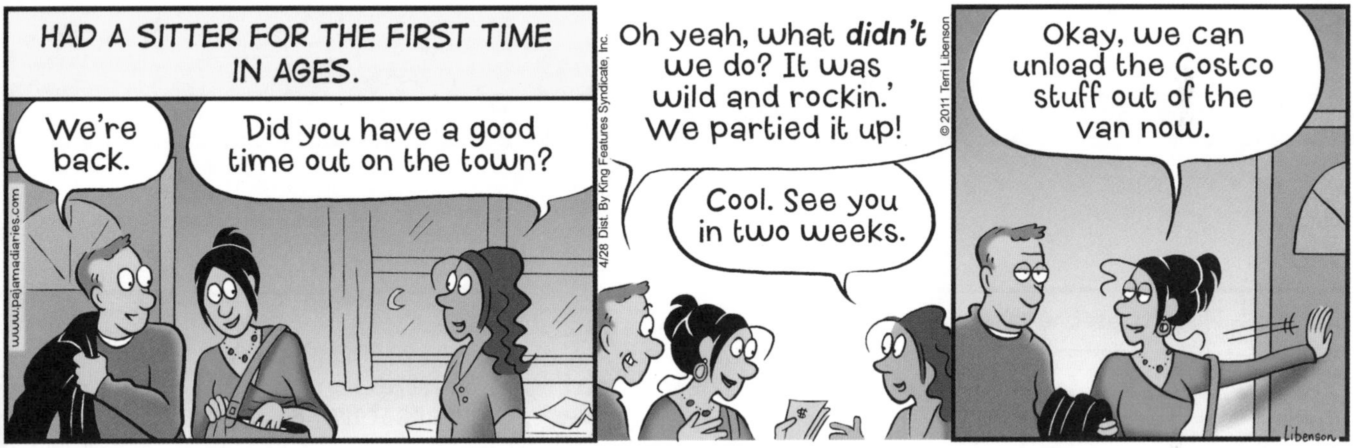
HAD A SITTER FOR THE FIRST TIME IN AGES.
We're back.
Did you have a good time out on the town?
www.pajamadiaries.com
4/28 Dist. By King Features Syndicate, Inc.
Oh yeah, what didn't we do? It was wild and rockin.' We partied it up!
Cool. See you in two weeks.
© 2011 Terri Libenson
Okay, we can unload the Costco stuff out of the van now.
Libenson

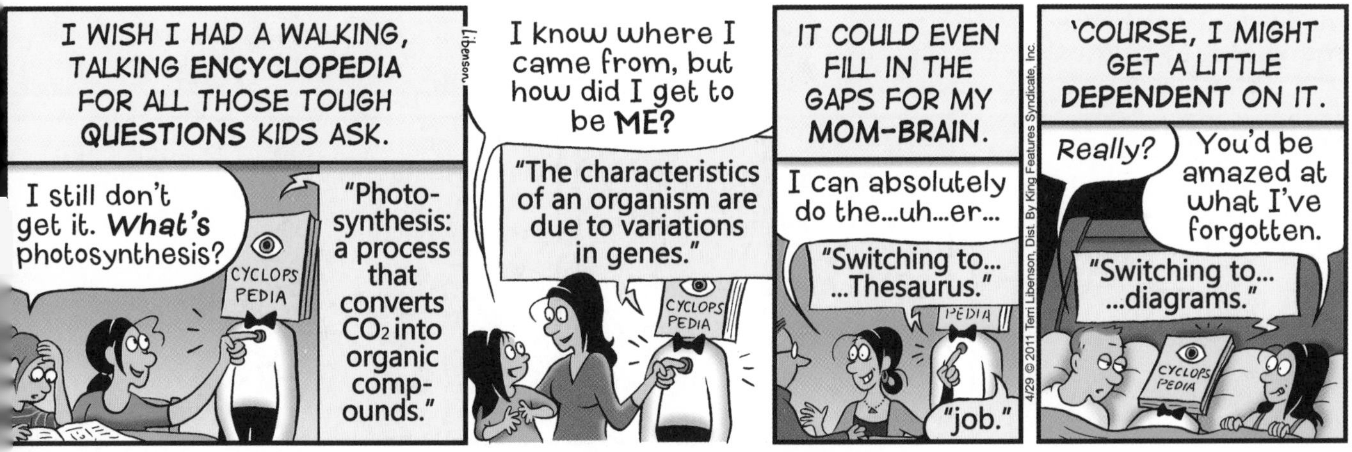
I WISH I HAD A WALKING, TALKING ENCYCLOPEDIA FOR ALL THOSE TOUGH QUESTIONS KIDS ASK.
I still don't get it. What's photosynthesis?
"Photo-synthesis: a process that converts CO2 into organic comp-ounds."
CYCLOPS PEDIA
Libenson
I know where I came from, but how did I get to be ME?
"The characteristics of an organism are due to variations in genes."
CYCLOPS PEDIA
IT COULD EVEN FILL IN THE GAPS FOR MY MOM-BRAIN.
I can absolutely do the...uh...er...
"Switching to... ...Thesaurus."
PEDIA
"job."
4/29 © 2011 Terri Libenson, Dist. By King Features Syndicate, Inc.
'COURSE, I MIGHT GET A LITTLE DEPENDENT ON IT.
Really?
You'd be amazed at what I've forgotten.
"Switching to... ...diagrams."
CYCLOPS PEDIA

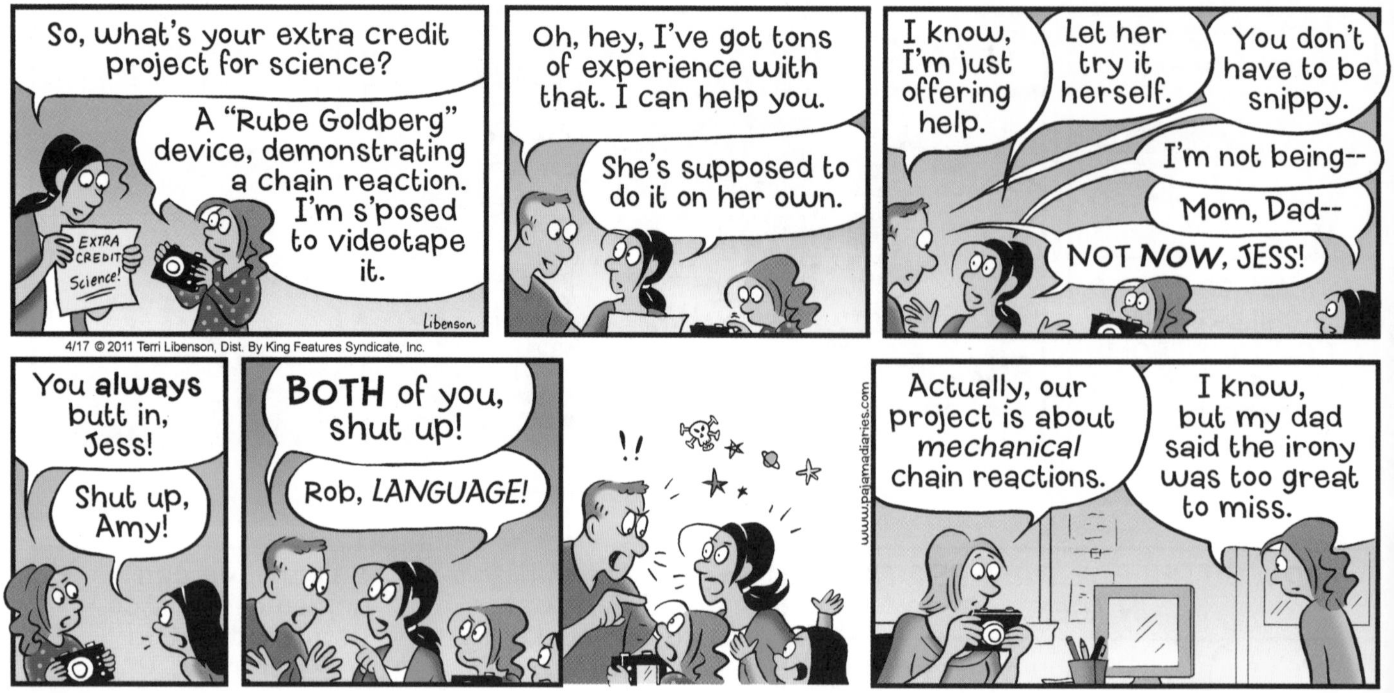
So, what's your extra credit project for science?
A "Rube Goldberg" device, demonstrating a chain reaction. I'm s'posed to videotape it.
EXTRA CREDIT Science!
Libenson
Oh, hey, I've got tons of experience with that. I can help you.
She's supposed to do it on her own.
I know, I'm just offering help.
Let her try it herself.
You don't have to be snippy.
I'm not being--
Mom, Dad--
NOT **NOW**, JESS!
4/17 © 2011 Terri Libenson, Dist. By King Features Syndicate, Inc.
You **always** butt in, Jess!
Shut up, Amy!
BOTH of you, shut up!
Rob, *LANGUAGE!*
!!
www.pajamadiaries.com
Actually, our project is about *mechanical* chain reactions.
I know, but my dad said the irony was too great to miss.

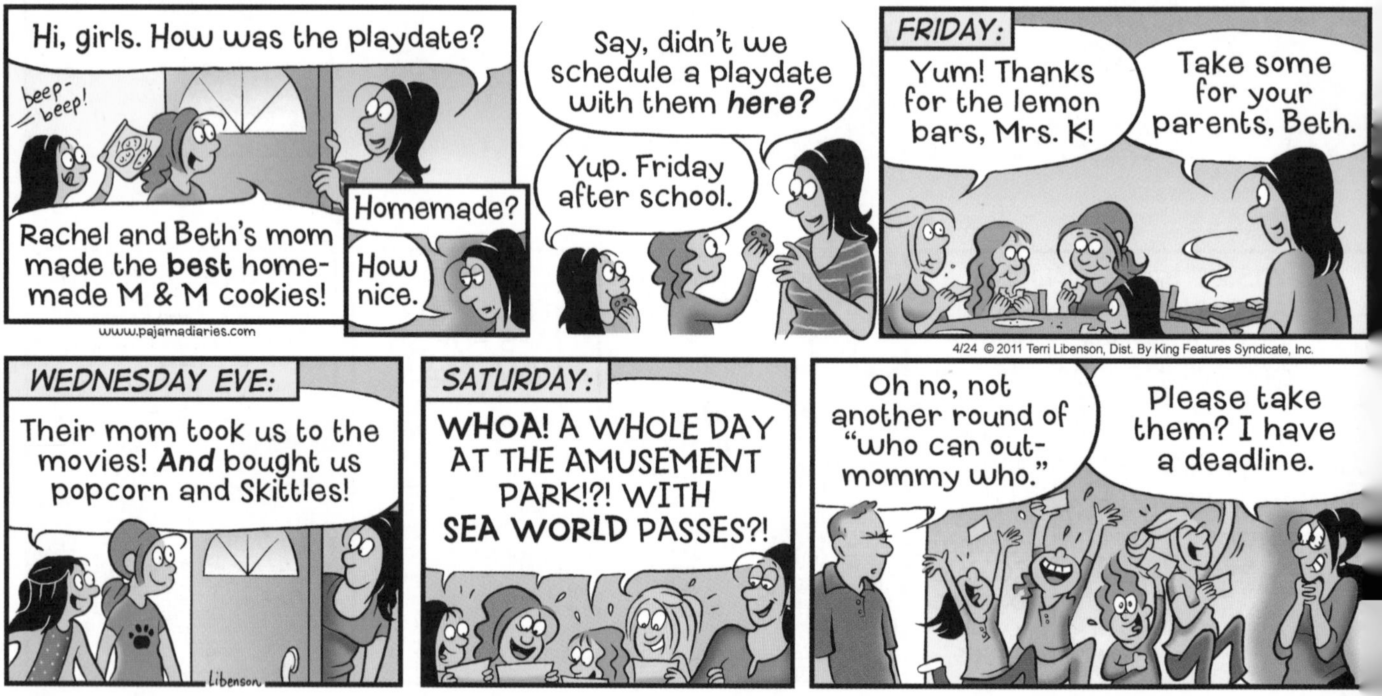
Hi, girls. How was the playdate?
beep-beep!
Rachel and Beth's mom made the **best** home-made M & M cookies!
Homemade?
How nice.
www.pajamadiaries.com
Say, didn't we schedule a playdate with them ***here?***
Yup. Friday after school.
FRIDAY:
Yum! Thanks for the lemon bars, Mrs. K!
Take some for your parents, Beth.
4/24 © 2011 Terri Libenson, Dist. By King Features Syndicate, Inc.
WEDNESDAY EVE:
Their mom took us to the movies! ***And*** bought us popcorn and Skittles!
Libenson
SATURDAY:
WHOA! A WHOLE DAY AT THE AMUSEMENT PARK!?! WITH **SEA WORLD** PASSES?!
Oh no, not another round of "who can out-mommy who."
Please take them? I have a deadline.

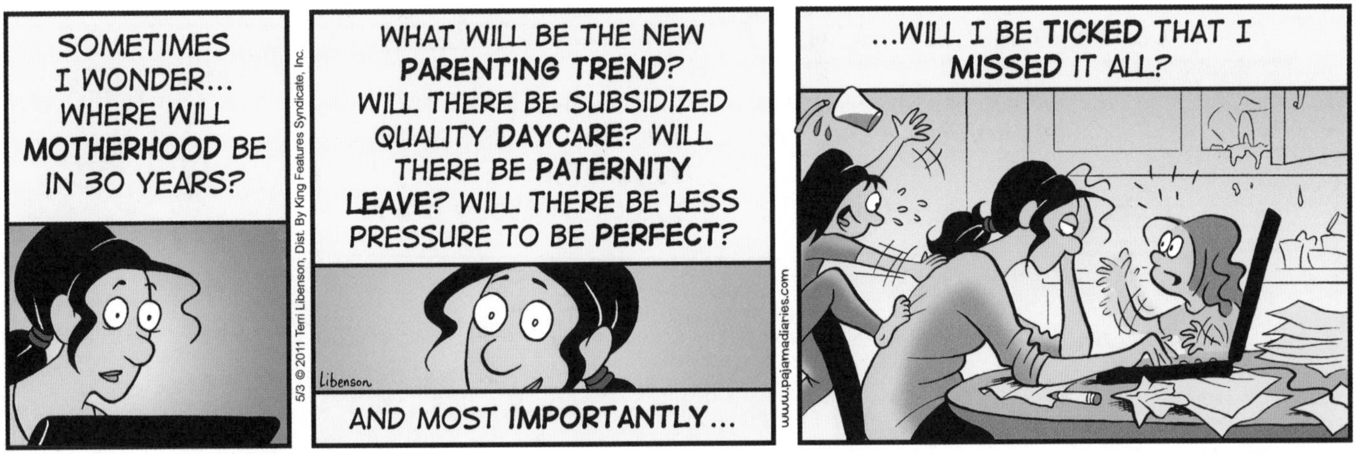
SOMETIMES I WONDER... WHERE WILL MOTHERHOOD BE IN 30 YEARS?
5/3 © 2011 Terri Libenson, Dist. By King Features Syndicate, Inc.
WHAT WILL BE THE NEW PARENTING TREND? WILL THERE BE SUBSIDIZED QUALITY DAYCARE? WILL THERE BE PATERNITY LEAVE? WILL THERE BE LESS PRESSURE TO BE PERFECT?
Libenson
AND MOST IMPORTANTLY...
www.pajamadiaries.com
...WILL I BE TICKED THAT I MISSED IT ALL?

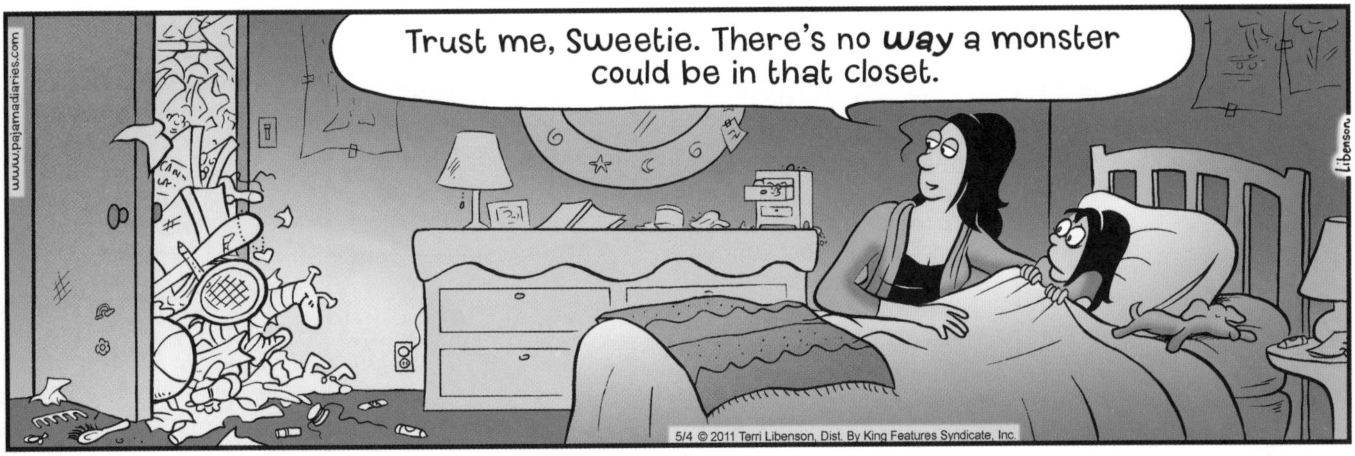
www.pajamadiaries.com
Trust me, Sweetie. There's no way a monster could be in that closet.
Libenson
5/4 © 2011 Terri Libenson, Dist. By King Features Syndicate, Inc.

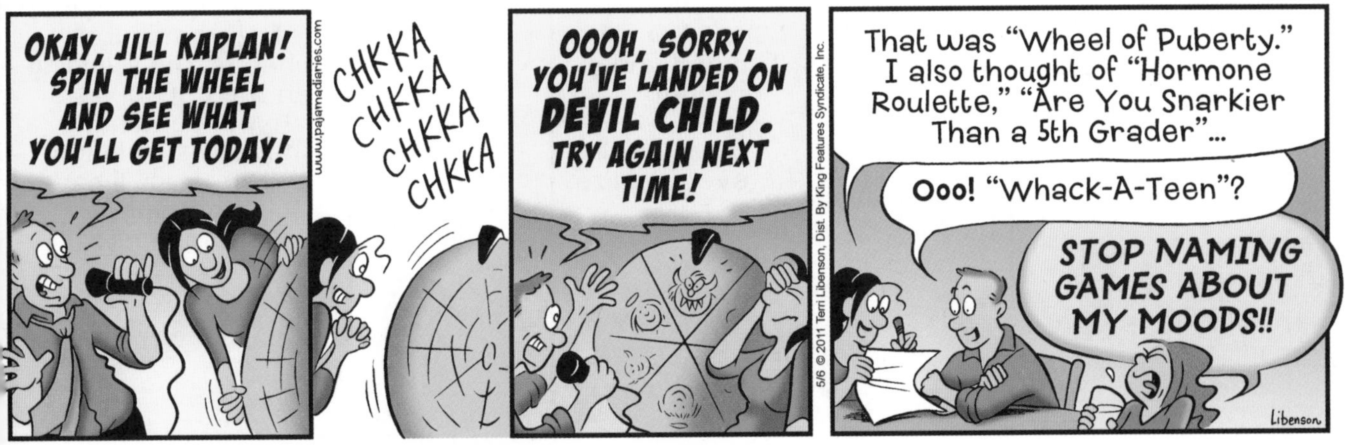
OKAY, JILL KAPLAN! SPIN THE WHEEL AND SEE WHAT YOU'LL GET TODAY!
www.pajamadiaries.com
CHKKA CHKKA CHKKA CHKKA
OOOH, SORRY, YOU'VE LANDED ON DEVIL CHILD. TRY AGAIN NEXT TIME!
5/6 © 2011 Terri Libenson, Dist. By King Features Syndicate, Inc.
That was "Wheel of Puberty." I also thought of "Hormone Roulette," "Are You Snarkier Than a 5th Grader"...
Ooo! "Whack-A-Teen"?
STOP NAMING GAMES ABOUT MY MOODS!!
Libenson

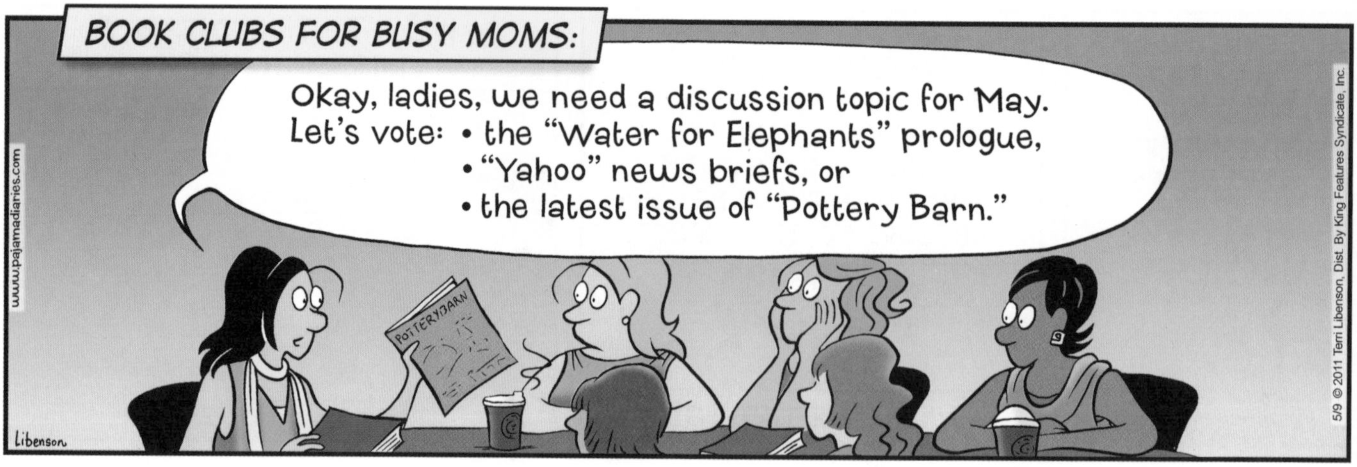
BOOK CLUBS FOR BUSY MOMS:
Okay, ladies, we need a discussion topic for May. Let's vote: • the "Water for Elephants" prologue, • "Yahoo" news briefs, or • the latest issue of "Pottery Barn."
POTTERY BARN
www.pajamadiaries.com
Libenson
5/9 © 2011 Terri Libenson, Dist. By King Features Syndicate, Inc.

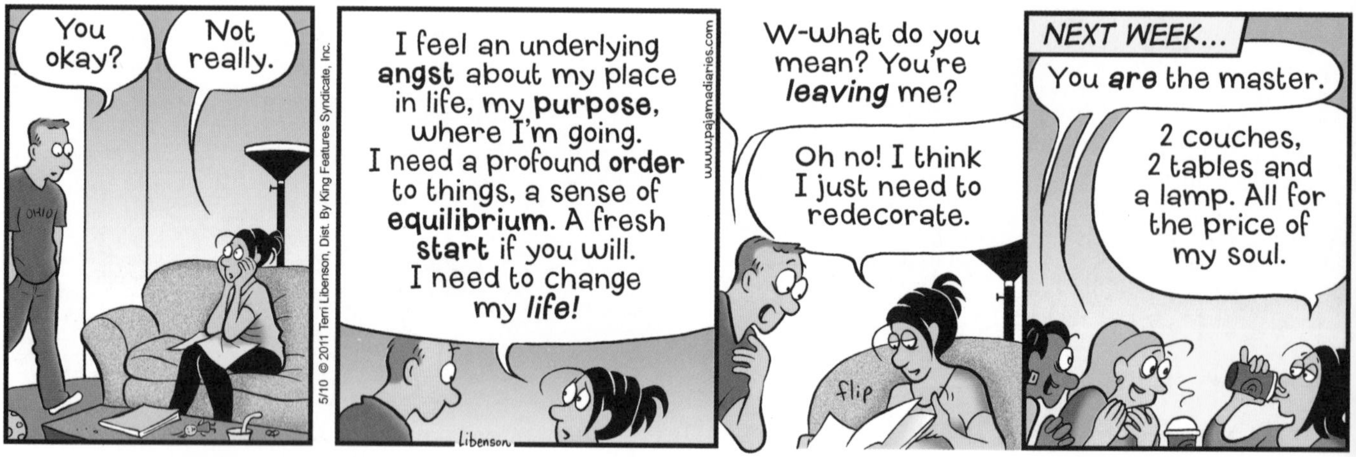
You okay?
Not really.
OHIO
5/10 © 2011 Terri Libenson, Dist. By King Features Syndicate, Inc.
I feel an underlying **angst** about my place in life, my **purpose**, where I'm going. I need a profound **order** to things, a sense of **equilibrium**. A fresh **start** if you will. I need to change my ***life!***
www.pajamadiaries.com
Libenson
W-what do you mean? You're ***leaving*** me?
Oh no! I think I just need to redecorate.
flip
NEXT WEEK...
You **are** the master.
2 couches, 2 tables and a lamp. All for the price of my soul.

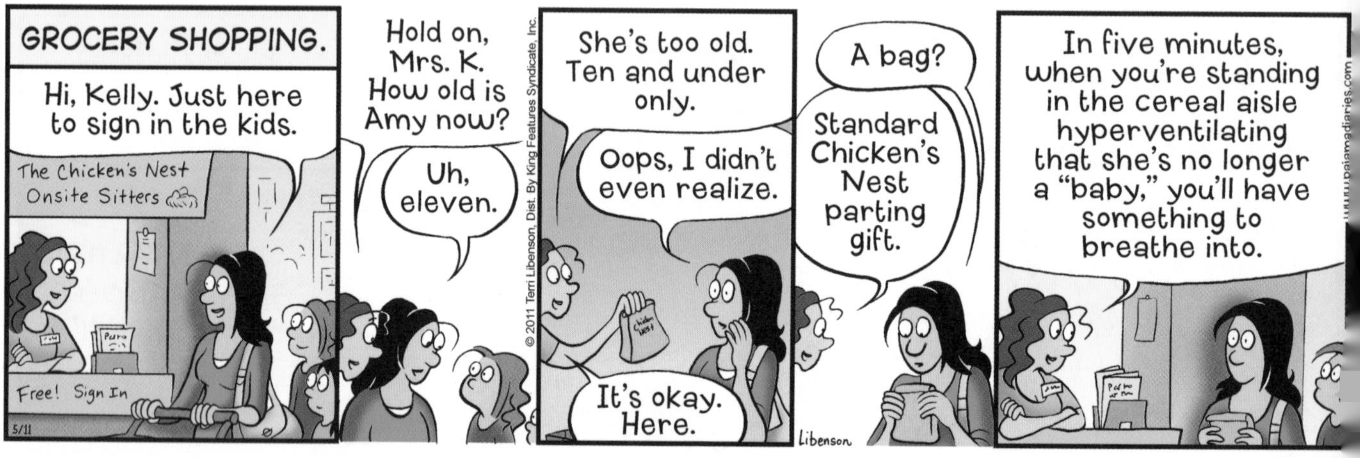
GROCERY SHOPPING.
Hi, Kelly. Just here to sign in the kids.
The Chicken's Nest Onsite Sitters
Free! Sign In
5/11
Hold on, Mrs. K. How old is Amy now?
Uh, eleven.
© 2011 Terri Libenson, Dist. By King Features Syndicate, Inc.
She's too old. Ten and under only.
Oops, I didn't even realize.
It's okay. Here.
A bag?
Standard Chicken's Nest parting gift.
Libenson
In five minutes, when you're standing in the cereal aisle hyperventilating that she's no longer a "baby," you'll have something to breathe into.
www.pajamadiaries.com

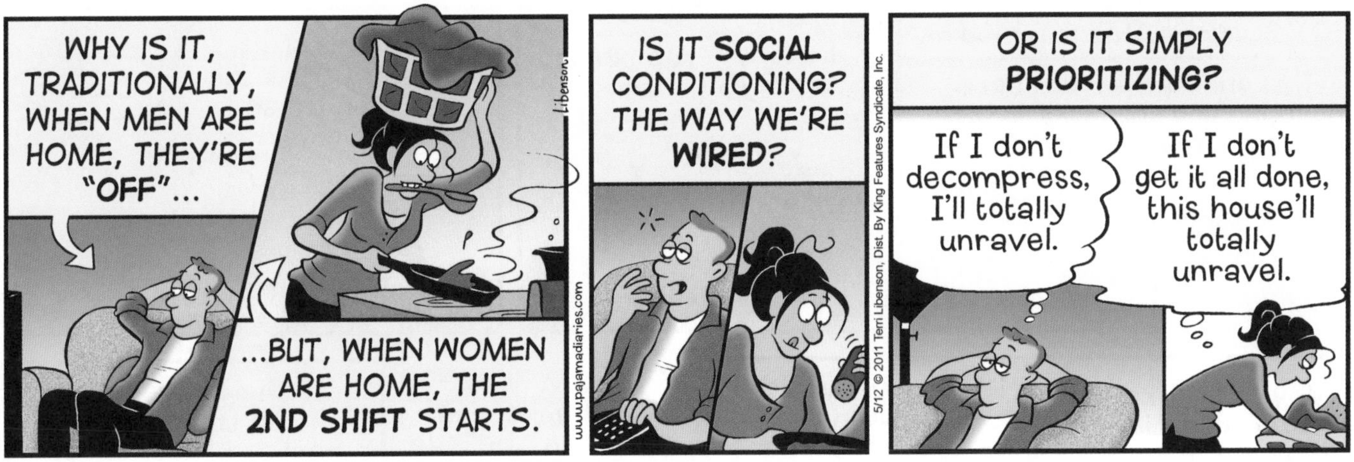
WHY IS IT, TRADITIONALLY, WHEN MEN ARE HOME, THEY'RE "OFF"...
...BUT, WHEN WOMEN ARE HOME, THE 2ND SHIFT STARTS.
Libenson
www.pajamadiaries.com
IS IT SOCIAL CONDITIONING? THE WAY WE'RE WIRED?
5/12 © 2011 Terri Libenson, Dist. By King Features Syndicate, Inc.
OR IS IT SIMPLY PRIORITIZING?
If I don't decompress, I'll totally unravel.
If I don't get it all done, this house'll totally unravel.

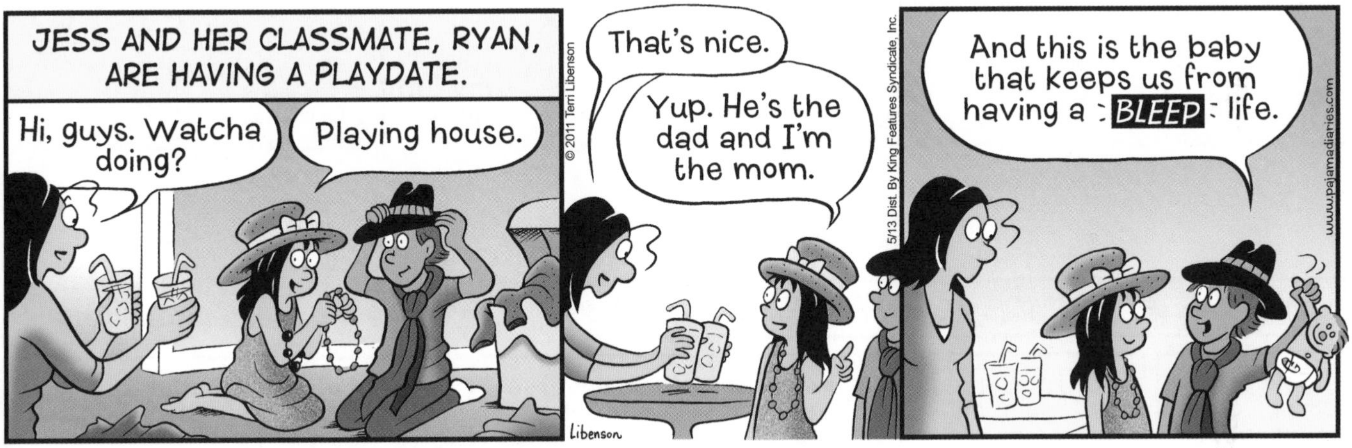
JESS AND HER CLASSMATE, RYAN, ARE HAVING A PLAYDATE.
Hi, guys. Watcha doing?
Playing house.
© 2011 Terri Libenson
That's nice.
Yup. He's the dad and I'm the mom.
Libenson
5/13 Dist. By King Features Syndicate, Inc.
And this is the baby that keeps us from having a BLEEP life.
www.pajamadiaries.com

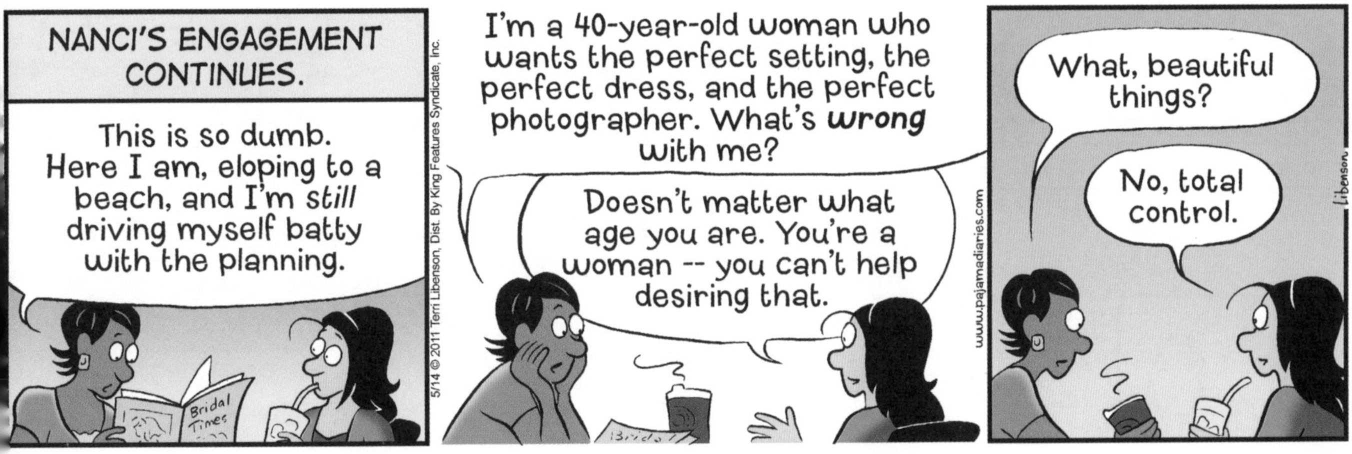
NANCI'S ENGAGEMENT CONTINUES.
This is so dumb. Here I am, eloping to a beach, and I'm *still* driving myself batty with the planning.
Bridal Times
5/14 © 2011 Terri Libenson, Dist. By King Features Syndicate, Inc.
I'm a 40-year-old woman who wants the perfect setting, the perfect dress, and the perfect photographer. What's **wrong** with me?
Doesn't matter what age you are. You're a woman -- you can't help desiring that.
www.pajamadiaries.com
What, beautiful things?
No, total control.
Libenson

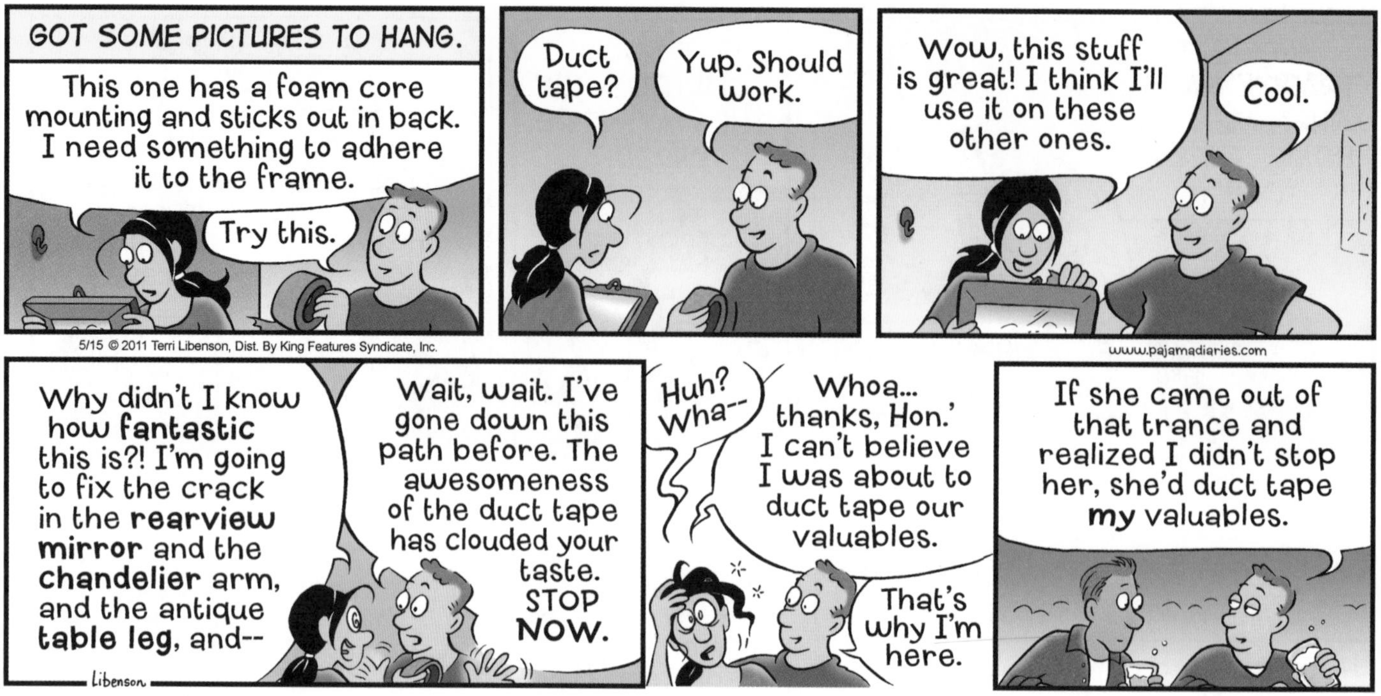
GOT SOME PICTURES TO HANG.
This one has a foam core mounting and sticks out in back. I need something to adhere it to the frame.
Try this.
Duct tape?
Yup. Should work.
Wow, this stuff is great! I think I'll use it on these other ones.
Cool.
Why didn't I know how **fantastic** this is?! I'm going to fix the crack in the **rearview mirror** and the **chandelier** arm, and the antique **table leg**, and--
Wait, wait. I've gone down this path before. The awesomeness of the duct tape has clouded your taste. STOP **NOW.**
Huh? Wha--
Whoa... thanks, Hon.' I can't believe I was about to duct tape our valuables.
That's why I'm here.
If she came out of that trance and realized I didn't stop her, she'd duct tape **my** valuables.
Libenson
www.pajamadiaries.com

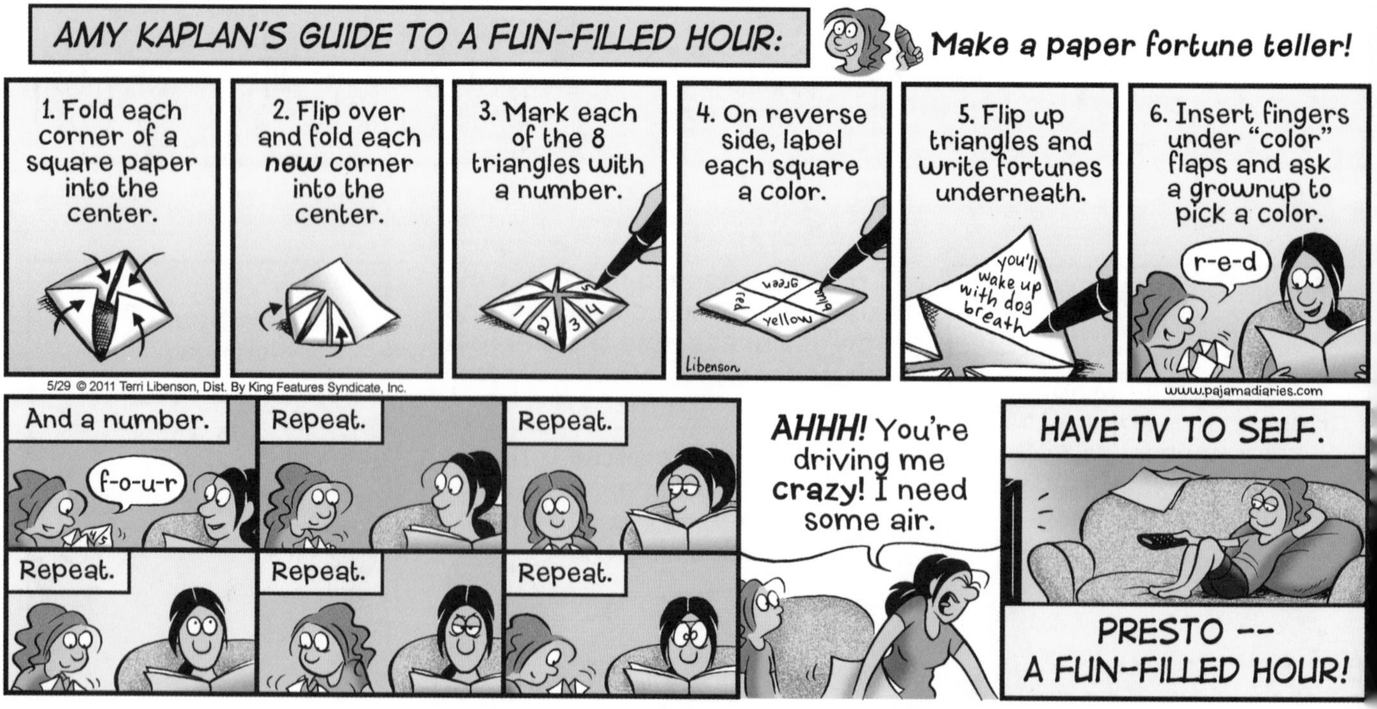
AMY KAPLAN'S GUIDE TO A FUN-FILLED HOUR:
Make a paper fortune teller!
1. Fold each corner of a square paper into the center.
2. Flip over and fold each *new* corner into the center.
3. Mark each of the 8 triangles with a number.
1 2 3 4 5
4. On reverse side, label each square a color.
green
blue
yellow
red
5. Flip up triangles and write fortunes underneath.
you'll wake up with dog breath
6. Insert fingers under "color" flaps and ask a grownup to pick a color.
r-e-d
Libenson
And a number.
f-o-u-r
Repeat.
Repeat.
Repeat.
Repeat.
Repeat.
AHHH! You're driving me **crazy!** I need some air.
HAVE TV TO SELF.
PRESTO -- A FUN-FILLED HOUR!
www.pajamadiaries.com

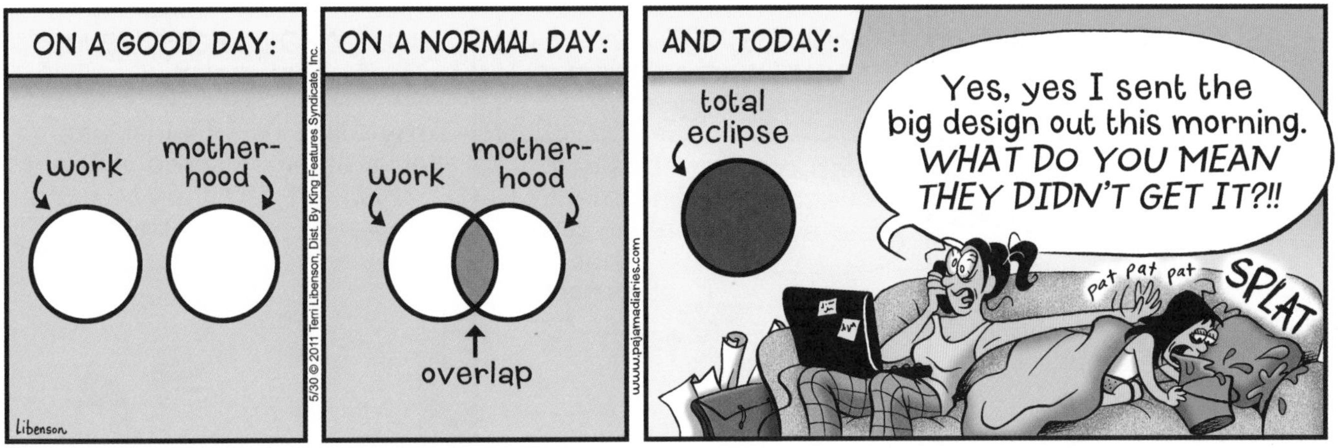
ON A GOOD DAY:
work
mother-hood
Libenson
5/30 © 2011 Terri Libenson, Dist. By King Features Syndicate, Inc.
ON A NORMAL DAY:
work
mother-hood
overlap
www.pajamadiaries.com
AND TODAY:
total eclipse
Yes, yes I sent the big design out this morning. WHAT DO YOU MEAN THEY DIDN'T GET IT?!!
pat pat pat
SPLAT

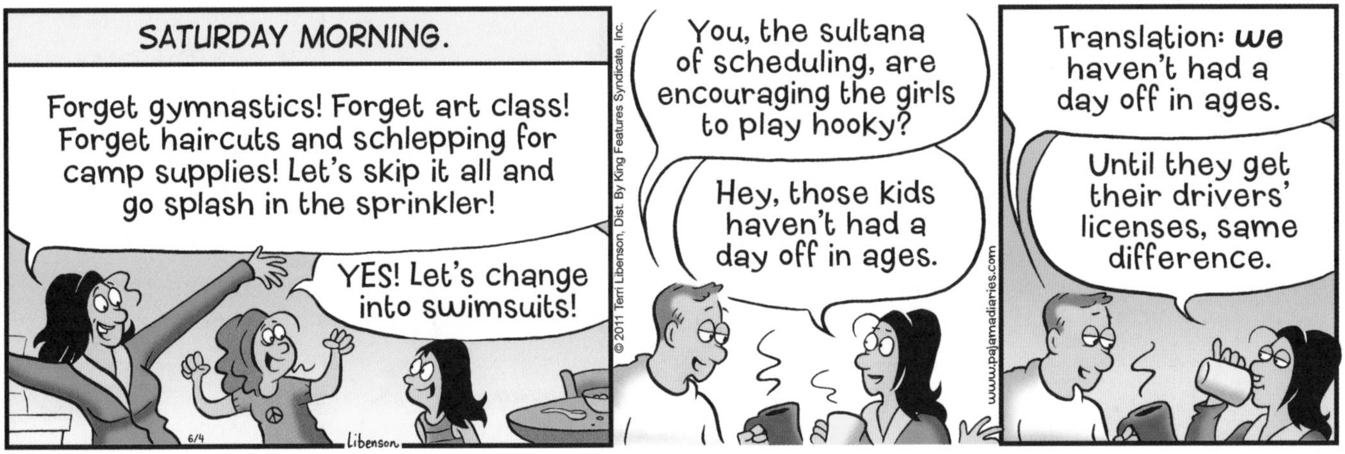
SATURDAY MORNING.
Forget gymnastics! Forget art class! Forget haircuts and schlepping for camp supplies! Let's skip it all and go splash in the sprinkler!
YES! Let's change into swimsuits!
6/4
Libenson
© 2011 Terri Libenson, Dist. By King Features Syndicate, Inc.
You, the sultana of scheduling, are encouraging the girls to play hooky?
Hey, those kids haven't had a day off in ages.
www.pajamadiaries.com
Translation: we haven't had a day off in ages.
Until they get their drivers' licenses, same difference.

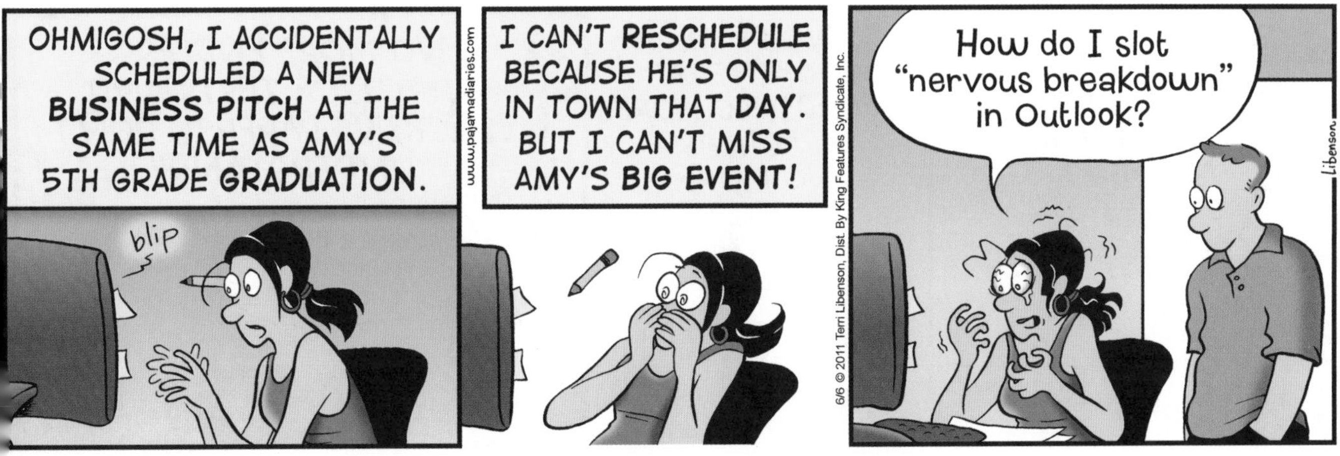
OHMIGOSH, I ACCIDENTALLY SCHEDULED A NEW BUSINESS PITCH AT THE SAME TIME AS AMY'S 5TH GRADE GRADUATION.
blip
www.pajamadiaries.com
I CAN'T RESCHEDULE BECAUSE HE'S ONLY IN TOWN THAT DAY. BUT I CAN'T MISS AMY'S BIG EVENT!
6/6 © 2011 Terri Libenson, Dist. By King Features Syndicate, Inc.
How do I slot "nervous breakdown" in Outlook?
Libenson

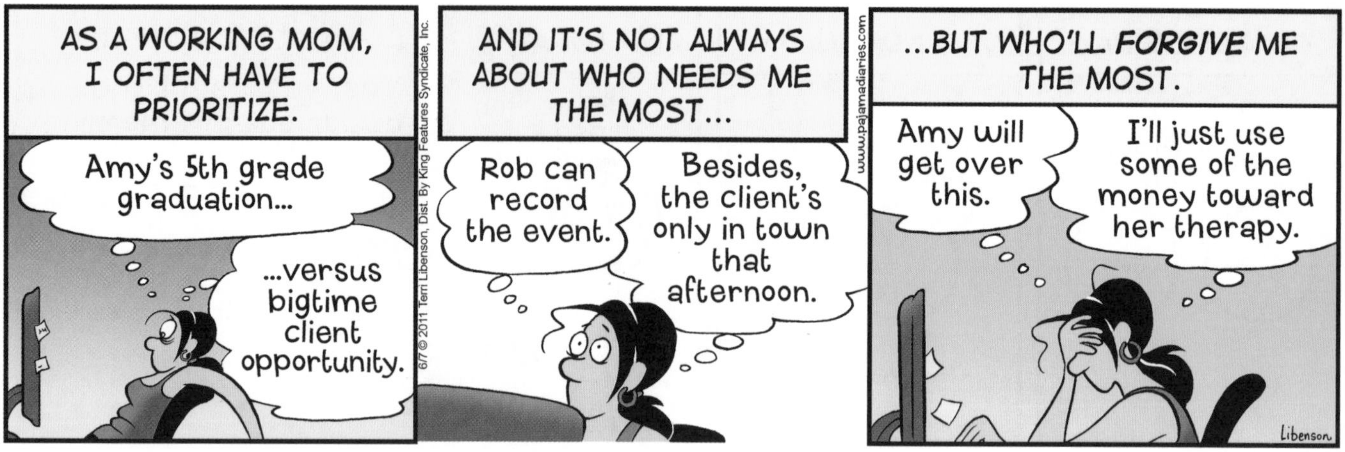
AS A WORKING MOM, I OFTEN HAVE TO PRIORITIZE.
Amy's 5th grade graduation...
...versus bigtime client opportunity.
6/7 © 2011 Terri Libenson, Dist. By King Features Syndicate, Inc.
AND IT'S NOT ALWAYS ABOUT WHO NEEDS ME THE MOST...
Rob can record the event.
Besides, the client's only in town that afternoon.
www.pajamadiaries.com
...BUT WHO'LL FORGIVE ME THE MOST.
Amy will get over this.
I'll just use some of the money toward her therapy.
Libenson

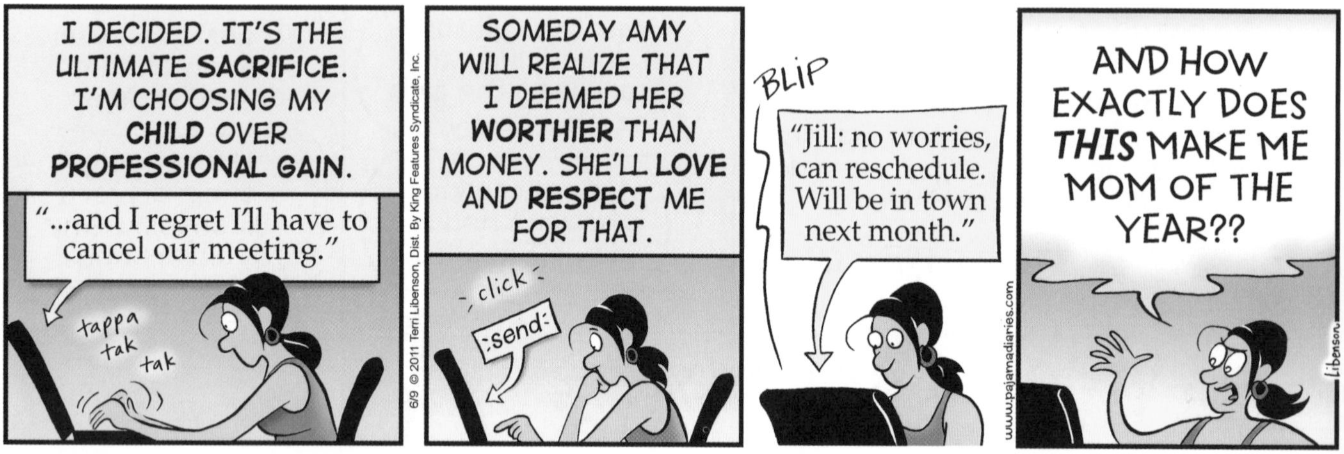
I DECIDED. IT'S THE ULTIMATE SACRIFICE. I'M CHOOSING MY CHILD OVER PROFESSIONAL GAIN.
"...and I regret I'll have to cancel our meeting."
tappa tak tak
6/9 © 2011 Terri Libenson, Dist. By King Features Syndicate, Inc.
SOMEDAY AMY WILL REALIZE THAT I DEEMED HER WORTHIER THAN MONEY. SHE'LL LOVE AND RESPECT ME FOR THAT.
click
send
BLIP
"Jill: no worries, can reschedule. Will be in town next month."
www.pajamadiaries.com
AND HOW EXACTLY DOES THIS MAKE ME MOM OF THE YEAR??
Libenson

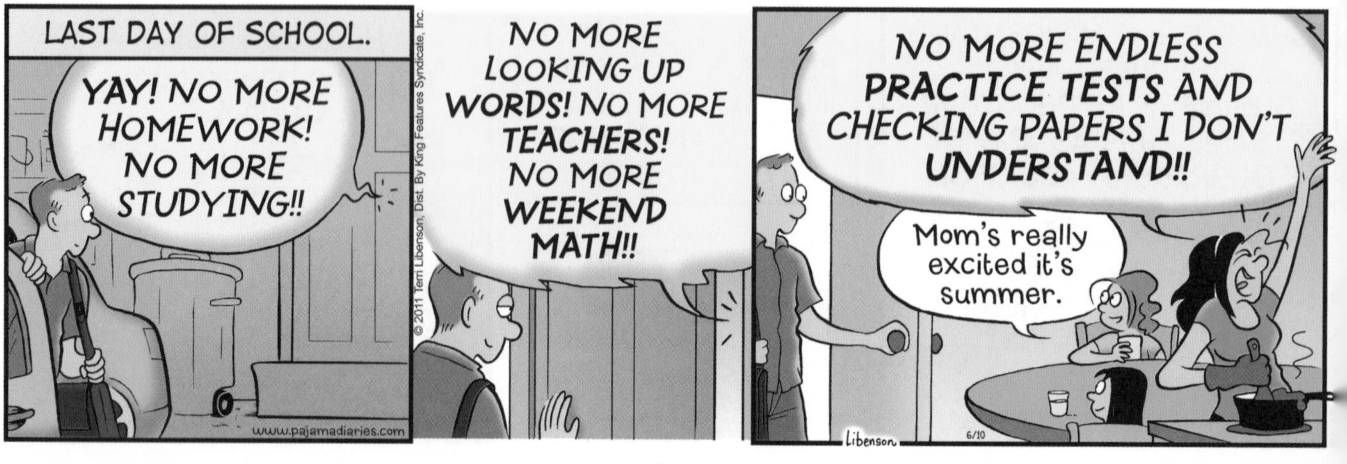
LAST DAY OF SCHOOL.
YAY! NO MORE HOMEWORK! NO MORE STUDYING!!
www.pajamadiaries.com
© 2011 Terri Libenson, Dist. By King Features Syndicate, Inc.
NO MORE LOOKING UP WORDS! NO MORE TEACHERS! NO MORE WEEKEND MATH!!
NO MORE ENDLESS PRACTICE TESTS AND CHECKING PAPERS I DON'T UNDERSTAND!!
Mom's really excited it's summer.
Libenson
6/10

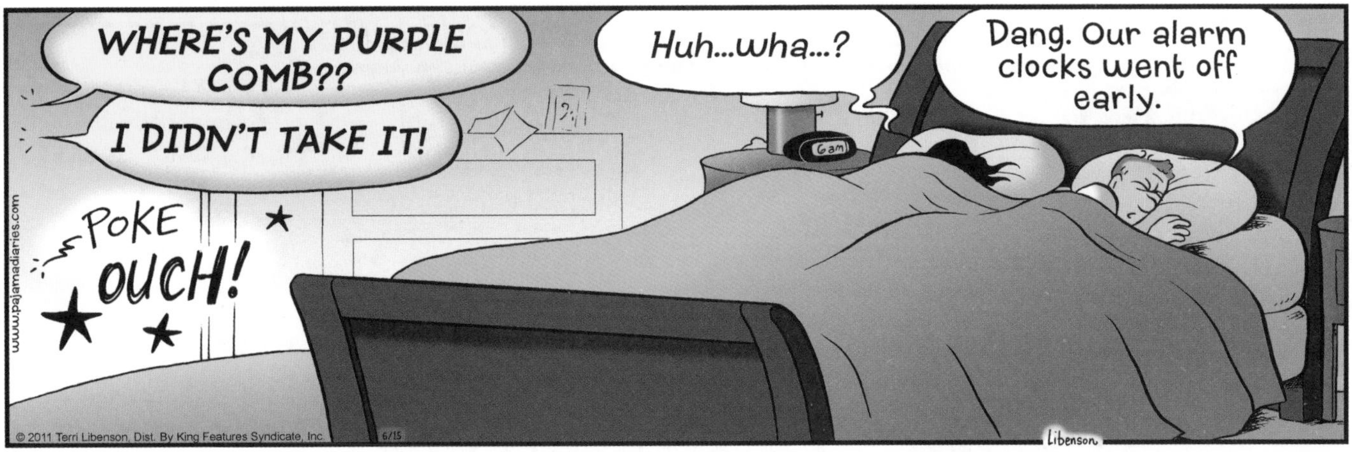
WHERE'S MY PURPLE COMB??
I DIDN'T TAKE IT!
POKE
OUCH!
Huh...wha...?
6am
Dang. Our alarm clocks went off early.
www.pajamadiaries.com
© 2011 Terri Libenson, Dist. By King Features Syndicate, Inc.
6/15
Libenson

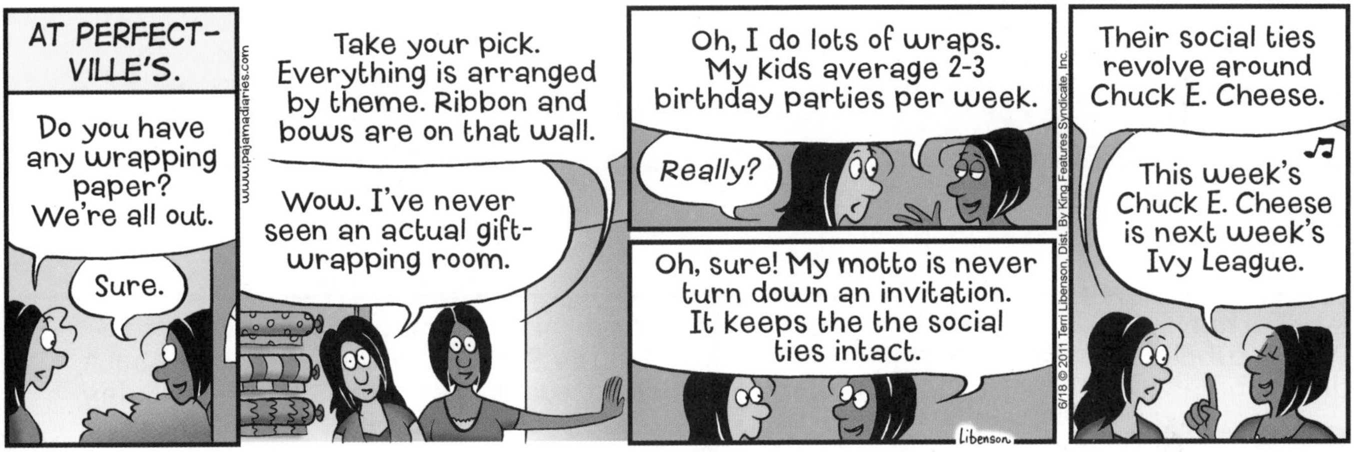
AT PERFECT-VILLE'S.
Do you have any wrapping paper? We're all out.
Sure.
www.pajamadiaries.com
Take your pick. Everything is arranged by theme. Ribbon and bows are on that wall.
Wow. I've never seen an actual gift-wrapping room.
Oh, I do lots of wraps. My kids average 2-3 birthday parties per week.
Really?
Oh, sure! My motto is never turn down an invitation. It keeps the the social ties intact.
Libenson
6/18 © 2011 Terri Libenson, Dist. By King Features Syndicate, Inc.
Their social ties revolve around Chuck E. Cheese.
This week's Chuck E. Cheese is next week's Ivy League.

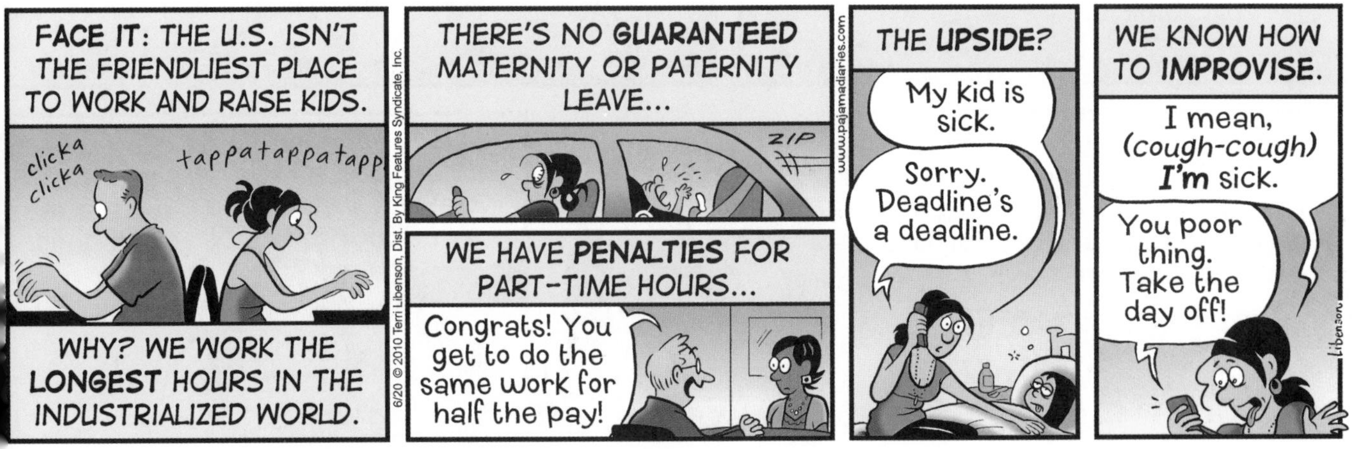
FACE IT: THE U.S. ISN'T THE FRIENDLIEST PLACE TO WORK AND RAISE KIDS.
clicka clicka
tappatappatapp
WHY? WE WORK THE LONGEST HOURS IN THE INDUSTRIALIZED WORLD.
6/20 © 2010 Terri Libenson, Dist. By King Features Syndicate, Inc.
THERE'S NO GUARANTEED MATERNITY OR PATERNITY LEAVE...
ZIP
WE HAVE PENALTIES FOR PART-TIME HOURS...
Congrats! You get to do the same work for half the pay!
www.pajamadiaries.com
THE UPSIDE?
My kid is sick.
Sorry. Deadline's a deadline.
WE KNOW HOW TO IMPROVISE.
I mean, (cough-cough) I'm sick.
You poor thing. Take the day off!
Libenson

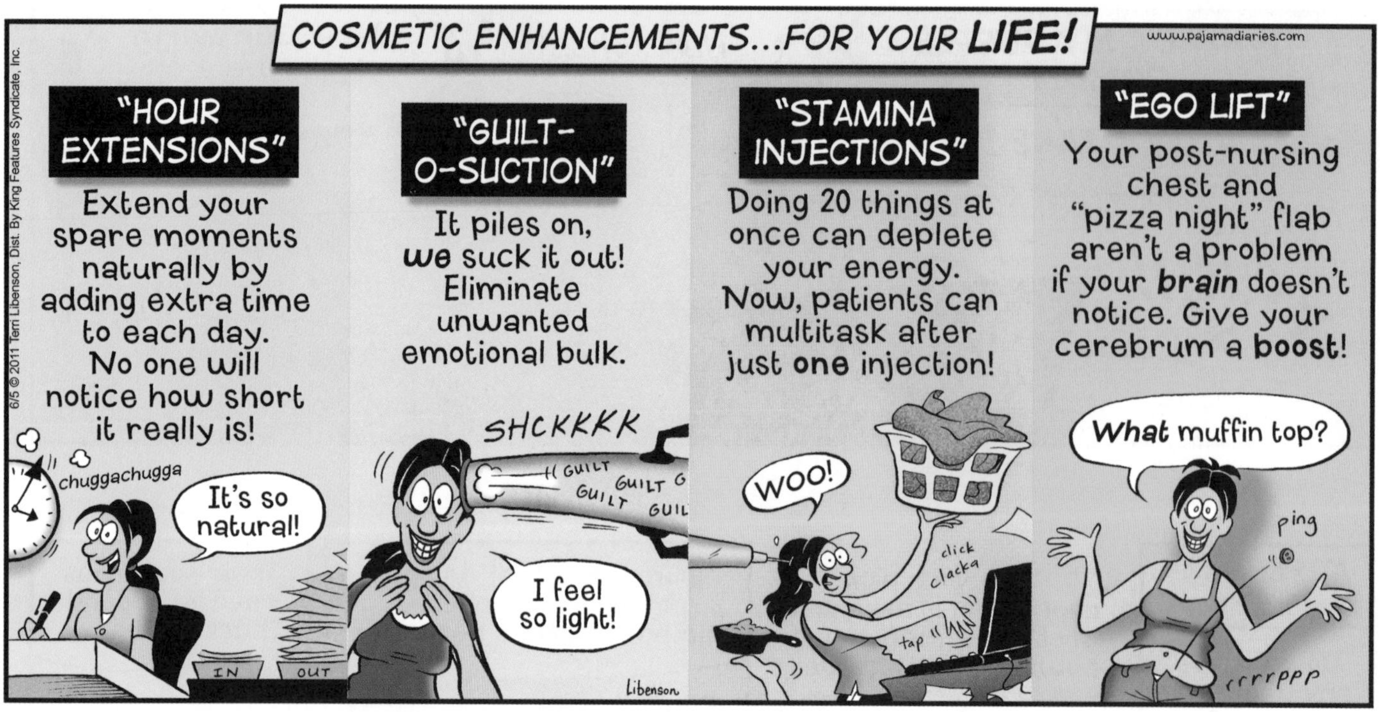
COSMETIC ENHANCEMENTS...FOR YOUR LIFE!
www.pajamadiaries.com
6/5 © 2011 Terri Libenson, Dist. By King Features Syndicate, Inc.
"HOUR EXTENSIONS"
Extend your spare moments naturally by adding extra time to each day. No one will notice how short it really is!
chuggachugga
It's so natural!
IN
OUT
"GUILT-O-SUCTION"
It piles on, we suck it out! Eliminate unwanted emotional bulk.
SHCKKKK
GUILT GUILT GUILT GUIL
I feel so light!
Libenson
"STAMINA INJECTIONS"
Doing 20 things at once can deplete your energy. Now, patients can multitask after just one injection!
WOO!
click clacka
tap
"EGO LIFT"
Your post-nursing chest and "pizza night" flab aren't a problem if your brain doesn't notice. Give your cerebrum a boost!
What muffin top?
ping
rrrppp

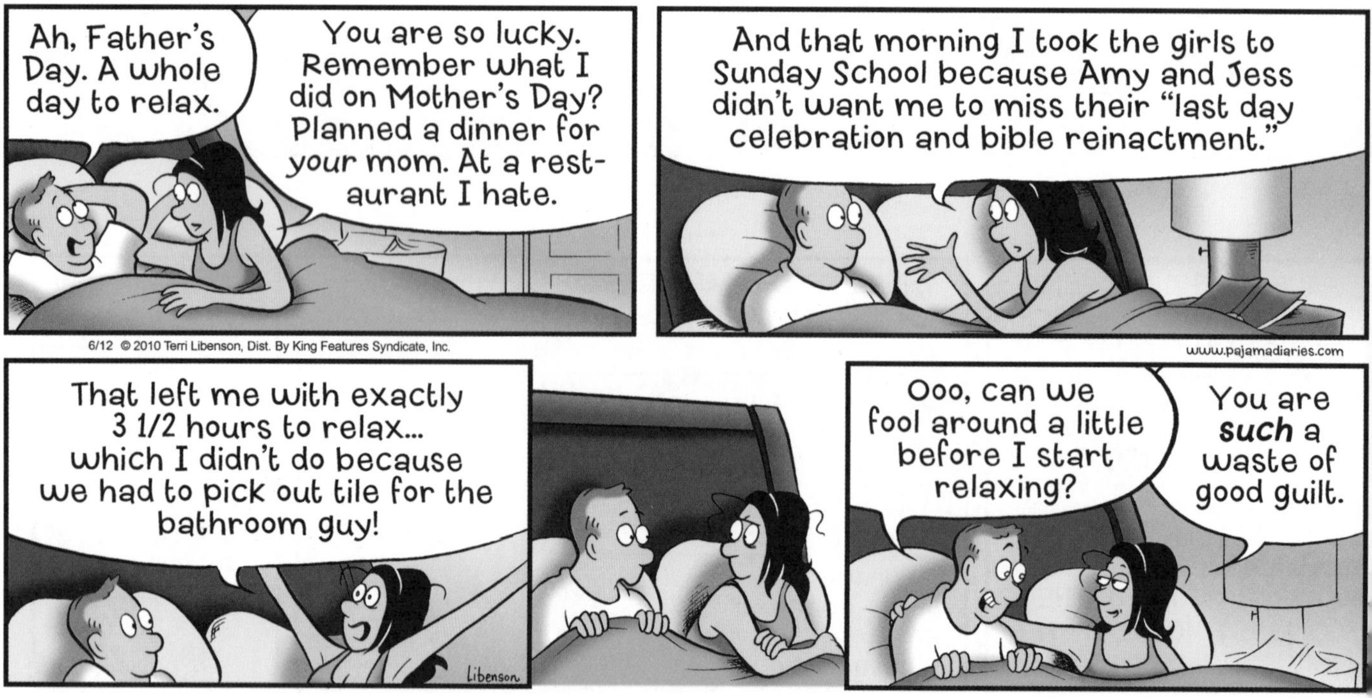
Ah, Father's Day. A whole day to relax.
You are so lucky. Remember what I did on Mother's Day? Planned a dinner for your mom. At a restaurant I hate.
And that morning I took the girls to Sunday School because Amy and Jess didn't want me to miss their "last day celebration and bible reinactment."
6/12 © 2010 Terri Libenson, Dist. By King Features Syndicate, Inc.
www.pajamadiaries.com
That left me with exactly 3 1/2 hours to relax... which I didn't do because we had to pick out tile for the bathroom guy!
Libenson
Ooo, can we fool around a little before I start relaxing?
You are such a waste of good guilt.

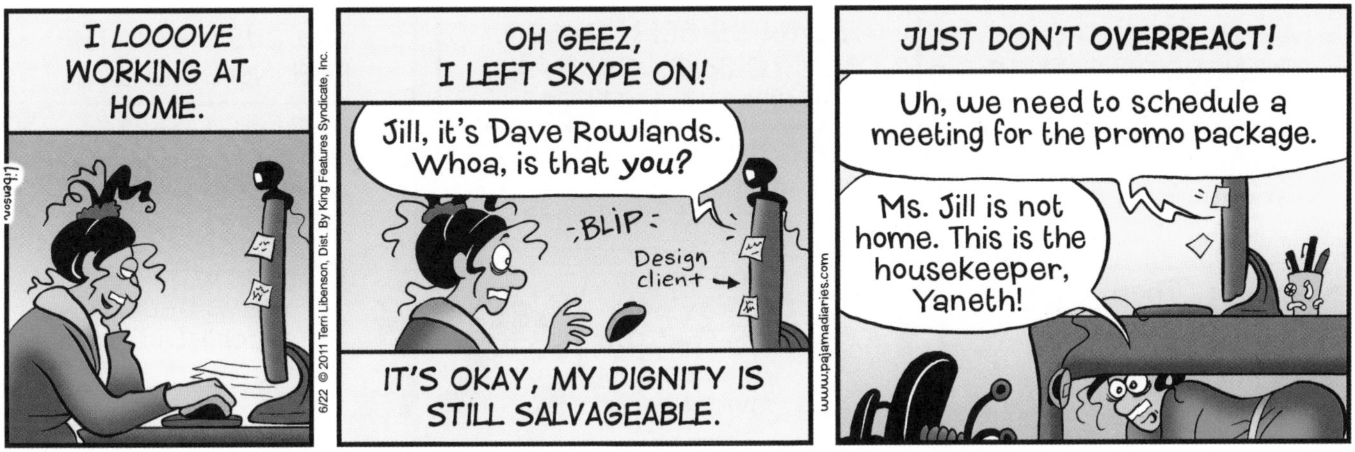
I LOOOVE WORKING AT HOME.
Libenson
6/22 © 2011 Terri Libenson, Dist. By King Features Syndicate, Inc.
OH GEEZ, I LEFT SKYPE ON!
Jill, it's Dave Rowlands. Whoa, is that *you?*
BLIP
Design client
IT'S OKAY, MY DIGNITY IS STILL SALVAGEABLE.
www.pajamadiaries.com
JUST DON'T OVERREACT!
Uh, we need to schedule a meeting for the promo package.
Ms. Jill is not home. This is the housekeeper, Yaneth!

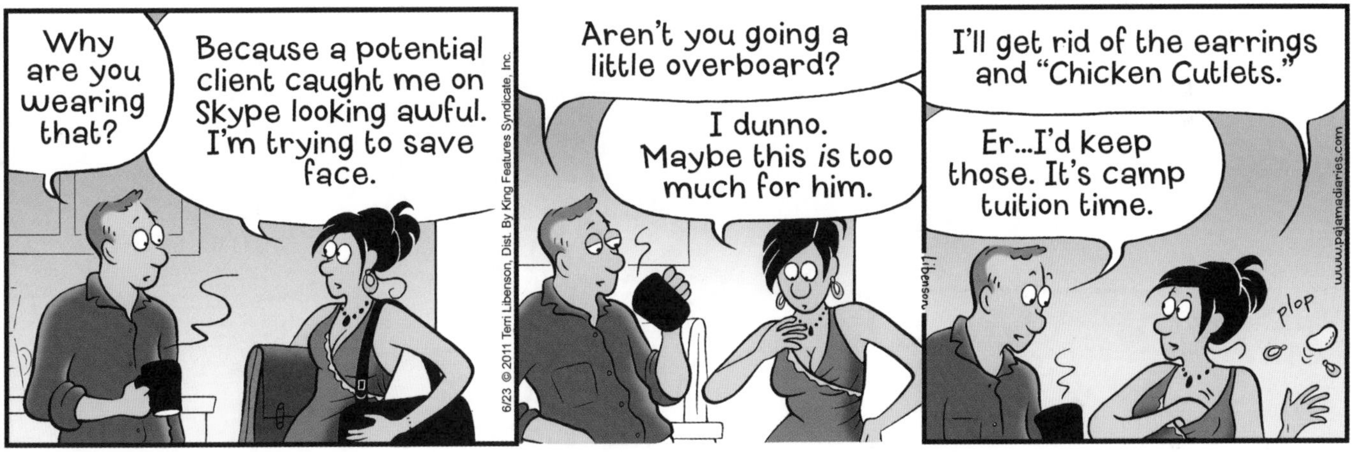
Why are you wearing that?
Because a potential client caught me on Skype looking awful. I'm trying to save face.
6/23 © 2011 Terri Libenson, Dist. By King Features Syndicate, Inc.
Aren't you going a little overboard?
I dunno. Maybe this *is* too much for him.
I'll get rid of the earrings and "Chicken Cutlets."
Er...I'd keep those. It's camp tuition time.
Libenson
plop
www.pajamadiaries.com

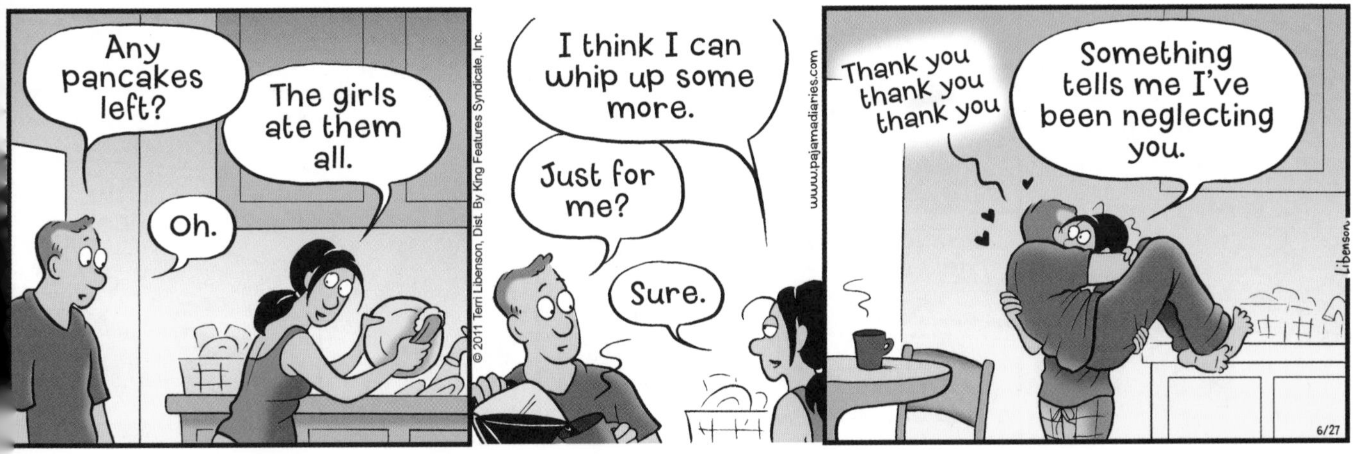
Any pancakes left?
The girls ate them all.
Oh.
© 2011 Terri Libenson, Dist. By King Features Syndicate, Inc.
I think I can whip up some more.
Just for me?
Sure.
www.pajamadiaries.com
Thank you thank you thank you
Something tells me I've been neglecting you.
Libenson
6/27

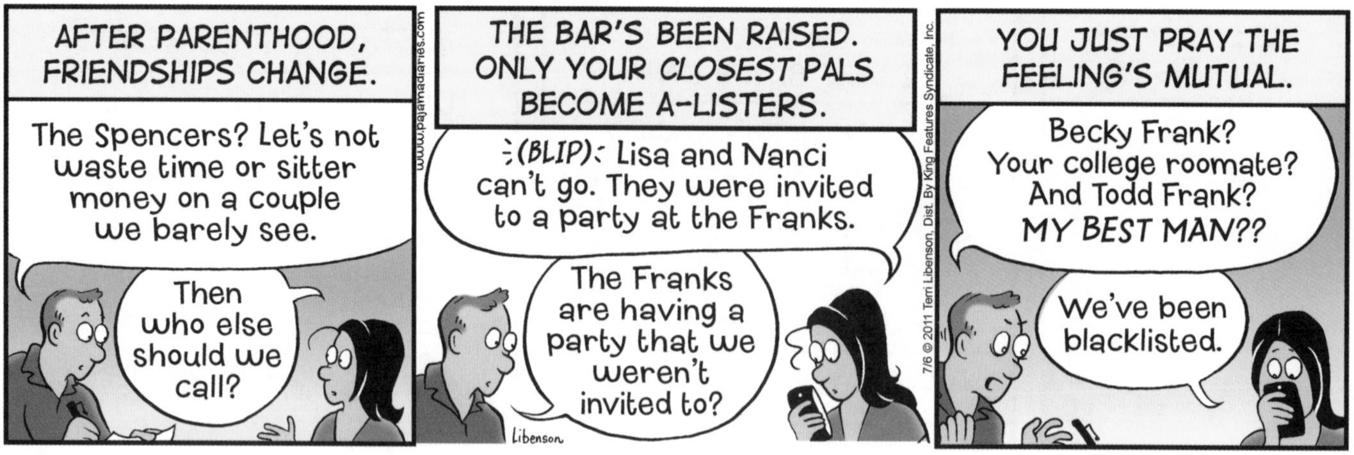
AFTER PARENTHOOD, FRIENDSHIPS CHANGE.
The Spencers? Let's not waste time or sitter money on a couple we barely see.
Then who else should we call?
www.pajamadiaries.com
THE BAR'S BEEN RAISED. ONLY YOUR CLOSEST PALS BECOME A-LISTERS.
(BLIP) Lisa and Nanci can't go. They were invited to a party at the Franks.
The Franks are having a party that we weren't invited to?
Libenson
7/6 © 2011 Terri Libenson, Dist. By King Features Syndicate, Inc.
YOU JUST PRAY THE FEELING'S MUTUAL.
Becky Frank? Your college roomate? And Todd Frank? MY BEST MAN??
We've been blacklisted.

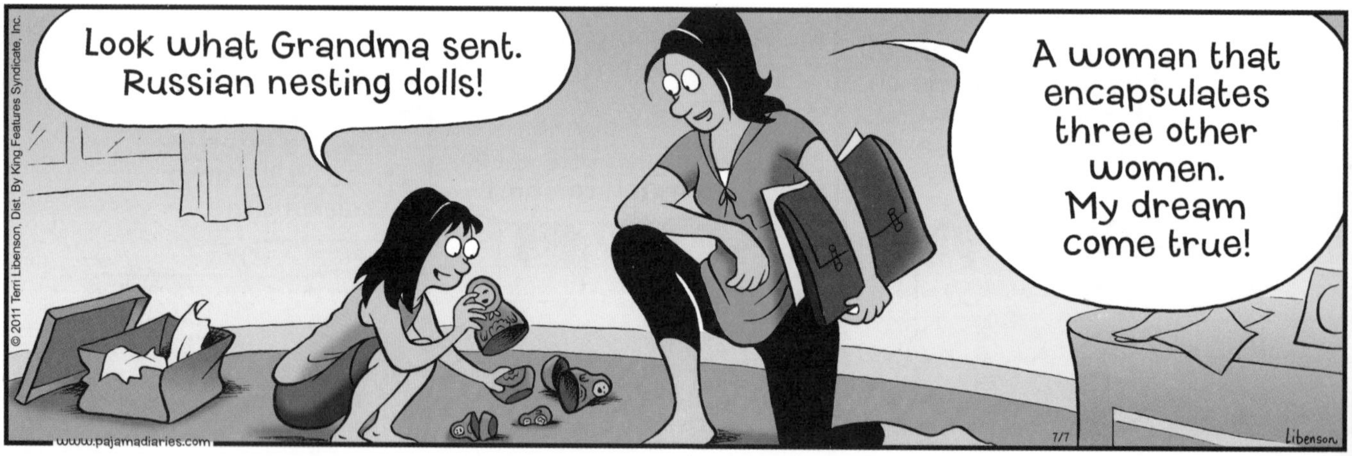
© 2011 Terri Libenson, Dist. By King Features Syndicate, Inc.
Look what Grandma sent. Russian nesting dolls!
A woman that encapsulates three other women. My dream come true!
www.pajamadiaries.com
7/7
Libenson

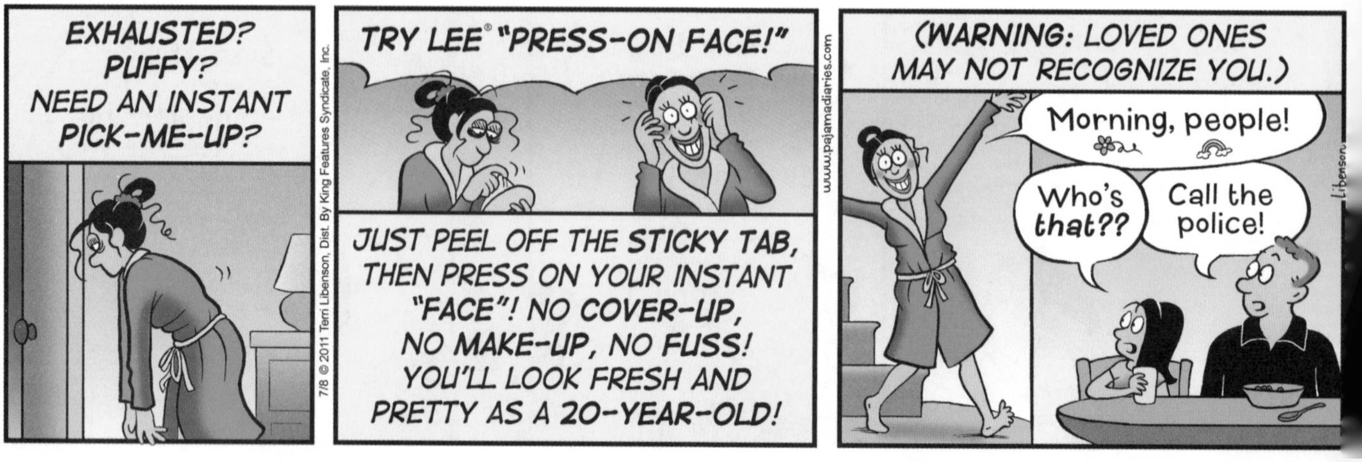
EXHAUSTED? PUFFY? NEED AN INSTANT PICK-ME-UP?
7/8 © 2011 Terri Libenson, Dist. By King Features Syndicate, Inc.
TRY LEE® "PRESS-ON FACE!"
JUST PEEL OFF THE STICKY TAB, THEN PRESS ON YOUR INSTANT "FACE"! NO COVER-UP, NO MAKE-UP, NO FUSS! YOU'LL LOOK FRESH AND PRETTY AS A 20-YEAR-OLD!
www.pajamadiaries.com
(WARNING: LOVED ONES MAY NOT RECOGNIZE YOU.)
Morning, people!
Who's that??
Call the police!
Libenson

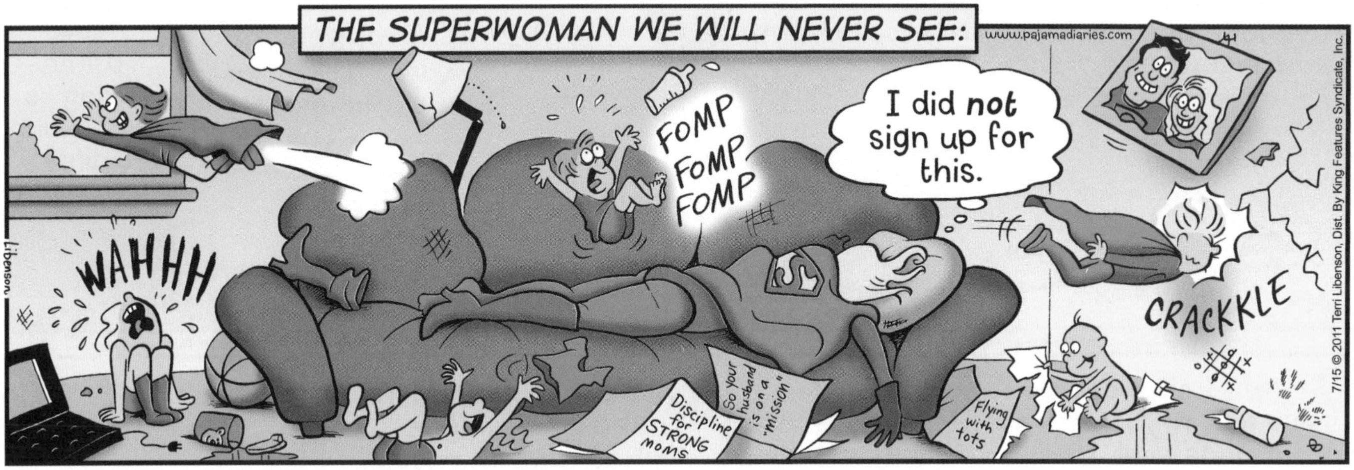
THE SUPERWOMAN WE WILL NEVER SEE:
www.pajamadiaries.com
WAHHH
FOMP FOMP FOMP
I did not sign up for this.
CRACKKLE
Discipline for STRONG moms
So your husband is on a "mission"
Flying with tots
Libenson
7/15 © 2011 Terri Libenson, Dist. By King Features Syndicate, Inc.

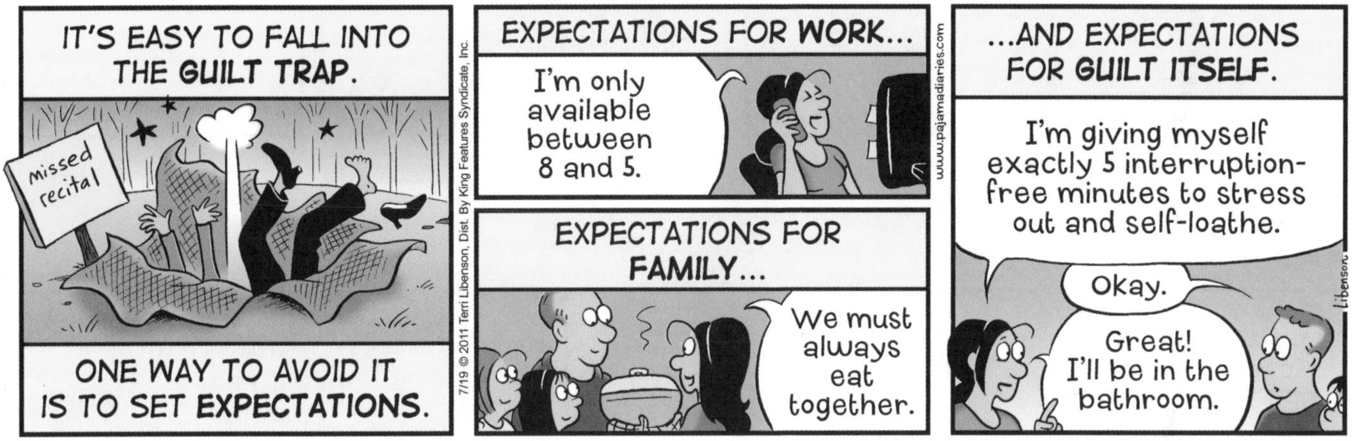
IT'S EASY TO FALL INTO THE GUILT TRAP.
missed recital
ONE WAY TO AVOID IT IS TO SET EXPECTATIONS.
7/19 © 2011 Terri Libenson, Dist. By King Features Syndicate, Inc.
EXPECTATIONS FOR WORK...
I'm only available between 8 and 5.
EXPECTATIONS FOR FAMILY...
We must always eat together.
www.pajamadiaries.com
...AND EXPECTATIONS FOR GUILT ITSELF.
I'm giving myself exactly 5 interruption-free minutes to stress out and self-loathe.
Okay.
Great! I'll be in the bathroom.
Libenson

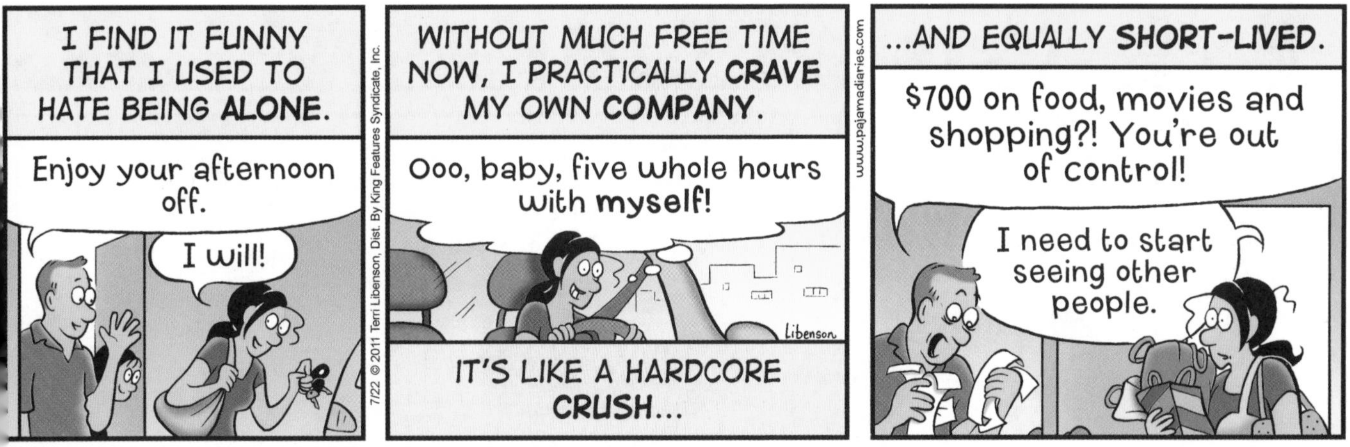
I FIND IT FUNNY THAT I USED TO HATE BEING ALONE.
Enjoy your afternoon off.
I will!
7/22 © 2011 Terri Libenson, Dist. By King Features Syndicate, Inc.
WITHOUT MUCH FREE TIME NOW, I PRACTICALLY CRAVE MY OWN COMPANY.
Ooo, baby, five whole hours with myself!
Libenson
IT'S LIKE A HARDCORE CRUSH...
www.pajamadiaries.com
...AND EQUALLY SHORT-LIVED.
$700 on food, movies and shopping?! You're out of control!
I need to start seeing other people.

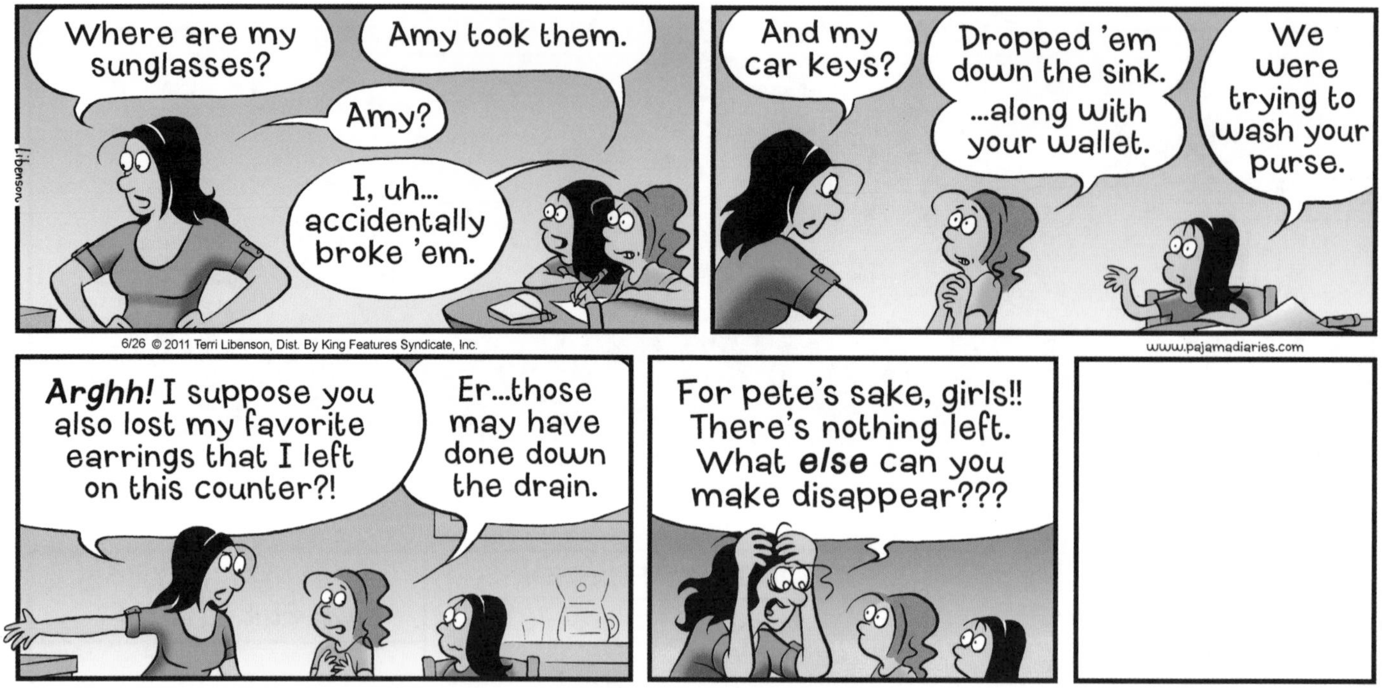
Libenson
Where are my sunglasses?
Amy took them.
Amy?
I, uh... accidentally broke 'em.
And my car keys?
Dropped 'em down the sink.
...along with your wallet.
We were trying to wash your purse.
6/26 © 2011 Terri Libenson, Dist. By King Features Syndicate, Inc.
www.pajamadiaries.com
Arghh! I suppose you also lost my favorite earrings that I left on this counter?!
Er...those may have done down the drain.
For pete's sake, girls!! There's nothing left. What else can you make disappear???

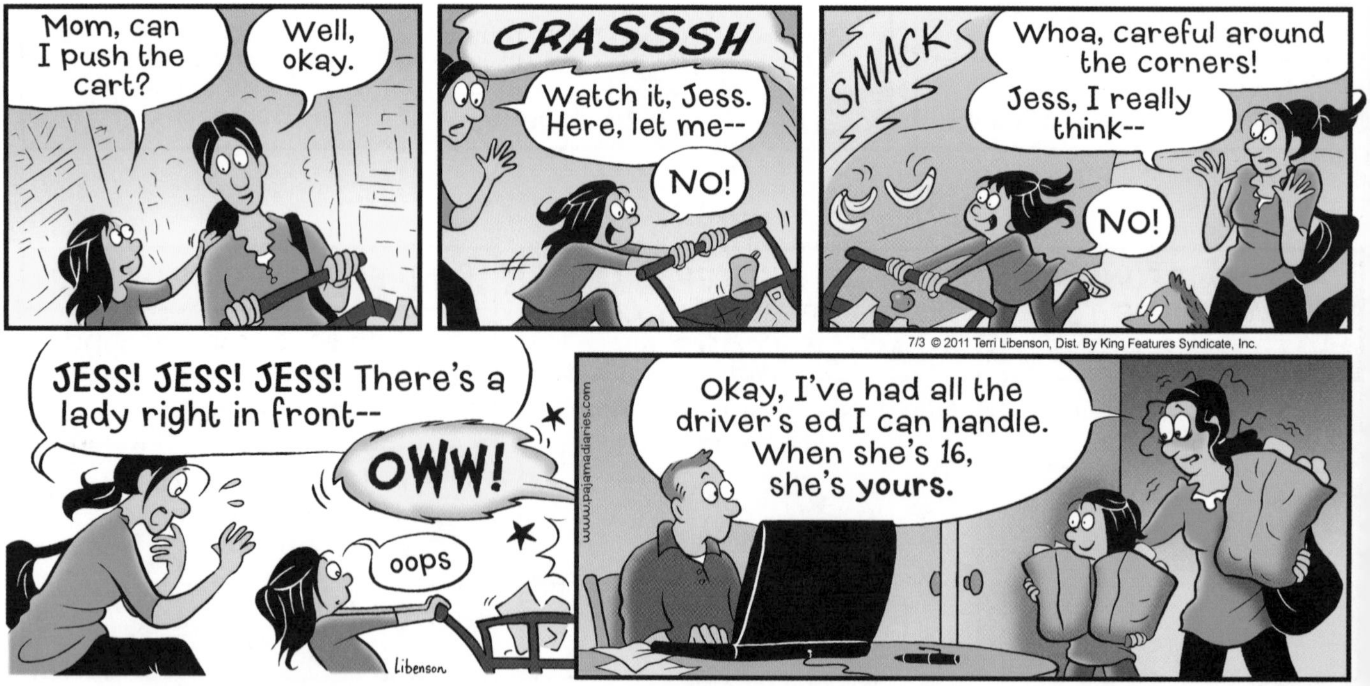
Mom, can I push the cart?
Well, okay.
CRASSSH
Watch it, Jess. Here, let me--
NO!
SMACK
Whoa, careful around the corners!
Jess, I really think--
NO!
7/3 © 2011 Terri Libenson, Dist. By King Features Syndicate, Inc.
JESS! JESS! JESS! There's a lady right in front--
OWW!
oops
Libenson
www.pajamadiaries.com
Okay, I've had all the driver's ed I can handle. When she's 16, she's yours.

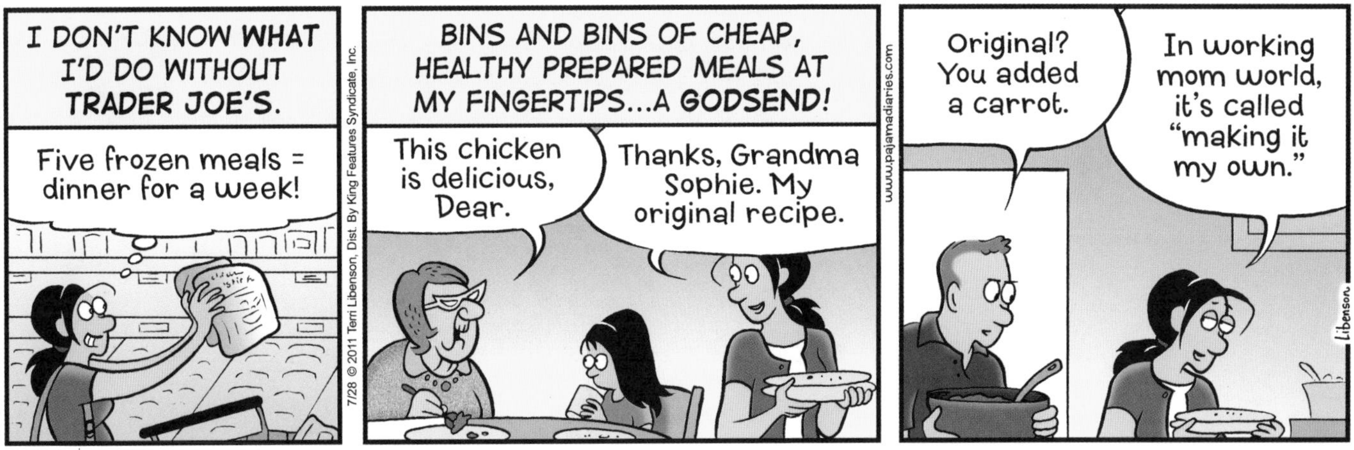
I DON'T KNOW **WHAT** I'D DO WITHOUT **TRADER JOE'S.**
Five frozen meals = dinner for a week!
7/28 © 2011 Terri Libenson, Dist. By King Features Syndicate, Inc.
BINS AND BINS OF CHEAP, HEALTHY PREPARED MEALS AT MY FINGERTIPS...A **GODSEND!**
This chicken is delicious, Dear.
Thanks, Grandma Sophie. My original recipe.
www.pajamadiaries.com
Original? You added a carrot.
In working mom world, it's called "making it my own."
Libenson

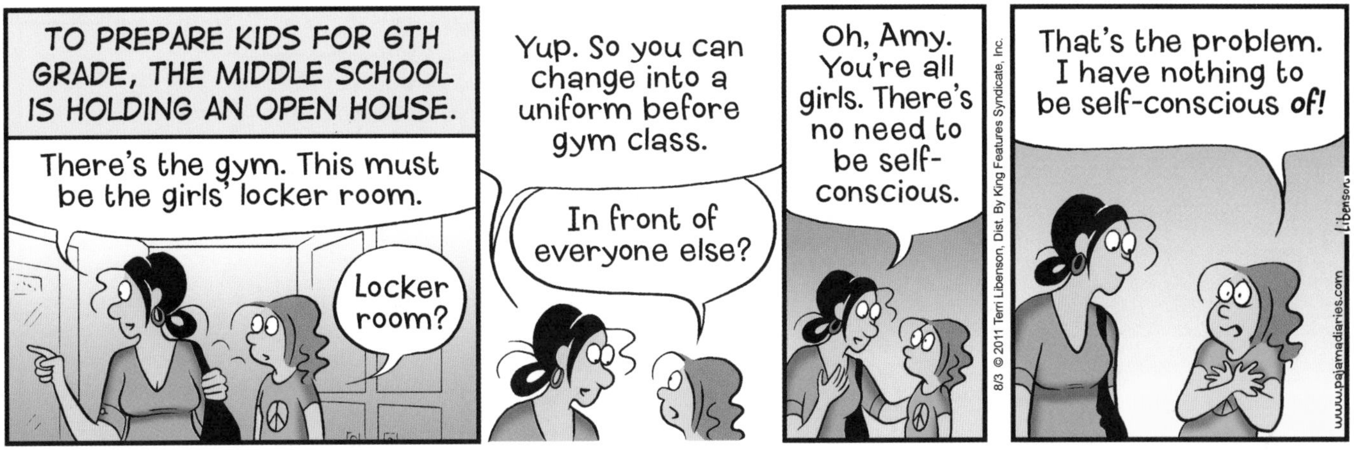
TO PREPARE KIDS FOR 6TH GRADE, THE MIDDLE SCHOOL IS HOLDING AN OPEN HOUSE.
There's the gym. This must be the girls' locker room.
Locker room?
Yup. So you can change into a uniform before gym class.
In front of everyone else?
Oh, Amy. You're all girls. There's no need to be self-conscious.
8/3 © 2011 Terri Libenson, Dist. By King Features Syndicate, Inc.
That's the problem. I have nothing to be self-conscious ***of!***
Libenson
www.pajamadiaries.com

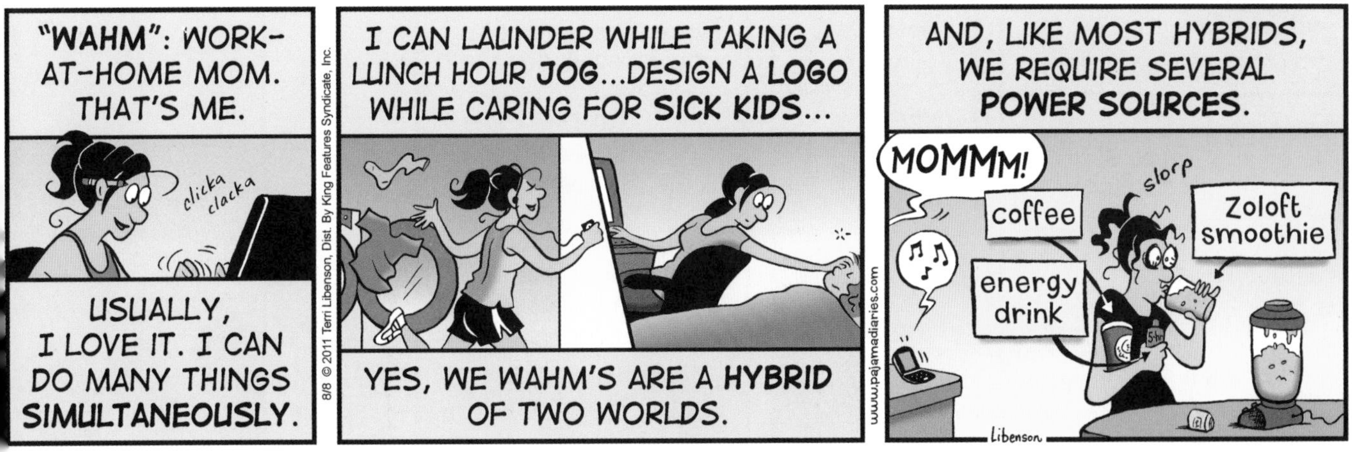
"WAHM": WORK-AT-HOME MOM. THAT'S ME.
clicka clacka
USUALLY, I LOVE IT. I CAN DO MANY THINGS **SIMULTANEOUSLY.**
8/8 © 2011 Terri Libenson, Dist. By King Features Syndicate, Inc.
I CAN LAUNDER WHILE TAKING A LUNCH HOUR **JOG**...DESIGN A **LOGO** WHILE CARING FOR **SICK KIDS**...
YES, WE WAHM'S ARE A **HYBRID** OF TWO WORLDS.
www.pajamadiaries.com
AND, LIKE MOST HYBRIDS, WE REQUIRE SEVERAL **POWER SOURCES.**
MOMMM!
coffee
slorp
Zoloft smoothie
energy drink
Libenson

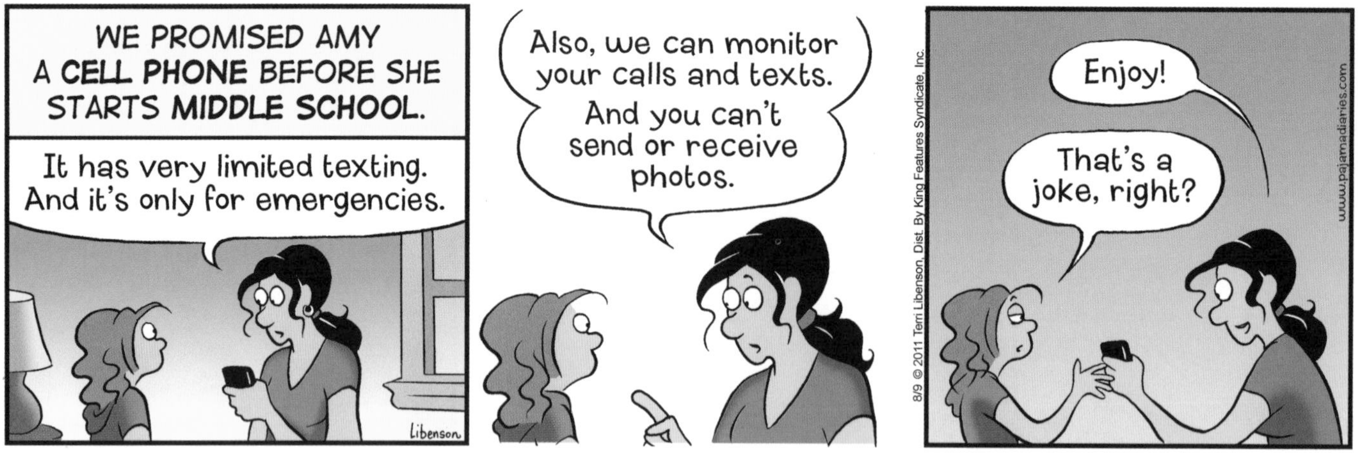
WE PROMISED AMY A CELL PHONE BEFORE SHE STARTS MIDDLE SCHOOL.
It has very limited texting. And it's only for emergencies.
Libenson
Also, we can monitor your calls and texts.
And you can't send or receive photos.
8/9 © 2011 Terri Libenson, Dist. By King Features Syndicate, Inc.
Enjoy!
That's a joke, right?
www.pajamadiaries.com

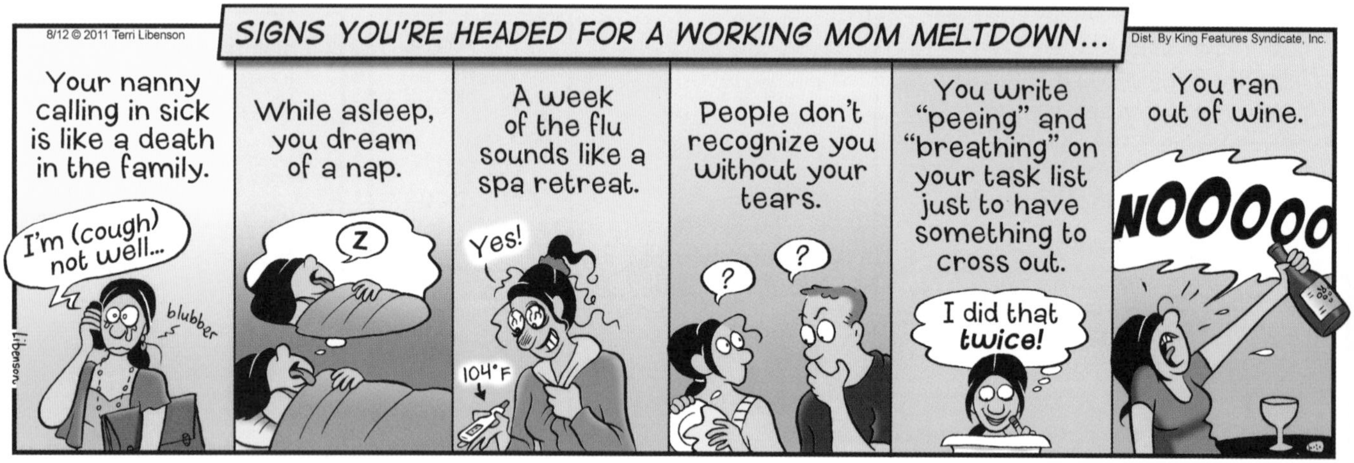
8/12 © 2011 Terri Libenson
SIGNS YOU'RE HEADED FOR A WORKING MOM MELTDOWN...
Dist. By King Features Syndicate, Inc.
Your nanny calling in sick is like a death in the family.
I'm (cough) not well...
blubber
Libenson
While asleep, you dream of a nap.
Z
A week of the flu sounds like a spa retreat.
Yes!
104°F
People don't recognize you without your tears.
?
?
You write "peeing" and "breathing" on your task list just to have something to cross out.
I did that twice!
You ran out of wine.
NOOOOO

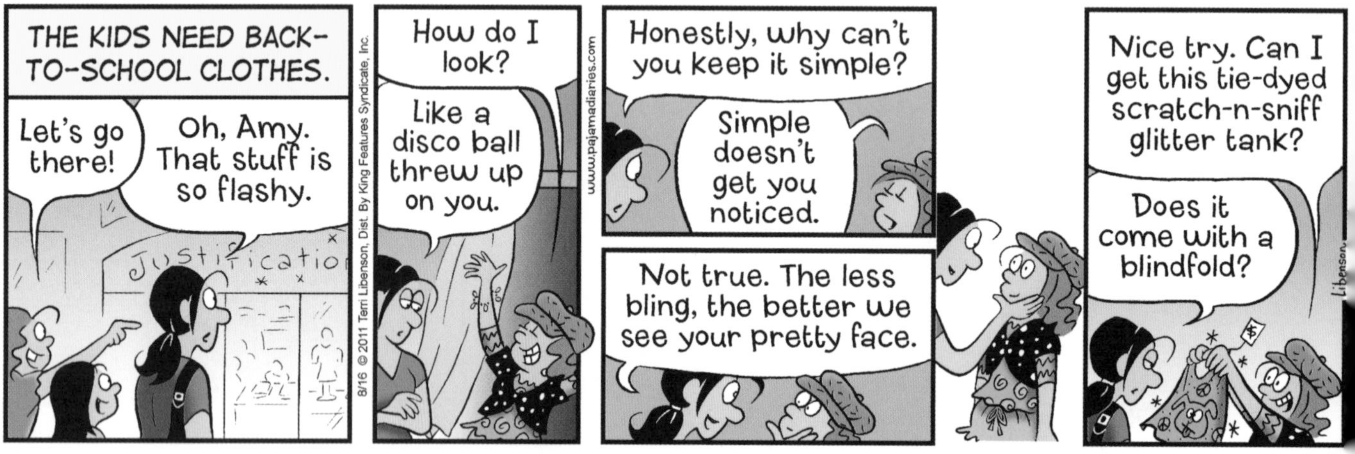
THE KIDS NEED BACK-TO-SCHOOL CLOTHES.
Let's go there!
Oh, Amy. That stuff is so flashy.
JUSTIfication
8/16 © 2011 Terri Libenson, Dist. By King Features Syndicate, Inc.
How do I look?
Like a disco ball threw up on you.
www.pajamadiaries.com
Honestly, why can't you keep it simple?
Simple doesn't get you noticed.
Not true. The less bling, the better we see your pretty face.
Nice try. Can I get this tie-dyed scratch-n-sniff glitter tank?
Does it come with a blindfold?
Libenson

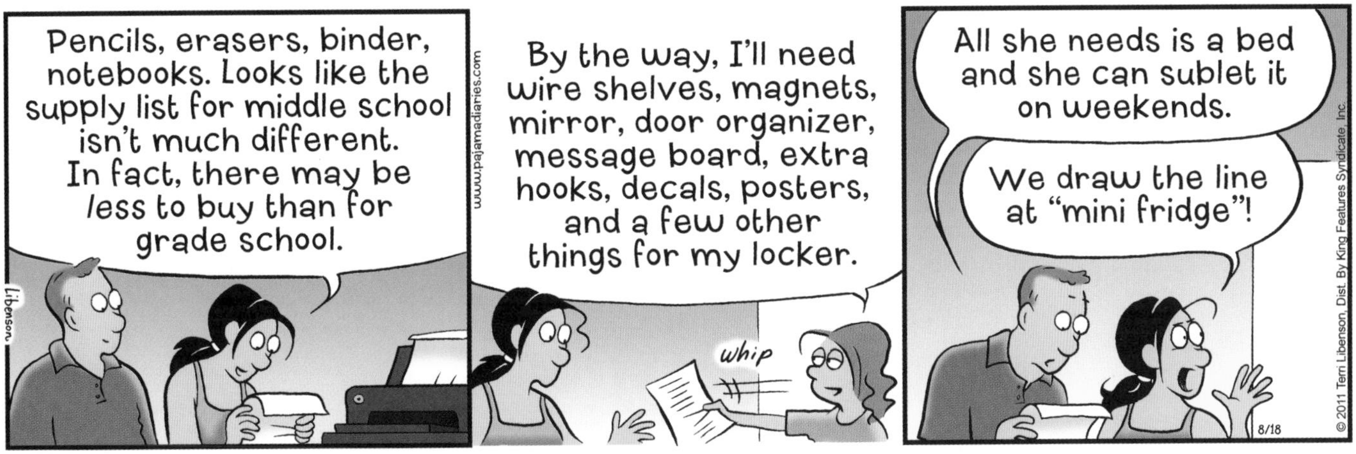
Pencils, erasers, binder, notebooks. Looks like the supply list for middle school isn't much different. In fact, there may be *less* to buy than for grade school.
Libenson
www.pajamadiaries.com
By the way, I'll need wire shelves, magnets, mirror, door organizer, message board, extra hooks, decals, posters, and a few other things for my locker.
whip
All she needs is a bed and she can sublet it on weekends.
We draw the line at "mini fridge"!
8/18
© 2011 Terri Libenson, Dist. By King Features Syndicate, Inc.

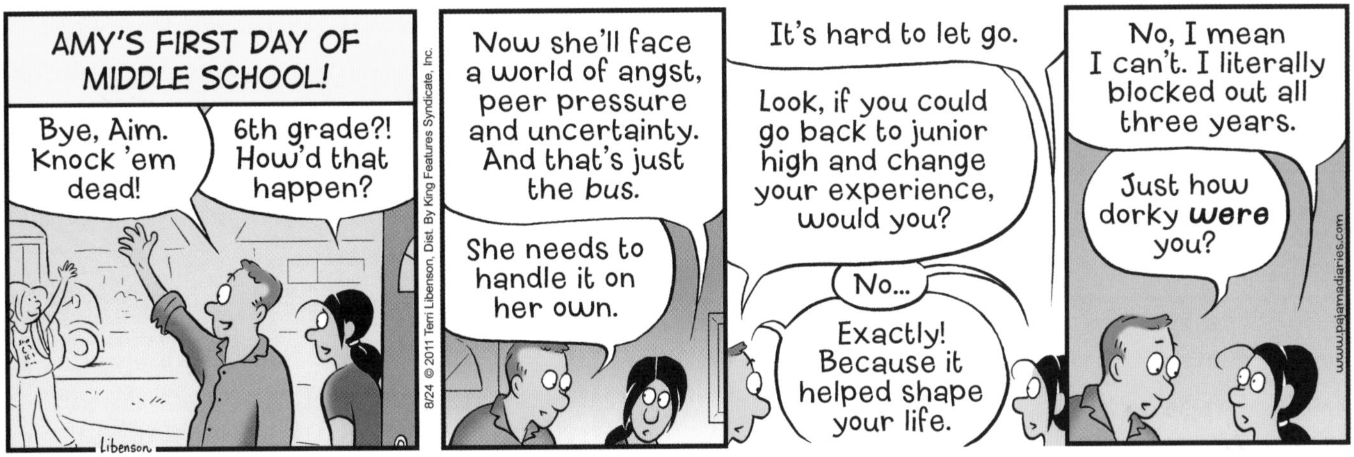
AMY'S FIRST DAY OF MIDDLE SCHOOL!
Bye, Aim. Knock 'em dead!
6th grade?! How'd that happen?
Libenson
8/24 © 2011 Terri Libenson, Dist. By King Features Syndicate, Inc.
Now she'll face a world of angst, peer pressure and uncertainty. And that's just the *bus*.
She needs to handle it on her own.
It's hard to let go.
Look, if you could go back to junior high and change your experience, would you?
No...
Exactly! Because it helped shape your life.
No, I mean I can't. I literally blocked out all three years.
Just how dorky ***were*** you?
www.pajamadiaries.com

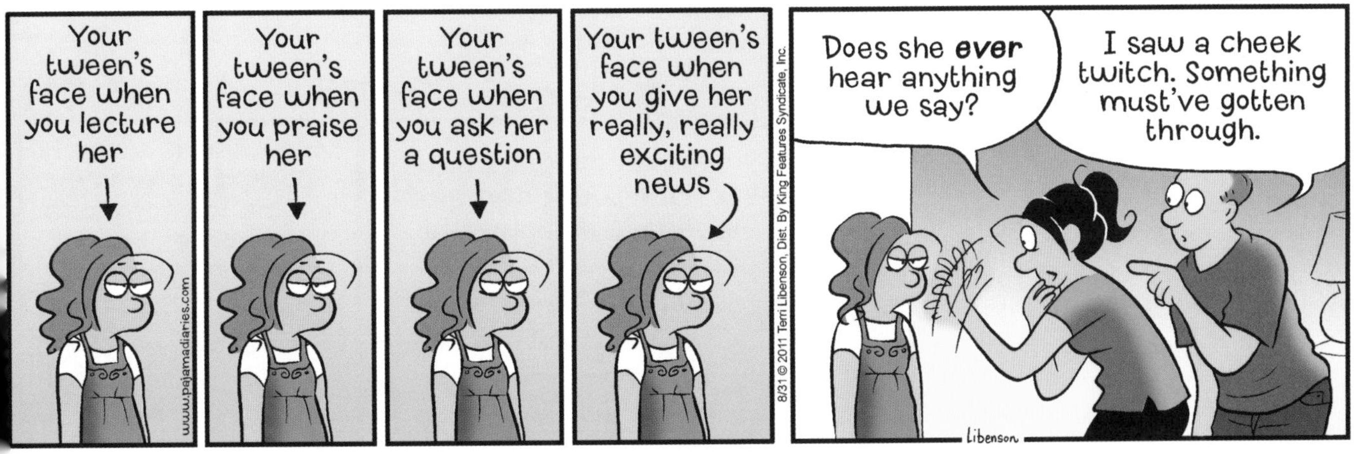
Your tween's face when you lecture her
www.pajamadiaries.com
Your tween's face when you praise her
Your tween's face when you ask her a question
Your tween's face when you give her really, really exciting news
8/31 © 2011 Terri Libenson, Dist. By King Features Syndicate, Inc.
Does she ***ever*** hear anything we say?
I saw a cheek twitch. Something must've gotten through.
Libenson

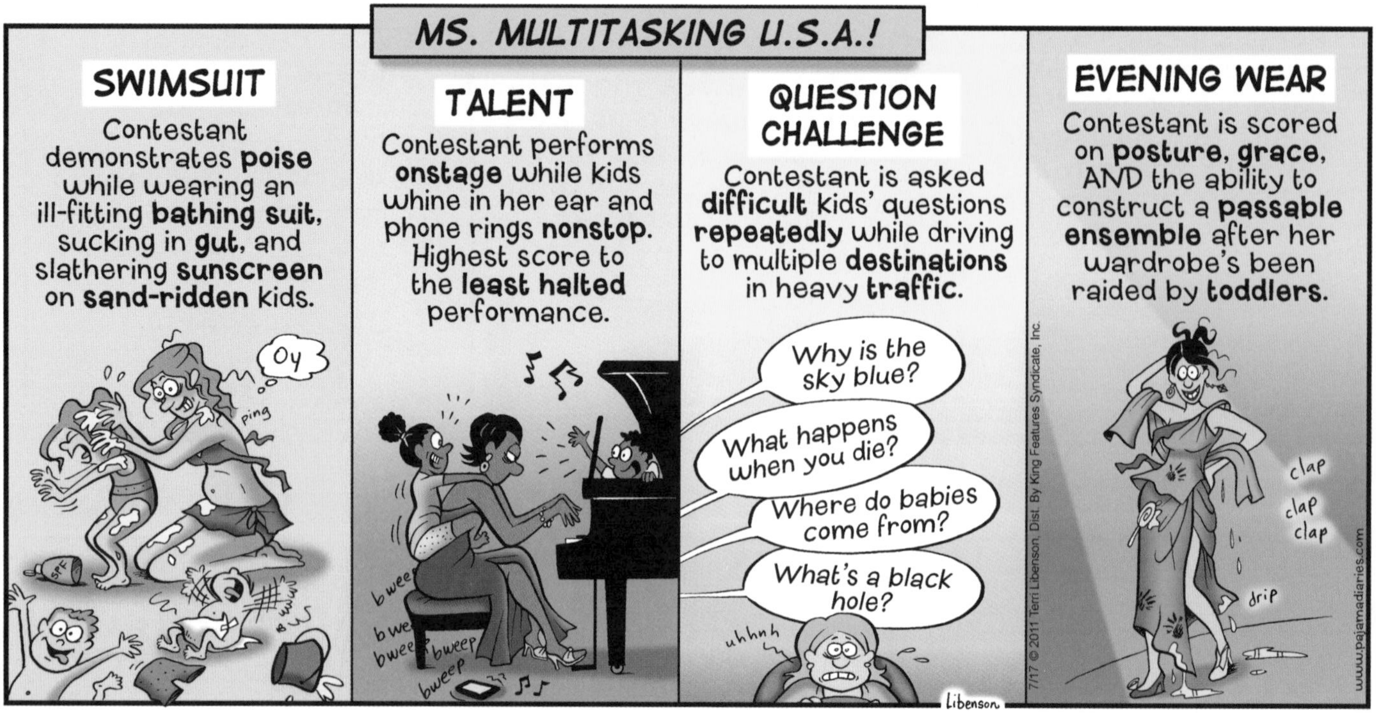
MS. MULTITASKING U.S.A.!
SWIMSUIT
Contestant demonstrates **poise** while wearing an ill-fitting **bathing suit**, sucking in **gut**, and slathering **sunscreen** on **sand-ridden** kids.
Oy
ping
TALENT
Contestant performs **onstage** while kids whine in her ear and phone rings **nonstop**. Highest score to the **least halted** performance.
bweep
bweep
bweep
bweep
QUESTION CHALLENGE
Contestant is asked **difficult** kids' questions **repeatedly** while driving to multiple **destinations** in heavy **traffic**.
Why is the sky blue?
What happens when you die?
Where do babies come from?
What's a black hole?
uhhnh
EVENING WEAR
Contestant is scored on **posture**, **grace**, AND the ability to construct a **passable ensemble** after her wardrobe's been raided by **toddlers**.
clap
clap
clap
drip
Libenson
7/17 © 2011 Terri Libenson, Dist. By King Features Syndicate, Inc.
www.pajamadiaries.com

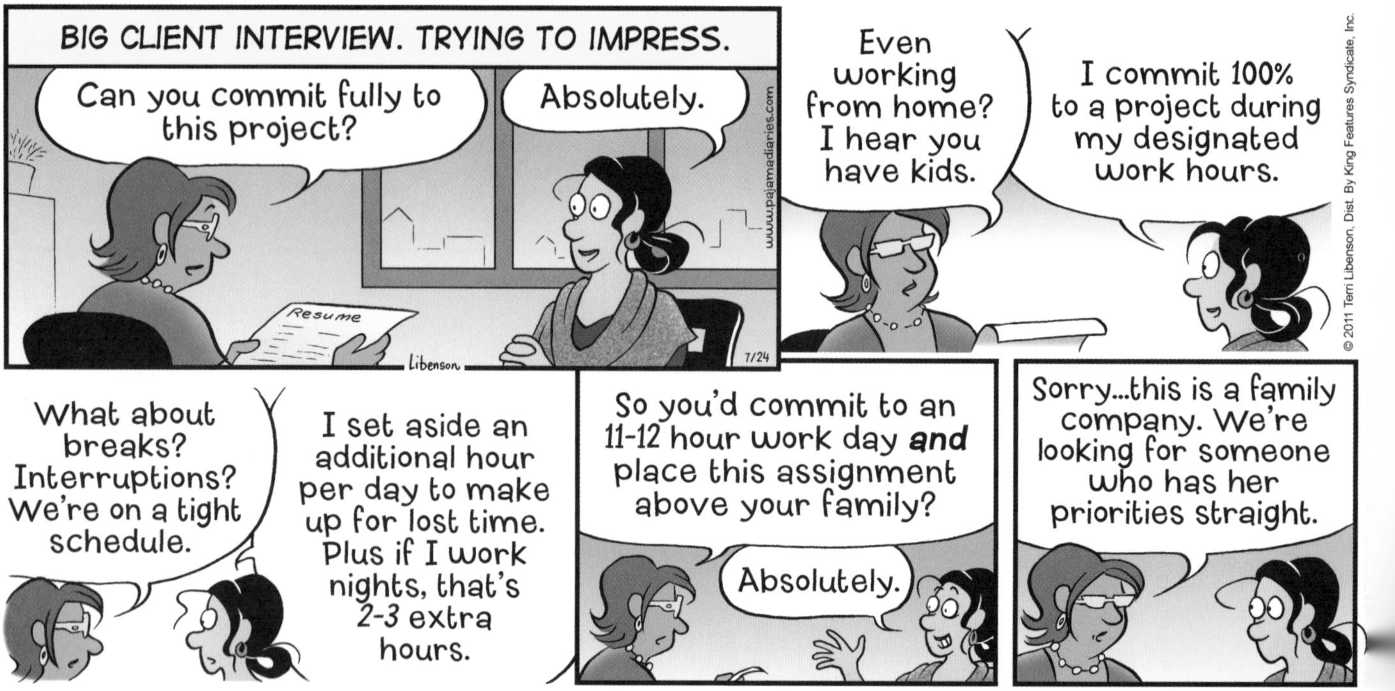
BIG CLIENT INTERVIEW. TRYING TO IMPRESS.
Can you commit fully to this project?
Absolutely.
Resume
Libenson
7/24
www.pajamadiaries.com
Even working from home? I hear you have kids.
I commit 100% to a project during my designated work hours.
What about breaks? Interruptions? We're on a tight schedule.
I set aside an additional hour per day to make up for lost time. Plus if I work nights, that's *2-3* extra hours.
So you'd commit to an 11-12 hour work day **and** place this assignment above your family?
Absolutely.
Sorry...this is a family company. We're looking for someone who has her priorities straight.
© 2011 Terri Libenson, Dist. By King Features Syndicate, Inc.

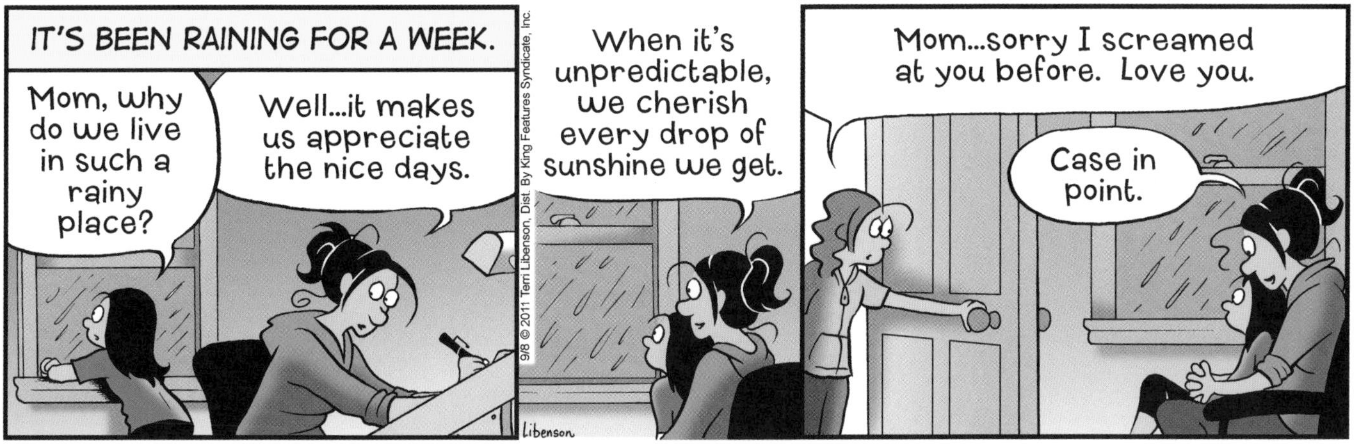
IT'S BEEN RAINING FOR A WEEK.
Mom, why do we live in such a rainy place?
Well...it makes us appreciate the nice days.
9/8 © 2011 Terri Libenson, Dist. By King Features Syndicate, Inc.
When it's unpredictable, we cherish every drop of sunshine we get.
Libenson
Mom...sorry I screamed at you before. Love you.
Case in point.

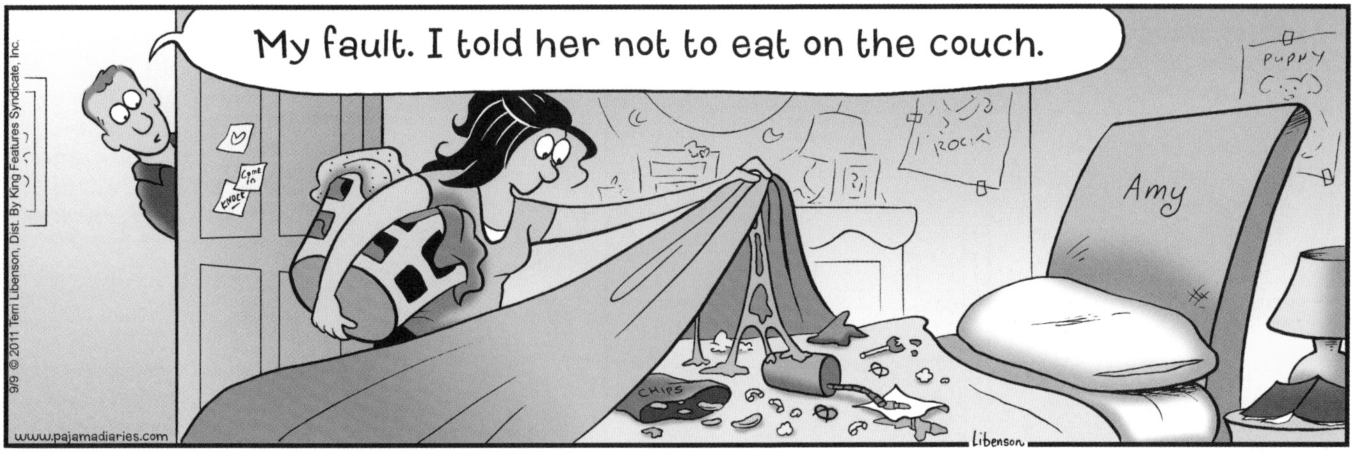
9/9 © 2011 Terri Libenson, Dist. By King Features Syndicate, Inc.
www.pajamadiaries.com
My fault. I told her not to eat on the couch.
PUPPY
Amy
CHIPS
Libenson

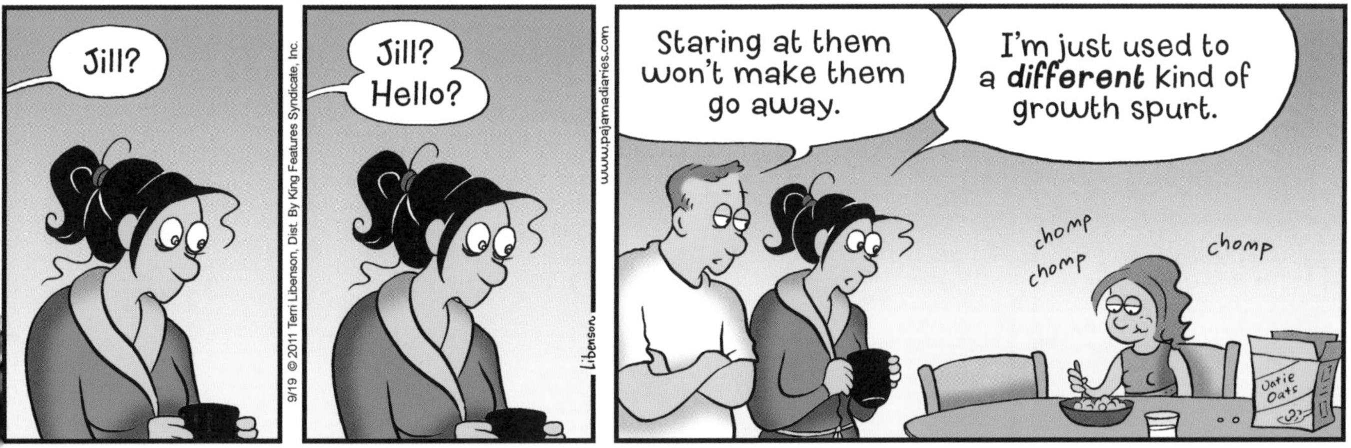
Jill?
Jill? Hello?
9/19 © 2011 Terri Libenson, Dist. By King Features Syndicate, Inc.
Libenson
www.pajamadiaries.com
Staring at them won't make them go away.
I'm just used to a **different** kind of growth spurt.
chomp
chomp
chomp
Oatie Oats

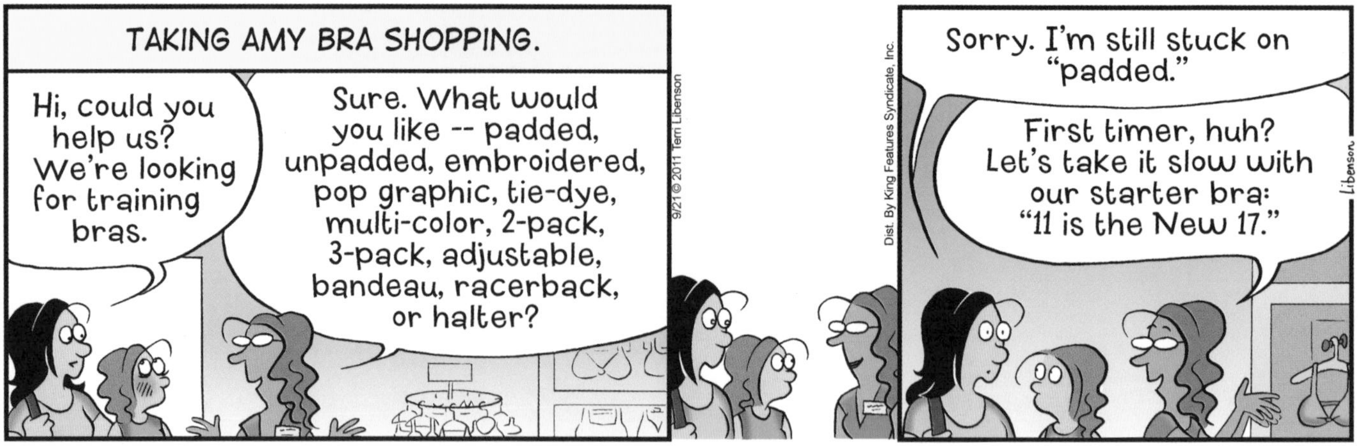
TAKING AMY BRA SHOPPING.
Hi, could you help us? We're looking for training bras.
Sure. What would you like -- padded, unpadded, embroidered, pop graphic, tie-dye, multi-color, 2-pack, 3-pack, adjustable, bandeau, racerback, or halter?
9/21 © 2011 Terri Libenson
Dist. By King Features Syndicate, Inc.
Sorry. I'm still stuck on "padded."
First timer, huh? Let's take it slow with our starter bra: "11 is the New 17."
Libenson

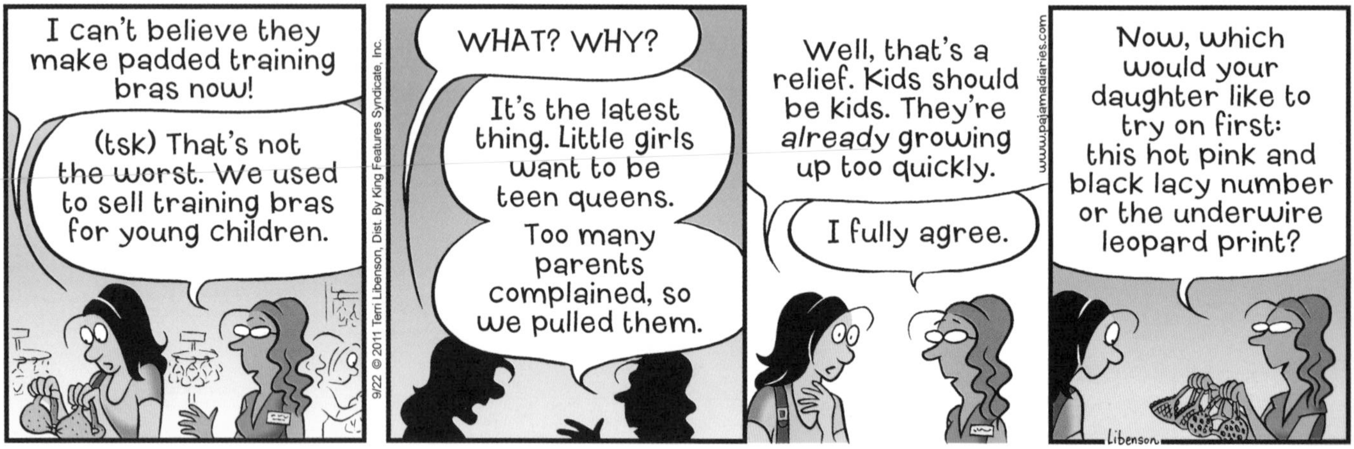
I can't believe they make padded training bras now!
(tsk) That's not the worst. We used to sell training bras for young children.
9/22 © 2011 Terri Libenson, Dist. By King Features Syndicate, Inc.
WHAT? WHY?
It's the latest thing. Little girls want to be teen queens.
Too many parents complained, so we pulled them.
Well, that's a relief. Kids should be kids. They're *already* growing up too quickly.
I fully agree.
www.pajamadiaries.com
Now, which would your daughter like to try on first: this hot pink and black lacy number or the underwire leopard print?
Libenson

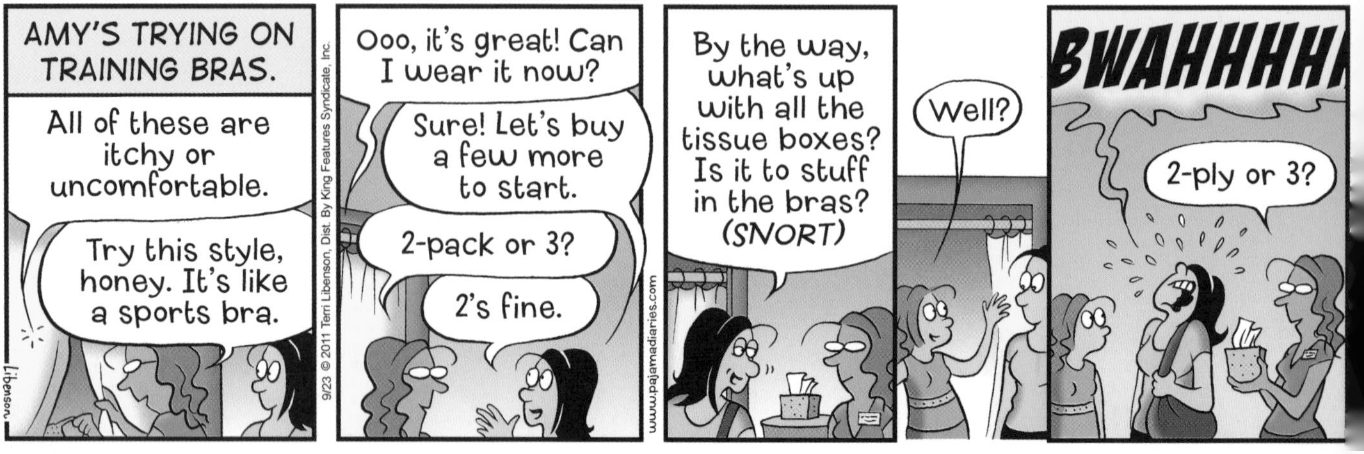
AMY'S TRYING ON TRAINING BRAS.
All of these are itchy or uncomfortable.
Try this style, honey. It's like a sports bra.
Libenson
9/23 © 2011 Terri Libenson, Dist. By King Features Syndicate, Inc.
Ooo, it's great! Can I wear it now?
Sure! Let's buy a few more to start.
2-pack or 3?
2's fine.
www.pajamadiaries.com
By the way, what's up with all the tissue boxes? Is it to stuff in the bras? *(SNORT)*
Well?
BWAHHHH
2-ply or 3?

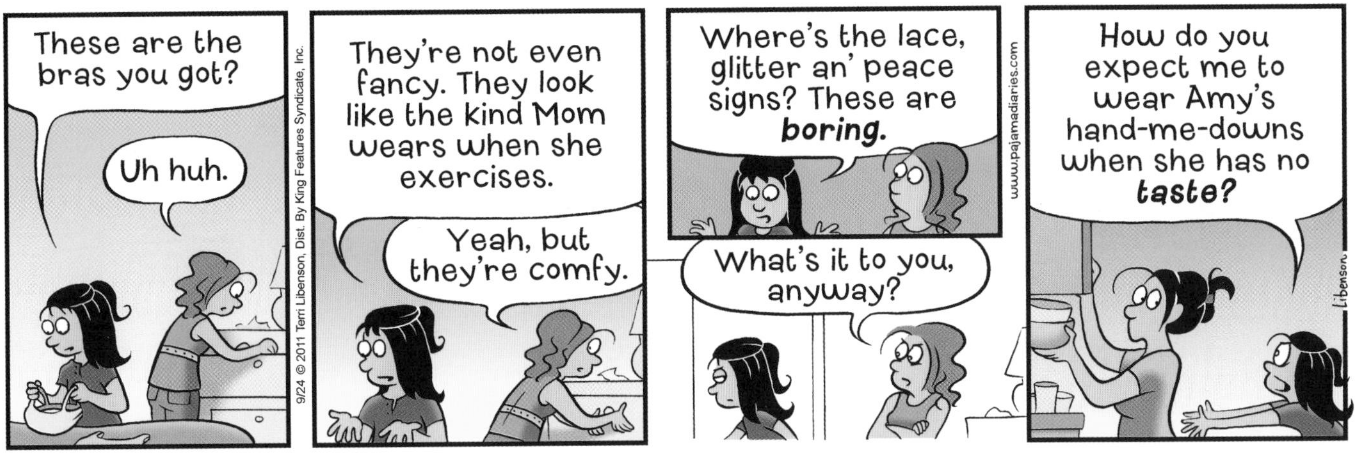
These are the bras you got?
Uh huh.
9/24 © 2011 Terri Libenson, Dist. By King Features Syndicate, Inc.
They're not even fancy. They look like the kind Mom wears when she exercises.
Yeah, but they're comfy.
Where's the lace, glitter an' peace signs? These are **boring.**
What's it to you, anyway?
www.pajamadiaries.com
How do you expect me to wear Amy's hand-me-downs when she has no ***taste?***
Libenson

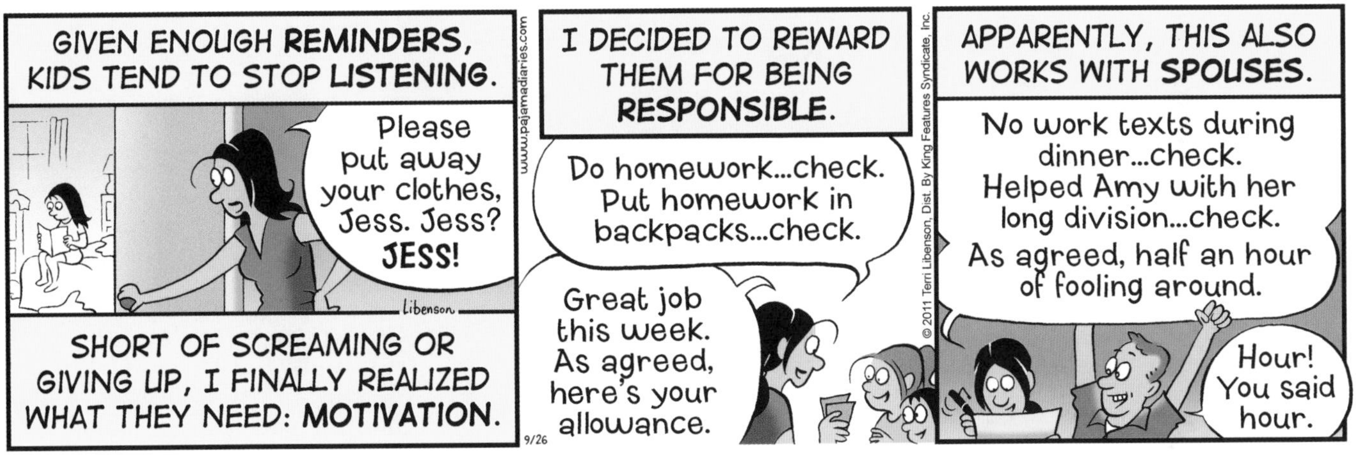
GIVEN ENOUGH **REMINDERS,** KIDS TEND TO STOP **LISTENING.**
Please put away your clothes, Jess. Jess? **JESS!**
Libenson
SHORT OF SCREAMING OR GIVING UP, I FINALLY REALIZED WHAT THEY NEED: **MOTIVATION.**
www.pajamadiaries.com
9/26
I DECIDED TO REWARD THEM FOR BEING **RESPONSIBLE.**
Do homework...check. Put homework in backpacks...check.
Great job this week. As agreed, here's your allowance.
© 2011 Terri Libenson, Dist. By King Features Syndicate, Inc.
APPARENTLY, THIS ALSO WORKS WITH **SPOUSES.**
No work texts during dinner...check. Helped Amy with her long division...check. As agreed, half an hour of fooling around.
Hour! You said hour.

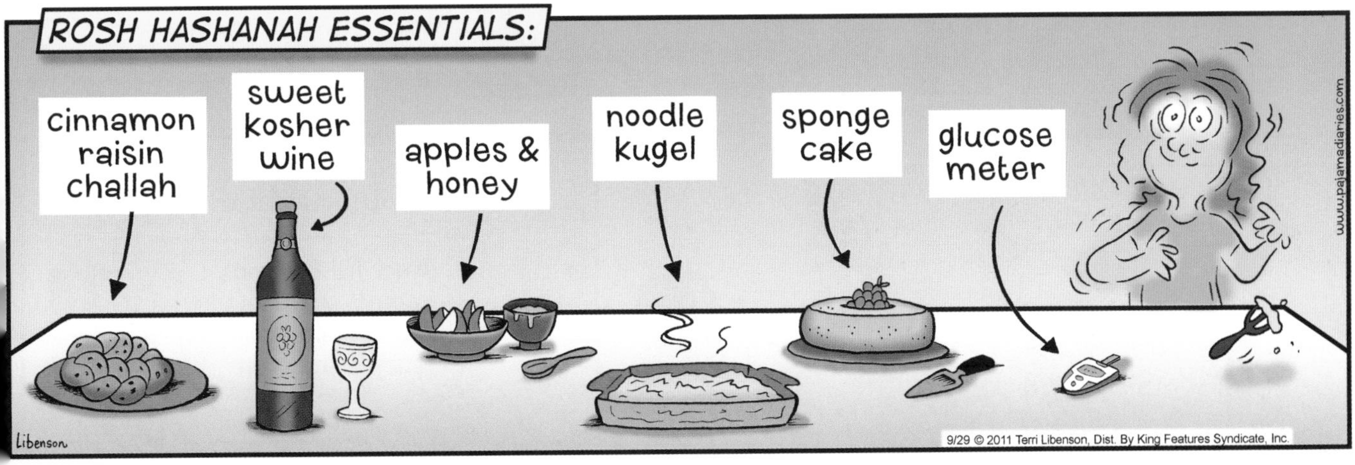
ROSH HASHANAH ESSENTIALS:
cinnamon raisin challah
sweet kosher wine
apples & honey
noodle kugel
sponge cake
glucose meter
www.pajamadiaries.com
Libenson
9/29 © 2011 Terri Libenson, Dist. By King Features Syndicate, Inc.

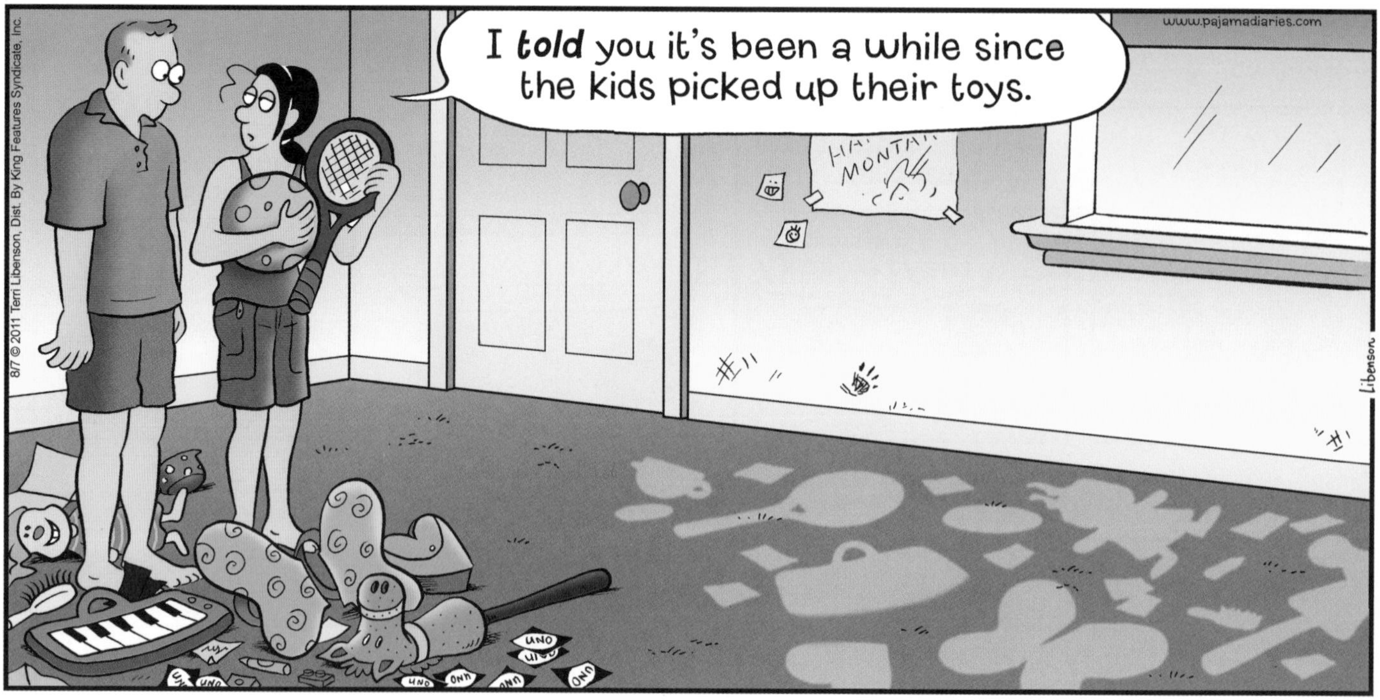
8/7 © 2011 Terri Libenson, Dist. By King Features Syndicate, Inc.
www.pajamadiaries.com
I *told* you it's been a while since the kids picked up their toys.
HA MONTA
UNO
Libenson

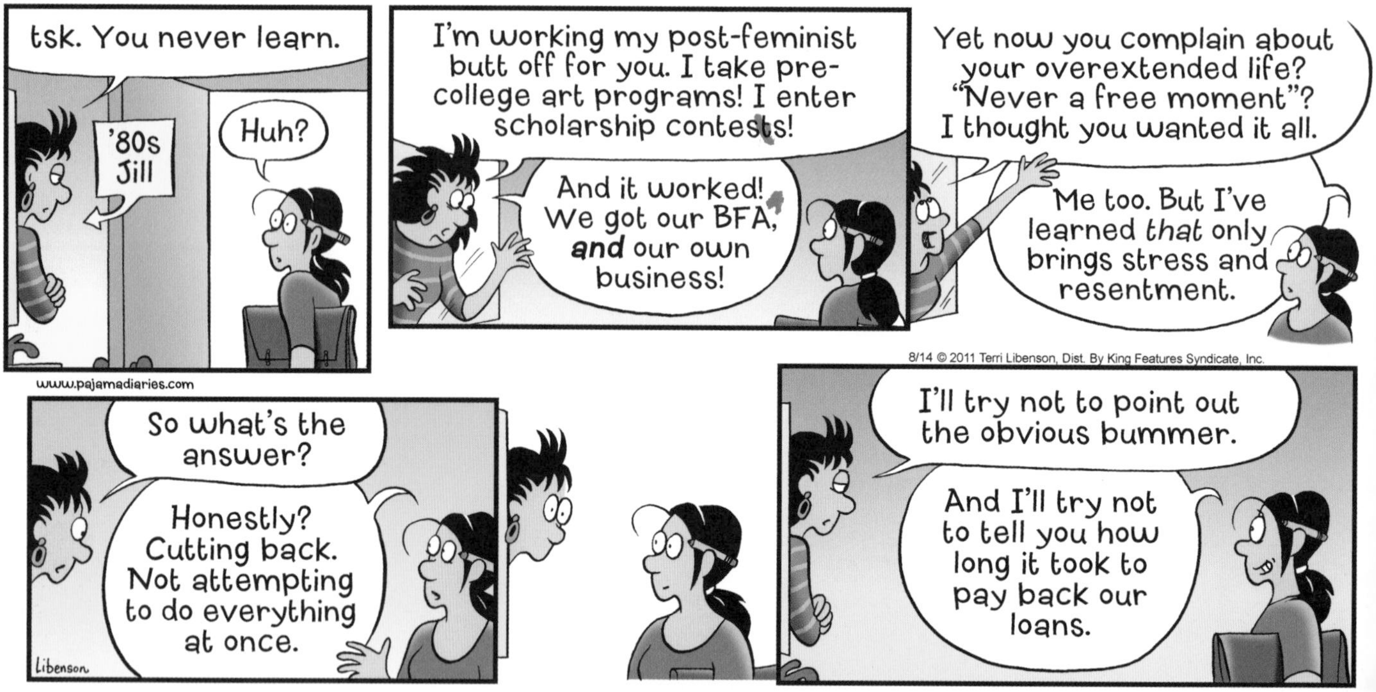
tsk. You never learn.
'80s Jill
Huh?
I'm working my post-feminist butt off for you. I take pre-college art programs! I enter scholarship contests!
And it worked! We got our BFA, **and** our own business!
Yet now you complain about your overextended life? "Never a free moment"? I thought you wanted it all.
Me too. But I've learned *that* only brings stress and resentment.
www.pajamadiaries.com
8/14 © 2011 Terri Libenson, Dist. By King Features Syndicate, Inc.
So what's the answer?
Honestly? Cutting back. Not attempting to do everything at once.
Libenson
I'll try not to point out the obvious bummer.
And I'll try not to tell you how long it took to pay back our loans.

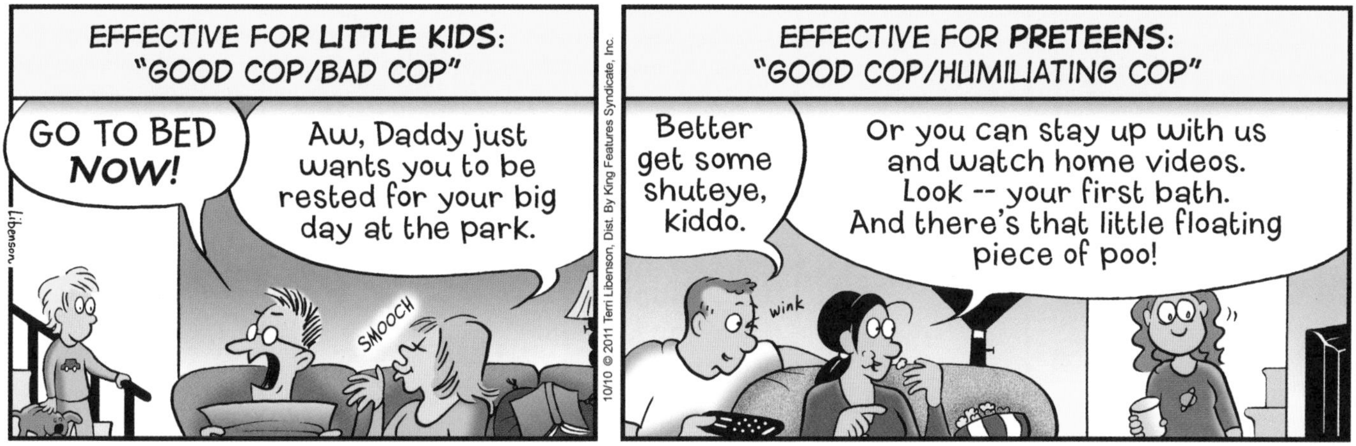
EFFECTIVE FOR LITTLE KIDS: "GOOD COP/BAD COP"
GO TO BED NOW!
Aw, Daddy just wants you to be rested for your big day at the park.
SMOOCH
EFFECTIVE FOR PRETEENS: "GOOD COP/HUMILIATING COP"
Better get some shuteye, kiddo.
wink
Or you can stay up with us and watch home videos. Look -- your first bath. And there's that little floating piece of poo!
Libenson
10/10 © 2011 Terri Libenson, Dist. By King Features Syndicate, Inc.

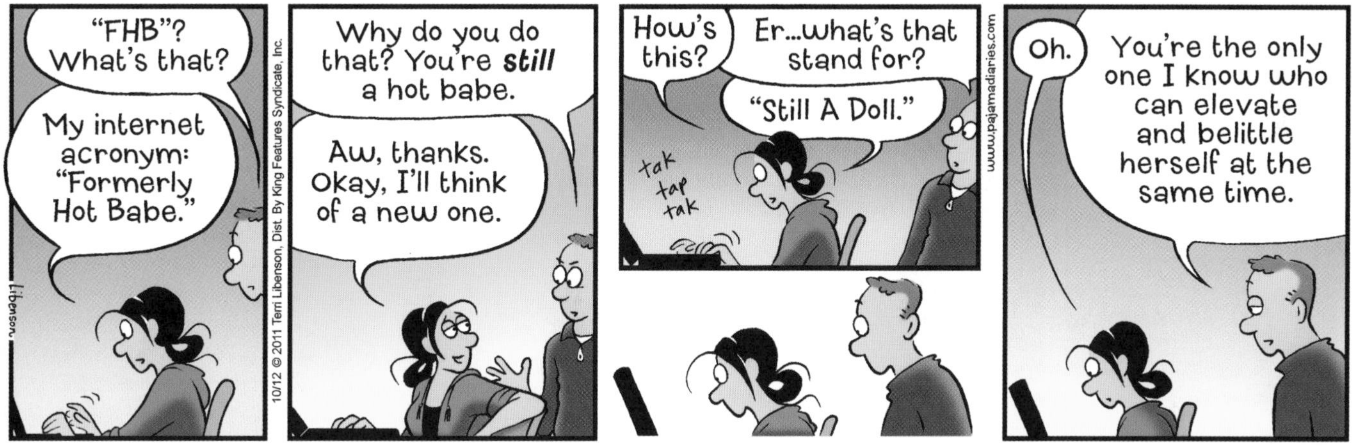
"FHB"? What's that?
My internet acronym: "Formerly Hot Babe."
Why do you do that? You're still a hot babe.
Aw, thanks. Okay, I'll think of a new one.
tak tap tak
How's this?
"Still A Doll."
Er...what's that stand for?
Oh.
You're the only one I know who can elevate and belittle herself at the same time.
Libenson
10/12 © 2011 Terri Libenson, Dist. By King Features Syndicate, Inc.
www.pajamadiaries.com

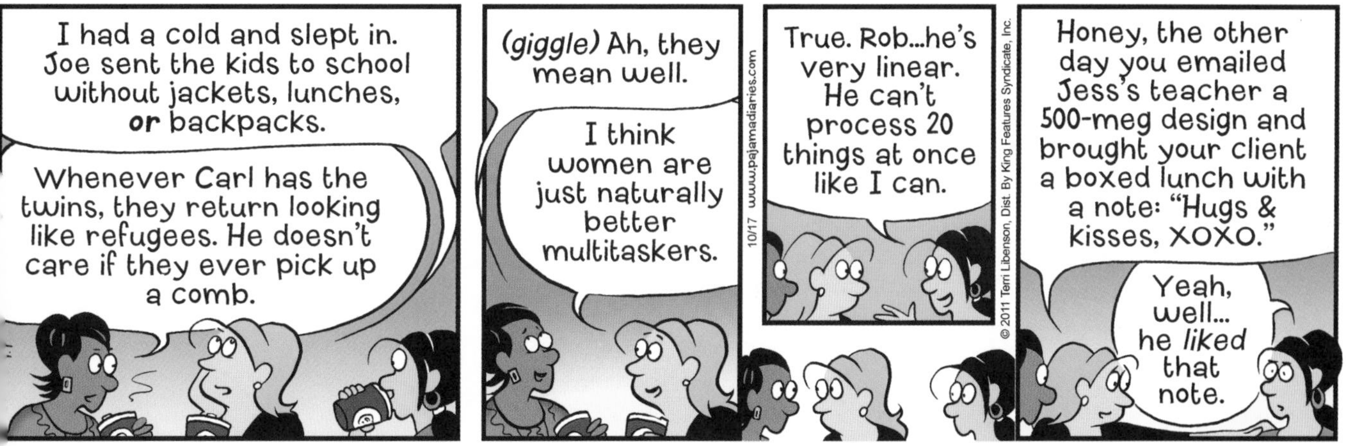
I had a cold and slept in. Joe sent the kids to school without jackets, lunches, or backpacks.
Whenever Carl has the twins, they return looking like refugees. He doesn't care if they ever pick up a comb.
(giggle) Ah, they mean well.
I think women are just naturally better multitaskers.
True. Rob...he's very linear. He can't process 20 things at once like I can.
Honey, the other day you emailed Jess's teacher a 500-meg design and brought your client a boxed lunch with a note: "Hugs & kisses, XOXO."
Yeah, well... he liked that note.
10/17 www.pajamadiaries.com
© 2011 Terri Libenson, Dist. By King Features Syndicate, Inc.

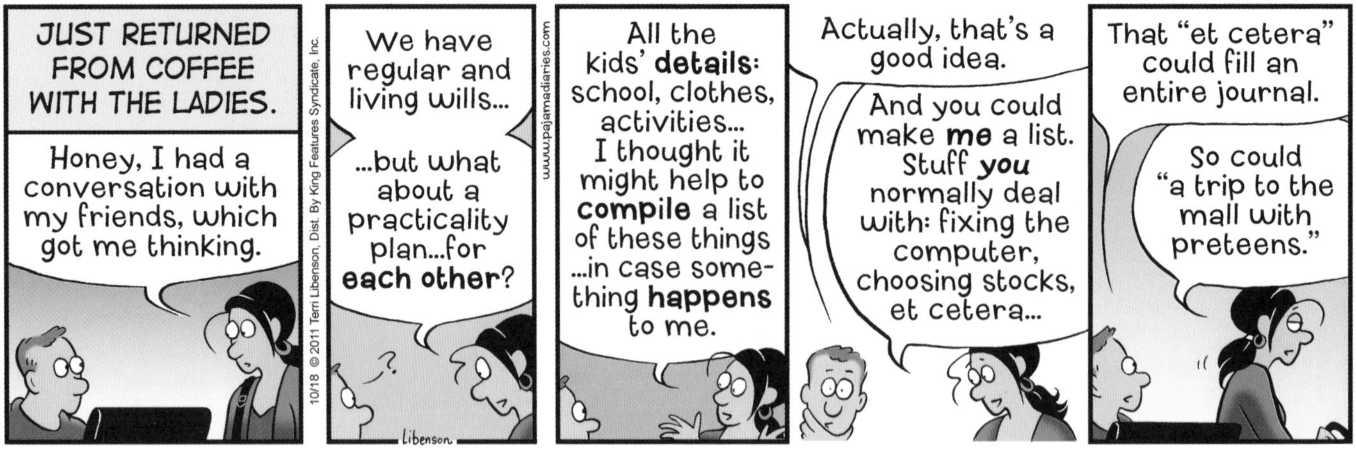
JUST RETURNED FROM COFFEE WITH THE LADIES.
Honey, I had a conversation with my friends, which got me thinking.
10/18 © 2011 Terri Libenson, Dist. By King Features Syndicate, Inc.
We have regular and living wills...
...but what about a practicality plan...for **each other**?
Libenson
www.pajamadiaries.com
All the kids' **details**: school, clothes, activities... I thought it might help to **compile** a list of these things ...in case something **happens** to me.
Actually, that's a good idea.
And you could make **me** a list. Stuff ***you*** normally deal with: fixing the computer, choosing stocks, et cetera...
That "et cetera" could fill an entire journal.
So could "a trip to the mall with preteens."

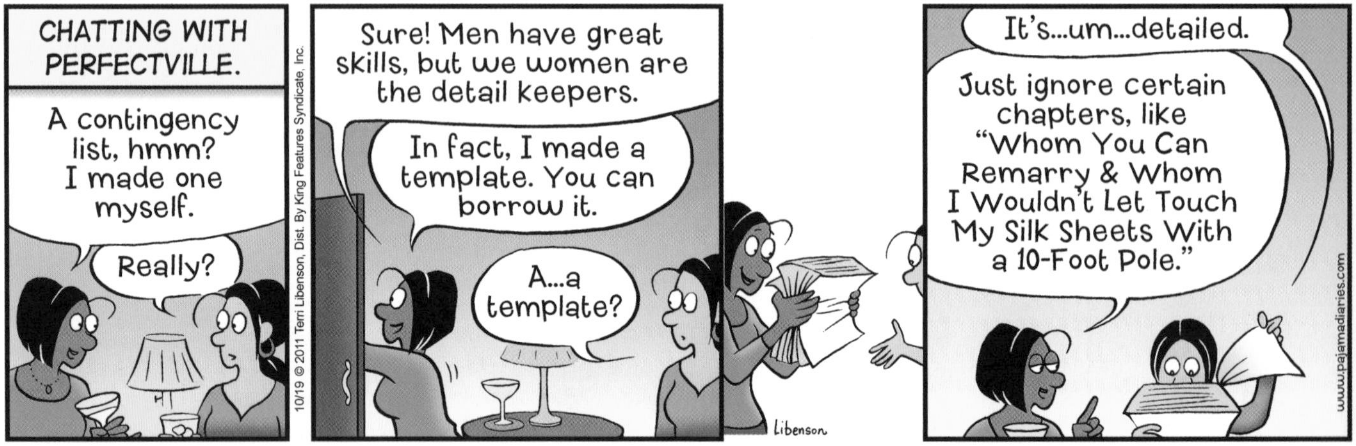
CHATTING WITH PERFECTVILLE.
A contingency list, hmm? I made one myself.
Really?
10/19 © 2011 Terri Libenson, Dist. By King Features Syndicate, Inc.
Sure! Men have great skills, but we women are the detail keepers.
In fact, I made a template. You can borrow it.
A...a template?
Libenson
It's...um...detailed.
Just ignore certain chapters, like "Whom You Can Remarry & Whom I Wouldn't Let Touch My Silk Sheets With a 10-Foot Pole."
www.pajamadiaries.com

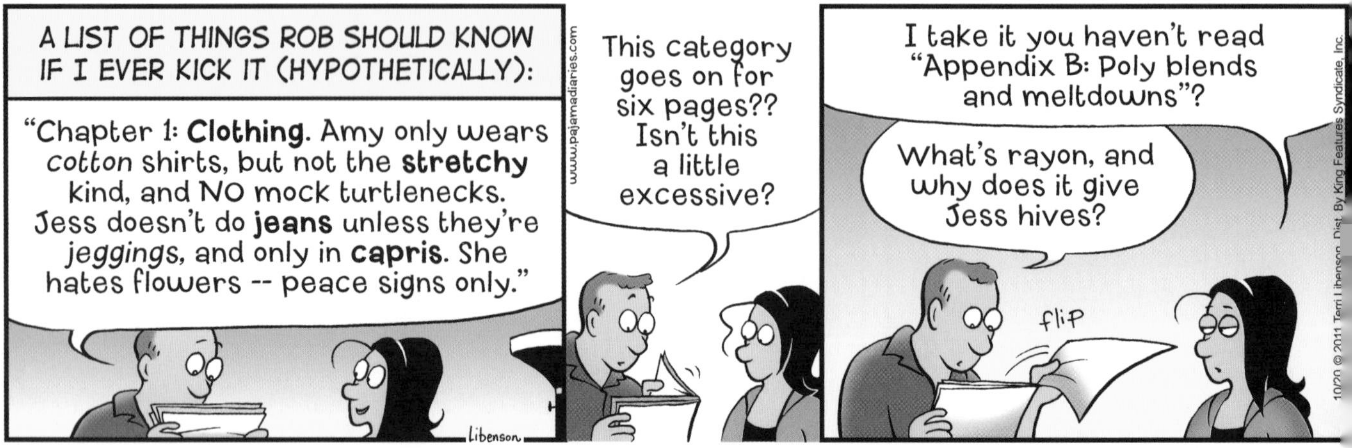
A LIST OF THINGS ROB SHOULD KNOW IF I EVER KICK IT (HYPOTHETICALLY):
"Chapter 1: **Clothing**. Amy only wears *cotton* shirts, but not the **stretchy** kind, and NO mock turtlenecks. Jess doesn't do **jeans** unless they're *jeggings*, and only in **capris**. She hates flowers -- peace signs only."
Libenson
www.pajamadiaries.com
This category goes on for six pages?? Isn't this a little excessive?
I take it you haven't read "Appendix B: Poly blends and meltdowns"?
What's rayon, and why does it give Jess hives?
flip
10/20 © 2011 Terri Libenson, Dist. By King Features Syndicate, Inc.

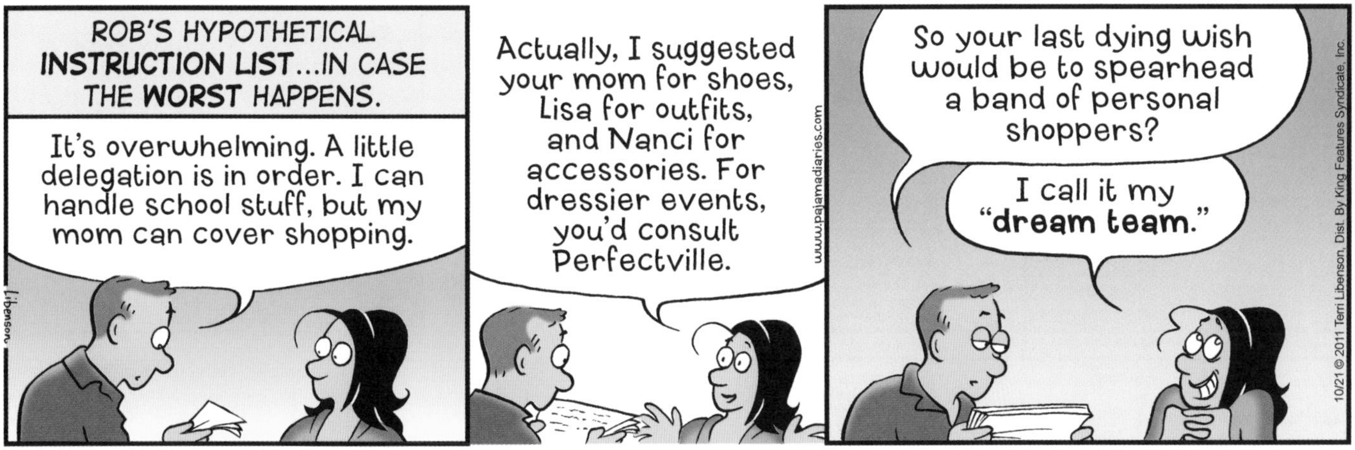
ROB'S HYPOTHETICAL INSTRUCTION LIST...IN CASE THE WORST HAPPENS.
It's overwhelming. A little delegation is in order. I can handle school stuff, but my mom can cover shopping.
Libenson
Actually, I suggested your mom for shoes, Lisa for outfits, and Nanci for accessories. For dressier events, you'd consult Perfectville.
www.pajamadiaries.com
So your last dying wish would be to spearhead a band of personal shoppers?
I call it my "dream team."
10/21 © 2011 Terri Libenson, Dist. By King Features Syndicate, Inc.

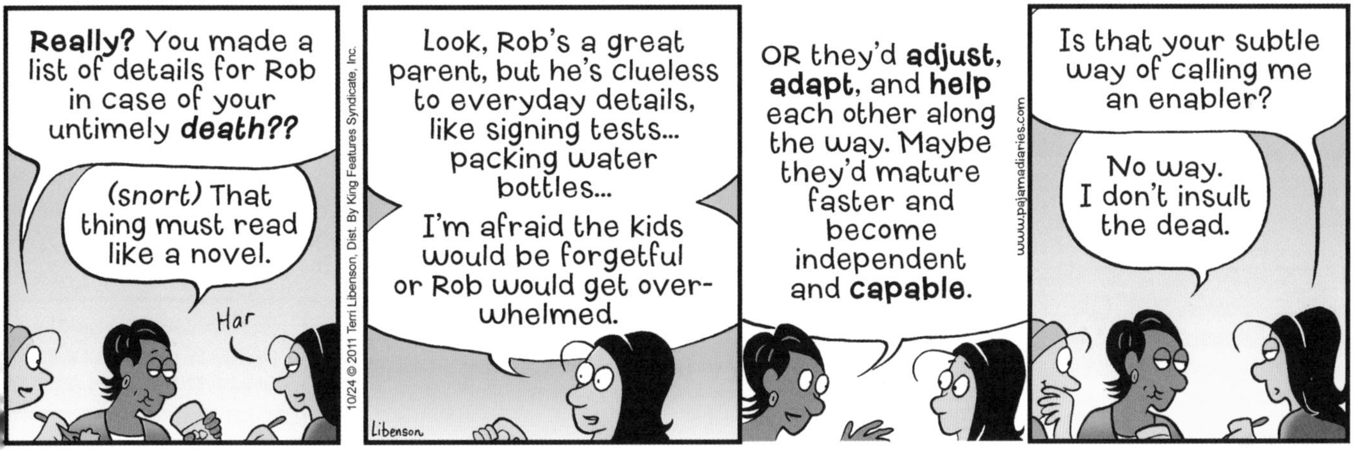
Really? You made a list of details for Rob in case of your untimely death??
(snort) That thing must read like a novel.
Har
10/24 © 2011 Terri Libenson, Dist. By King Features Syndicate, Inc.
Look, Rob's a great parent, but he's clueless to everyday details, like signing tests... packing water bottles...
I'm afraid the kids would be forgetful or Rob would get over-whelmed.
Libenson
OR they'd adjust, adapt, and help each other along the way. Maybe they'd mature faster and become independent and capable.
www.pajamadiaries.com
Is that your subtle way of calling me an enabler?
No way. I don't insult the dead.

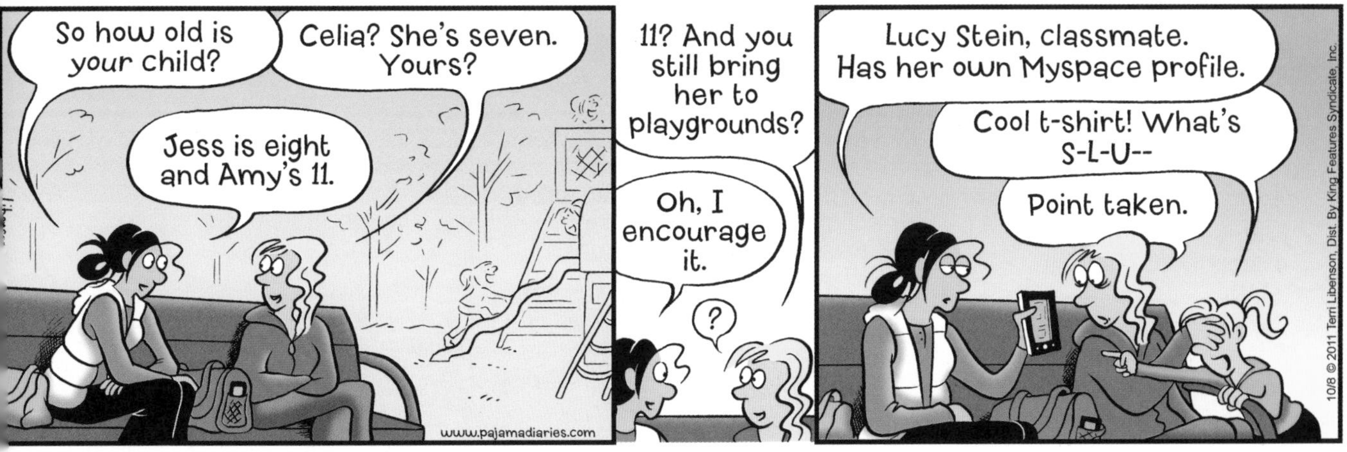
So how old is your child?
Celia? She's seven. Yours?
Jess is eight and Amy's 11.
www.pajamadiaries.com
11? And you still bring her to playgrounds?
Oh, I encourage it.
?
Lucy Stein, classmate. Has her own Myspace profile.
Cool t-shirt! What's S-L-U--
Point taken.
10/8 © 2011 Terri Libenson, Dist. By King Features Syndicate, Inc.

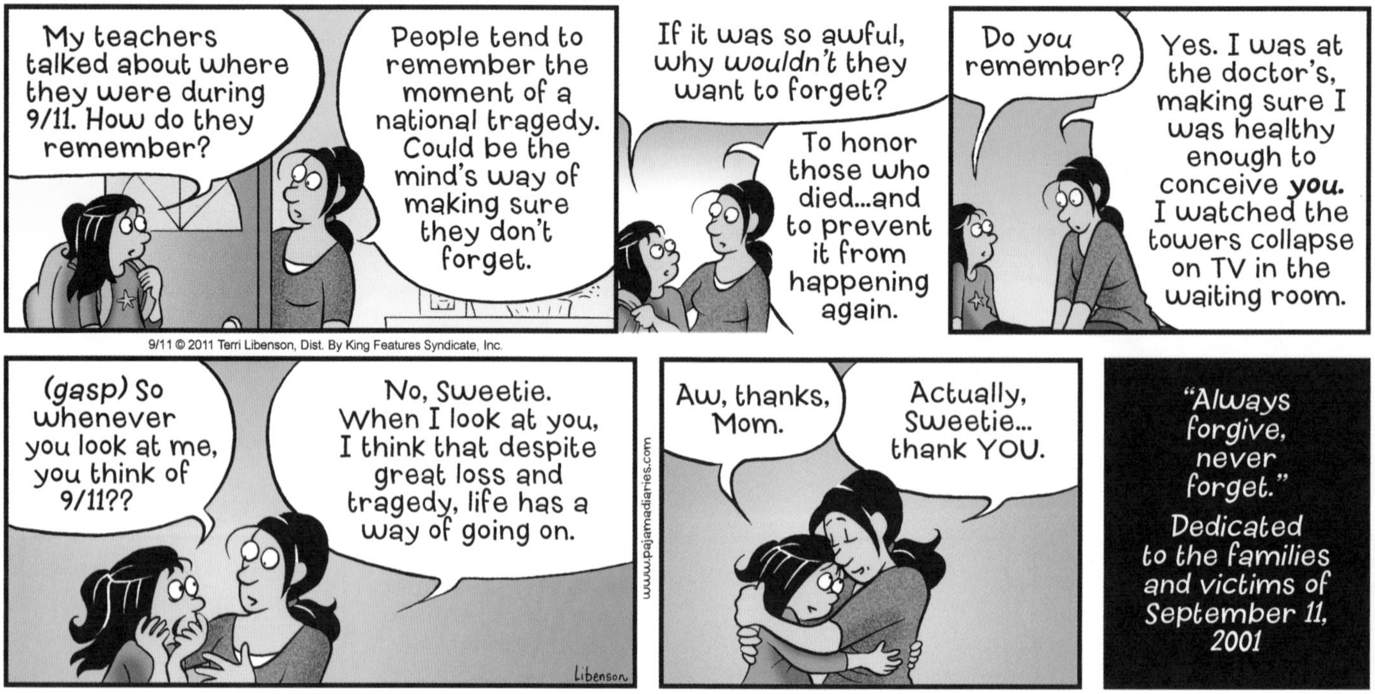

My teachers talked about where they were during 9/11. How do they remember?
People tend to remember the moment of a national tragedy. Could be the mind's way of making sure they don't forget.
If it was so awful, why *wouldn't* they want to forget?
To honor those who died...and to prevent it from happening again.
Do *you* remember?
Yes. I was at the doctor's, making sure I was healthy enough to conceive **you.** I watched the towers collapse on TV in the waiting room.
(*gasp*) So whenever you look at me, you think of 9/11??
No, Sweetie. When I look at you, I think that despite great loss and tragedy, life has a way of going on.
www.pajamadiaries.com
Aw, thanks, Mom.
Actually, Sweetie... thank YOU.
Libenson
"Always forgive, never forget."
Dedicated to the families and victims of September 11, 2001

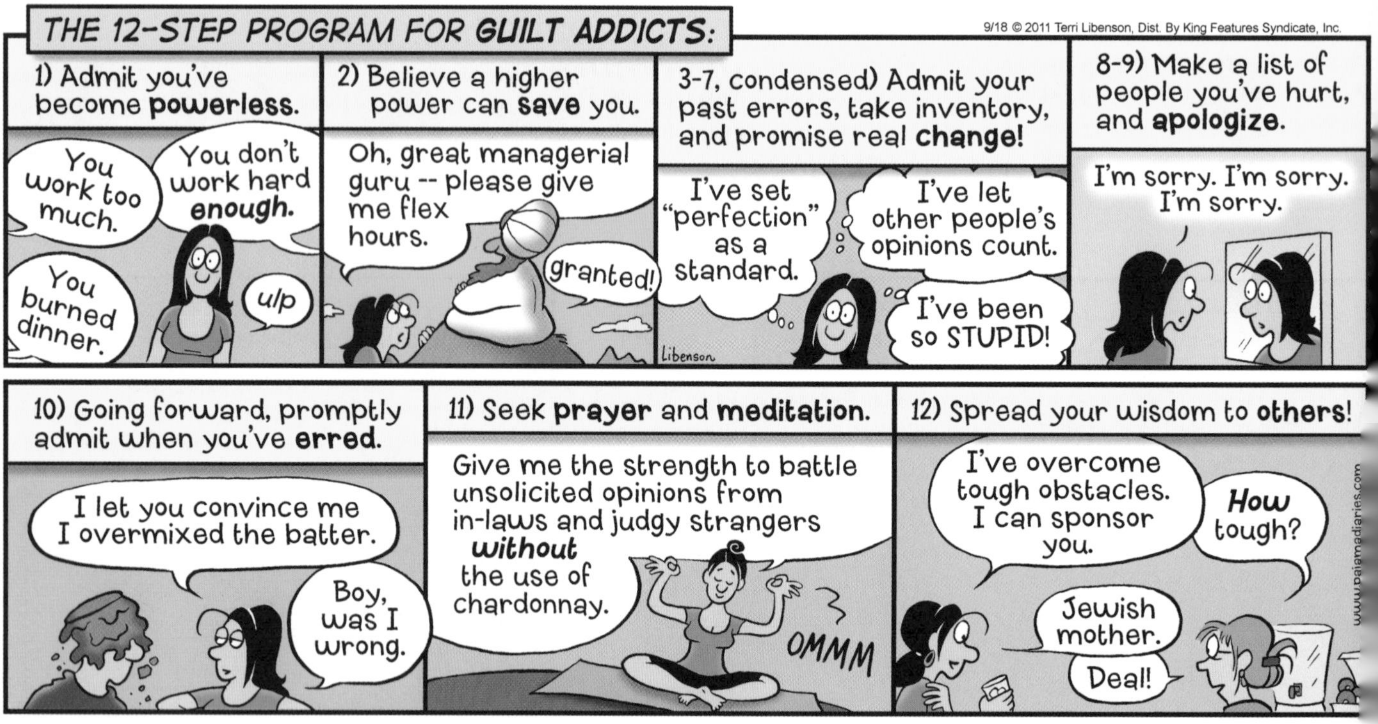

THE 12-STEP PROGRAM FOR **GUILT ADDICTS**:
1) Admit you've become **powerless**.
You work too much.
You don't work hard **enough.**
You burned dinner.
u/p
2) Believe a higher power can **save** you.
Oh, great managerial guru -- please give me flex hours.
granted!
3-7, condensed) Admit your past errors, take inventory, and promise real **change!**
I've set "perfection" as a standard.
I've let other people's opinions count.
I've been so STUPID!
Libenson
8-9) Make a list of people you've hurt, and **apologize**.
I'm sorry. I'm sorry. I'm sorry.
10) Going forward, promptly admit when you've **erred**.
I let you convince me I overmixed the batter.
Boy, was I wrong.
11) Seek **prayer** and **meditation**.
Give me the strength to battle unsolicited opinions from in-laws and judgy strangers ***without*** the use of chardonnay.
OMMM
12) Spread your wisdom to **others**!
I've overcome tough obstacles. I can sponsor you.
How tough?
Jewish mother.
Deal!
www.pajamadiaries.com

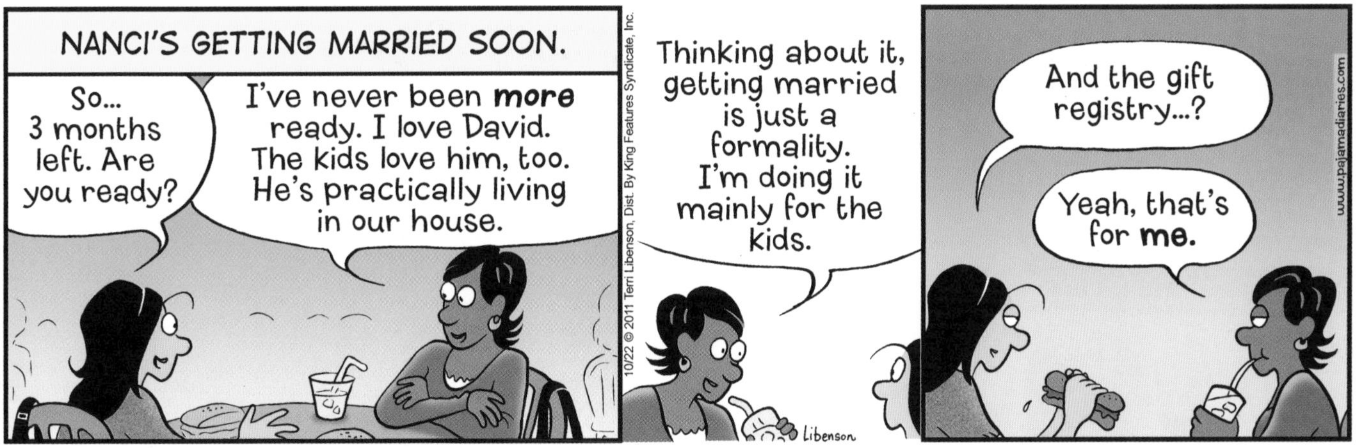
NANCI'S GETTING MARRIED SOON.
So... 3 months left. Are you ready?
I've never been **more** ready. I love David. The kids love him, too. He's practically living in our house.
10/22 © 2011 Terri Libenson, Dist. By King Features Syndicate, Inc.
Thinking about it, getting married is just a formality. I'm doing it mainly for the kids.
Libenson
And the gift registry...?
Yeah, that's for **me.**
www.pajamadiaries.com

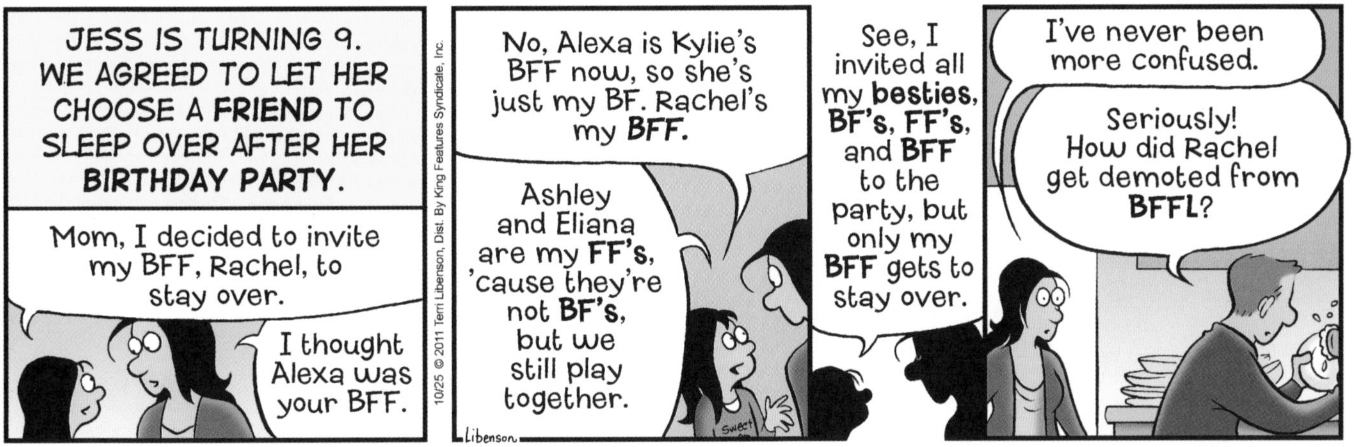
JESS IS TURNING 9. WE AGREED TO LET HER CHOOSE A **FRIEND** TO SLEEP OVER AFTER HER **BIRTHDAY PARTY**.
Mom, I decided to invite my BFF, Rachel, to stay over.
I thought Alexa was your BFF.
10/25 © 2011 Terri Libenson, Dist. By King Features Syndicate, Inc.
No, Alexa is Kylie's BFF now, so she's just my BF. Rachel's my **BFF**.
Ashley and Eliana are my **FF's**, 'cause they're not **BF's**, but we still play together.
Libenson
See, I invited all my **besties**, **BF's**, **FF's**, and **BFF** to the party, but only my **BFF** gets to stay over.
I've never been more confused.
Seriously! How did Rachel get demoted from **BFFL**?

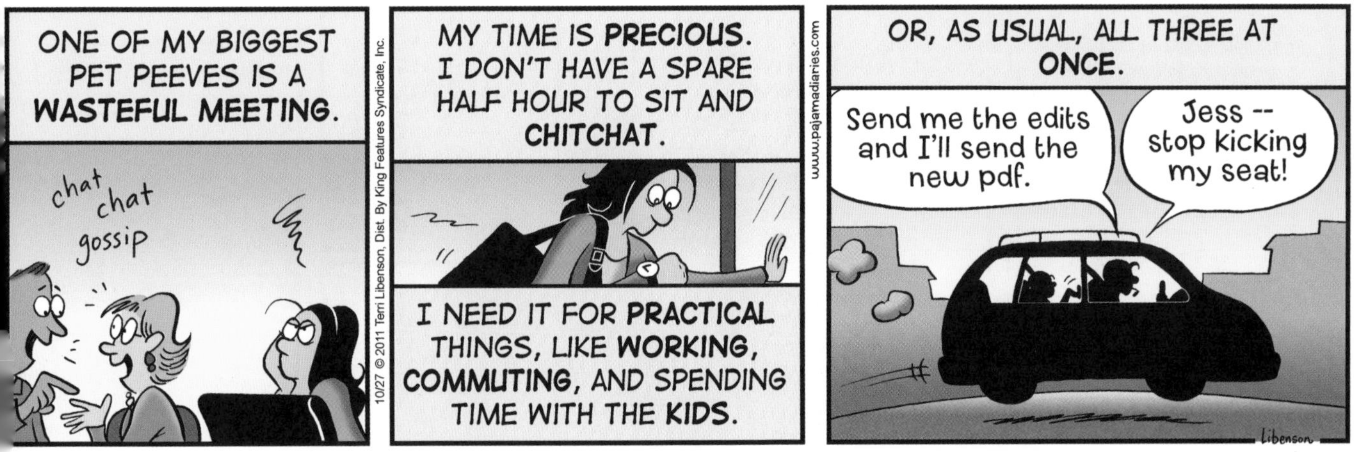
ONE OF MY BIGGEST PET PEEVES IS A **WASTEFUL MEETING**.
chat chat gossip
10/27 © 2011 Terri Libenson, Dist. By King Features Syndicate, Inc.
MY TIME IS **PRECIOUS**. I DON'T HAVE A SPARE HALF HOUR TO SIT AND **CHITCHAT**.
I NEED IT FOR **PRACTICAL** THINGS, LIKE **WORKING**, **COMMUTING**, AND SPENDING TIME WITH THE **KIDS**.
www.pajamadiaries.com
OR, AS USUAL, ALL THREE AT **ONCE**.
Send me the edits and I'll send the new pdf.
Jess -- stop kicking my seat!
Libenson

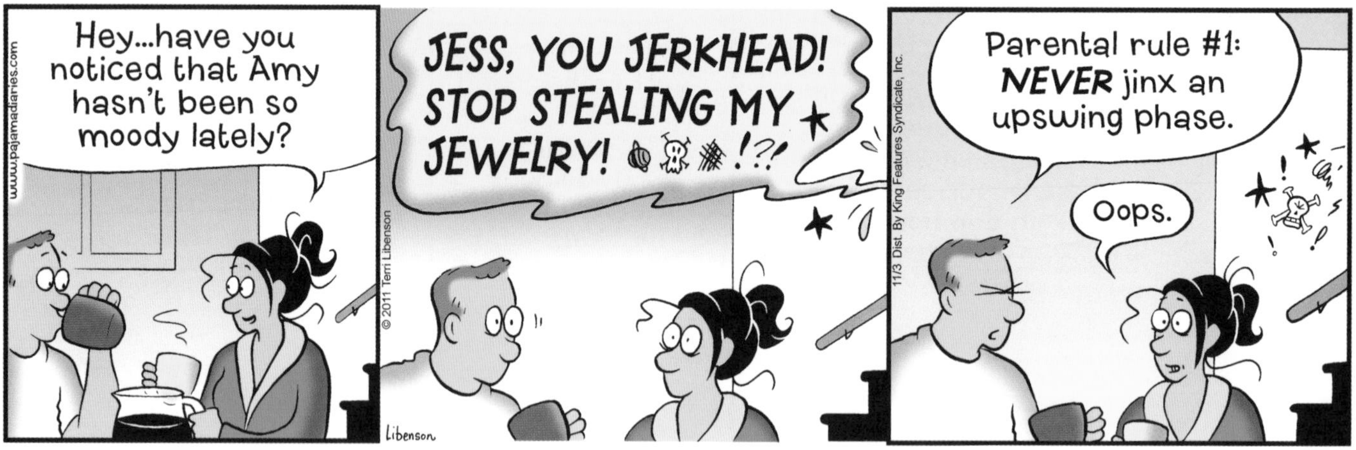
Hey...have you noticed that Amy hasn't been so moody lately?
JESS, YOU JERKHEAD! STOP STEALING MY JEWELRY! !?!
Parental rule #1: NEVER jinx an upswing phase.
Oops.
www.pajamadiaries.com
© 2011 Terri Libenson
11/3 Dist. By King Features Syndicate, Inc.
Libenson

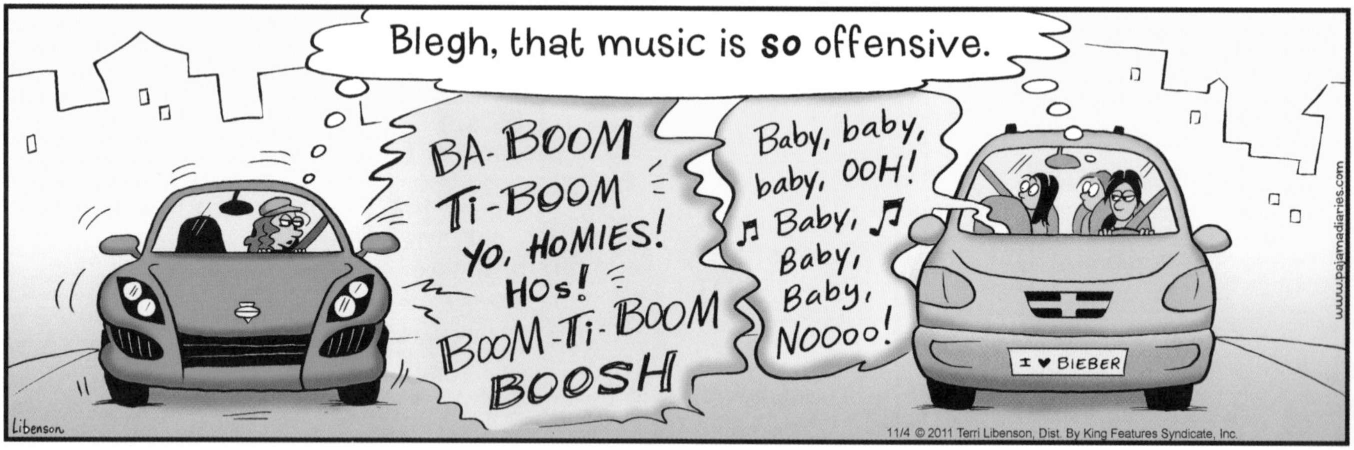
Blegh, that music is so offensive.
BA-BOOM TI-BOOM YO, HOMIES! HOs! BOOM-TI-BOOM BOOSH
Baby, baby, baby, OOH! ♫ Baby, ♫ Baby, Baby, NOOOO!
I ♥ BIEBER
www.pajamadiaries.com
Libenson
11/4 © 2011 Terri Libenson, Dist. By King Features Syndicate, Inc.

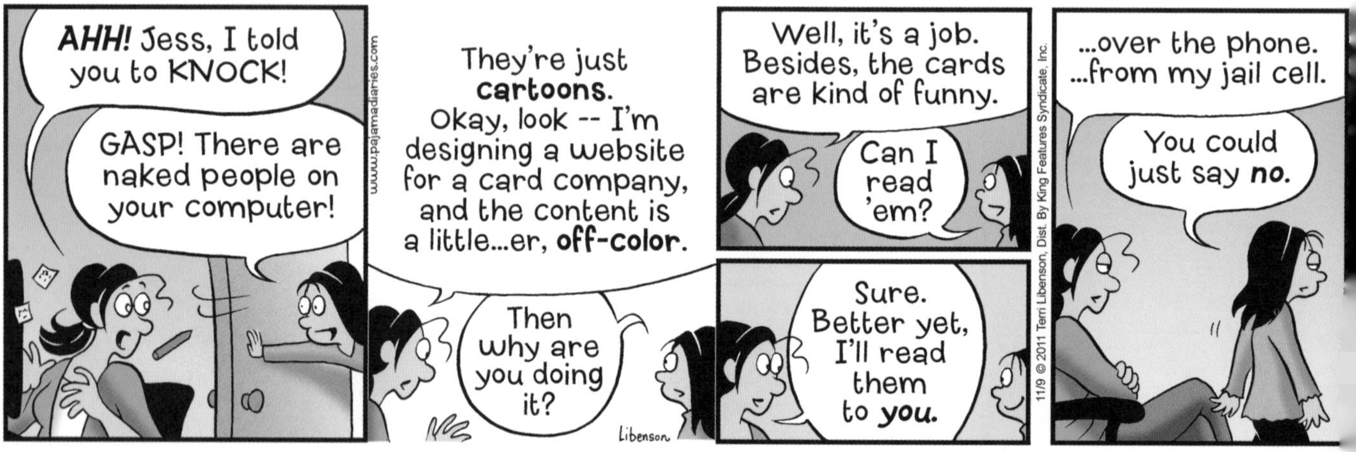
AHH! Jess, I told you to KNOCK!
GASP! There are naked people on your computer!
They're just cartoons. Okay, look -- I'm designing a website for a card company, and the content is a little...er, off-color.
Then why are you doing it?
Well, it's a job. Besides, the cards are kind of funny.
Can I read 'em?
Sure. Better yet, I'll read them to you.
...over the phone. ...from my jail cell.
You could just say no.
www.pajamadiaries.com
11/9 © 2011 Terri Libenson, Dist. By King Features Syndicate, Inc.
Libenson

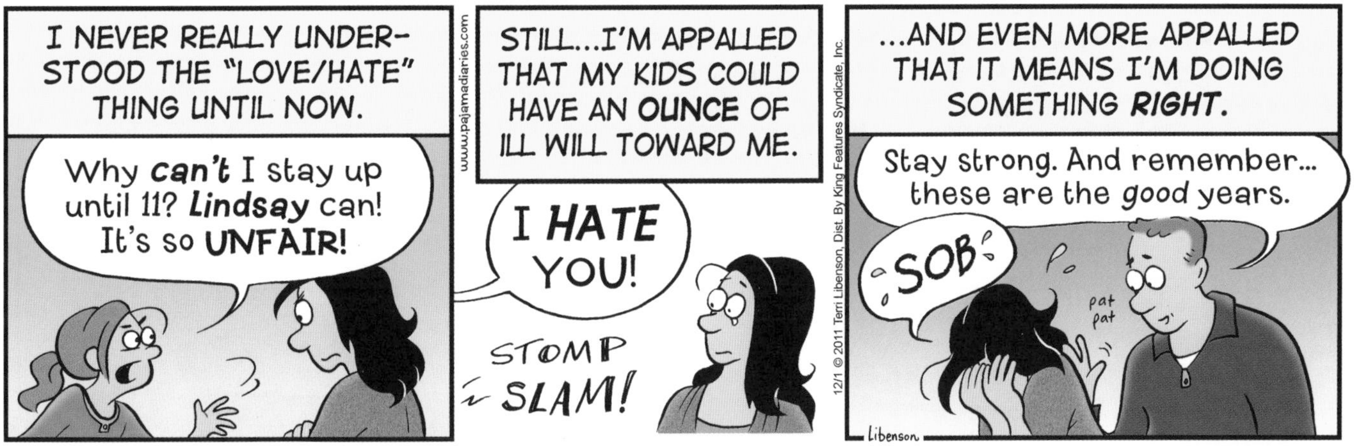
I NEVER REALLY UNDERSTOOD THE "LOVE/HATE" THING UNTIL NOW.
Why **can't** I stay up until 11? ***Lindsay*** can! It's so **UNFAIR!**
www.pajamadiaries.com
STILL...I'M APPALLED THAT MY KIDS COULD HAVE AN **OUNCE** OF ILL WILL TOWARD ME.
I ***HATE*** YOU!
STOMP
SLAM!
12/1 © 2011 Terri Libenson, Dist. By King Features Syndicate, Inc.
...AND EVEN MORE APPALLED THAT IT MEANS I'M DOING SOMETHING ***RIGHT***.
Stay strong. And remember... these are the *good* years.
SOB
pat pat
Libenson

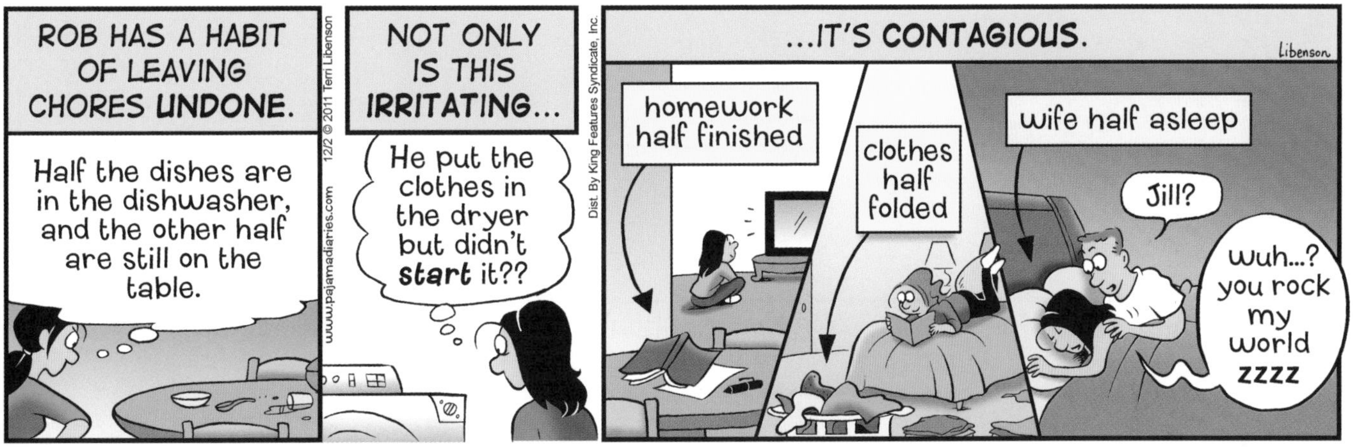
ROB HAS A HABIT OF LEAVING CHORES **UNDONE**.
Half the dishes are in the dishwasher, and the other half are still on the table.
12/2 © 2011 Terri Libenson
www.pajamadiaries.com
NOT ONLY IS THIS **IRRITATING**...
He put the clothes in the dryer but didn't **start** it??
Dist. By King Features Syndicate, Inc.
...IT'S **CONTAGIOUS**.
Libenson
homework half finished
clothes half folded
wife half asleep
Jill?
wuh...? you rock my world **zzzz**

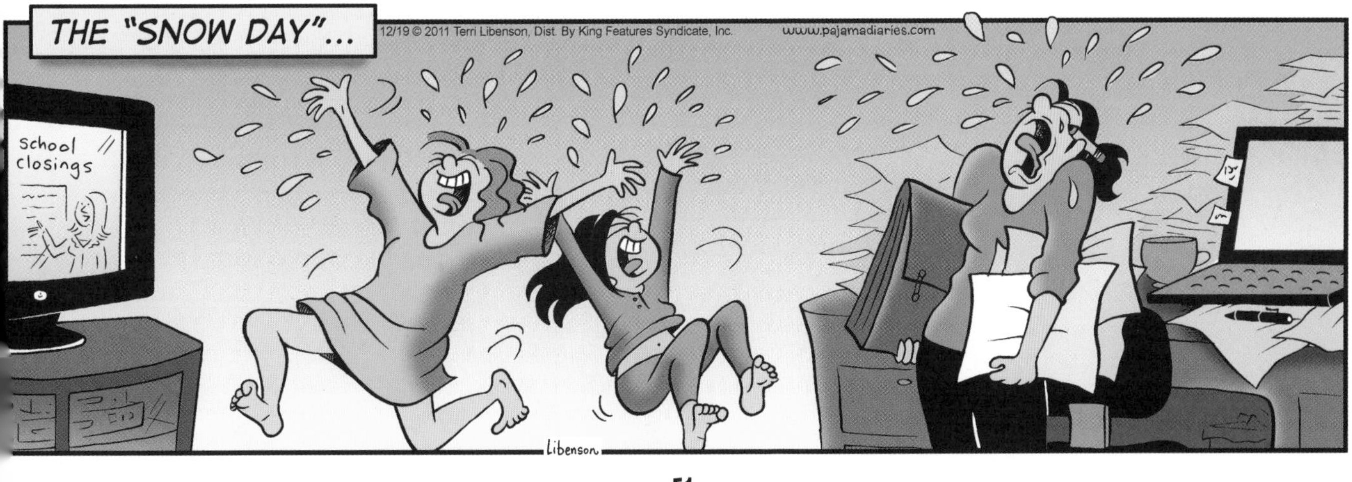
THE "SNOW DAY"...
12/19 © 2011 Terri Libenson, Dist. By King Features Syndicate, Inc.
www.pajamadiaries.com
School closings
Libenson

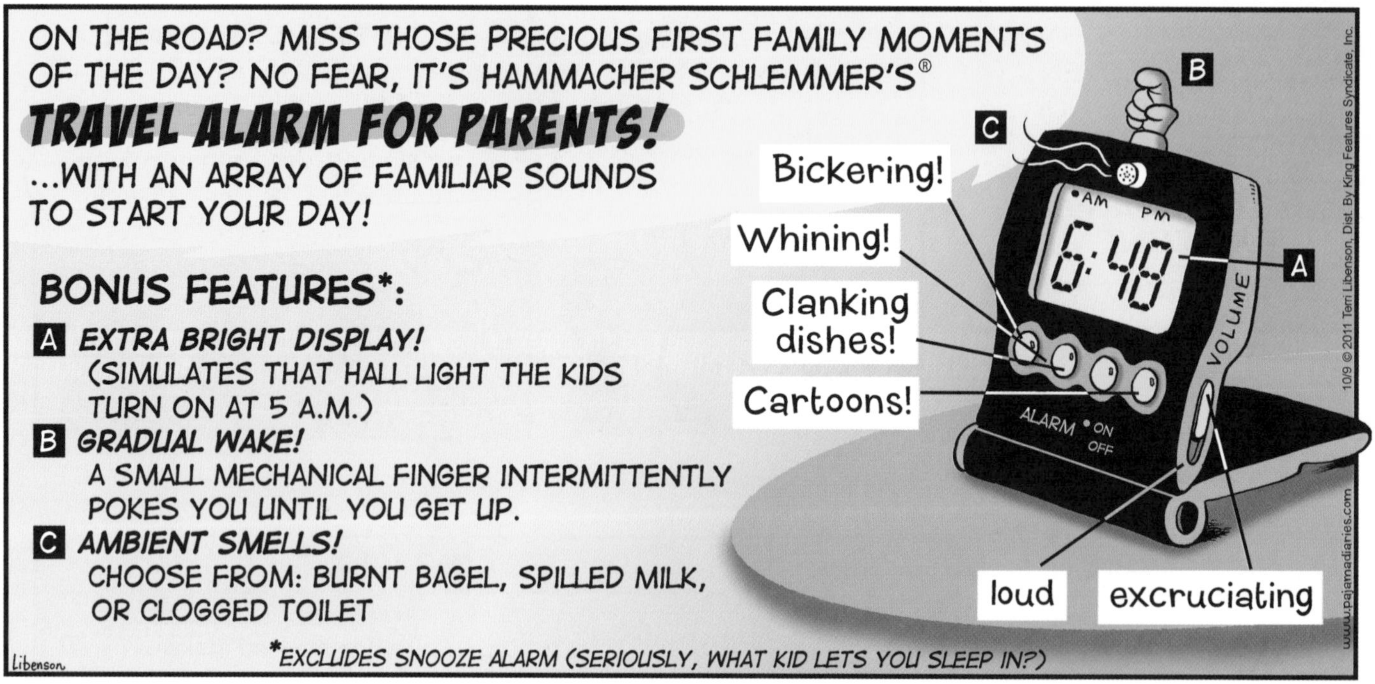
ON THE ROAD? MISS THOSE PRECIOUS FIRST FAMILY MOMENTS OF THE DAY? NO FEAR, IT'S HAMMACHER SCHLEMMER'S®
TRAVEL ALARM FOR PARENTS!
...WITH AN ARRAY OF FAMILIAR SOUNDS TO START YOUR DAY!
BONUS FEATURES*:
A EXTRA BRIGHT DISPLAY! (SIMULATES THAT HALL LIGHT THE KIDS TURN ON AT 5 A.M.)
B GRADUAL WAKE! A SMALL MECHANICAL FINGER INTERMITTENTLY POKES YOU UNTIL YOU GET UP.
C AMBIENT SMELLS! CHOOSE FROM: BURNT BAGEL, SPILLED MILK, OR CLOGGED TOILET
*EXCLUDES SNOOZE ALARM (SERIOUSLY, WHAT KID LETS YOU SLEEP IN?)
Bickering!
Whining!
Clanking dishes!
Cartoons!
6:48
AM PM
VOLUME
ALARM ON OFF
loud
excruciating
A
B
C
Libenson
10/9 © 2011 Terri Libenson, Dist. By King Features Syndicate, Inc.
www.pajamadiaries.com

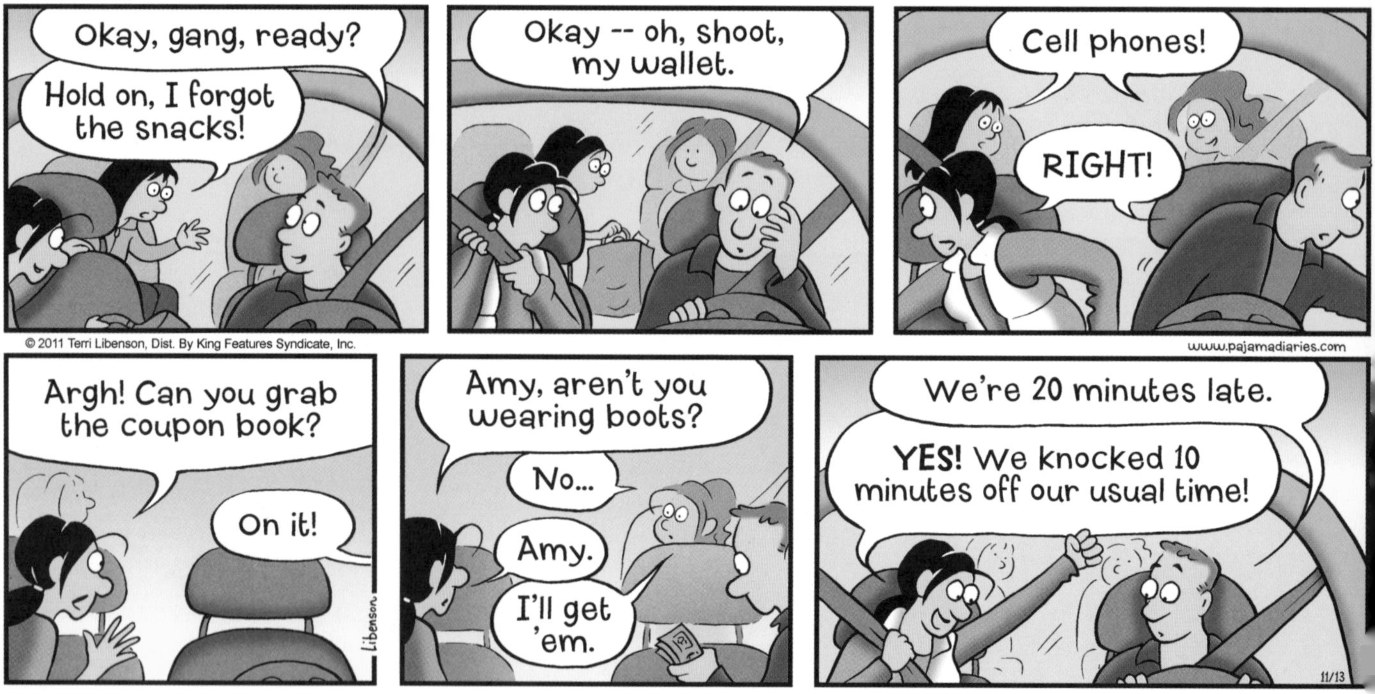
Okay, gang, ready?
Hold on, I forgot the snacks!
Okay -- oh, shoot, my wallet.
Cell phones!
RIGHT!
© 2011 Terri Libenson, Dist. By King Features Syndicate, Inc.
www.pajamadiaries.com
Argh! Can you grab the coupon book?
On it!
Libenson
Amy, aren't you wearing boots?
No...
Amy.
I'll get 'em.
We're 20 minutes late.
YES! We knocked 10 minutes off our usual time!
11/13

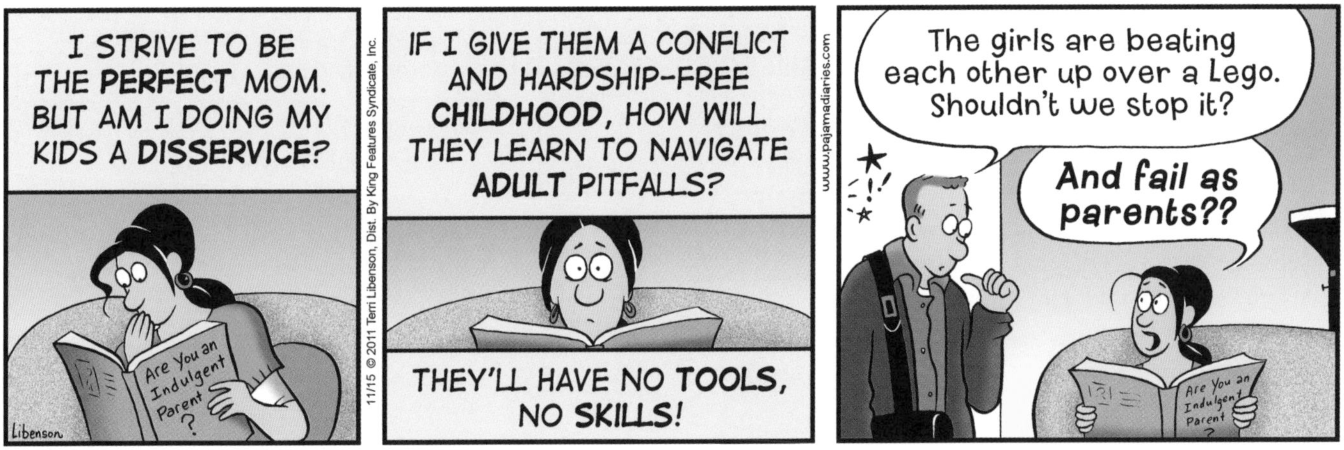
I STRIVE TO BE THE PERFECT MOM. BUT AM I DOING MY KIDS A DISSERVICE?
Are You an Indulgent Parent ?
Libenson
11/15 © 2011 Terri Libenson, Dist. By King Features Syndicate, Inc.
IF I GIVE THEM A CONFLICT AND HARDSHIP-FREE CHILDHOOD, HOW WILL THEY LEARN TO NAVIGATE ADULT PITFALLS?
THEY'LL HAVE NO TOOLS, NO SKILLS!
www.pajamadiaries.com
The girls are beating each other up over a Lego. Shouldn't we stop it?
And fail as parents??
Are You an Indulgent Parent ?

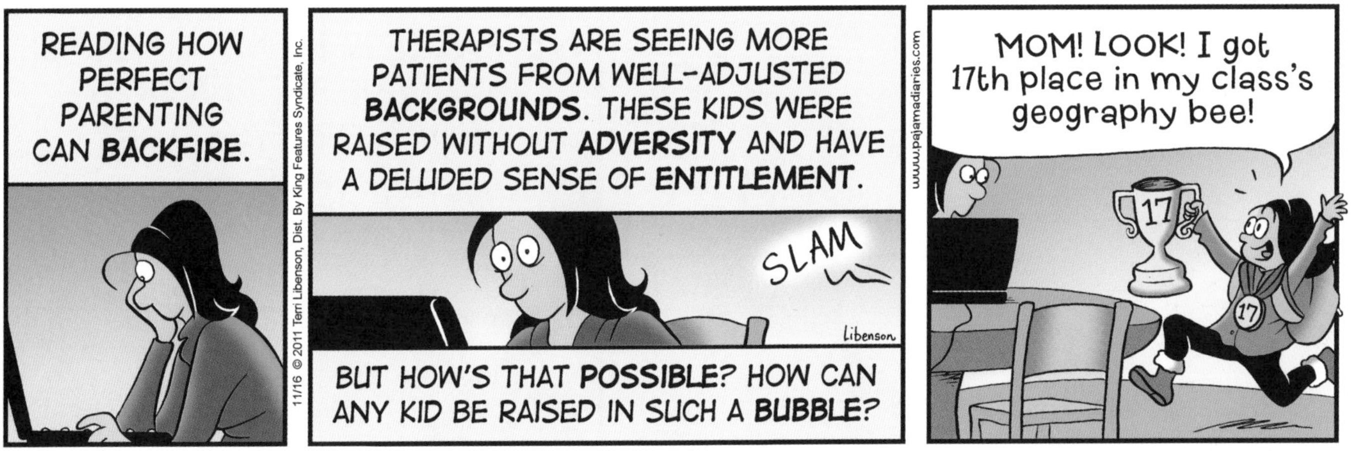
READING HOW PERFECT PARENTING CAN BACKFIRE.
11/16 © 2011 Terri Libenson, Dist. By King Features Syndicate, Inc.
THERAPISTS ARE SEEING MORE PATIENTS FROM WELL-ADJUSTED BACKGROUNDS. THESE KIDS WERE RAISED WITHOUT ADVERSITY AND HAVE A DELUDED SENSE OF ENTITLEMENT.
SLAM
Libenson
BUT HOW'S THAT POSSIBLE? HOW CAN ANY KID BE RAISED IN SUCH A BUBBLE?
www.pajamadiaries.com
MOM! LOOK! I got 17th place in my class's geography bee!
17
17

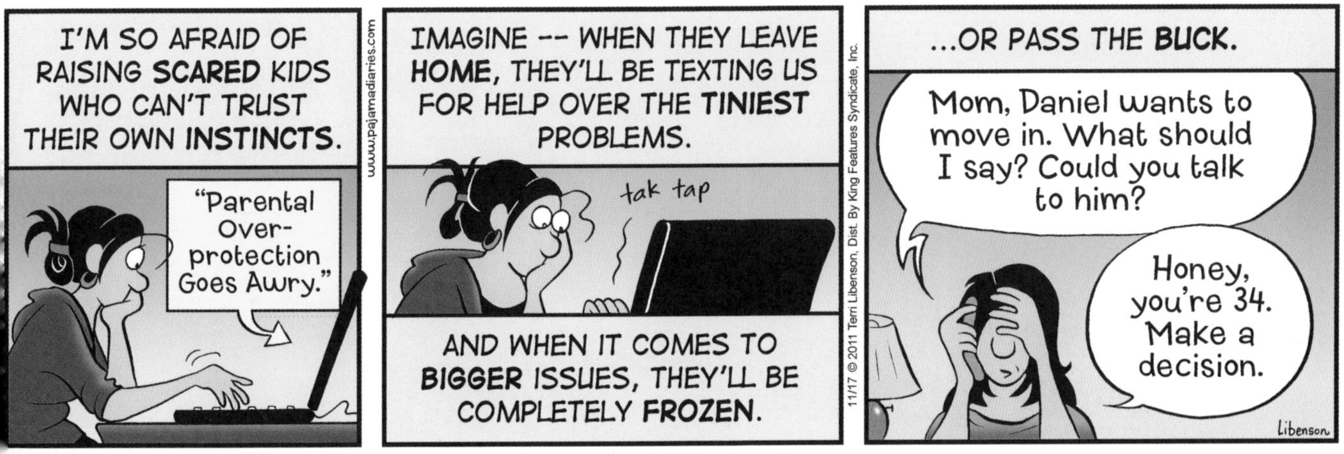
I'M SO AFRAID OF RAISING SCARED KIDS WHO CAN'T TRUST THEIR OWN INSTINCTS.
"Parental Over-protection Goes Awry."
www.pajamadiaries.com
IMAGINE -- WHEN THEY LEAVE HOME, THEY'LL BE TEXTING US FOR HELP OVER THE TINIEST PROBLEMS.
tak tap
AND WHEN IT COMES TO BIGGER ISSUES, THEY'LL BE COMPLETELY FROZEN.
11/17 © 2011 Terri Libenson, Dist. By King Features Syndicate, Inc.
...OR PASS THE BUCK.
Mom, Daniel wants to move in. What should I say? Could you talk to him?
Honey, you're 34. Make a decision.
Libenson

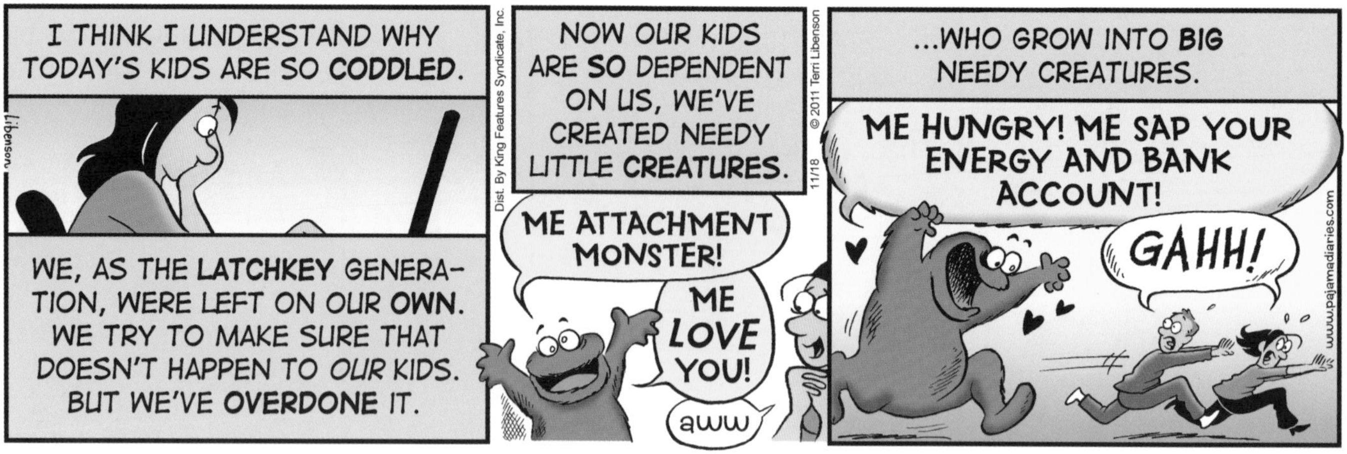
I THINK I UNDERSTAND WHY TODAY'S KIDS ARE SO **CODDLED**.
WE, AS THE **LATCHKEY** GENERATION, WERE LEFT ON OUR **OWN**. WE TRY TO MAKE SURE THAT DOESN'T HAPPEN TO *OUR* KIDS. BUT WE'VE **OVERDONE** IT.
NOW OUR KIDS ARE **SO** DEPENDENT ON US, WE'VE CREATED NEEDY LITTLE **CREATURES**.
ME ATTACHMENT MONSTER!
ME *LOVE* YOU!
aww
...WHO GROW INTO **BIG** NEEDY CREATURES.
ME HUNGRY! ME SAP YOUR ENERGY AND BANK ACCOUNT!
GAHH!
Libenson
Dist. By King Features Syndicate, Inc.
11/18 © 2011 Terri Libenson
www.pajamadiaries.com

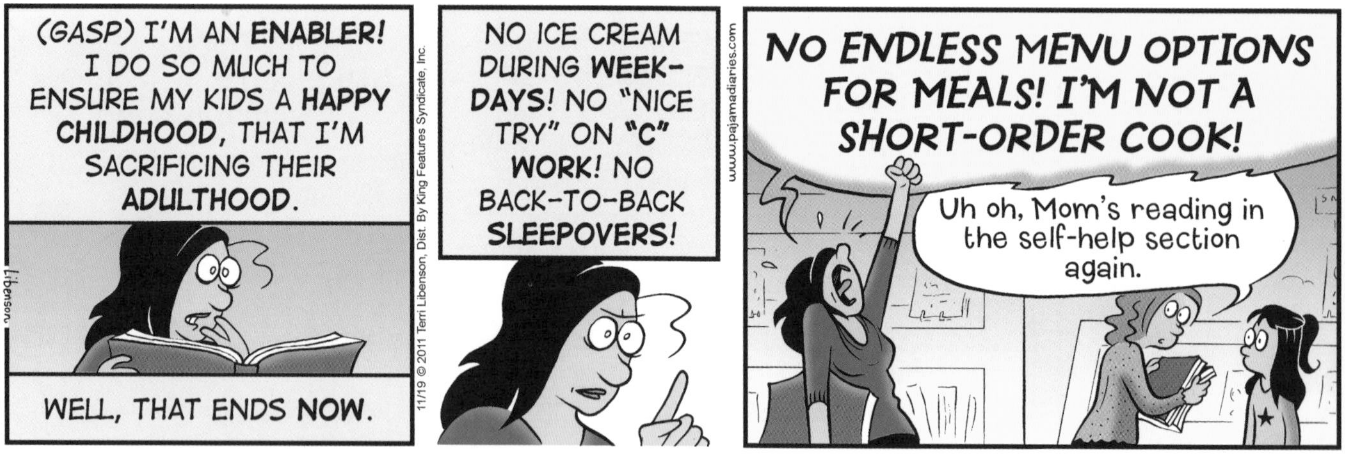
(GASP) I'M AN **ENABLER**! I DO SO MUCH TO ENSURE MY KIDS A **HAPPY CHILDHOOD**, THAT I'M SACRIFICING THEIR **ADULTHOOD**.
WELL, THAT ENDS **NOW**.
NO ICE CREAM DURING **WEEKDAYS**! NO "NICE TRY" ON **"C" WORK**! NO BACK-TO-BACK **SLEEPOVERS**!
NO ENDLESS MENU OPTIONS FOR MEALS! I'M NOT A SHORT-ORDER COOK!
Uh oh, Mom's reading in the self-help section again.
Libenson
11/19 © 2011 Terri Libenson, Dist. By King Features Syndicate, Inc.
www.pajamadiaries.com

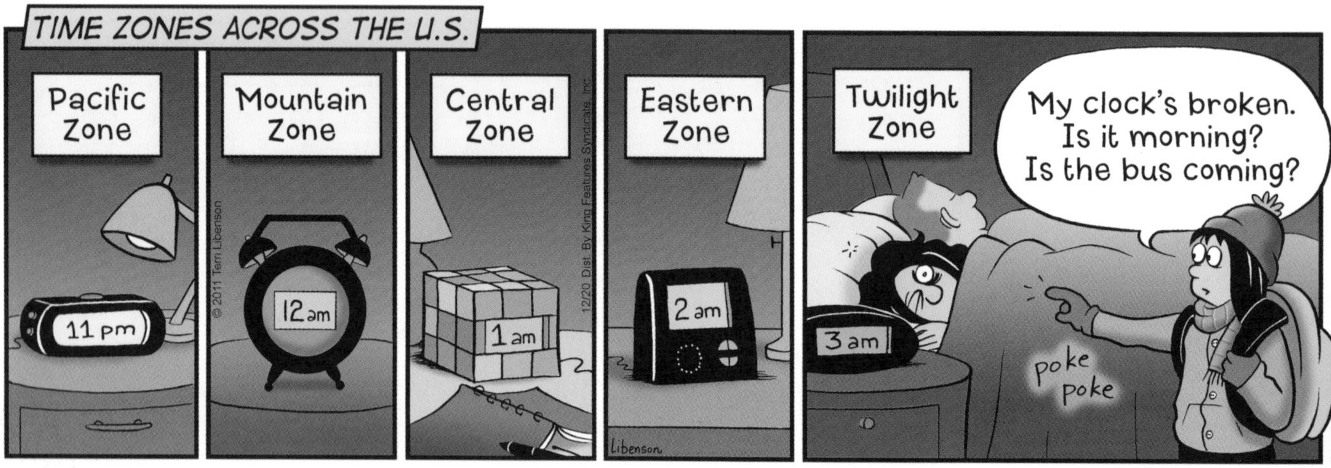
TIME ZONES ACROSS THE U.S.
Pacific Zone
11 pm
Mountain Zone
12 am
Central Zone
1 am
Eastern Zone
2 am
Twilight Zone
3 am
My clock's broken. Is it morning? Is the bus coming?
poke poke
© 2011 Terri Libenson
12/20 Dist. By King Features Syndicate, Inc.
Libenson

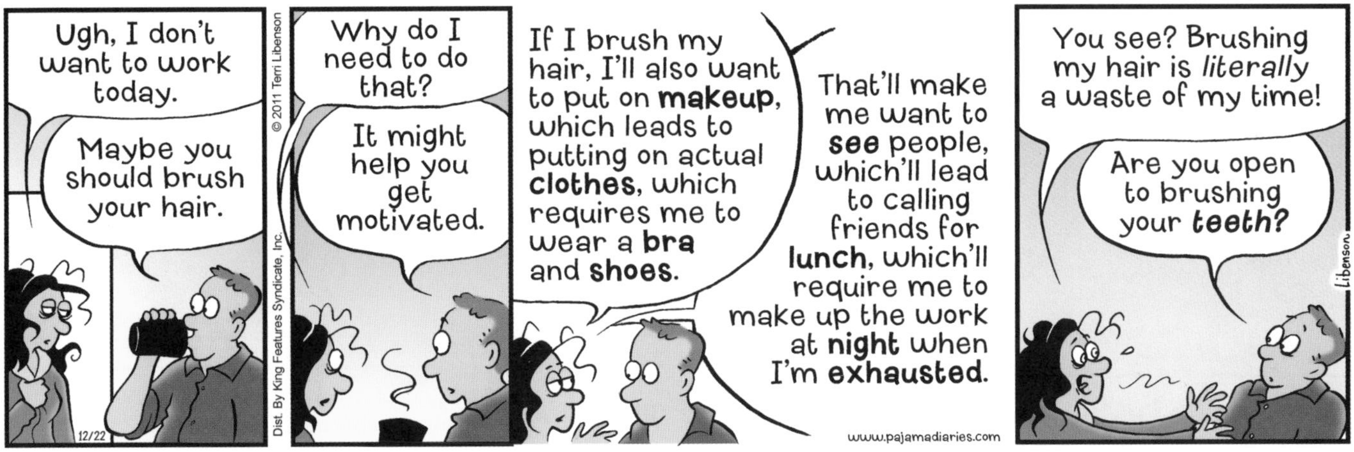
Ugh, I don't want to work today.
Maybe you should brush your hair.
Why do I need to do that?
It might help you get motivated.
If I brush my hair, I'll also want to put on **makeup**, which leads to putting on actual **clothes**, which requires me to wear a **bra** and **shoes**.
That'll make me want to **see** people, which'll lead to calling friends for **lunch**, which'll require me to make up the work at **night** when I'm **exhausted**.
You see? Brushing my hair is *literally* a waste of my time!
Are you open to brushing your ***teeth?***
12/22
© 2011 Terri Libenson
Dist. By King Features Syndicate, Inc.
www.pajamadiaries.com
Libenson

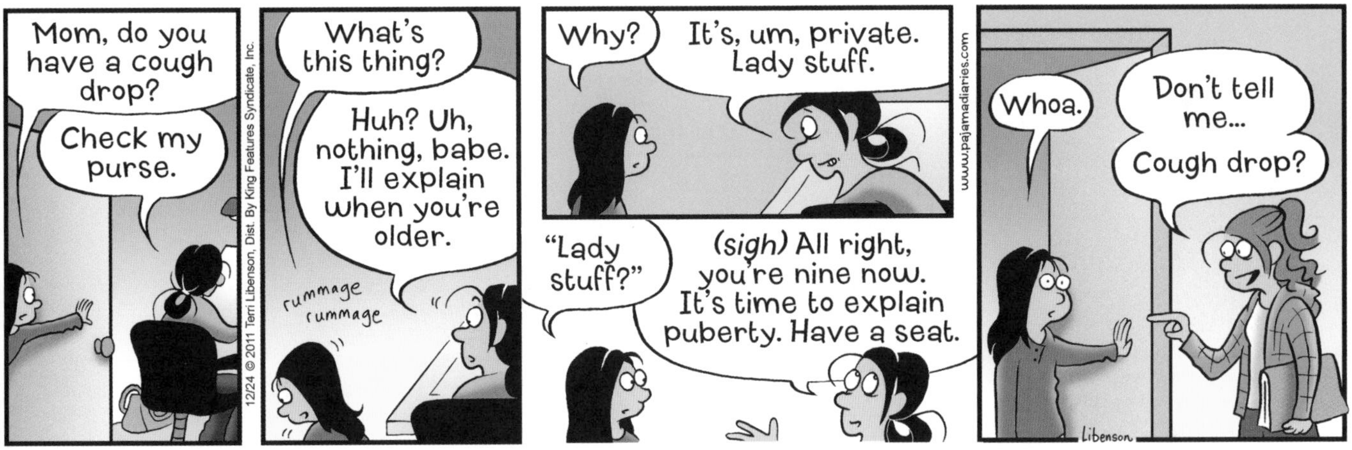
Mom, do you have a cough drop?
Check my purse.
What's this thing?
Huh? Uh, nothing, babe. I'll explain when you're older.
rummage rummage
Why?
It's, um, private. Lady stuff.
"Lady stuff?"
(sigh) All right, you're nine now. It's time to explain puberty. Have a seat.
Whoa.
Don't tell me...
Cough drop?
12/24 © 2011 Terri Libenson, Dist. By King Features Syndicate, Inc.
www.pajamadiaries.com
Libenson

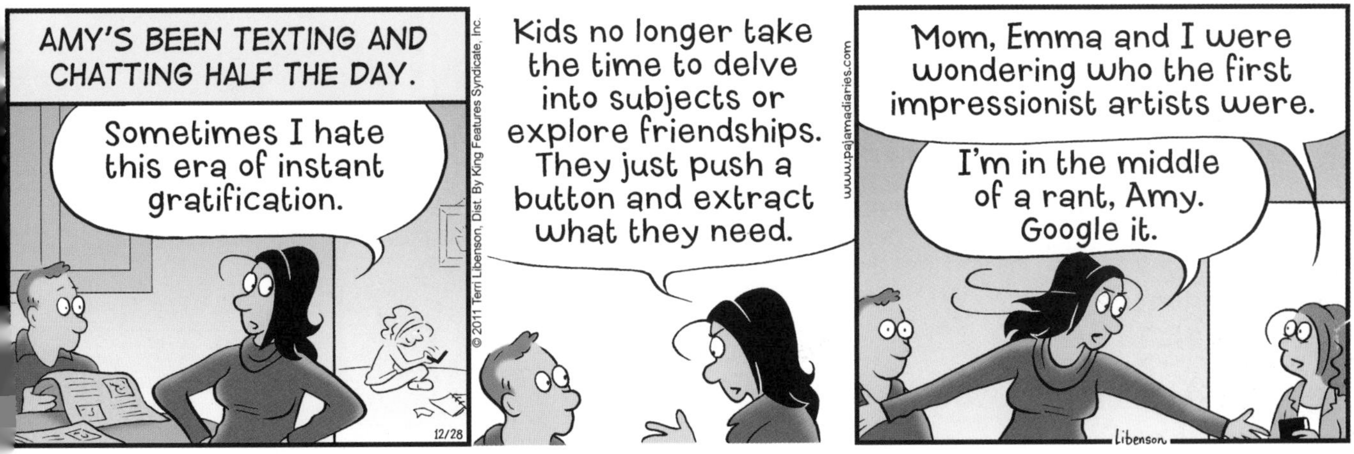
AMY'S BEEN TEXTING AND CHATTING HALF THE DAY.
Sometimes I hate this era of instant gratification.
Kids no longer take the time to delve into subjects or explore friendships. They just push a button and extract what they need.
Mom, Emma and I were wondering who the first impressionist artists were.
I'm in the middle of a rant, Amy. Google it.
12/28
© 2011 Terri Libenson, Dist. By King Features Syndicate, Inc.
www.pajamadiaries.com
Libenson

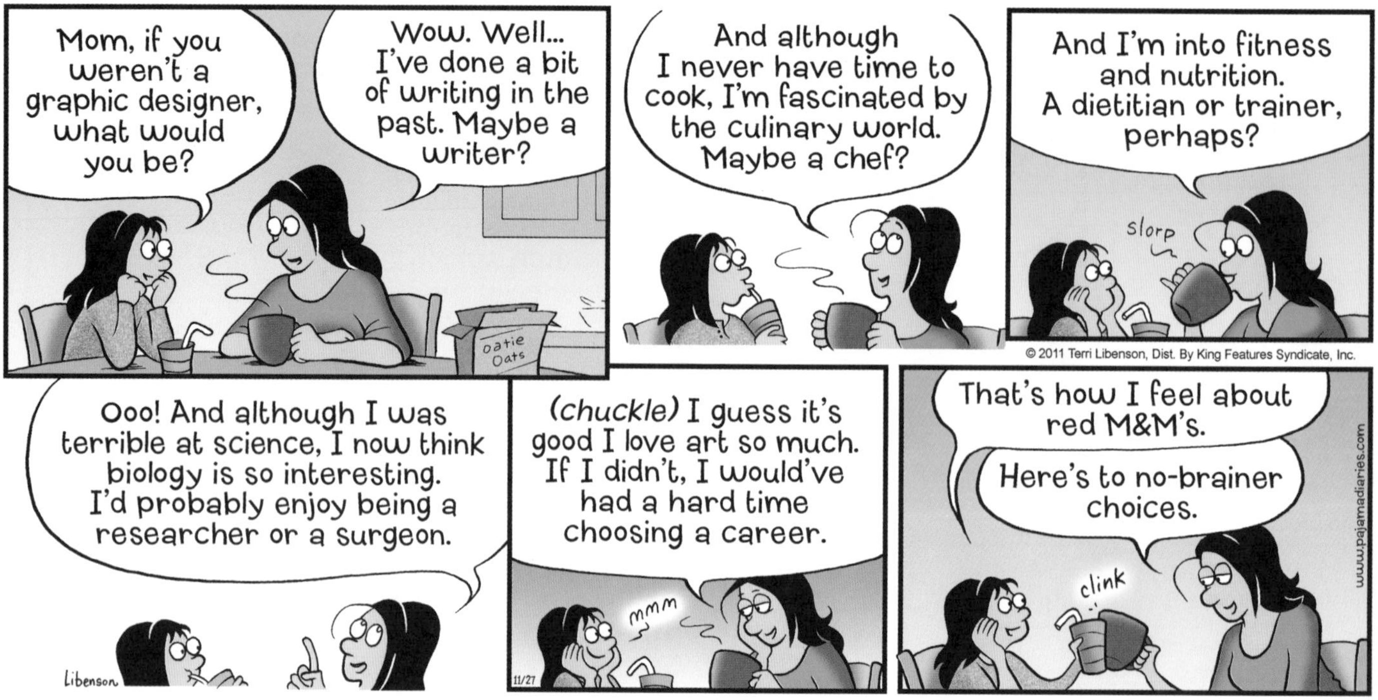
Mom, if you weren't a graphic designer, what would you be?
Wow. Well... I've done a bit of writing in the past. Maybe a writer?
And although I never have time to cook, I'm fascinated by the culinary world. Maybe a chef?
And I'm into fitness and nutrition. A dietitian or trainer, perhaps?
slorp
oatie Oats
© 2011 Terri Libenson, Dist. By King Features Syndicate, Inc.
Ooo! And although I was terrible at science, I now think biology is so interesting. I'd probably enjoy being a researcher or a surgeon.
Libenson
(chuckle) I guess it's good I love art so much. If I didn't, I would've had a hard time choosing a career.
mmm
11/27
That's how I feel about red M&M's.
Here's to no-brainer choices.
clink
www.pajamadiaries.com

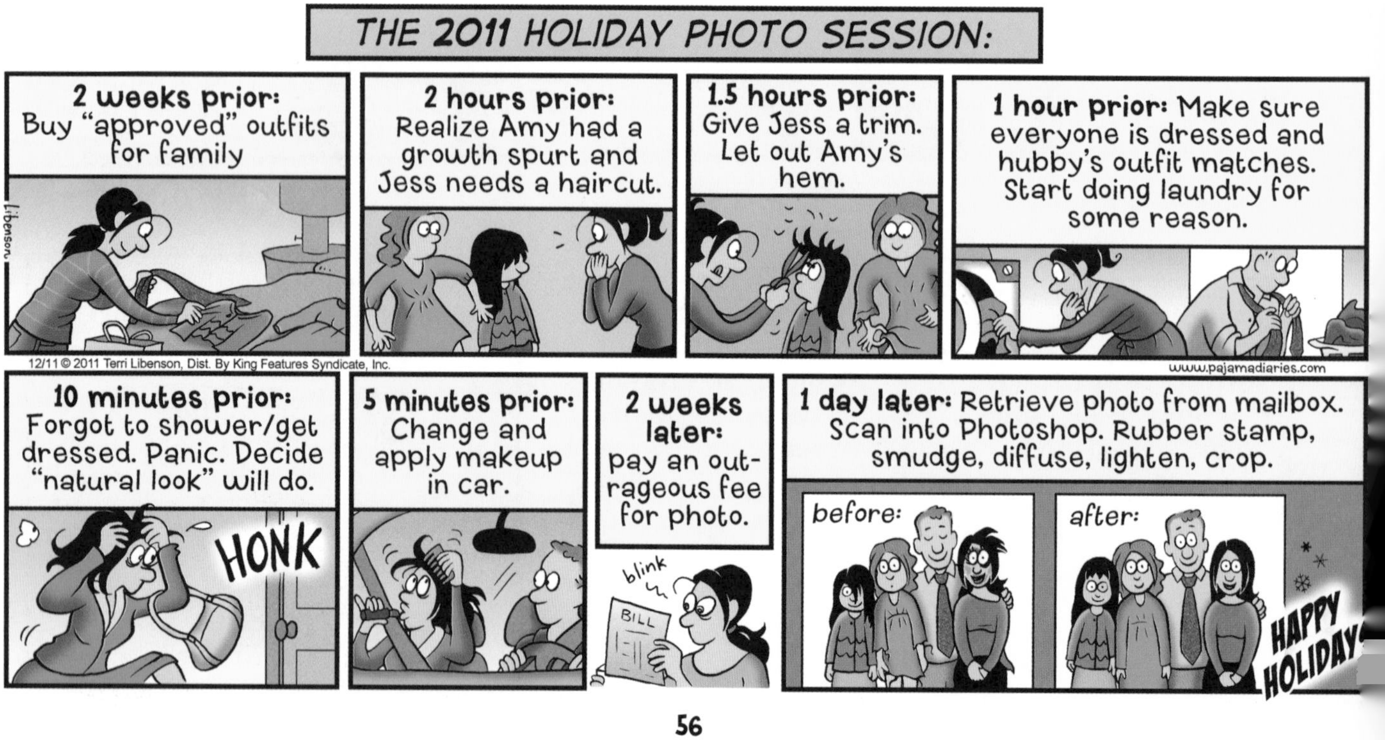
THE 2011 HOLIDAY PHOTO SESSION:
2 weeks prior: Buy "approved" outfits for family
Libenson
2 hours prior: Realize Amy had a growth spurt and Jess needs a haircut.
1.5 hours prior: Give Jess a trim. Let out Amy's hem.
1 hour prior: Make sure everyone is dressed and hubby's outfit matches. Start doing laundry for some reason.
12/11 © 2011 Terri Libenson, Dist. By King Features Syndicate, Inc.
www.pajamadiaries.com
10 minutes prior: Forgot to shower/get dressed. Panic. Decide "natural look" will do.
HONK
5 minutes prior: Change and apply makeup in car.
2 weeks later: pay an outrageous fee for photo.
blink
BILL
1 day later: Retrieve photo from mailbox. Scan into Photoshop. Rubber stamp, smudge, diffuse, lighten, crop.
before:
after:
HAPPY HOLIDAYS

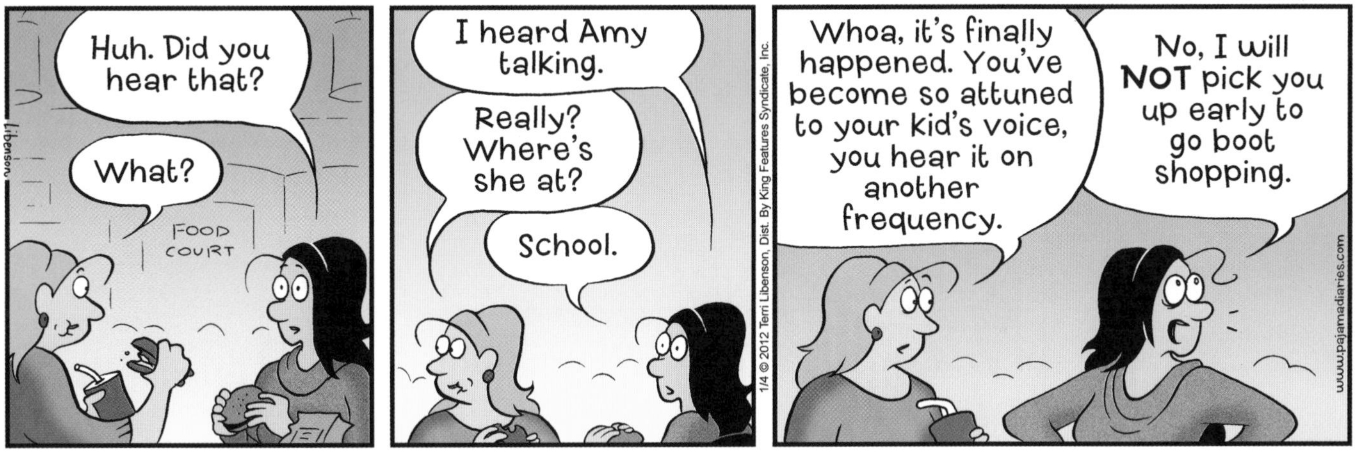
Huh. Did you hear that?
What?
FOOD COURT
Libenson
I heard Amy talking.
Really? Where's she at?
School.
1/4 © 2012 Terri Libenson, Dist. By King Features Syndicate, Inc.
Whoa, it's finally happened. You've become so attuned to your kid's voice, you hear it on another frequency.
No, I will **NOT** pick you up early to go boot shopping.
www.pajamadiaries.com

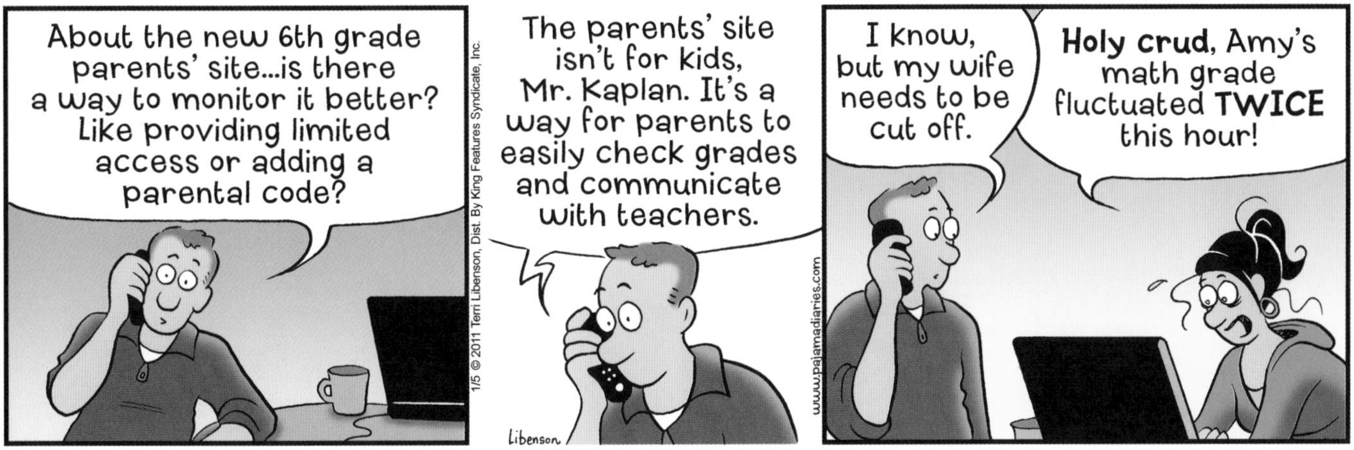
About the new 6th grade parents' site...is there a way to monitor it better? Like providing limited access or adding a parental code?
1/5 © 2011 Terri Libenson, Dist. By King Features Syndicate, Inc.
The parents' site isn't for kids, Mr. Kaplan. It's a way for parents to easily check grades and communicate with teachers.
Libenson
www.pajamadiaries.com
I know, but my wife needs to be cut off.
Holy crud, Amy's math grade fluctuated **TWICE** this hour!

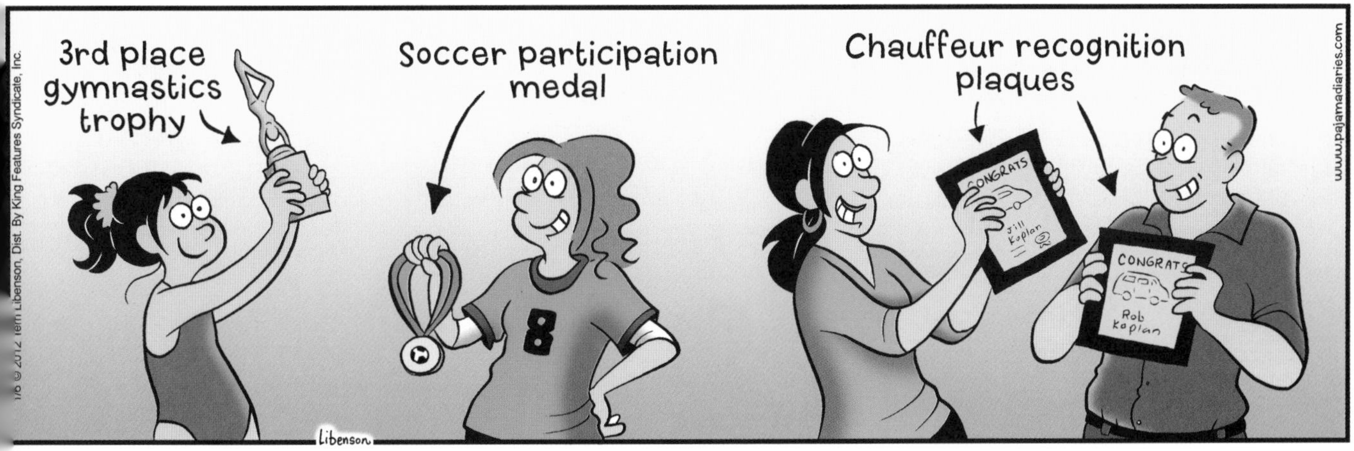
1/6 © 2012 Terri Libenson, Dist. By King Features Syndicate, Inc.
3rd place gymnastics trophy
Soccer participation medal
Chauffeur recognition plaques
CONGRATS
Jill Kaplan
CONGRATS
Rob Kaplan
Libenson
www.pajamadiaries.com

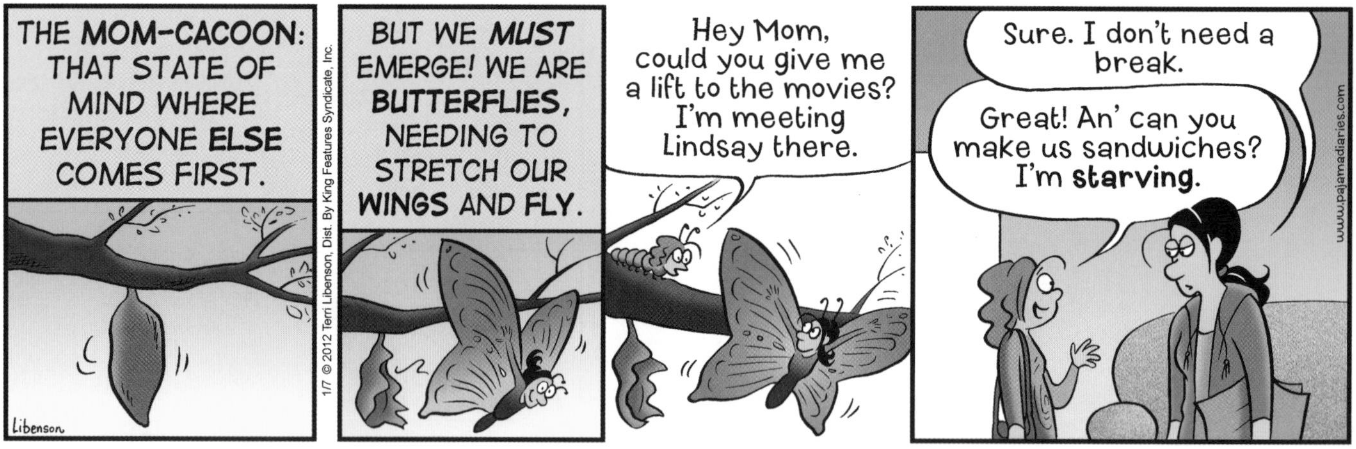
THE MOM-CACOON: THAT STATE OF MIND WHERE EVERYONE ELSE COMES FIRST.
Libenson
1/7 © 2012 Terri Libenson, Dist. By King Features Syndicate, Inc.
BUT WE MUST EMERGE! WE ARE BUTTERFLIES, NEEDING TO STRETCH OUR WINGS AND FLY.
Hey Mom, could you give me a lift to the movies? I'm meeting Lindsay there.
Sure. I don't need a break.
Great! An' can you make us sandwiches? I'm starving.
www.pajamadiaries.com

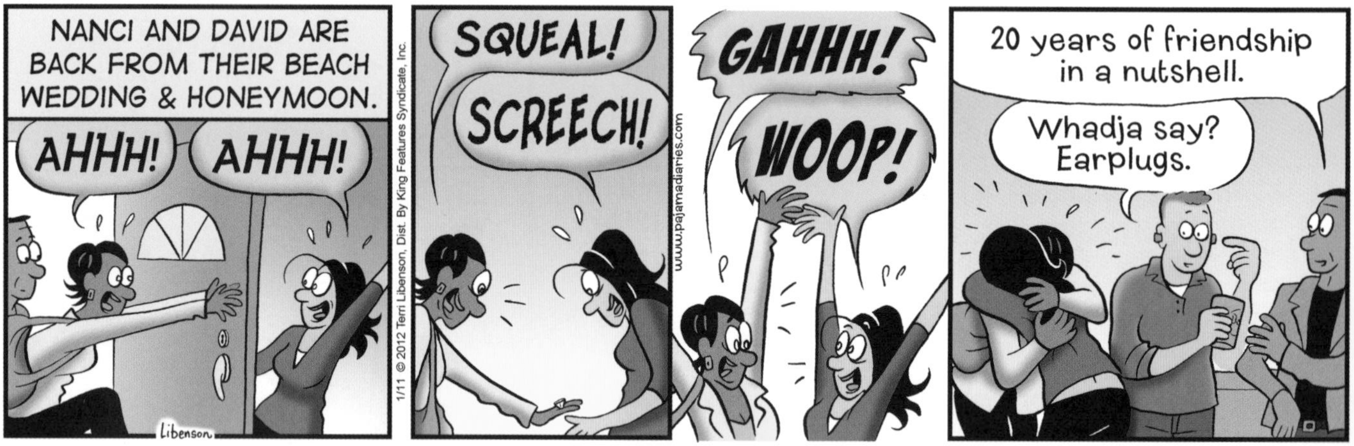
NANCI AND DAVID ARE BACK FROM THEIR BEACH WEDDING & HONEYMOON.
AHHH!
AHHH!
Libenson
1/11 © 2012 Terri Libenson, Dist. By King Features Syndicate, Inc.
SQUEAL!
SCREECH!
www.pajamadiaries.com
GAHHH!
WOOP!
20 years of friendship in a nutshell.
Whadja say? Earplugs.

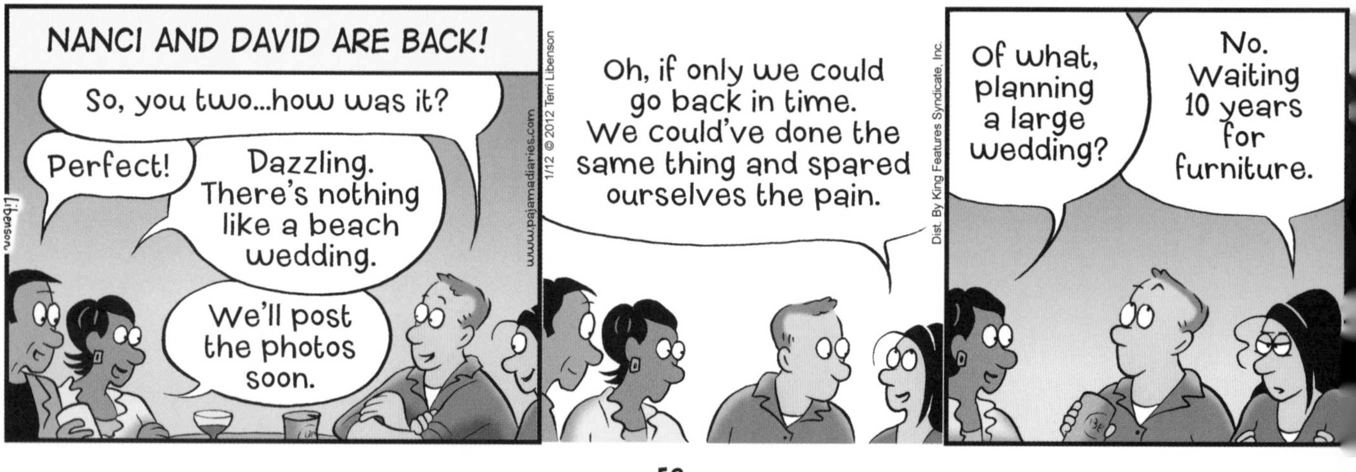
NANCI AND DAVID ARE BACK!
So, you two...how was it?
Perfect!
Dazzling. There's nothing like a beach wedding.
We'll post the photos soon.
Libenson
www.pajamadiaries.com
1/12 © 2012 Terri Libenson
Oh, if only we could go back in time. We could've done the same thing and spared ourselves the pain.
Dist. By King Features Syndicate, Inc.
Of what, planning a large wedding?
No. Waiting 10 years for furniture.

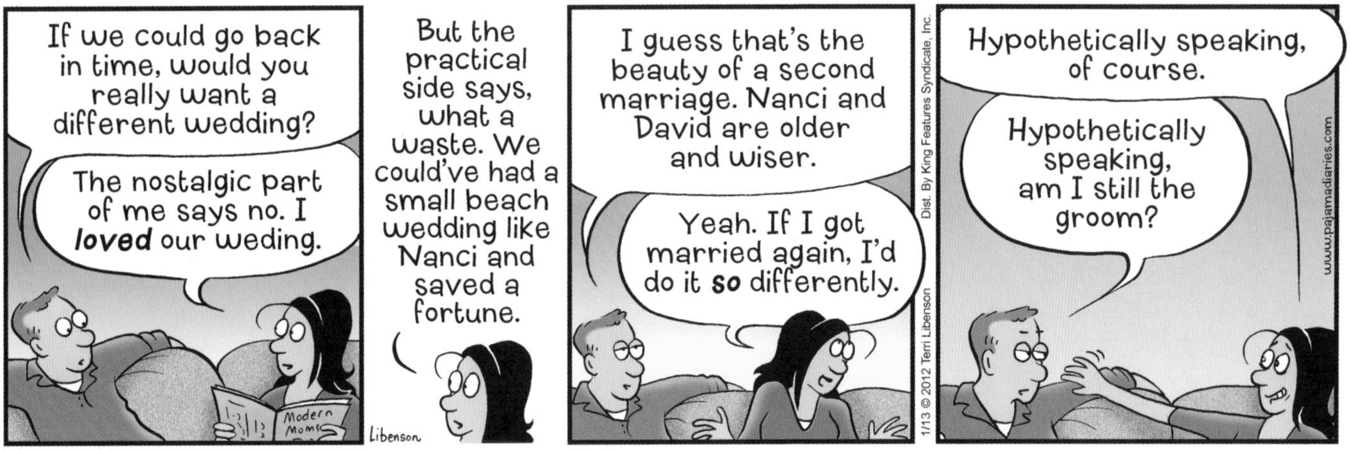
If we could go back in time, would you really want a different wedding?
The nostalgic part of me says no. I ***loved*** our weding.
Modern Moms
But the practical side says, what a waste. We could've had a small beach wedding like Nanci and saved a fortune.
Libenson
I guess that's the beauty of a second marriage. Nanci and David are older and wiser.
Yeah. If I got married again, I'd do it **so** differently.
1/13 © 2012 Terri Libenson Dist. By King Features Syndicate, Inc.
Hypothetically speaking, of course.
Hypothetically speaking, am I still the groom?
www.pajamadiaries.com

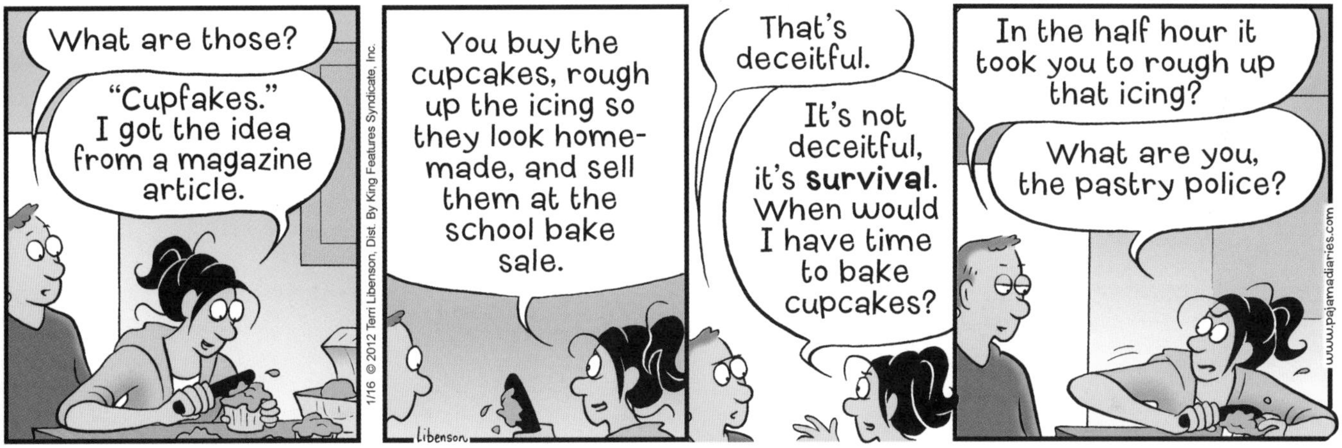
What are those?
"Cupfakes." I got the idea from a magazine article.
1/16 © 2012 Terri Libenson, Dist. By King Features Syndicate, Inc.
You buy the cupcakes, rough up the icing so they look home-made, and sell them at the school bake sale.
Libenson
That's deceitful.
It's not deceitful, it's **survival**. When would I have time to bake cupcakes?
In the half hour it took you to rough up that icing?
What are you, the pastry police?
www.pajamadiaries.com

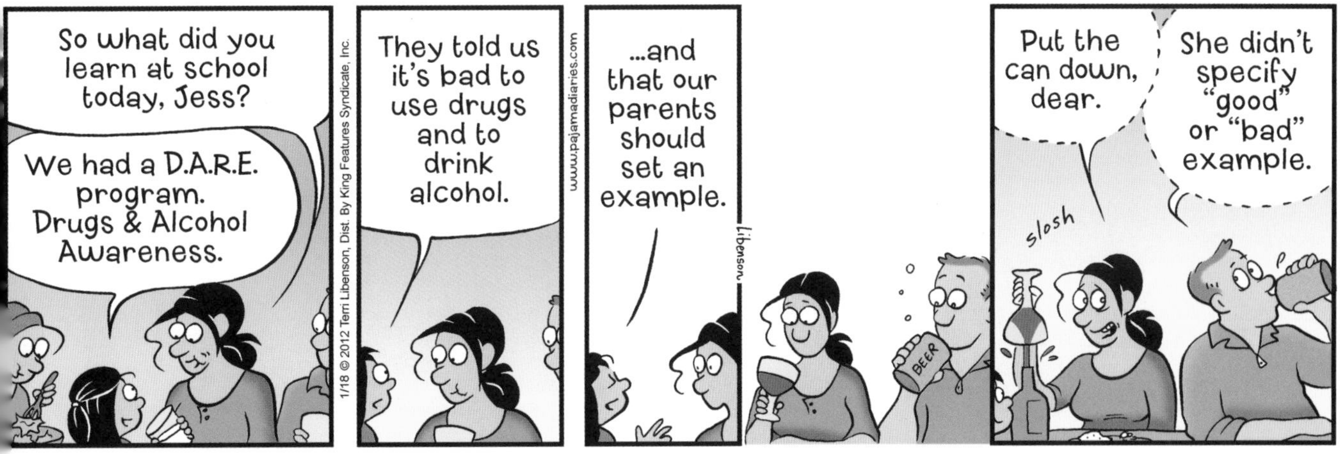
So what did you learn at school today, Jess?
We had a D.A.R.E. program. Drugs & Alcohol Awareness.
1/18 © 2012 Terri Libenson, Dist. By King Features Syndicate, Inc.
They told us it's bad to use drugs and to drink alcohol.
www.pajamadiaries.com
...and that our parents should set an example.
Libenson
BEER
Put the can down, dear.
She didn't specify "good" or "bad" example.
slosh

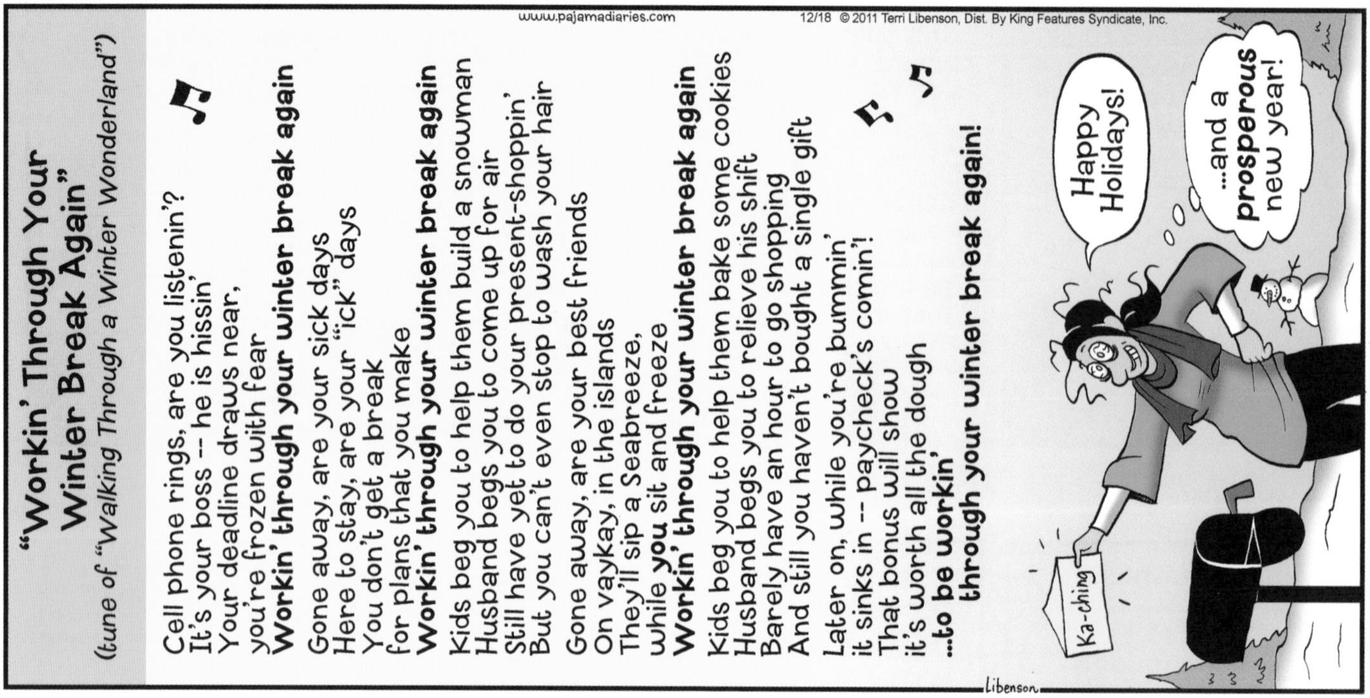

www.pajamadiaries.com
12/18 © 2011 Terri Libenson, Dist. By King Features Syndicate, Inc.
"Workin' Through Your Winter Break Again"
(tune of "Walking Through a Winter Wonderland")
Cell phone rings, are you listenin'?
It's your boss -- he is hissin'
Your deadline draws near,
you're frozen with fear
Workin' through your winter break again
Gone away, are your sick days
Here to stay, are your "ick" days
You don't get a break
for plans that you make
Workin' through your winter break again
Kids beg you to help them build a snowman
Husband begs you to come up for air
Still have yet to do your present-shoppin'
But you can't even stop to wash your hair
Gone away, are your best friends
On vaykay, in the islands
They'll sip a Seabreeze,
while you sit and freeze
Workin' through your winter break again
Kids beg you to help them bake some cookies
Husband begs you to relieve his shift
Barely have an hour to go shopping
And still you haven't bought a single gift
Later on, while you're bummin'
it sinks in -- paycheck's comin'!
That bonus will show
it's worth all the dough
...to be workin'
through your winter break again!
Happy Holidays!
...and a prosperous new year!
Ka-ching
Libenson

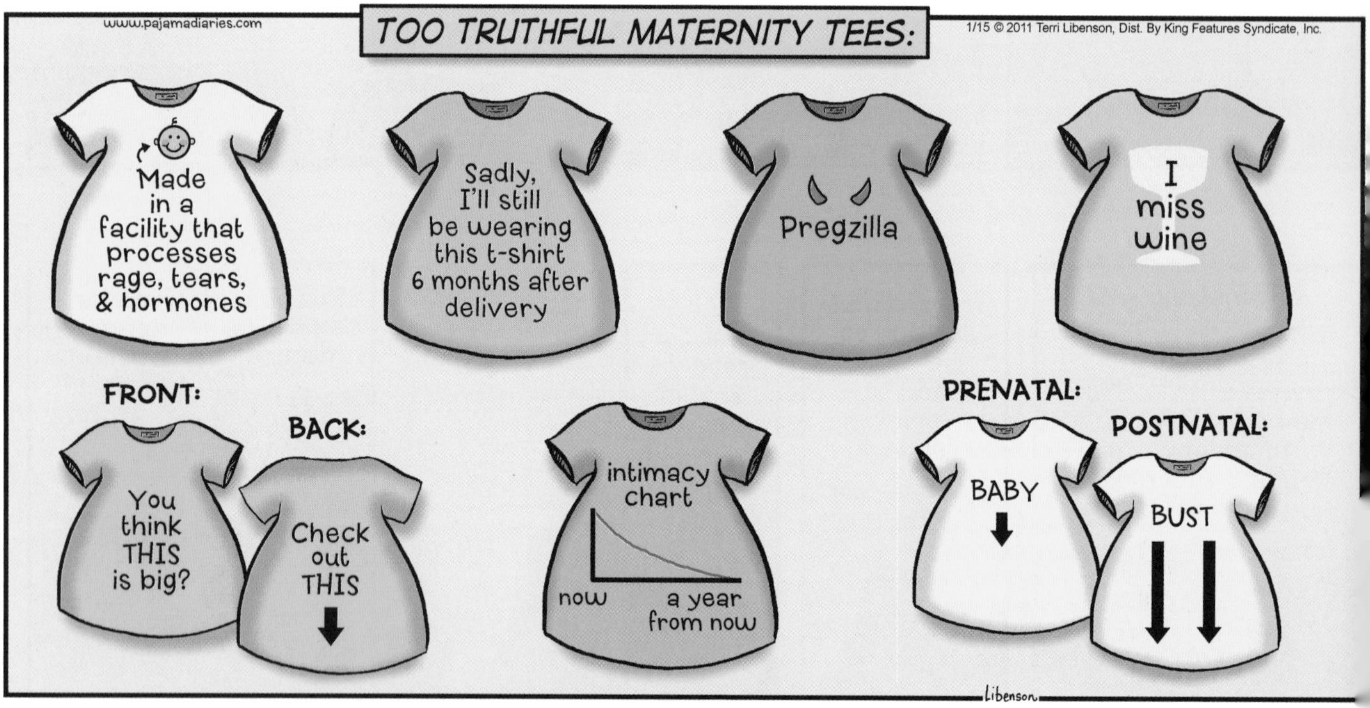

www.pajamadiaries.com
TOO TRUTHFUL MATERNITY TEES:
1/15 © 2011 Terri Libenson, Dist. By King Features Syndicate, Inc.
Made in a facility that processes rage, tears, & hormones
Sadly, I'll still be wearing this t-shirt 6 months after delivery
Pregzilla
I miss wine
FRONT:
You think THIS is big?
BACK:
Check out THIS
intimacy chart
now
a year from now
PRENATAL:
BABY
POSTNATAL:
BUST
Libenson

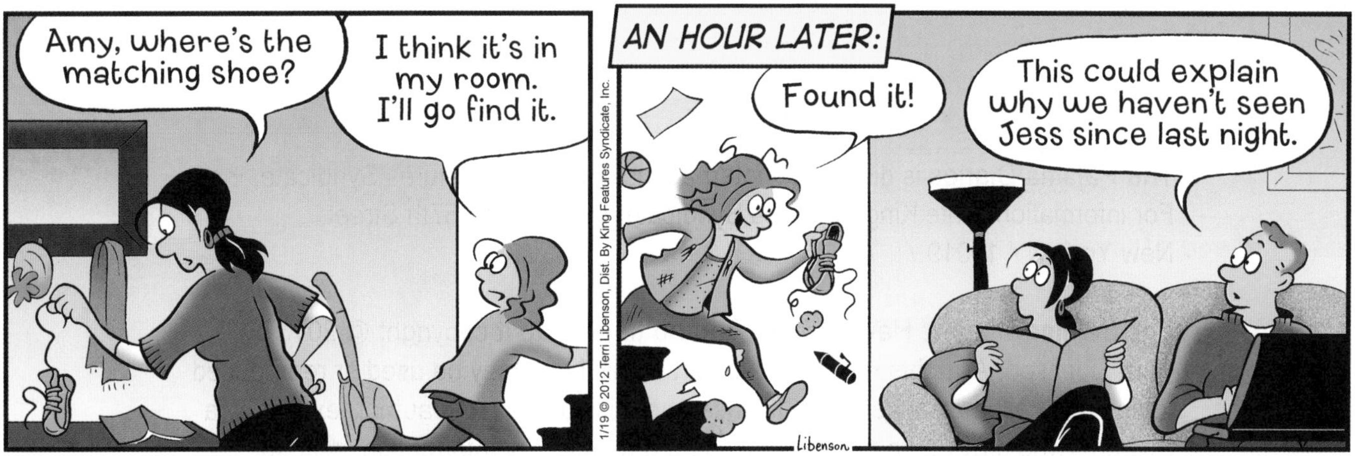
Amy, where's the matching shoe?
I think it's in my room. I'll go find it.
1/19 © 2012 Terri Libenson, Dist. By King Features Syndicate, Inc.
AN HOUR LATER:
Found it!
This could explain why we haven't seen Jess since last night.
Libenson

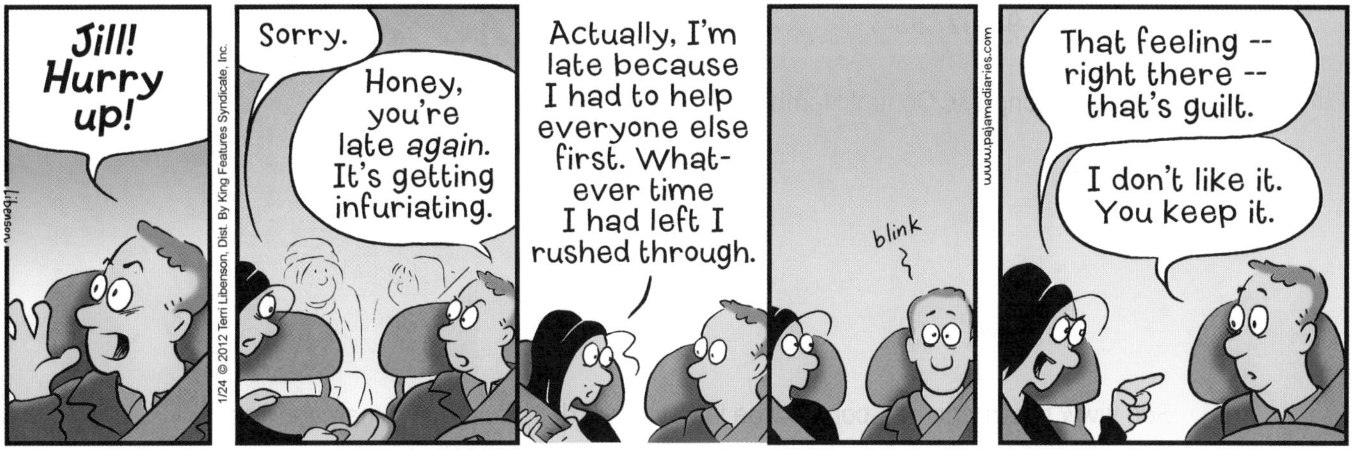
Jill! Hurry up!
Libenson
1/24 © 2012 Terri Libenson, Dist. By King Features Syndicate, Inc.
Sorry.
Honey, you're late *again*. It's getting infuriating.
Actually, I'm late because I had to help everyone else first. Whatever time I had left I rushed through.
blink
www.pajamadiaries.com
That feeling -- right there -- that's guilt.
I don't like it. You keep it.

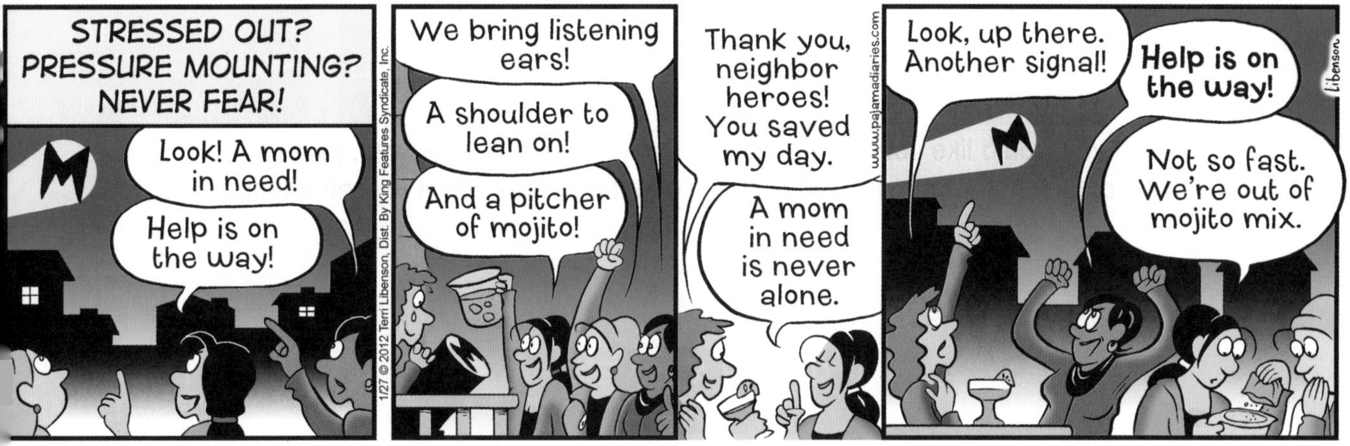
STRESSED OUT? PRESSURE MOUNTING? NEVER FEAR!
Look! A mom in need!
Help is on the way!
1/27 © 2012 Terri Libenson, Dist. By King Features Syndicate, Inc.
We bring listening ears!
A shoulder to lean on!
And a pitcher of mojito!
Thank you, neighbor heroes! You saved my day.
A mom in need is never alone.
www.pajamadiaries.com
Look, up there. Another signal!
Help is on the way!
Not so fast. We're out of mojito mix.
Libenson

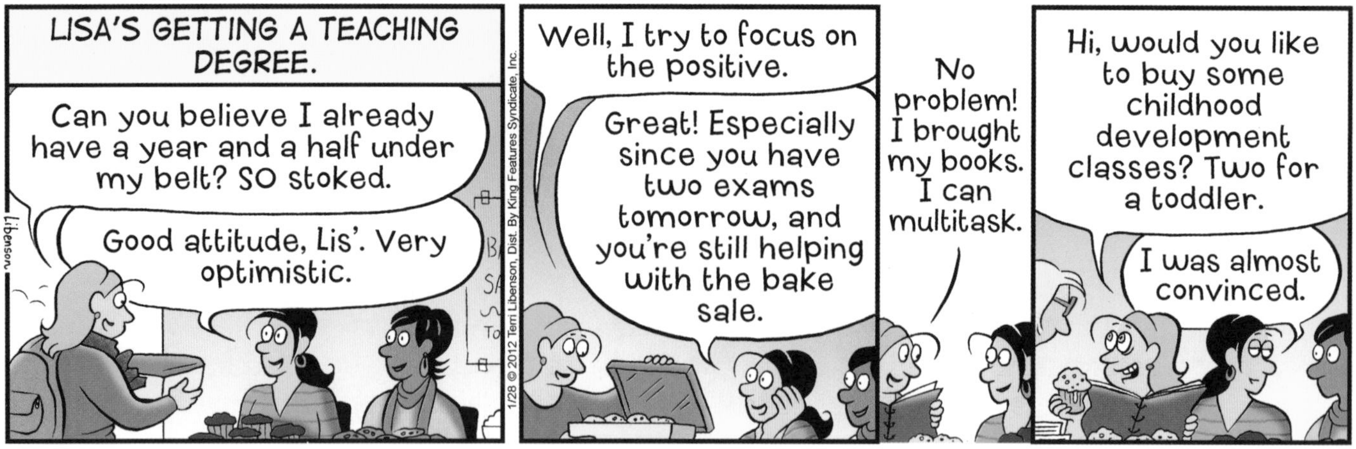
LISA'S GETTING A TEACHING DEGREE.
Can you believe I already have a year and a half under my belt? SO stoked.
Good attitude, Lis'. Very optimistic.
Well, I try to focus on the positive.
Great! Especially since you have two exams tomorrow, and you're still helping with the bake sale.
No problem! I brought my books. I can multitask.
Hi, would you like to buy some childhood development classes? Two for a toddler.
I was almost convinced.
Libenson
1/28 © 2012 Terri Libenson, Dist. By King Features Syndicate, Inc.

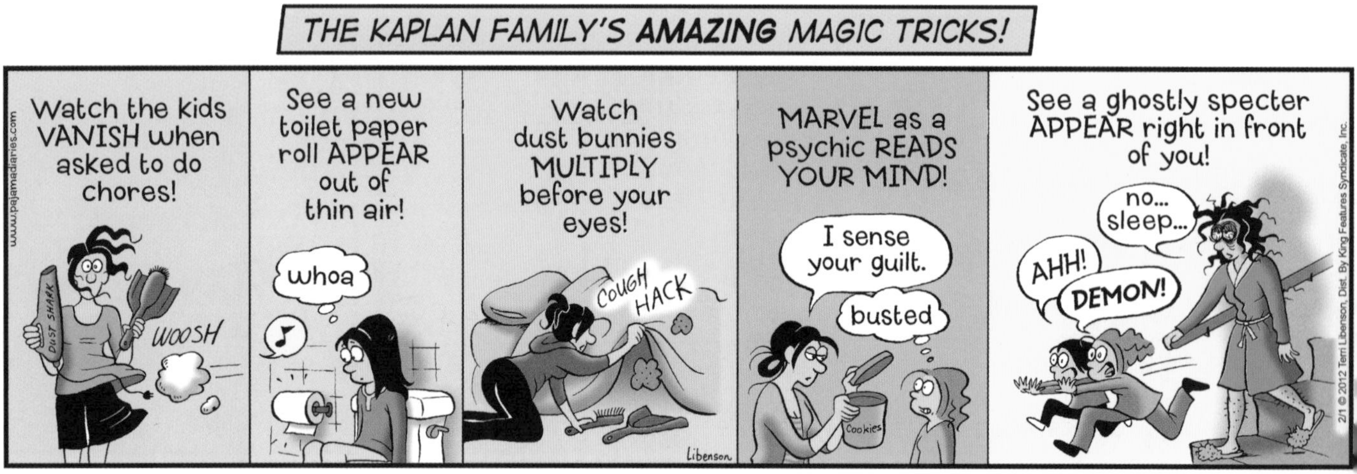
THE KAPLAN FAMILY'S AMAZING MAGIC TRICKS!
Watch the kids VANISH when asked to do chores!
DUST SHARK
WOOSH
See a new toilet paper roll APPEAR out of thin air!
whoa
Watch dust bunnies MULTIPLY before your eyes!
COUGH HACK
MARVEL as a psychic READS YOUR MIND!
I sense your guilt.
busted
Cookies
See a ghostly specter APPEAR right in front of you!
no... sleep...
AHH!
DEMON!
Libenson
www.pajamadiaries.com
2/1 © 2012 Terri Libenson, Dist. By King Features Syndicate, Inc.

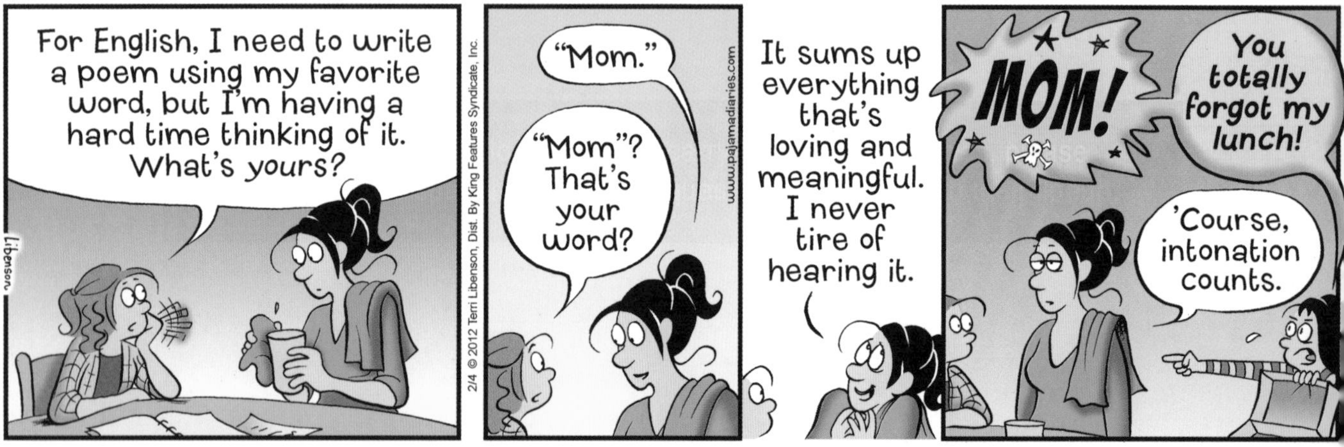
For English, I need to write a poem using my favorite word, but I'm having a hard time thinking of it. What's yours?
"Mom."
"Mom"? That's your word?
It sums up everything that's loving and meaningful. I never tire of hearing it.
MOM!
You totally forgot my lunch!
'Course, intonation counts.
Libenson
www.pajamadiaries.com
2/4 © 2012 Terri Libenson, Dist. By King Features Syndicate, Inc.

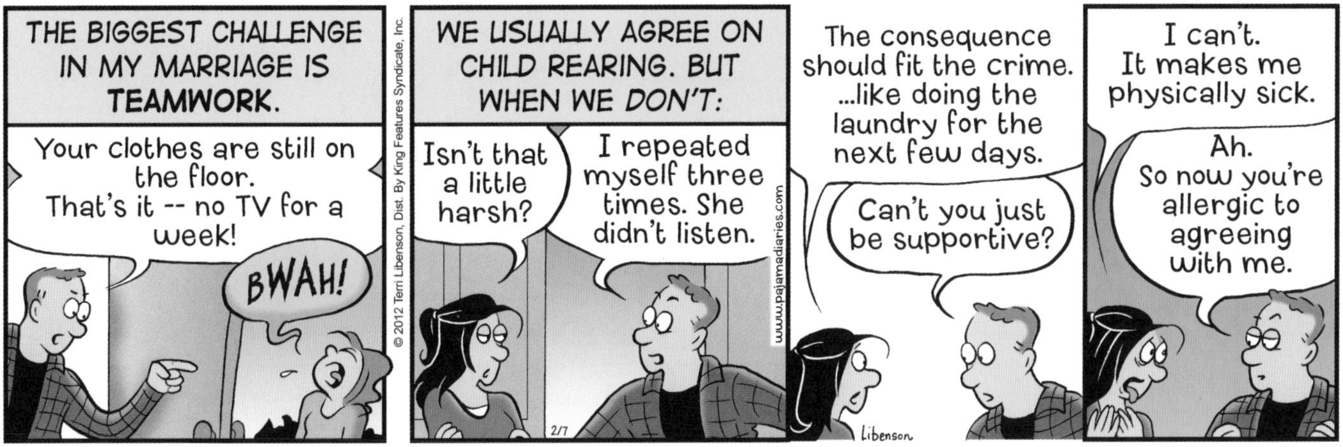
THE BIGGEST CHALLENGE IN MY MARRIAGE IS **TEAMWORK**.
Your clothes are still on the floor. That's it -- no TV for a week!
BWAH!
© 2012 Terri Libenson, Dist. By King Features Syndicate, Inc.
WE USUALLY AGREE ON CHILD REARING. BUT WHEN WE *DON'T*:
Isn't that a little harsh?
I repeated myself three times. She didn't listen.
2/7
www.pajamadiaries.com
The consequence should fit the crime. ...like doing the laundry for the next few days.
Can't you just be supportive?
Libenson
I can't. It makes me physically sick.
Ah. So now you're allergic to agreeing with me.

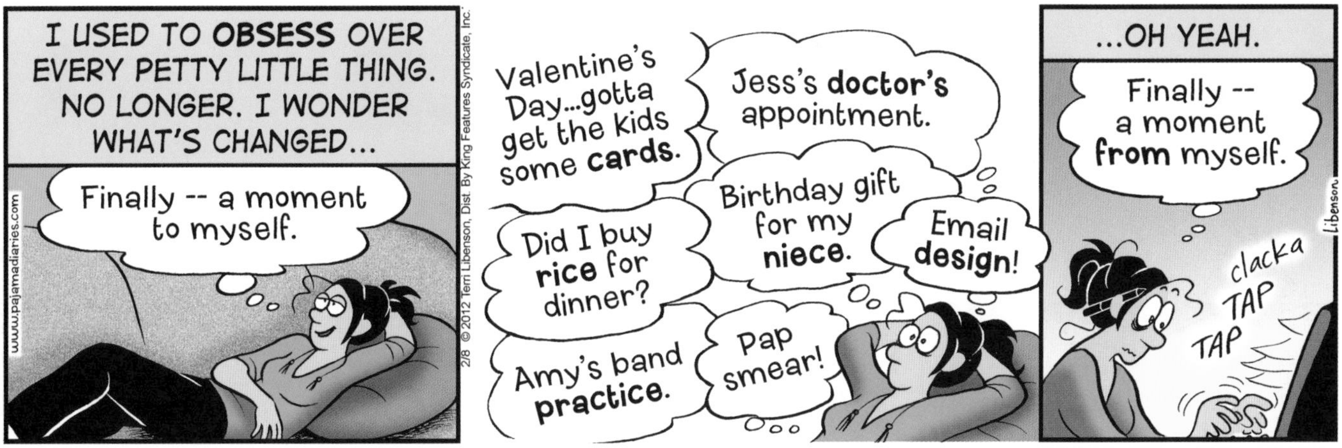
I USED TO **OBSESS** OVER EVERY PETTY LITTLE THING. NO LONGER. I WONDER WHAT'S CHANGED...
Finally -- a moment to myself.
www.pajamadiaries.com
2/8 © 2012 Terri Libenson, Dist. By King Features Syndicate, Inc.
Valentine's Day...gotta get the kids some **cards**.
Jess's **doctor's** appointment.
Birthday gift for my **niece**.
Email **design**!
Did I buy **rice** for dinner?
Amy's band **practice**.
Pap smear!
...OH YEAH.
Finally -- a moment **from** myself.
clacka
TAP
TAP
Libenson

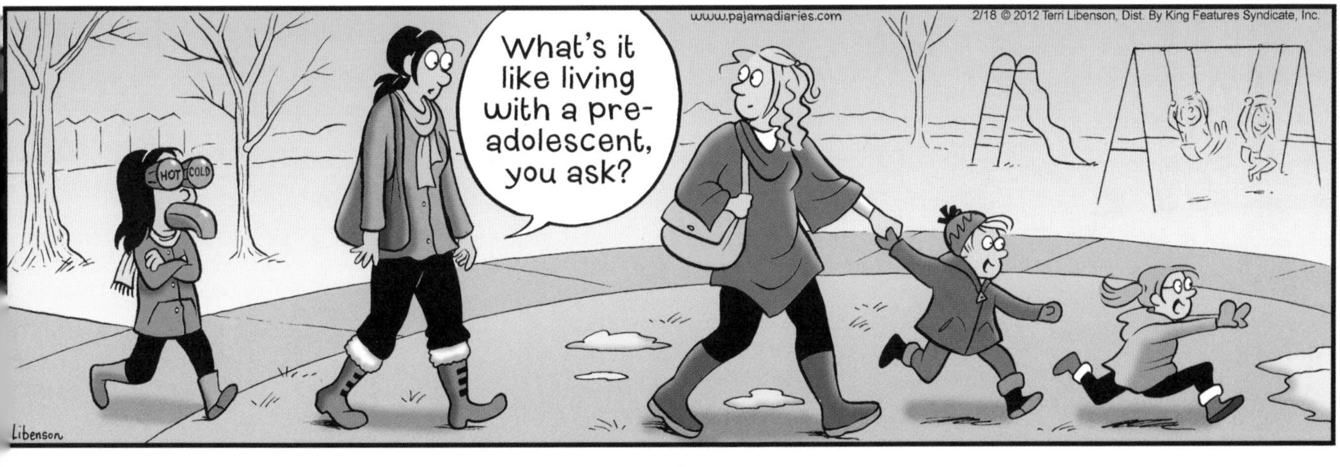
www.pajamadiaries.com
2/18 © 2012 Terri Libenson, Dist. By King Features Syndicate, Inc.
What's it like living with a pre-adolescent, you ask?
HOT
COLD
Libenson

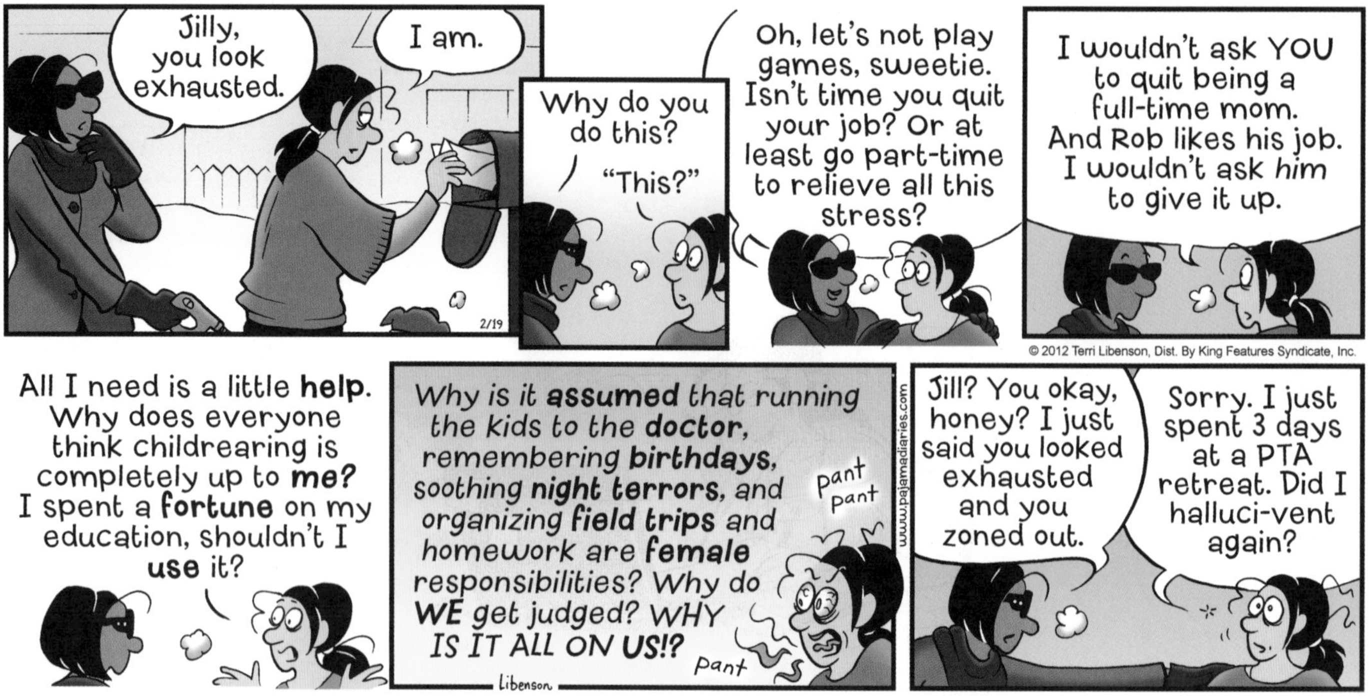

Jilly, you look exhausted.
I am.
2/19
Why do you do this?
"This?"
Oh, let's not play games, sweetie. Isn't time you quit your job? Or at least go part-time to relieve all this stress?
I wouldn't ask YOU to quit being a full-time mom. And Rob likes his job. I wouldn't ask *him* to give it up.
© 2012 Terri Libenson, Dist. By King Features Syndicate, Inc.
All I need is a little **help**. Why does everyone think childrearing is completely up to **me?** I spent a **fortune** on my education, shouldn't I **use** it?
*Why is it **assumed** that running the kids to the **doctor**, remembering **birthdays**, soothing **night terrors**, and organizing **field trips** and homework are **female** responsibilities? Why do **WE** get judged? WHY IS IT ALL ON **US**!?*
pant pant
pant
www.pajamadiaries.com
Libenson
Jill? You okay, honey? I just said you looked exhausted and you zoned out.
Sorry. I just spent 3 days at a PTA retreat. Did I halluci-vent again?

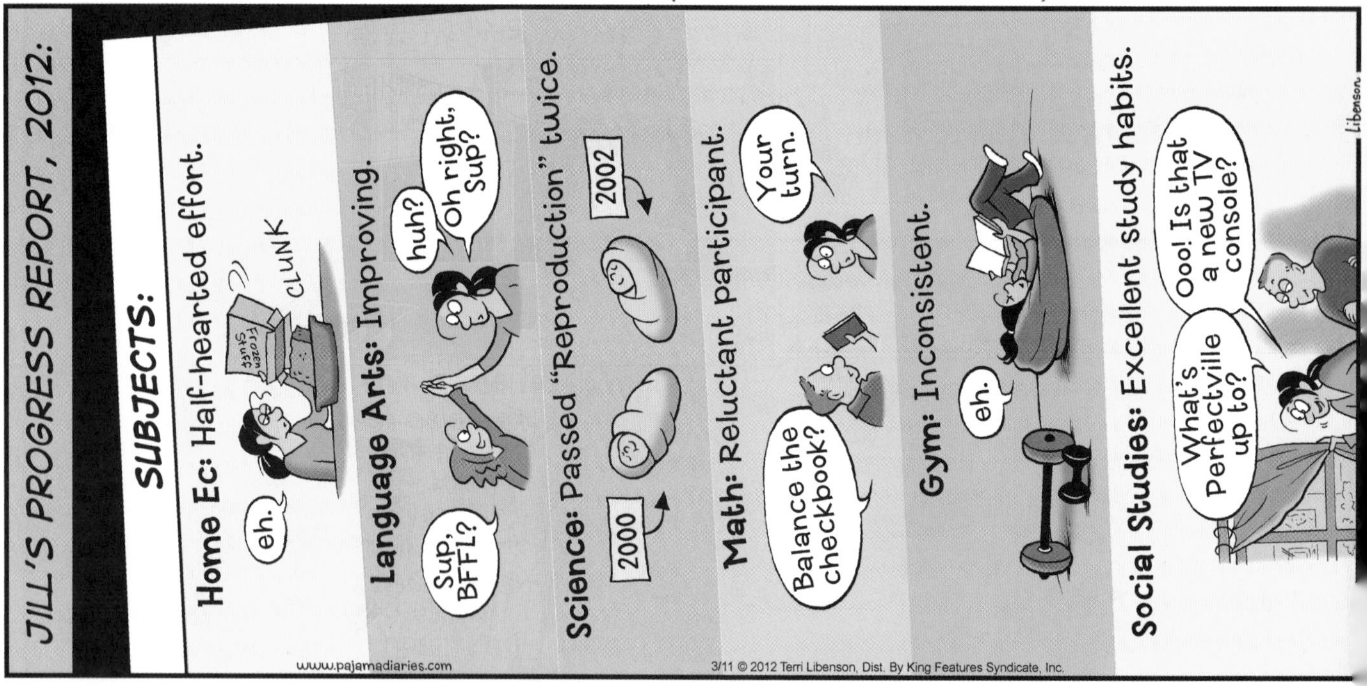

JILL'S PROGRESS REPORT, 2012:
SUBJECTS:
Home Ec: Half-hearted effort.
eh.
Frozen Stuff
CLUNK
Language Arts: Improving.
Sup, BFFL?
huh?
Oh right, Sup?
Science: Passed "Reproduction" twice.
2000
2002
Math: Reluctant participant.
Balance the checkbook?
Your turn.
Gym: Inconsistent.
eh.
Social Studies: Excellent study habits.
What's Perfectville up to?
Ooo! Is that a new TV console?
Libenson
www.pajamadiaries.com
3/11 © 2012 Terri Libenson, Dist. By King Features Syndicate, Inc.

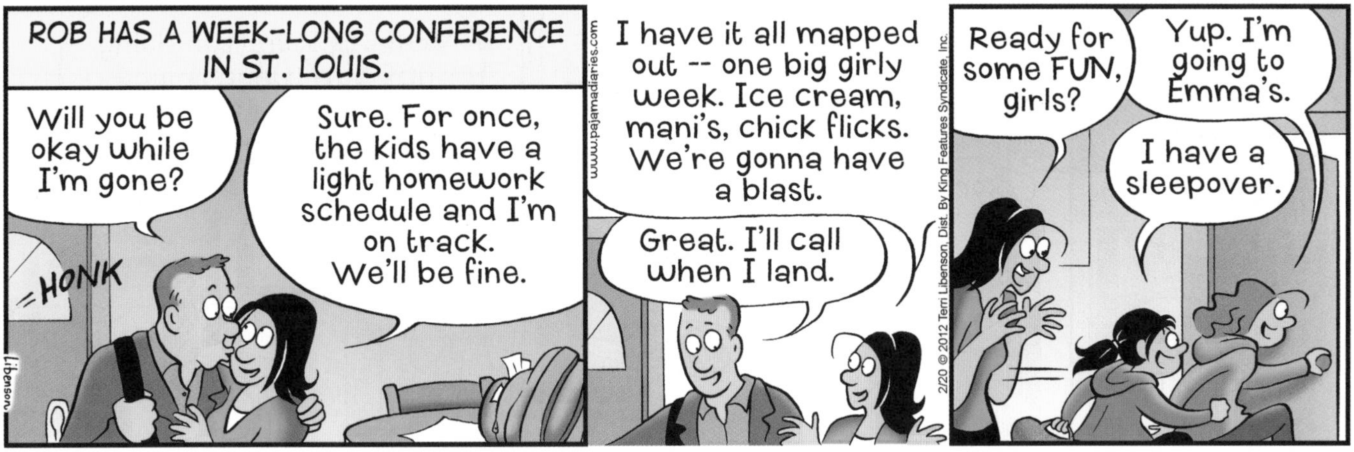
ROB HAS A WEEK-LONG CONFERENCE IN ST. LOUIS.
Will you be okay while I'm gone?
Sure. For once, the kids have a light homework schedule and I'm on track. We'll be fine.
HONK
Libenson
www.pajamadiaries.com
I have it all mapped out -- one big girly week. Ice cream, mani's, chick flicks. We're gonna have a blast.
Great. I'll call when I land.
2/20 © 2012 Terri Libenson, Dist. By King Features Syndicate, Inc.
Ready for some FUN, girls?
Yup. I'm going to Emma's.
I have a sleepover.

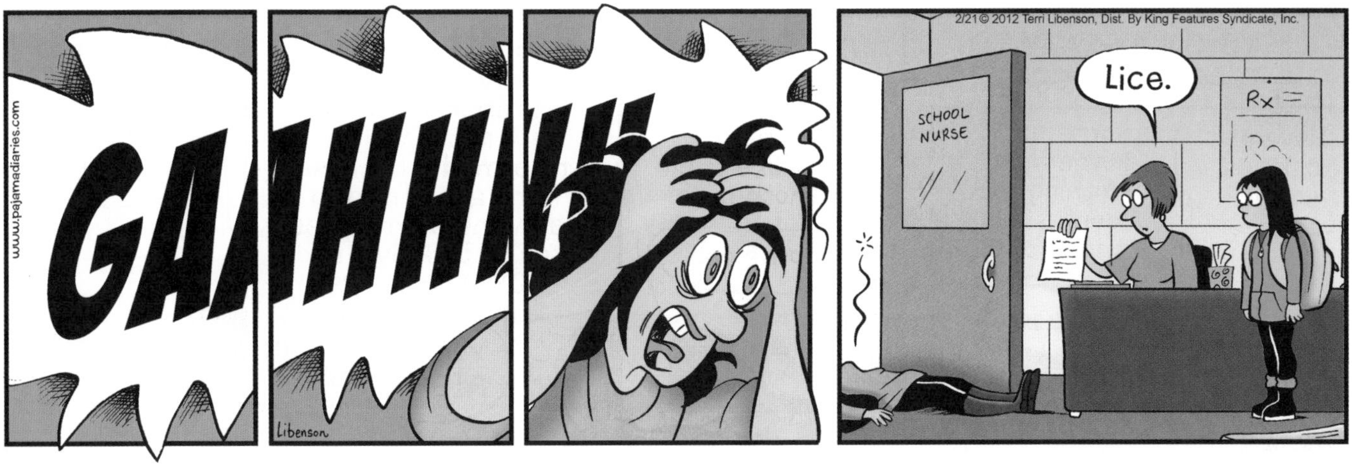
www.pajamadiaries.com
GAAHHH!!
Libenson
2/21 © 2012 Terri Libenson, Dist. By King Features Syndicate, Inc.
SCHOOL NURSE
Lice.
Rx

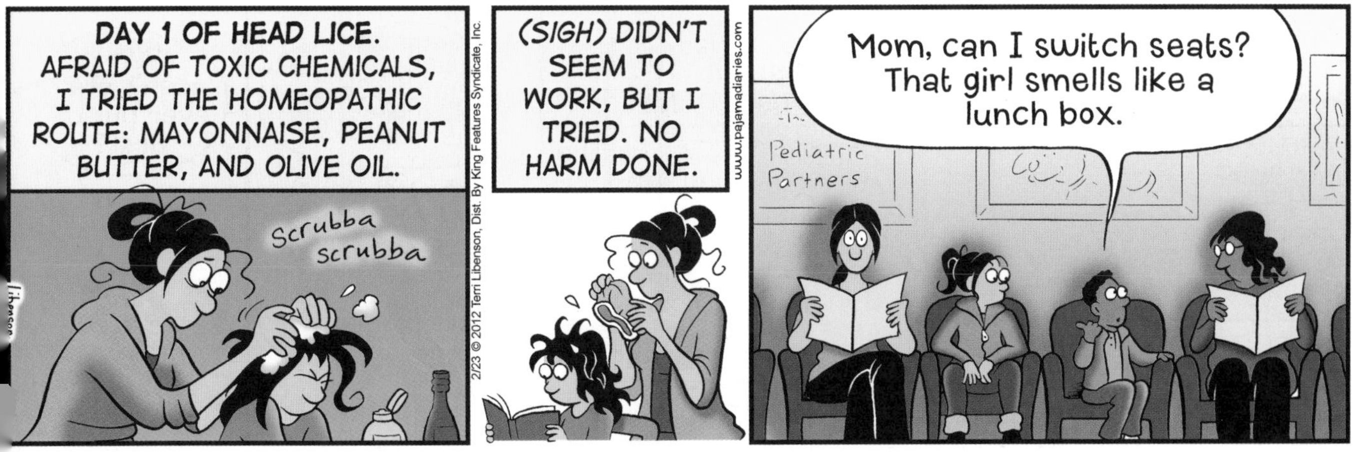
DAY 1 OF HEAD LICE. AFRAID OF TOXIC CHEMICALS, I TRIED THE HOMEOPATHIC ROUTE: MAYONNAISE, PEANUT BUTTER, AND OLIVE OIL.
Scrubba scrubba
2/23 © 2012 Terri Libenson, Dist. By King Features Syndicate, Inc.
(SIGH) DIDN'T SEEM TO WORK, BUT I TRIED. NO HARM DONE.
www.pajamadiaries.com
Mom, can I switch seats? That girl smells like a lunch box.
Pediatric Partners

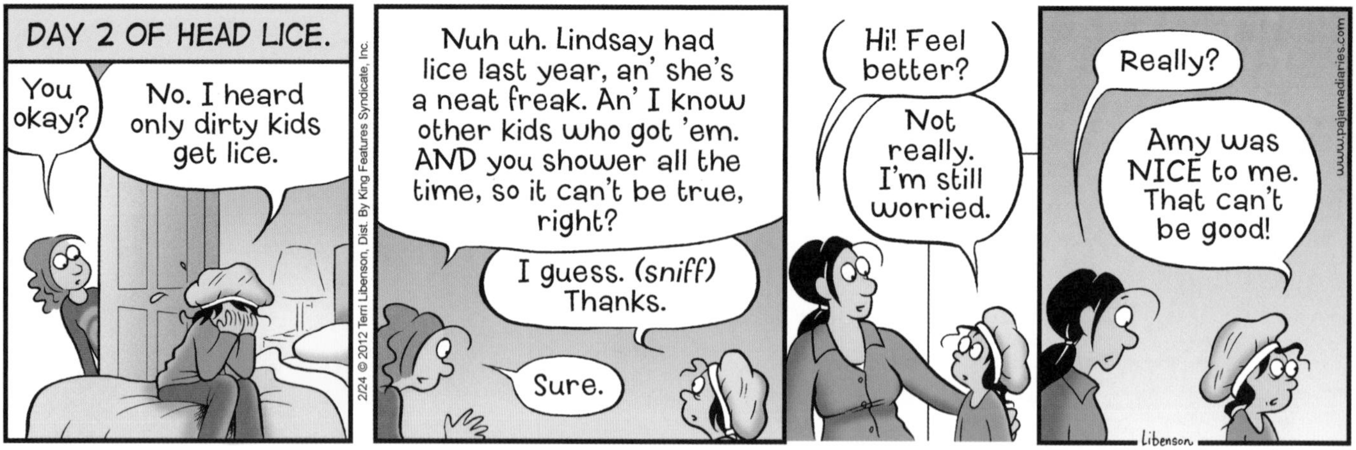
DAY 2 OF HEAD LICE.
You okay?
No. I heard only dirty kids get lice.
2/24 © 2012 Terri Libenson, Dist. By King Features Syndicate, Inc.
Nuh uh. Lindsay had lice last year, an' she's a neat freak. An' I know other kids who got 'em. AND you shower all the time, so it can't be true, right?
I guess. (sniff) Thanks.
Sure.
Hi! Feel better?
Not really. I'm still worried.
Really?
Amy was NICE to me. That can't be good!
www.pajamadiaries.com
Libenson

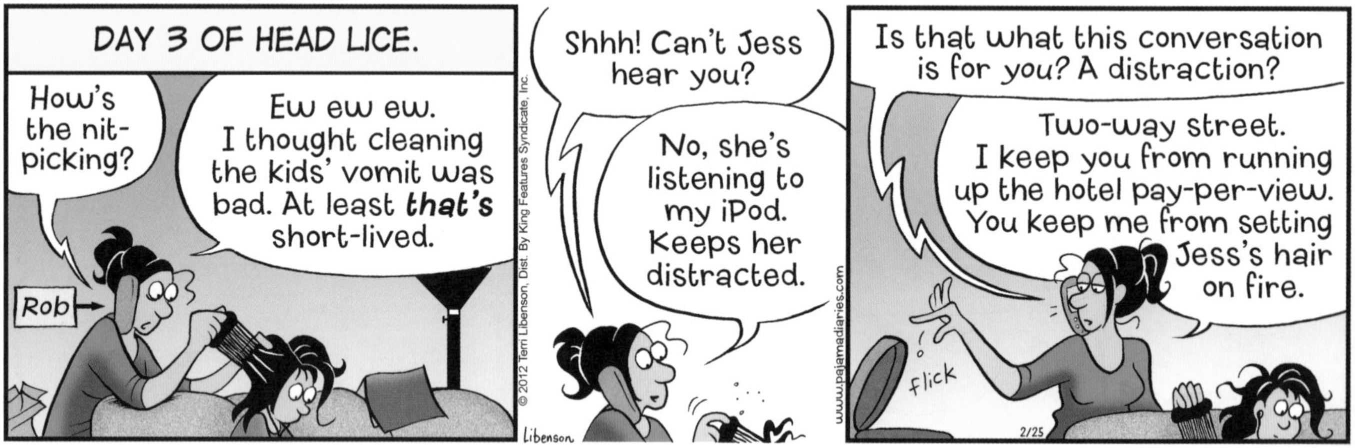
DAY 3 OF HEAD LICE.
How's the nit-picking?
Ew ew ew. I thought cleaning the kids' vomit was bad. At least **that's** short-lived.
Rob
Libenson
© 2012 Terri Libenson, Dist. By King Features Syndicate, Inc.
Shhh! Can't Jess hear you?
No, she's listening to my iPod. Keeps her distracted.
www.pajamadiaries.com
Is that what this conversation is for *you*? A distraction?
Two-way street. I keep you from running up the hotel pay-per-view. You keep me from setting Jess's hair on fire.
flick
2/25

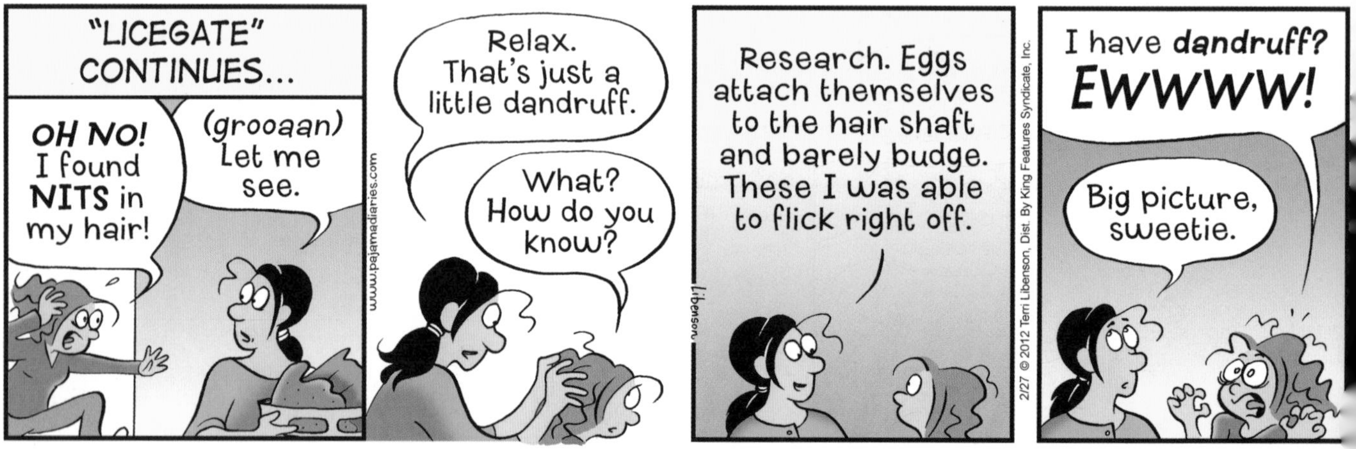
"LICEGATE" CONTINUES...
OH NO! I found **NITS** in my hair!
(grooaan) Let me see.
www.pajamadiaries.com
Relax. That's just a little dandruff.
What? How do you know?
Libenson
Research. Eggs attach themselves to the hair shaft and barely budge. These I was able to flick right off.
2/27 © 2012 Terri Libenson, Dist. By King Features Syndicate, Inc.
I have **dandruff? EWWWW!**
Big picture, sweetie.

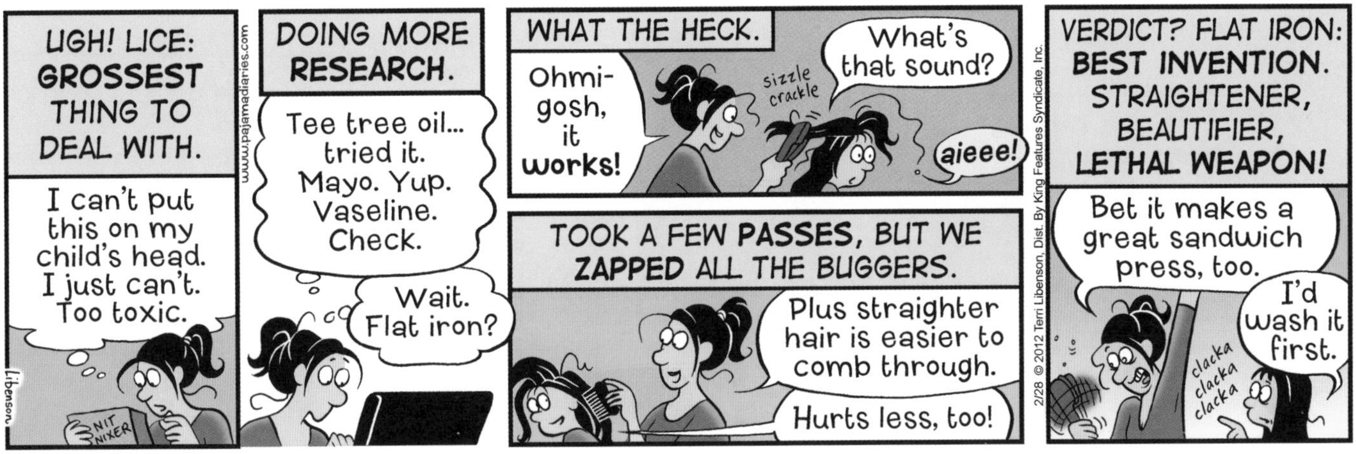
UGH! LICE: **GROSSEST** THING TO DEAL WITH.
I can't put this on my child's head. I just can't. Too toxic.
NIT NIXER
Libenson
www.pajamadiaries.com
DOING MORE **RESEARCH**.
Tee tree oil... tried it. Mayo. Yup. Vaseline. Check.
Wait. Flat iron?
WHAT THE HECK.
Ohmi-gosh, it **works!**
What's that sound?
sizzle crackle
aieee!
TOOK A FEW **PASSES**, BUT WE **ZAPPED** ALL THE BUGGERS.
Plus straighter hair is easier to comb through.
Hurts less, too!
2/28 © 2012 Terri Libenson, Dist. By King Features Syndicate, Inc.
VERDICT? FLAT IRON: **BEST INVENTION**. STRAIGHTENER, BEAUTIFIER, **LETHAL WEAPON!**
Bet it makes a great sandwich press, too.
I'd wash it first.
clacka clacka clacka

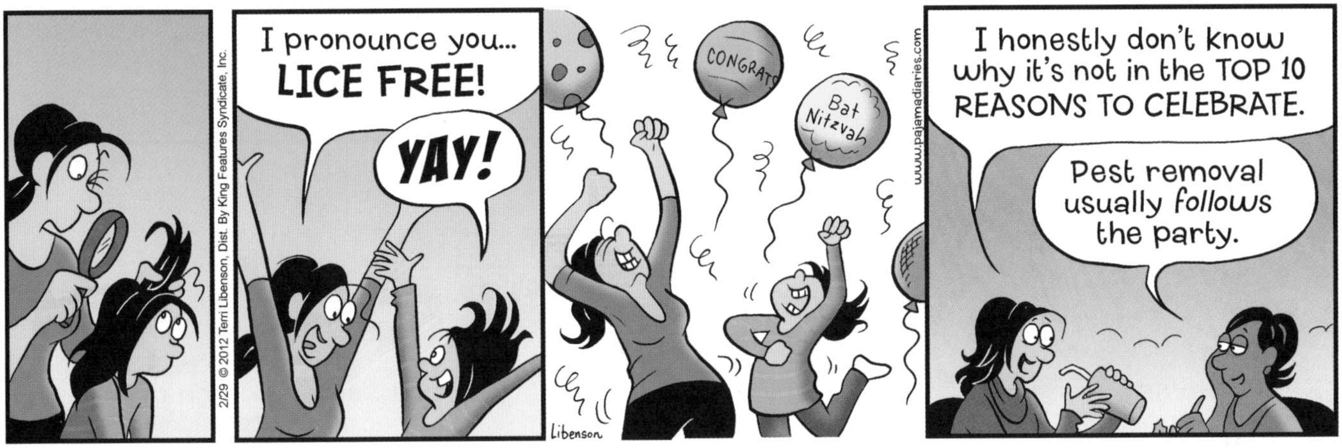
2/29 © 2012 Terri Libenson, Dist. By King Features Syndicate, Inc.
I pronounce you... **LICE FREE!**
YAY!
CONGRATS
Bat Nitzvah
Libenson
www.pajamadiaries.com
I honestly don't know why it's not in the TOP 10 REASONS TO CELEBRATE.
Pest removal usually *follows* the party.

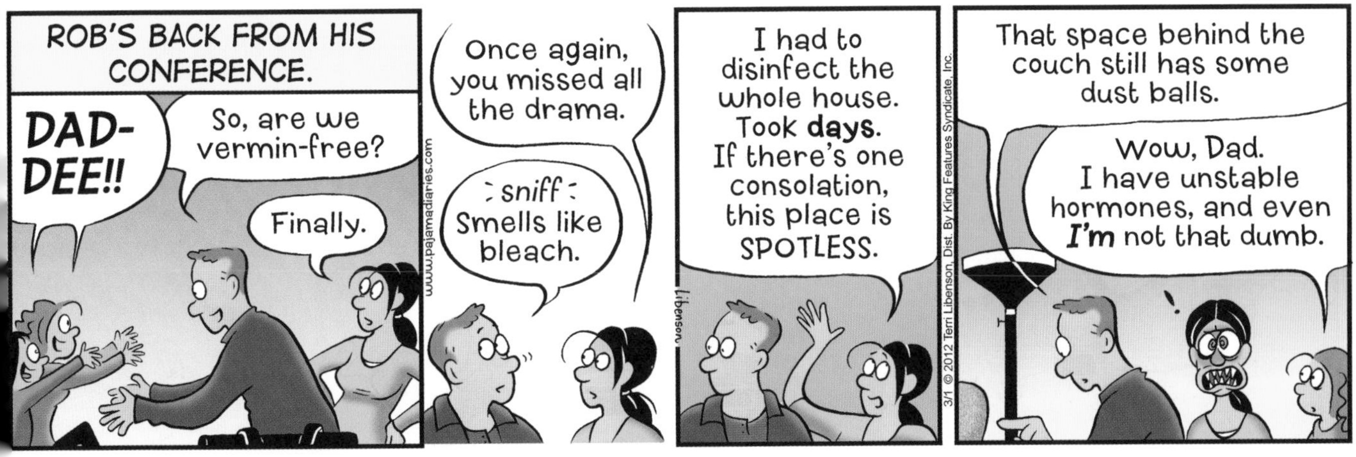
ROB'S BACK FROM HIS CONFERENCE.
DAD-DEE!!
So, are we vermin-free?
Finally.
www.pajamadiaries.com
Once again, you missed all the drama.
sniff
Smells like bleach.
Libenson
I had to disinfect the whole house. Took **days**. If there's one consolation, this place is SPOTLESS.
3/1 © 2012 Terri Libenson, Dist. By King Features Syndicate, Inc.
That space behind the couch still has some dust balls.
Wow, Dad. I have unstable hormones, and even ***I'm*** not that dumb.

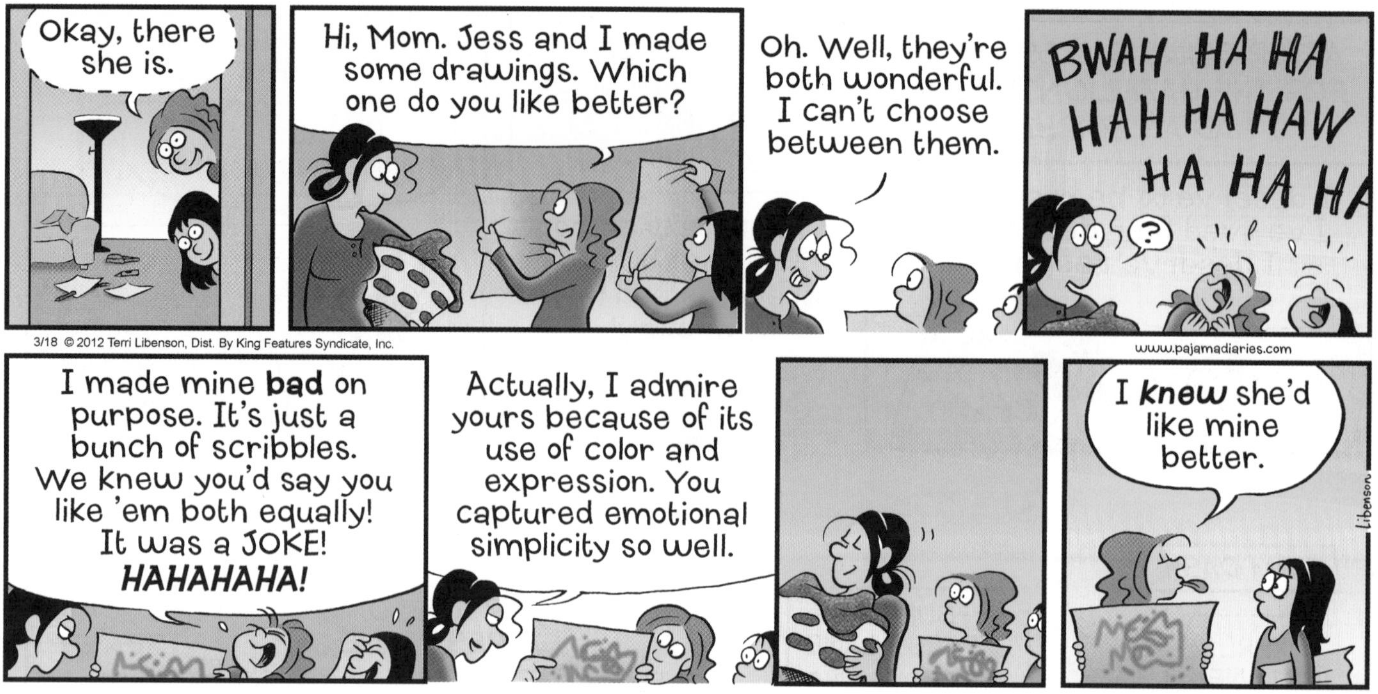
Okay, there she is.
Hi, Mom. Jess and I made some drawings. Which one do you like better?
Oh. Well, they're both wonderful. I can't choose between them.
BWAH HA HA HAH HA HAW HA HA HA
?
3/18 © 2012 Terri Libenson, Dist. By King Features Syndicate, Inc.
www.pajamadiaries.com
I made mine **bad** on purpose. It's just a bunch of scribbles. We knew you'd say you like 'em both equally! It was a JOKE! HAHAHAHA!
Actually, I admire yours because of its use of color and expression. You captured emotional simplicity so well.
I **knew** she'd like mine better.
Libenson

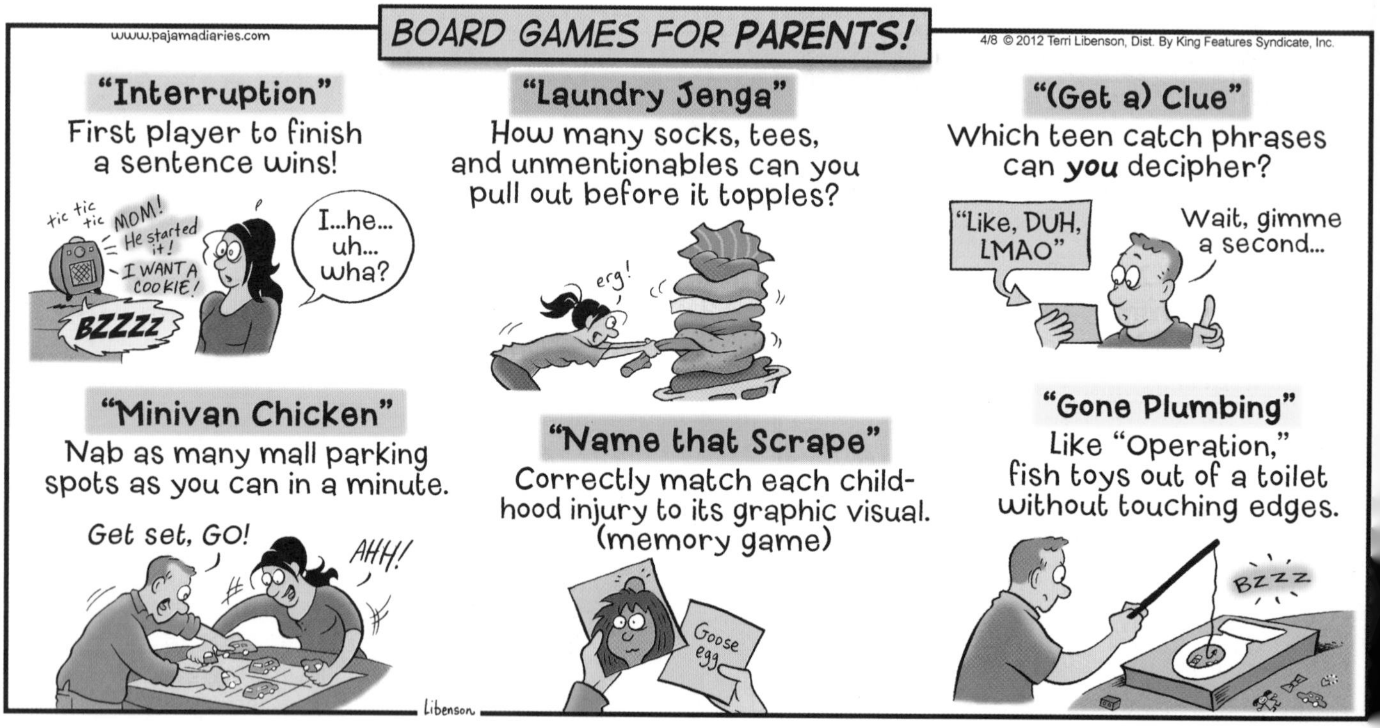
www.pajamadiaries.com
BOARD GAMES FOR PARENTS!
4/8 © 2012 Terri Libenson, Dist. By King Features Syndicate, Inc.
"Interruption"
First player to finish a sentence wins!
tic tic tic
MOM!
He started it!
I WANT A COOKIE!
BZZZz
I...he... uh... wha?
"Laundry Jenga"
How many socks, tees, and unmentionables can you pull out before it topples?
erg!
"(Get a) Clue"
Which teen catch phrases can **you** decipher?
"Like, DUH, LMAO"
Wait, gimme a second...
"Minivan Chicken"
Nab as many mall parking spots as you can in a minute.
Get set, GO!
AHH!
"Name that Scrape"
Correctly match each childhood injury to its graphic visual. (memory game)
Goose egg
"Gone Plumbing"
Like "Operation," fish toys out of a toilet without touching edges.
BZZZ
Libenson

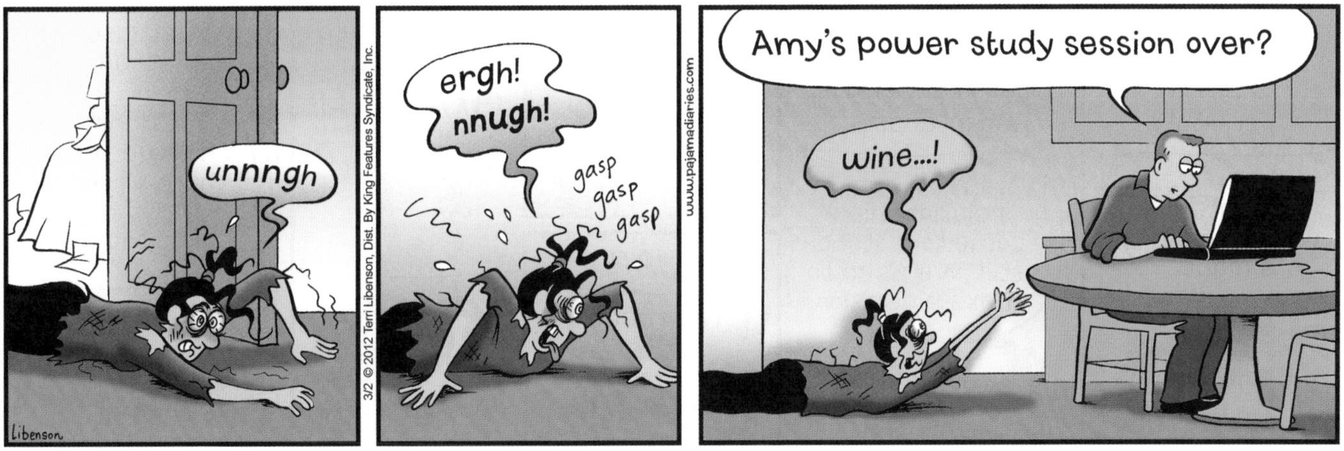
unnngh
Libenson
3/2 © 2012 Terri Libenson, Dist. By King Features Syndicate, Inc.
ergh! nnugh!
gasp gasp gasp
www.pajamadiaries.com
Amy's power study session over?
wine...!

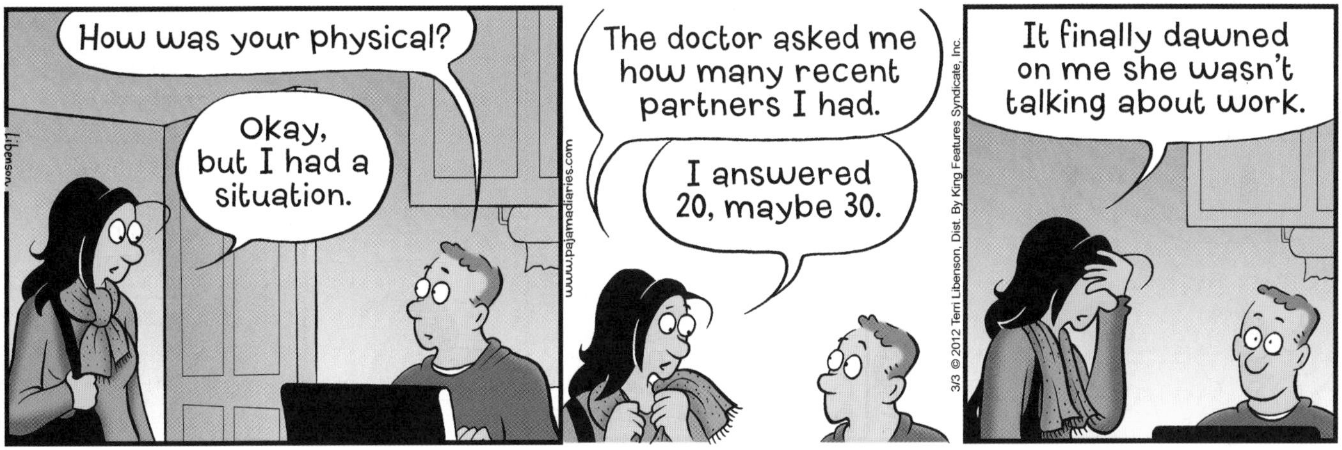
How was your physical?
Okay, but I had a situation.
Libenson
www.pajamadiaries.com
The doctor asked me how many recent partners I had.
I answered 20, maybe 30.
3/3 © 2012 Terri Libenson, Dist. By King Features Syndicate, Inc.
It finally dawned on me she wasn't talking about work.

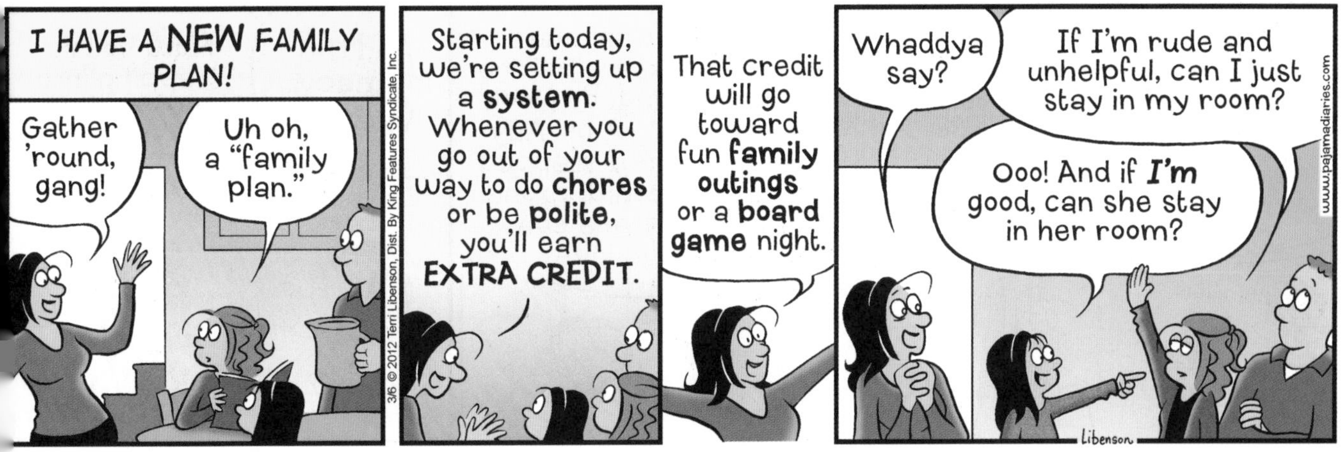
I HAVE A NEW FAMILY PLAN!
Gather 'round, gang!
Uh oh, a "family plan."
3/6 © 2012 Terri Libenson, Dist. By King Features Syndicate, Inc.
Starting today, we're setting up a system. Whenever you go out of your way to do chores or be polite, you'll earn EXTRA CREDIT.
That credit will go toward fun family outings or a board game night.
Whaddya say?
If I'm rude and unhelpful, can I just stay in my room?
Ooo! And if I'm good, can she stay in her room?
www.pajamadiaries.com
Libenson

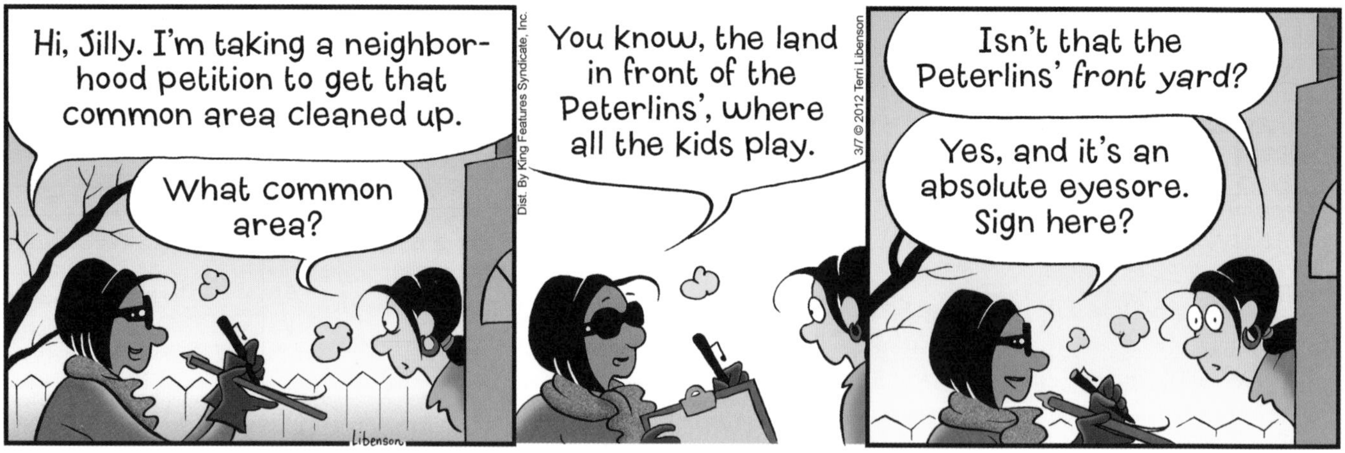
Hi, Jilly. I'm taking a neighborhood petition to get that common area cleaned up.
What common area?
You know, the land in front of the Peterlins', where all the kids play.
Isn't that the Peterlins' front yard?
Yes, and it's an absolute eyesore. Sign here?
Libenson
Dist. By King Features Syndicate, Inc.
3/7 © 2012 Terri Libenson

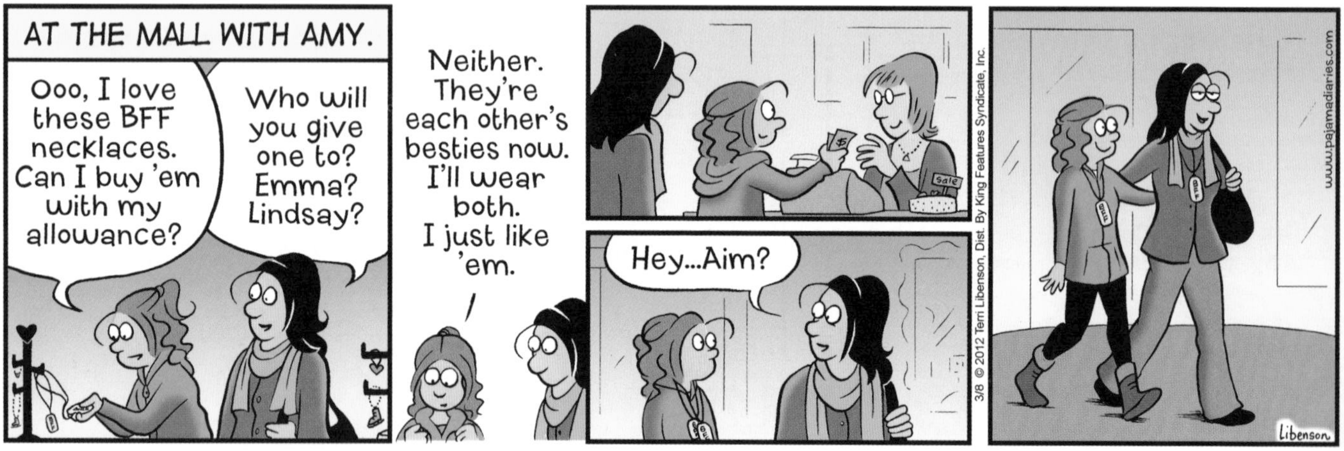
AT THE MALL WITH AMY.
Ooo, I love these BFF necklaces. Can I buy 'em with my allowance?
Who will you give one to? Emma? Lindsay?
Neither. They're each other's besties now. I'll wear both. I just like 'em.
Hey...Aim?
3/8 © 2012 Terri Libenson, Dist. By King Features Syndicate, Inc.
www.pajamadiaries.com
Libenson

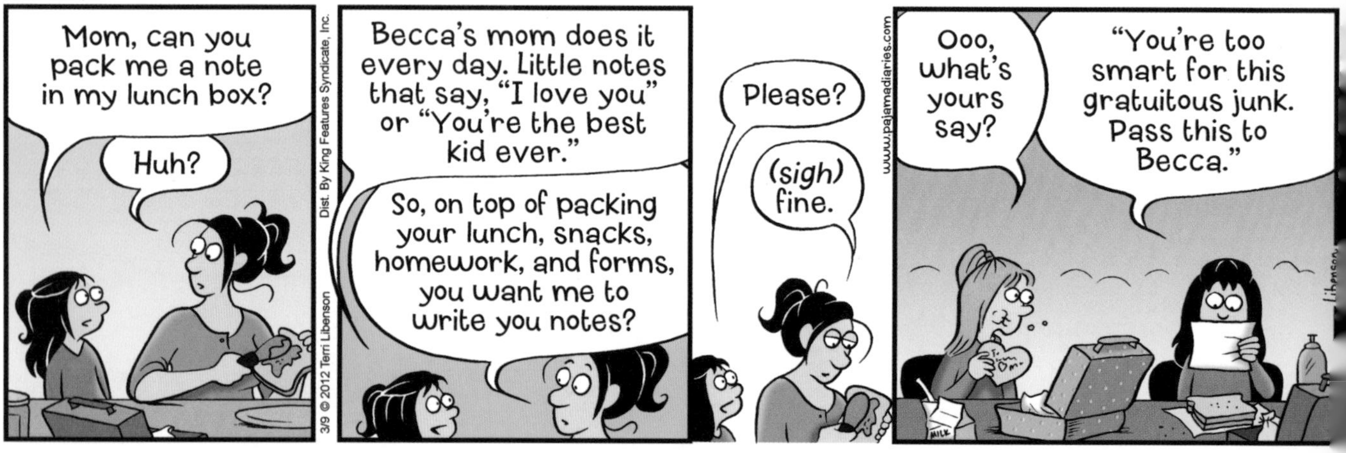
Mom, can you pack me a note in my lunch box?
Huh?
Becca's mom does it every day. Little notes that say, "I love you" or "You're the best kid ever."
So, on top of packing your lunch, snacks, homework, and forms, you want me to write you notes?
Please?
(sigh) fine.
Ooo, what's yours say?
"You're too smart for this gratuitous junk. Pass this to Becca."
Dist. By King Features Syndicate, Inc.
3/9 © 2012 Terri Libenson
www.pajamadiaries.com

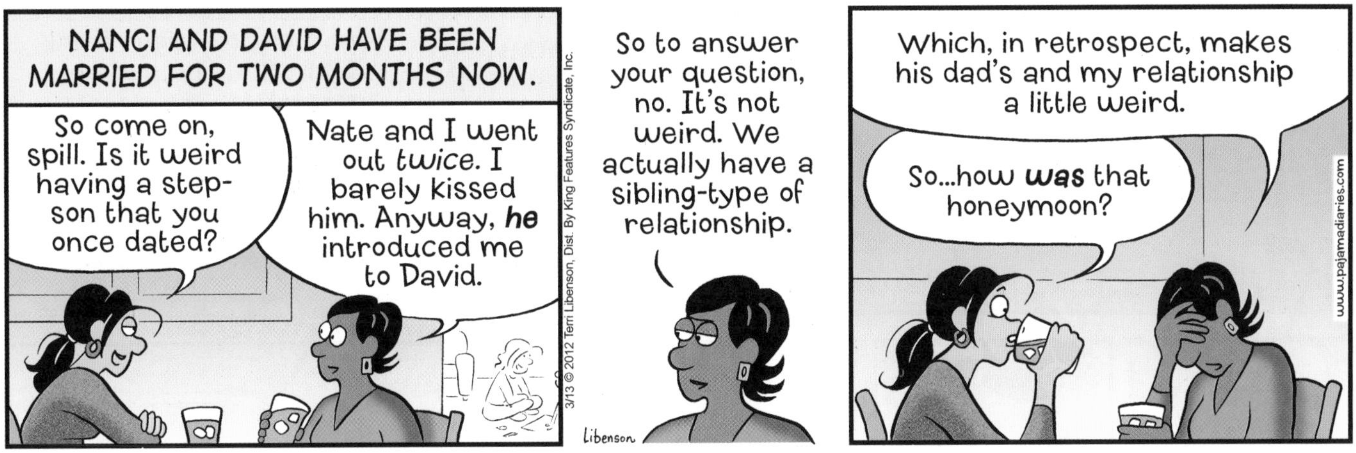
NANCI AND DAVID HAVE BEEN MARRIED FOR TWO MONTHS NOW.
So come on, spill. Is it weird having a step-son that you once dated?
Nate and I went out *twice*. I barely kissed him. Anyway, **he** introduced me to David.
3/13 © 2012 Terri Libenson, Dist. By King Features Syndicate, Inc.
So to answer your question, no. It's not weird. We actually have a sibling-type of relationship.
Libenson
Which, in retrospect, makes his dad's and my relationship a little weird.
So...how **was** that honeymoon?
www.pajamadiaries.com

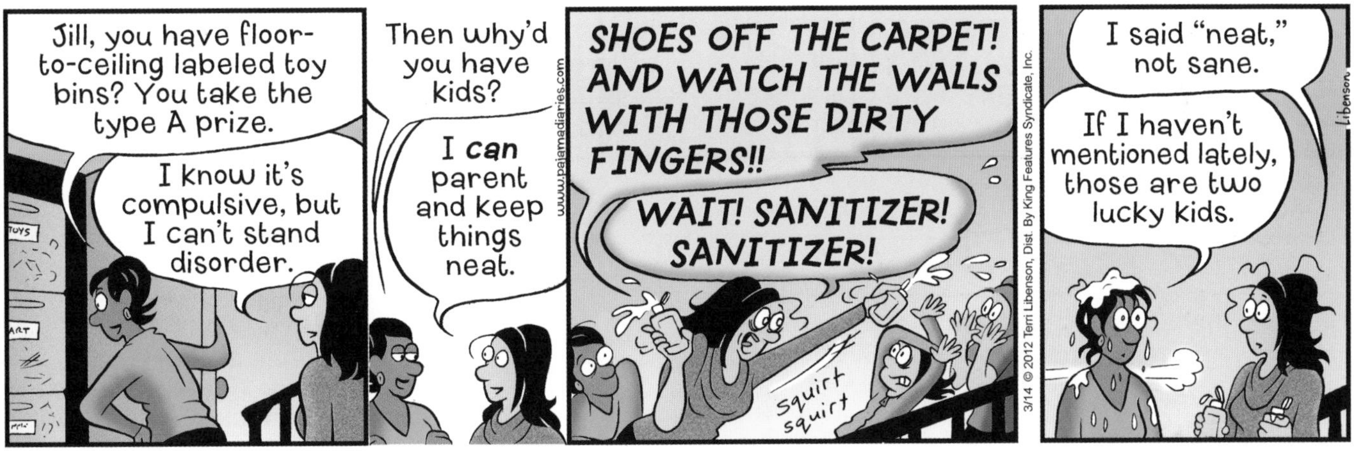
Jill, you have floor-to-ceiling labeled toy bins? You take the type A prize.
I know it's compulsive, but I can't stand disorder.
TOYS
ART
Then why'd you have kids?
I **can** parent and keep things neat.
www.pajamadiaries.com
SHOES OFF THE CARPET! AND WATCH THE WALLS WITH THOSE DIRTY FINGERS!!
WAIT! SANITIZER! SANITIZER!
squirt squirt
3/14 © 2012 Terri Libenson, Dist. By King Features Syndicate, Inc.
I said "neat," not sane.
If I haven't mentioned lately, those are two lucky kids.
Libenson

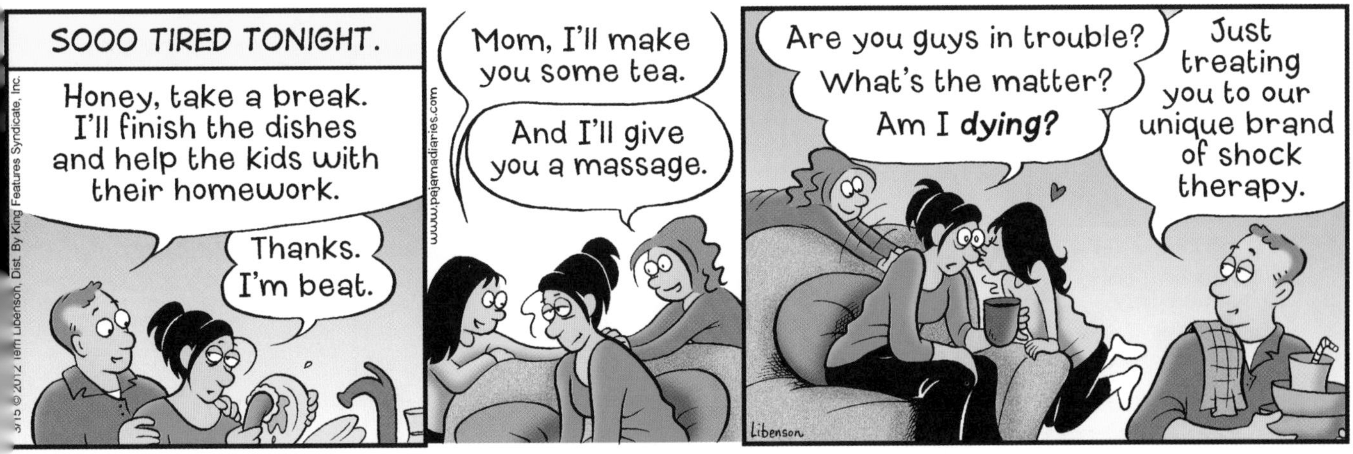
SOOO TIRED TONIGHT.
Honey, take a break. I'll finish the dishes and help the kids with their homework.
Thanks. I'm beat.
3/15 © 2012 Terri Libenson, Dist. By King Features Syndicate, Inc.
Mom, I'll make you some tea.
And I'll give you a massage.
www.pajamadiaries.com
Are you guys in trouble?
What's the matter?
Am I ***dying?***
Just treating you to our unique brand of shock therapy.
Libenson

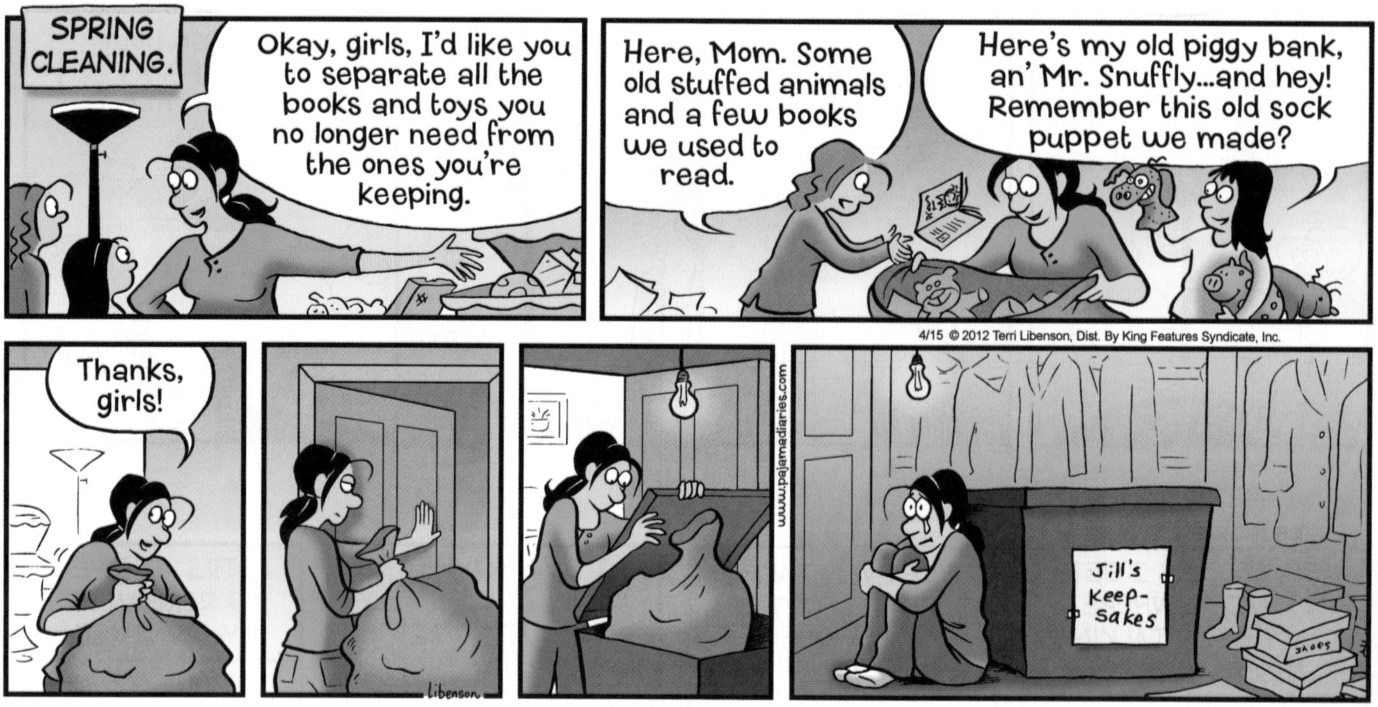
SPRING CLEANING.
Okay, girls, I'd like you to separate all the books and toys you no longer need from the ones you're keeping.
Here, Mom. Some old stuffed animals and a few books we used to read.
Here's my old piggy bank, an' Mr. Snuffly...and hey! Remember this old sock puppet we made?
Thanks, girls!
www.pajamadiaries.com
Libenson
Jill's Keep-sakes
SHOES

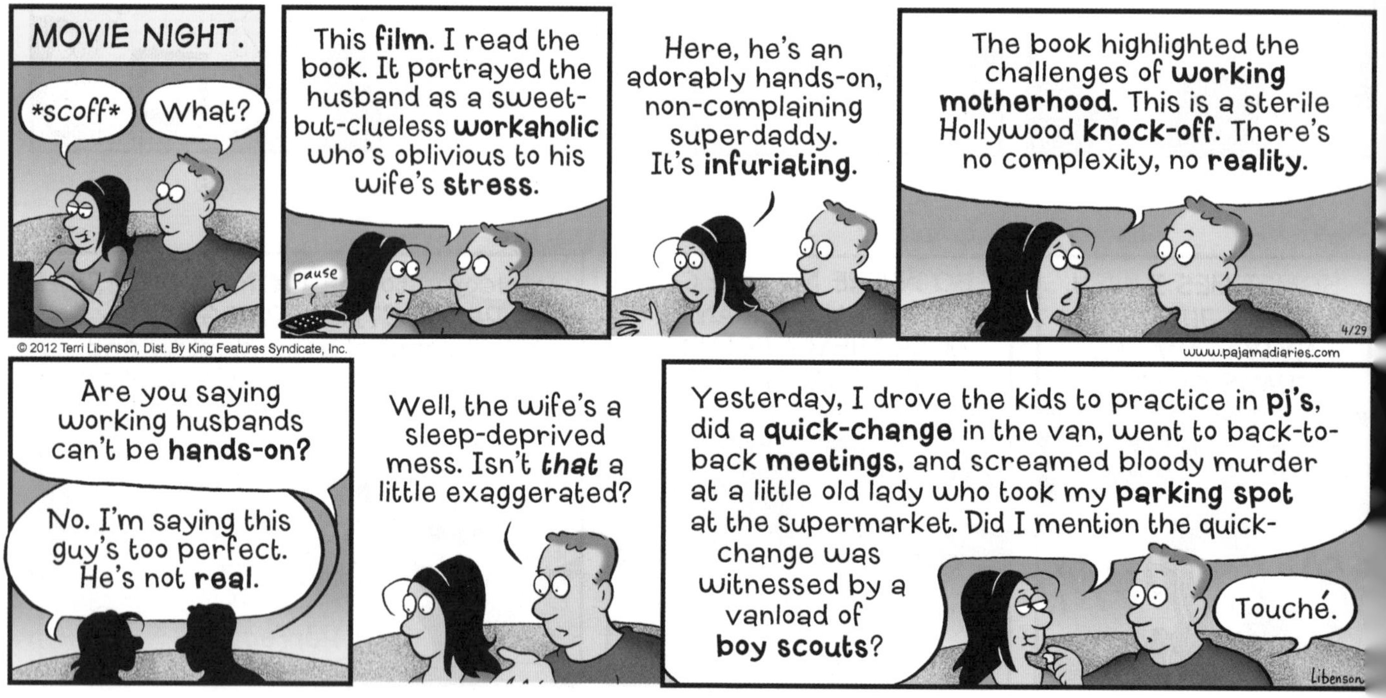
MOVIE NIGHT.
scoff
What?
This **film**. I read the book. It portrayed the husband as a sweet-but-clueless **workaholic** who's oblivious to his wife's **stress**.
pause
Here, he's an adorably hands-on, non-complaining superdaddy. It's **infuriating**.
The book highlighted the challenges of **working motherhood**. This is a sterile Hollywood **knock-off**. There's no complexity, no **reality**.
4/29
Are you saying working husbands can't be **hands-on?**
No. I'm saying this guy's too perfect. He's not **real**.
Well, the wife's a sleep-deprived mess. Isn't ***that*** a little exaggerated?
Yesterday, I drove the kids to practice in **pj's**, did a **quick-change** in the van, went to back-to-back **meetings**, and screamed bloody murder at a little old lady who took my **parking spot** at the supermarket. Did I mention the quick-change was witnessed by a vanload of **boy scouts**?
Touché.
Libenson

www.pajamadiaries.com

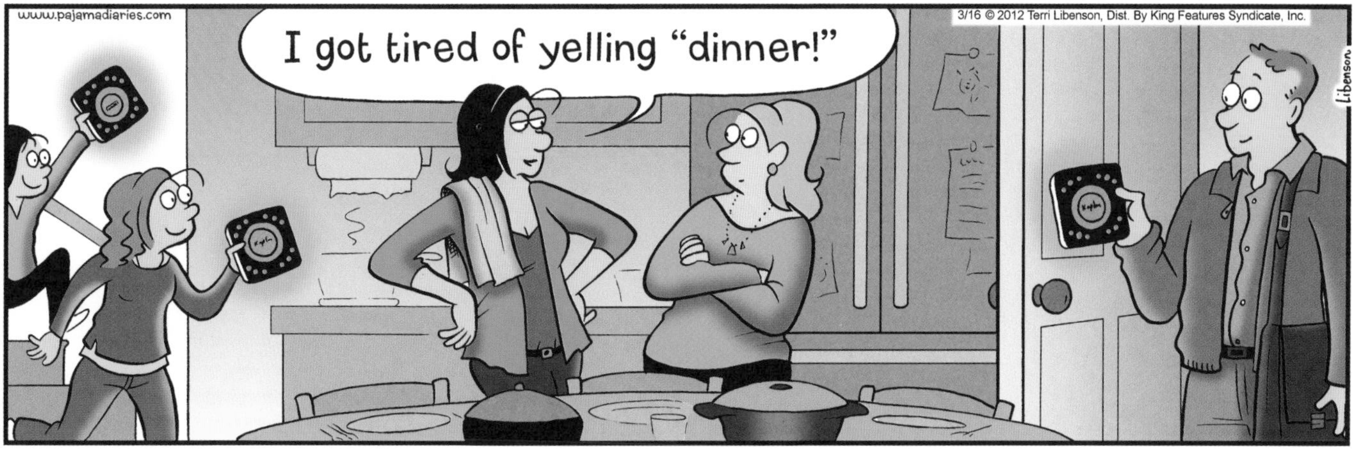
www.pajamadiaries.com
3/16 © 2012 Terri Libenson, Dist. By King Features Syndicate, Inc.
I got tired of yelling "dinner!"
Libenson

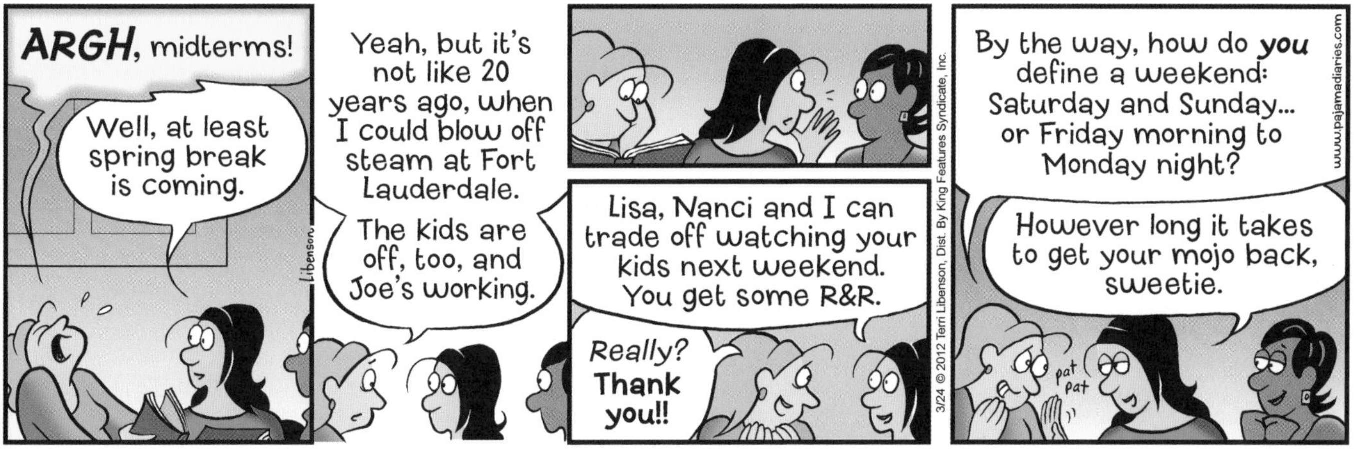
ARGH, midterms!
Well, at least spring break is coming.
Libenson
Yeah, but it's not like 20 years ago, when I could blow off steam at Fort Lauderdale.
The kids are off, too, and Joe's working.
Lisa, Nanci and I can trade off watching your kids next weekend. You get some R&R.
Really? **Thank you!!**
3/24 © 2012 Terri Libenson, Dist. By King Features Syndicate, Inc.
By the way, how do **you** define a weekend: Saturday and Sunday... or Friday morning to Monday night?
However long it takes to get your mojo back, sweetie.
pat pat
www.pajamadiaries.com

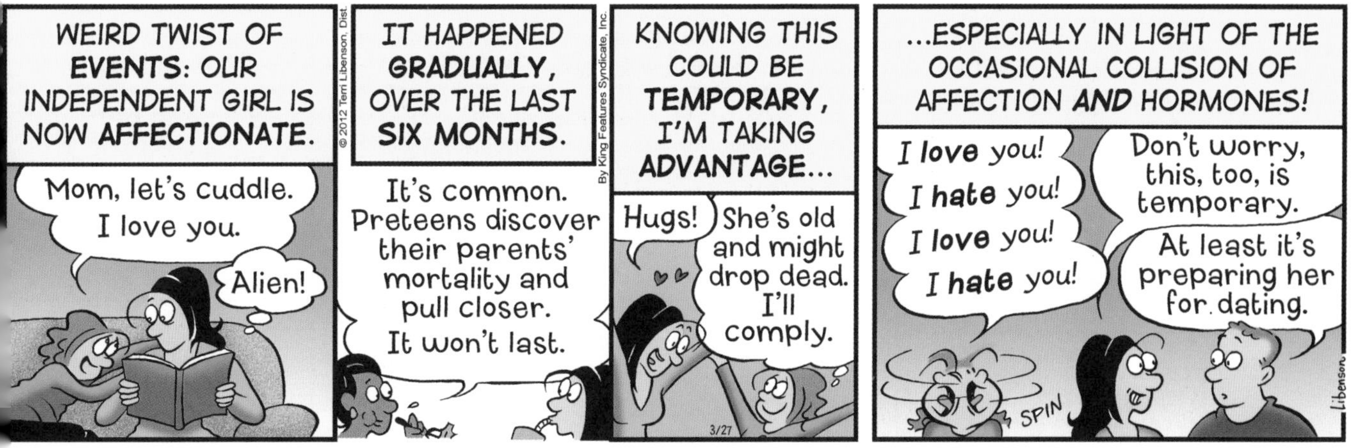
WEIRD TWIST OF **EVENTS**: OUR INDEPENDENT GIRL IS NOW **AFFECTIONATE**.
Mom, let's cuddle. I love you.
Alien!
© 2012 Terri Libenson, Dist.
IT HAPPENED **GRADUALLY**, OVER THE LAST **SIX MONTHS**.
It's common. Preteens discover their parents' mortality and pull closer.
It won't last.
By King Features Syndicate, Inc.
KNOWING THIS COULD BE **TEMPORARY**, I'M TAKING **ADVANTAGE**...
Hugs!
She's old and might drop dead. I'll comply.
3/27
...ESPECIALLY IN LIGHT OF THE OCCASIONAL COLLISION OF AFFECTION ***AND*** HORMONES!
I love *you!*
I hate *you!*
I love *you!*
I hate *you!*
Don't worry, this, too, is temporary.
At least it's preparing her for dating.
SPIN
Libenson

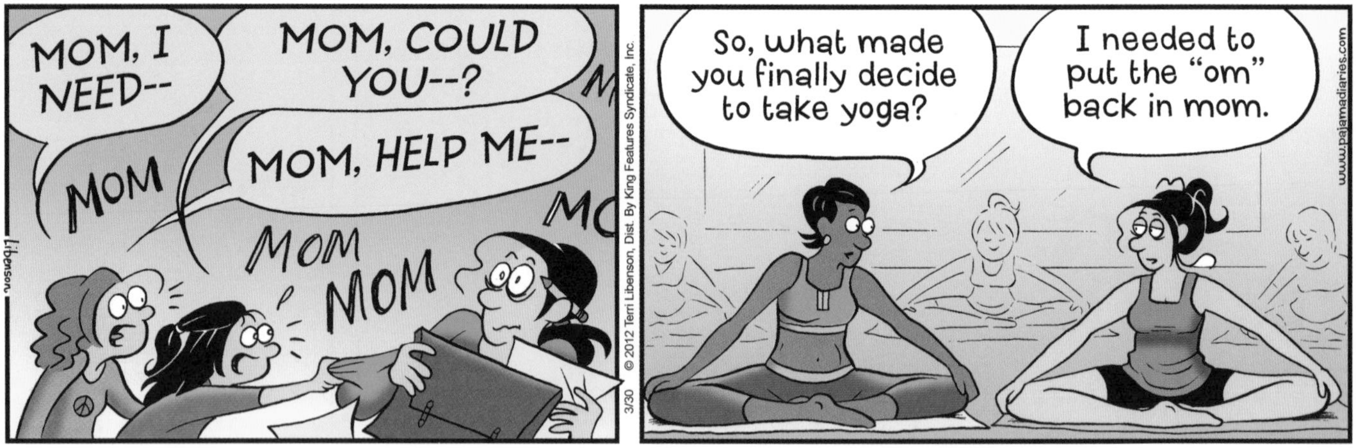
MOM, I NEED--
MOM, COULD YOU--?
MOM
MOM, HELP ME--
MOM
MOM
Libenson
3/30 © 2012 Terri Libenson, Dist. By King Features Syndicate, Inc.
So, what made you finally decide to take yoga?
I needed to put the "om" back in mom.
www.pajamadiaries.com

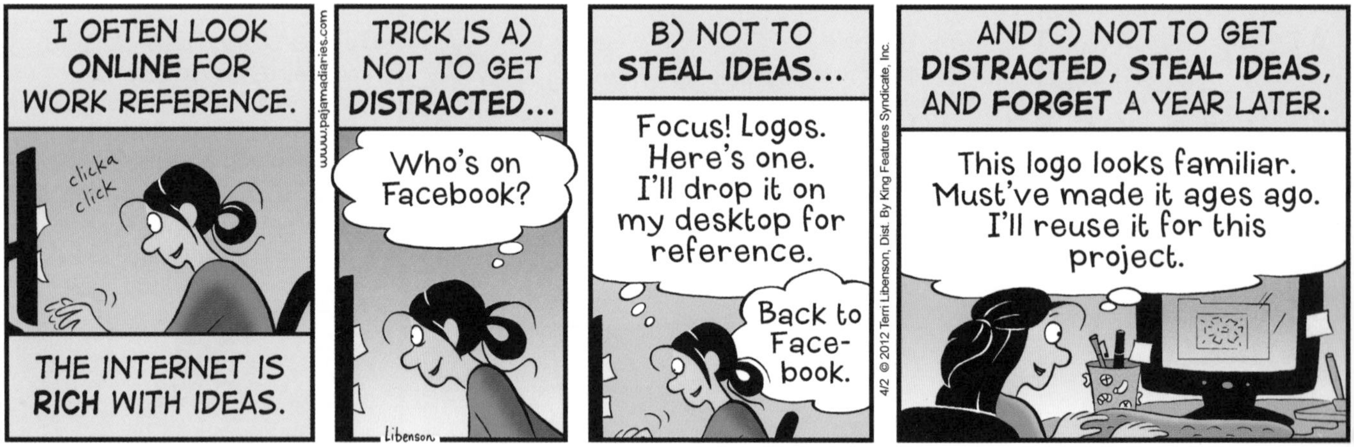
I OFTEN LOOK **ONLINE** FOR WORK REFERENCE.
clicka click
THE INTERNET IS **RICH** WITH IDEAS.
www.pajamadiaries.com
TRICK IS A) NOT TO GET **DISTRACTED**...
Who's on Facebook?
Libenson
B) NOT TO **STEAL IDEAS**...
Focus! Logos. Here's one. I'll drop it on my desktop for reference.
Back to Face-book.
4/2 © 2012 Terri Libenson, Dist. By King Features Syndicate, Inc.
AND C) NOT TO GET **DISTRACTED, STEAL IDEAS,** AND **FORGET** A YEAR LATER.
This logo looks familiar. Must've made it ages ago. I'll reuse it for this project.

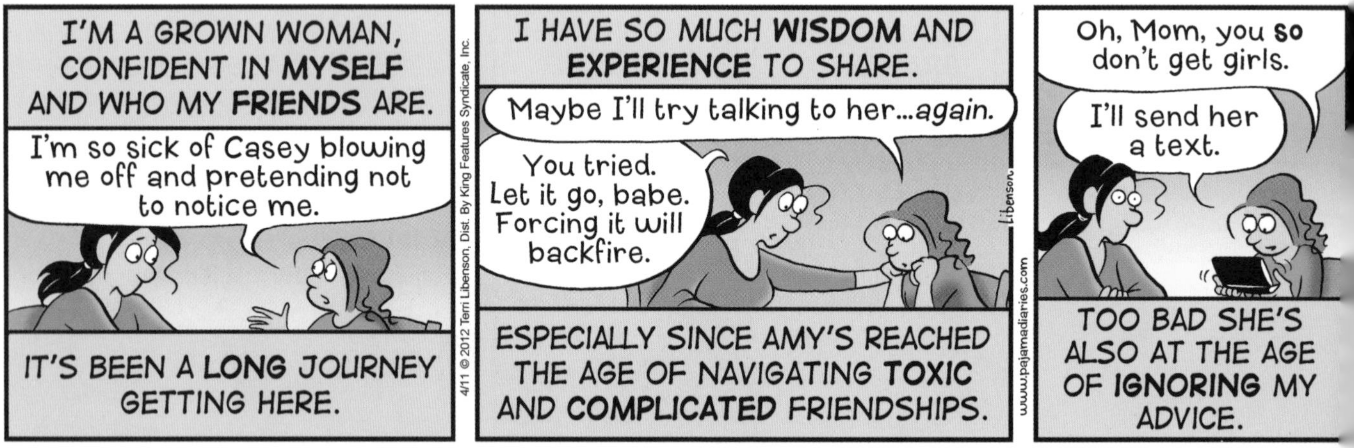
I'M A GROWN WOMAN, CONFIDENT IN **MYSELF** AND WHO MY **FRIENDS** ARE.
I'm so sick of Casey blowing me off and pretending not to notice me.
IT'S BEEN A **LONG** JOURNEY GETTING HERE.
4/11 © 2012 Terri Libenson, Dist. By King Features Syndicate, Inc.
I HAVE SO MUCH **WISDOM** AND **EXPERIENCE** TO SHARE.
Maybe I'll try talking to her...*again.*
You tried. Let it go, babe. Forcing it will backfire.
Libenson
ESPECIALLY SINCE AMY'S REACHED THE AGE OF NAVIGATING **TOXIC** AND **COMPLICATED** FRIENDSHIPS.
www.pajamadiaries.com
Oh, Mom, you **so** don't get girls.
I'll send her a text.
TOO BAD SHE'S ALSO AT THE AGE OF **IGNORING** MY ADVICE.

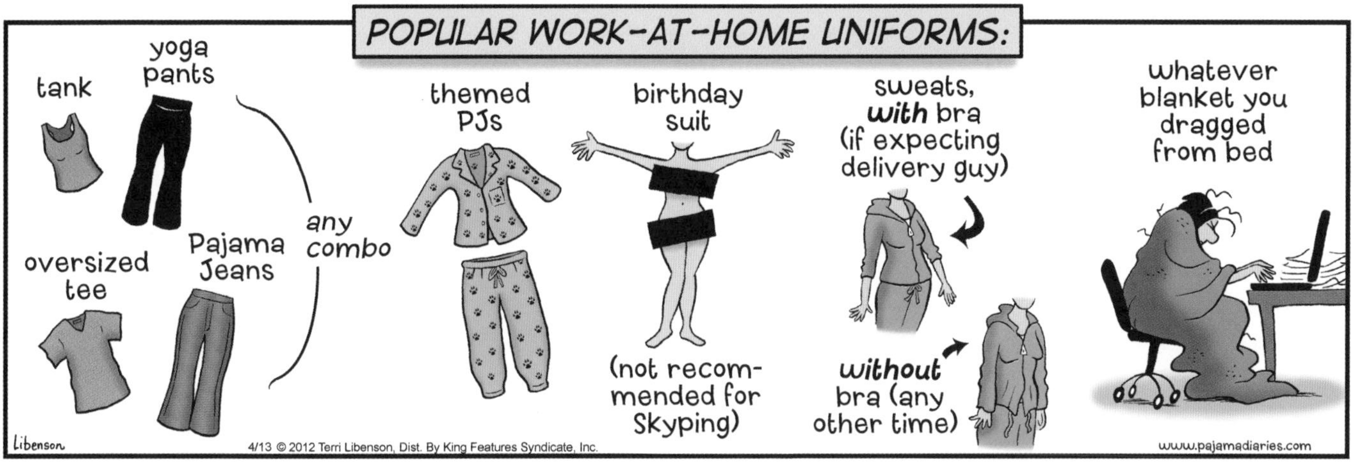
POPULAR WORK-AT-HOME UNIFORMS:
tank
yoga pants
oversized tee
Pajama Jeans
any combo
themed PJs
birthday suit
(not recommended for Skyping)
sweats, with bra (if expecting delivery guy)
without bra (any other time)
whatever blanket you dragged from bed
Libenson
4/13 © 2012 Terri Libenson, Dist. By King Features Syndicate, Inc.
www.pajamadiaries.com

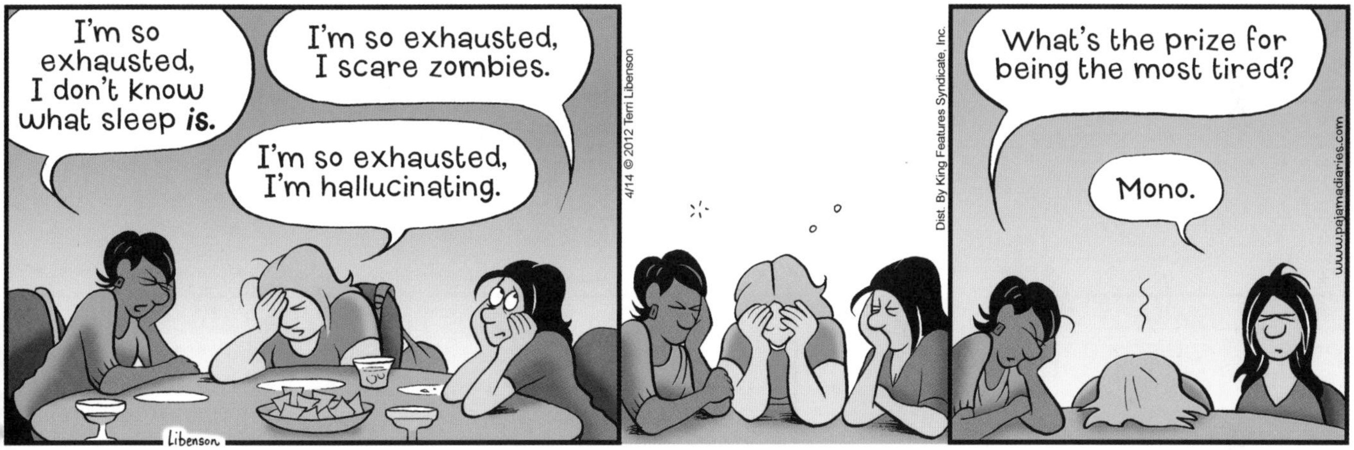
I'm so exhausted, I don't know what sleep is.
I'm so exhausted, I scare zombies.
I'm so exhausted, I'm hallucinating.
4/14 © 2012 Terri Libenson
Libenson
Dist. By King Features Syndicate, Inc.
What's the prize for being the most tired?
Mono.
www.pajamadiaries.com

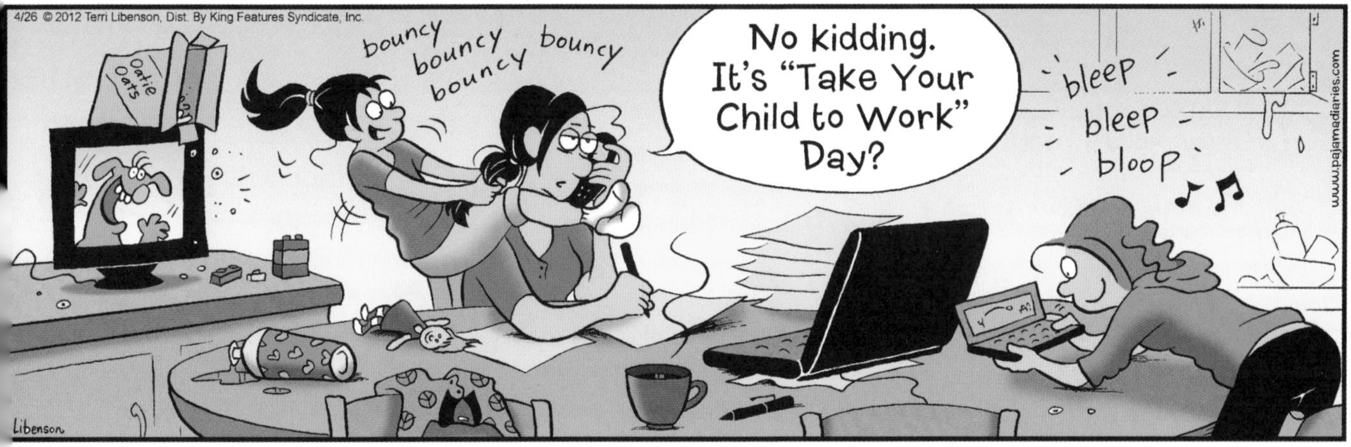
4/26 © 2012 Terri Libenson, Dist. By King Features Syndicate, Inc.
Oatie Oats
bouncy bouncy bouncy bouncy
No kidding. It's "Take Your Child to Work" Day?
bleep bleep bloop
www.pajamadiaries.com
Libenson

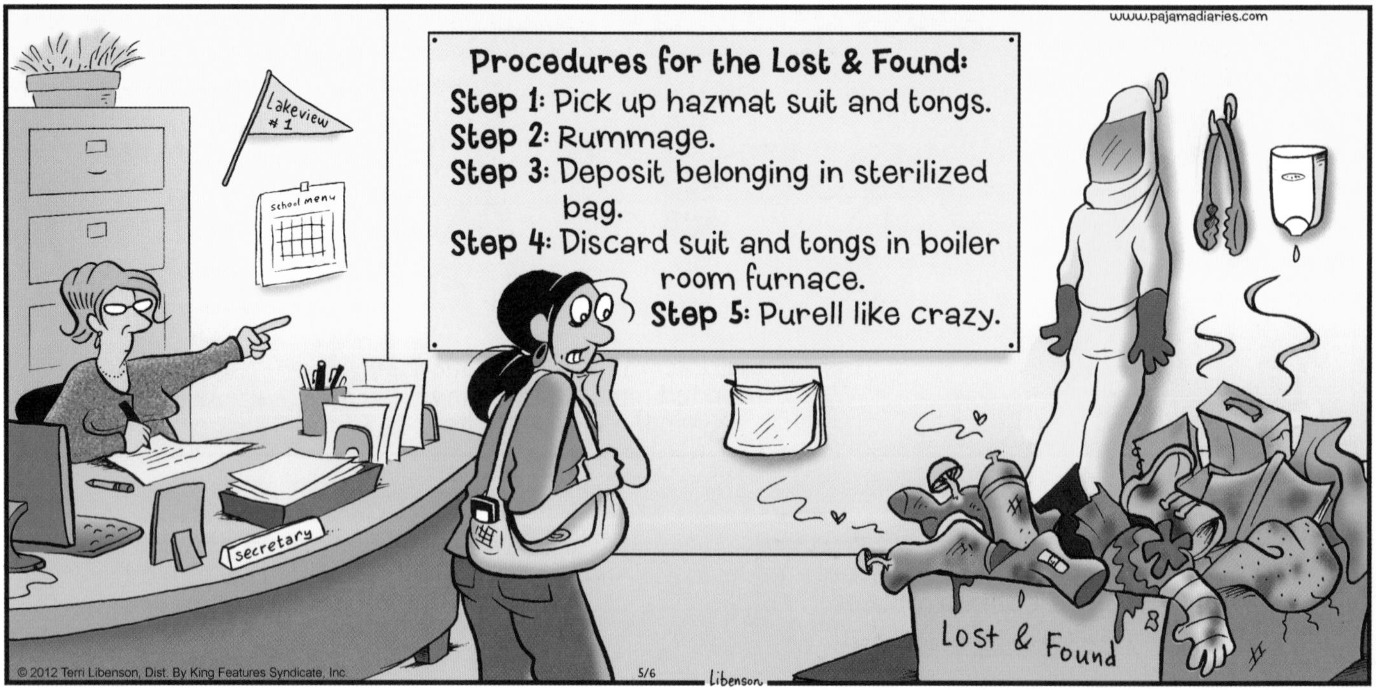
www.pajamadiaries.com
Procedures for the Lost & Found:
Step 1: Pick up hazmat suit and tongs.
Step 2: Rummage.
Step 3: Deposit belonging in sterilized bag.
Step 4: Discard suit and tongs in boiler room furnace.
Step 5: Purell like crazy.
Lakeview #1
School menu
secretary
Lost & Found
© 2012 Terri Libenson, Dist. By King Features Syndicate, Inc.
5/6
Libenson

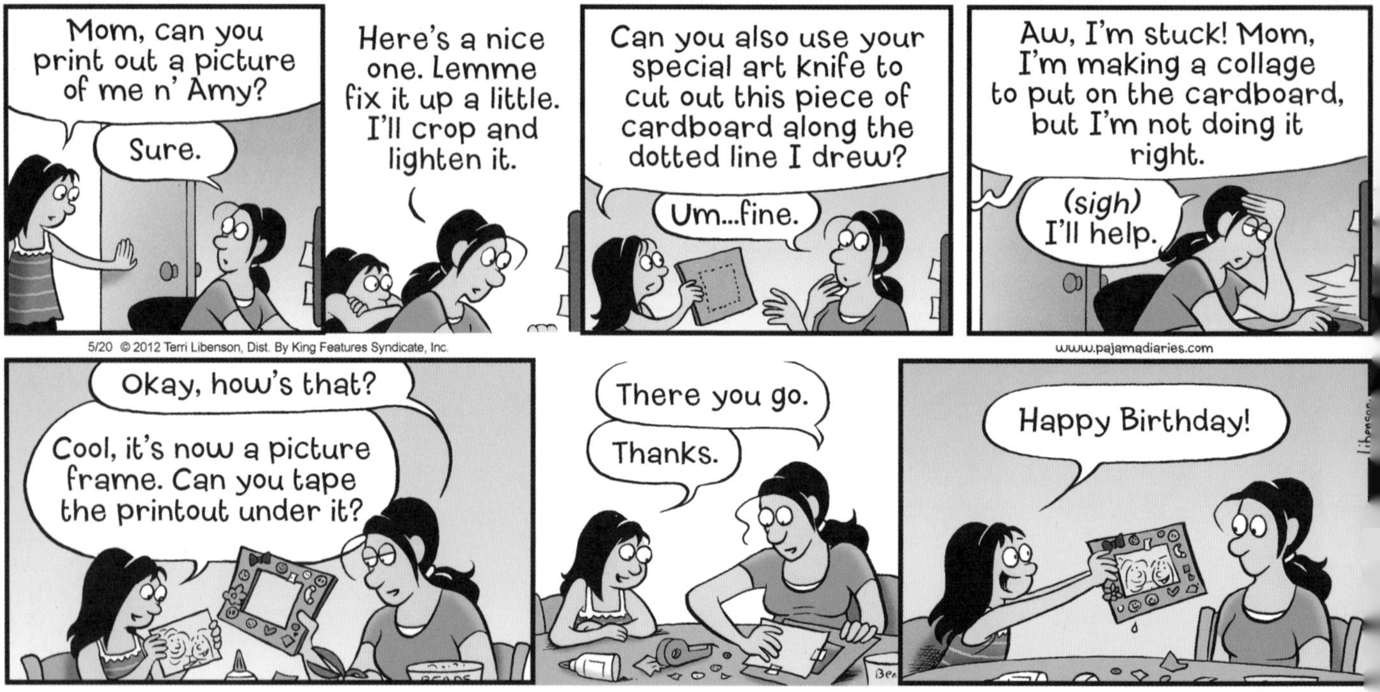
Mom, can you print out a picture of me n' Amy?
Sure.
Here's a nice one. Lemme fix it up a little. I'll crop and lighten it.
Can you also use your special art knife to cut out this piece of cardboard along the dotted line I drew?
Um...fine.
Aw, I'm stuck! Mom, I'm making a collage to put on the cardboard, but I'm not doing it right.
(sigh) I'll help.
5/20 © 2012 Terri Libenson, Dist. By King Features Syndicate, Inc.
www.pajamadiaries.com
Okay, how's that?
Cool, it's now a picture frame. Can you tape the printout under it?
There you go.
Thanks.
Happy Birthday!

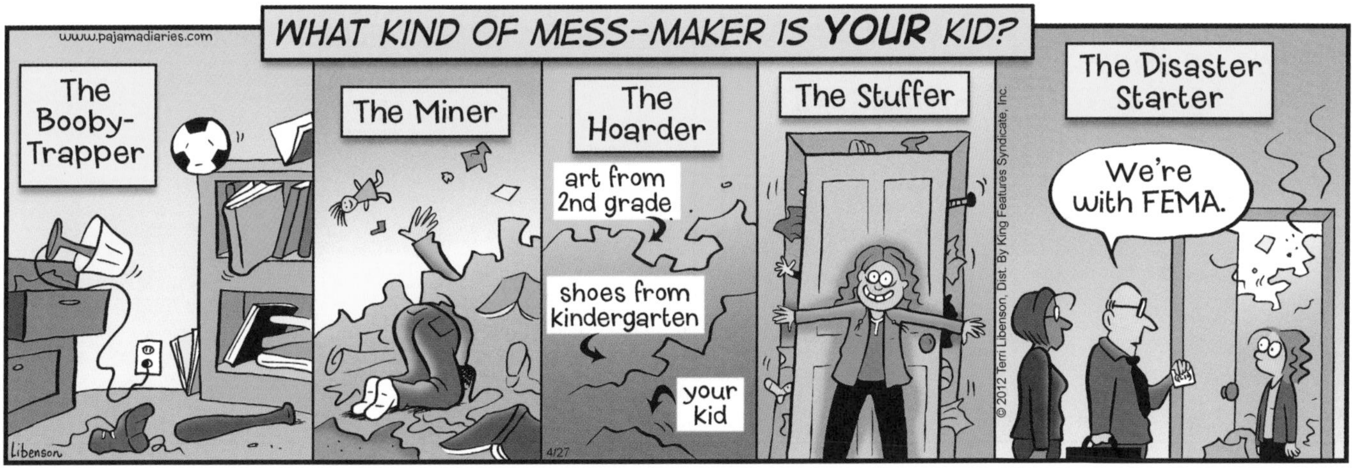
www.pajamadiaries.com
WHAT KIND OF MESS-MAKER IS YOUR KID?
The Booby-Trapper
Libenson
The Miner
The Hoarder
art from 2nd grade
shoes from kindergarten
your kid
4/27
The Stuffer
© 2012 Terri Libenson, Dist. By King Features Syndicate, Inc.
The Disaster Starter
We're with FEMA.

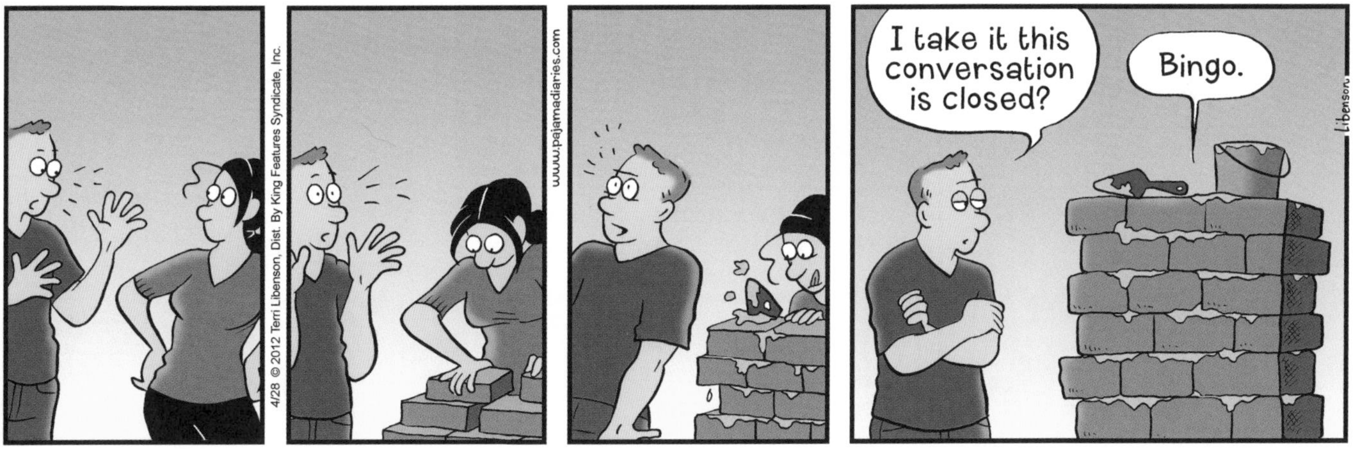
4/28 © 2012 Terri Libenson, Dist. By King Features Syndicate, Inc.
www.pajamadiaries.com
I take it this conversation is closed?
Bingo.
Libenson

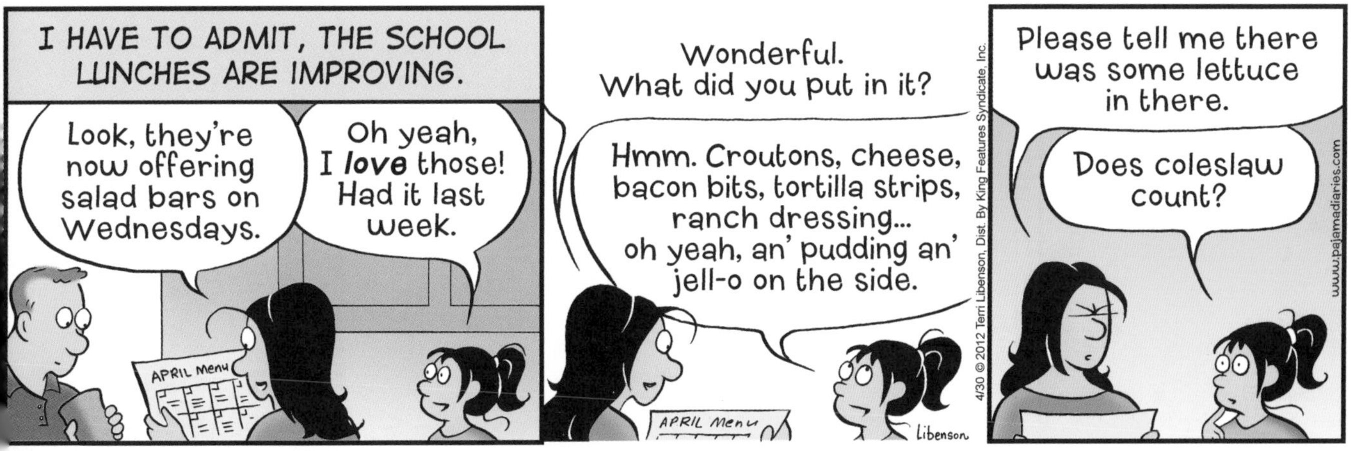
I HAVE TO ADMIT, THE SCHOOL LUNCHES ARE IMPROVING.
Look, they're now offering salad bars on Wednesdays.
Oh yeah, I *love* those! Had it last week.
APRIL Menu
Wonderful. What did you put in it?
Hmm. Croutons, cheese, bacon bits, tortilla strips, ranch dressing... oh yeah, an' pudding an' jell-o on the side.
APRIL Menu
Libenson
4/30 © 2012 Terri Libenson, Dist. By King Features Syndicate, Inc.
Please tell me there was some lettuce in there.
Does coleslaw count?
www.pajamadiaries.com

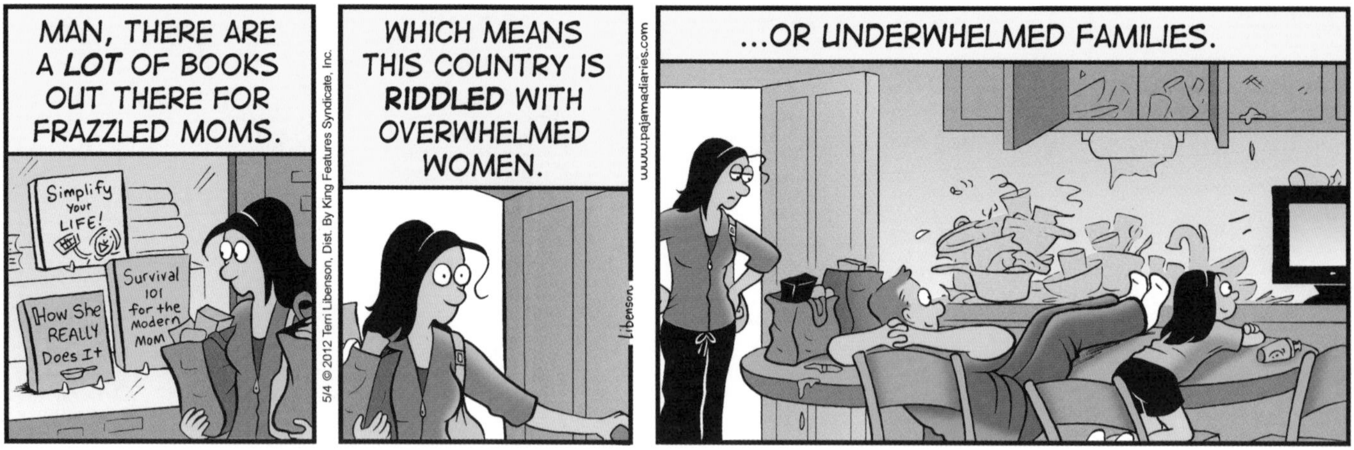
MAN, THERE ARE A LOT OF BOOKS OUT THERE FOR FRAZZLED MOMS.
Simplify Your LIFE!
How She REALLY Does It
Survival 101 for the Modern Mom
5/4 © 2012 Terri Libenson, Dist. By King Features Syndicate, Inc.
WHICH MEANS THIS COUNTRY IS RIDDLED WITH OVERWHELMED WOMEN.
www.pajamadiaries.com
Libenson
...OR UNDERWHELMED FAMILIES.

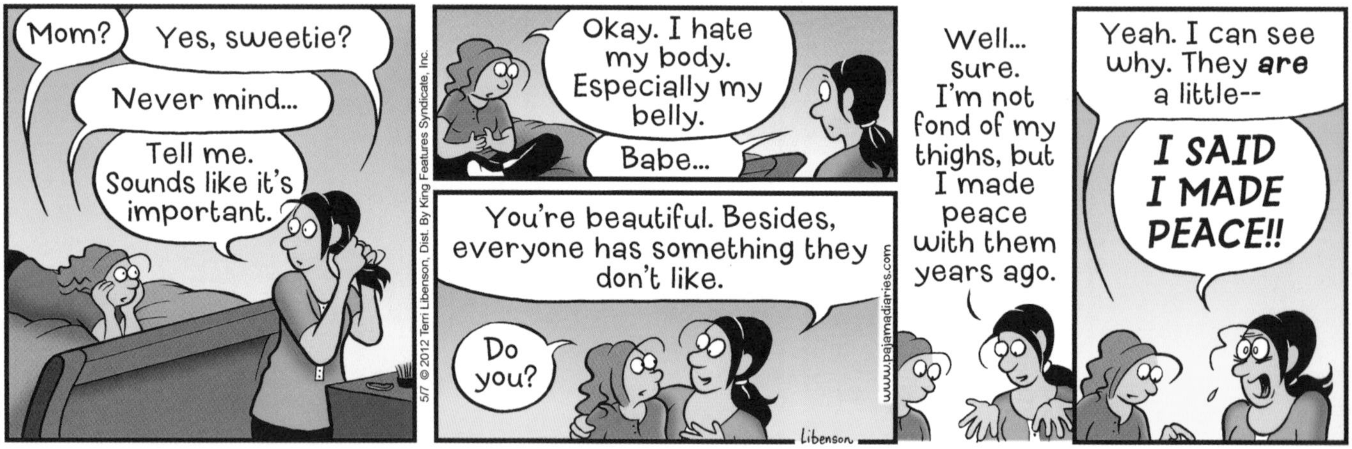
Mom?
Yes, sweetie?
Never mind...
Tell me. Sounds like it's important.
5/7 © 2012 Terri Libenson, Dist. By King Features Syndicate, Inc.
Okay. I hate my body. Especially my belly.
Babe...
You're beautiful. Besides, everyone has something they don't like.
Do you?
www.pajamadiaries.com
Libenson
Well... sure. I'm not fond of my thighs, but I made peace with them years ago.
Yeah. I can see why. They are a little--
I SAID I MADE PEACE!!

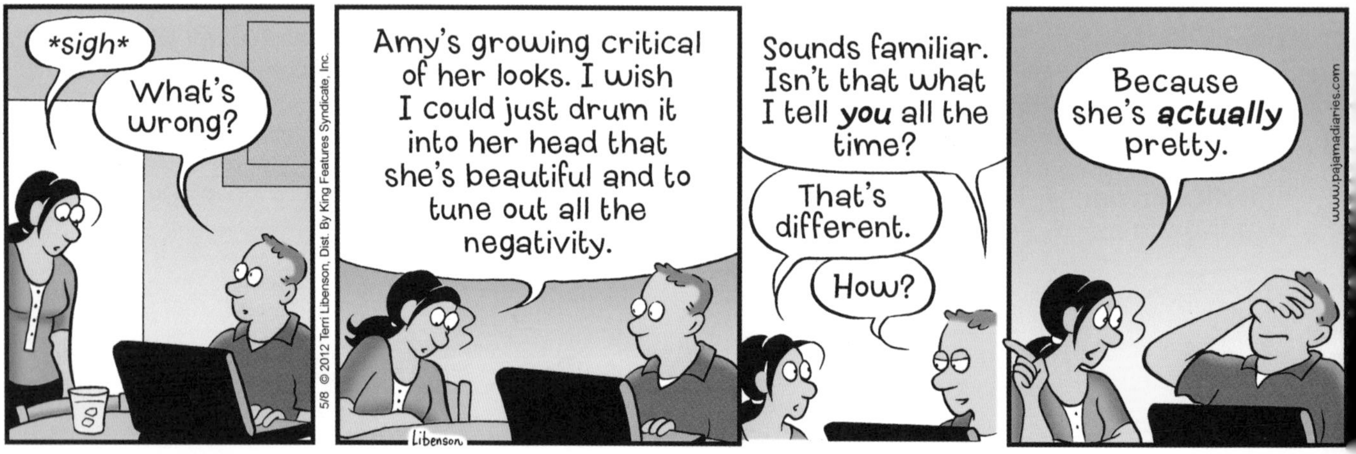
sigh
What's wrong?
5/8 © 2012 Terri Libenson, Dist. By King Features Syndicate, Inc.
Amy's growing critical of her looks. I wish I could just drum it into her head that she's beautiful and to tune out all the negativity.
Libenson
Sounds familiar. Isn't that what I tell you all the time?
That's different.
How?
Because she's actually pretty.
www.pajamadiaries.com

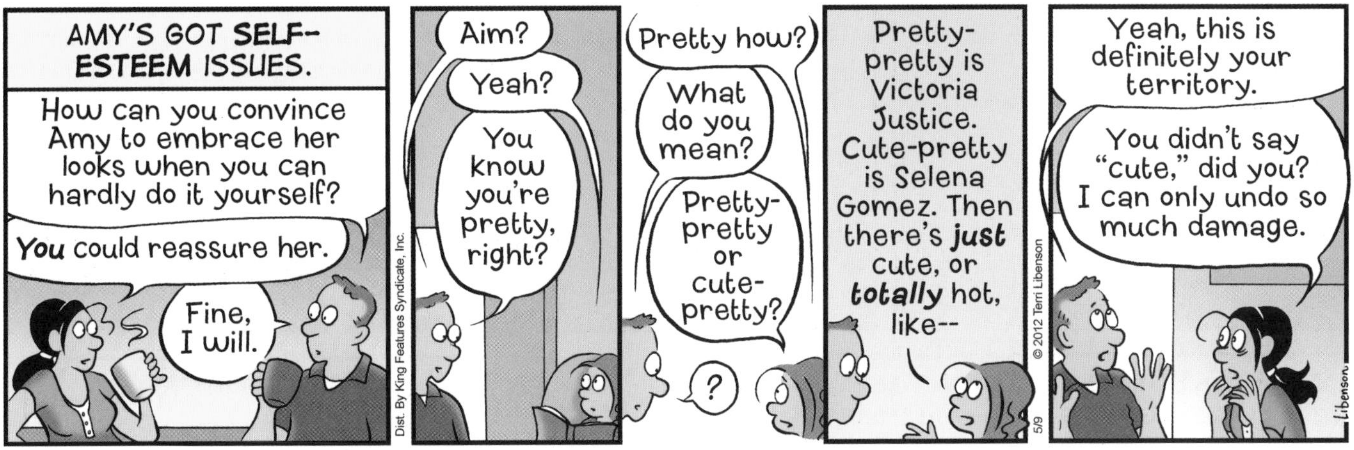
AMY'S GOT **SELF-ESTEEM** ISSUES.
How can you convince Amy to embrace her looks when you can hardly do it yourself?
You could reassure her.
Fine, I will.
Dist. By King Features Syndicate, Inc.
Aim?
Yeah?
You know you're pretty, right?
Pretty how?
What do you mean?
Pretty-pretty or cute-pretty?
?
Pretty-pretty is Victoria Justice. Cute-pretty is Selena Gomez. Then there's ***just*** cute, or ***totally*** hot, like--
© 2012 Terri Libenson
5/9
Yeah, this is definitely your territory.
You didn't say "cute," did you? I can only undo so much damage.
Libenson

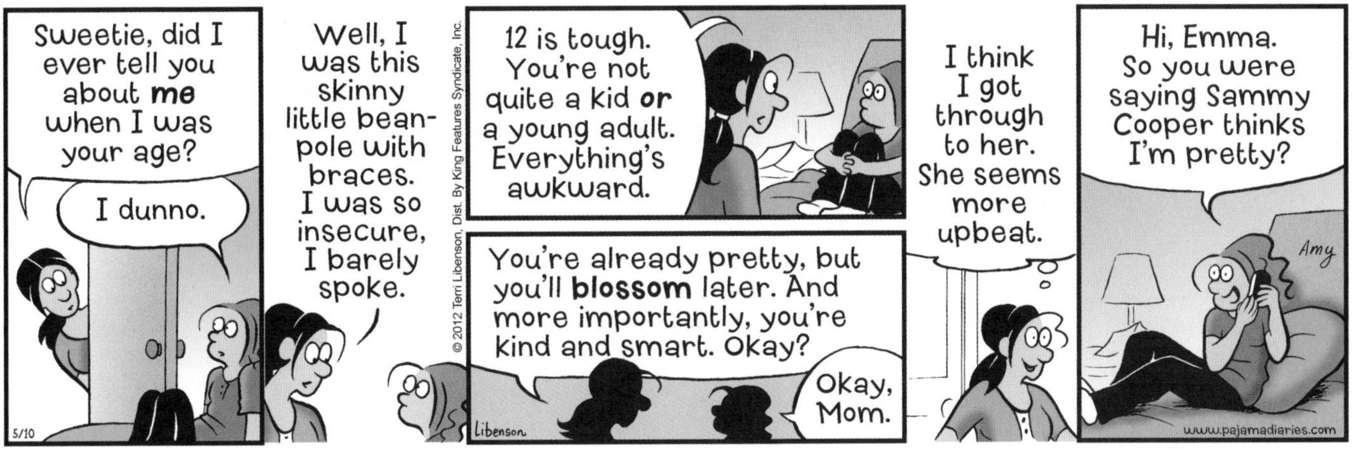
Sweetie, did I ever tell you about **me** when I was your age?
I dunno.
5/10
Well, I was this skinny little bean-pole with braces. I was so insecure, I barely spoke.
© 2012 Terri Libenson, Dist. By King Features Syndicate, Inc.
12 is tough. You're not quite a kid ***or*** a young adult. Everything's awkward.
You're already pretty, but you'll **blossom** later. And more importantly, you're kind and smart. Okay?
Okay, Mom.
Libenson
I think I got through to her. She seems more upbeat.
Hi, Emma. So you were saying Sammy Cooper thinks I'm pretty?
Amy
www.pajamadiaries.com

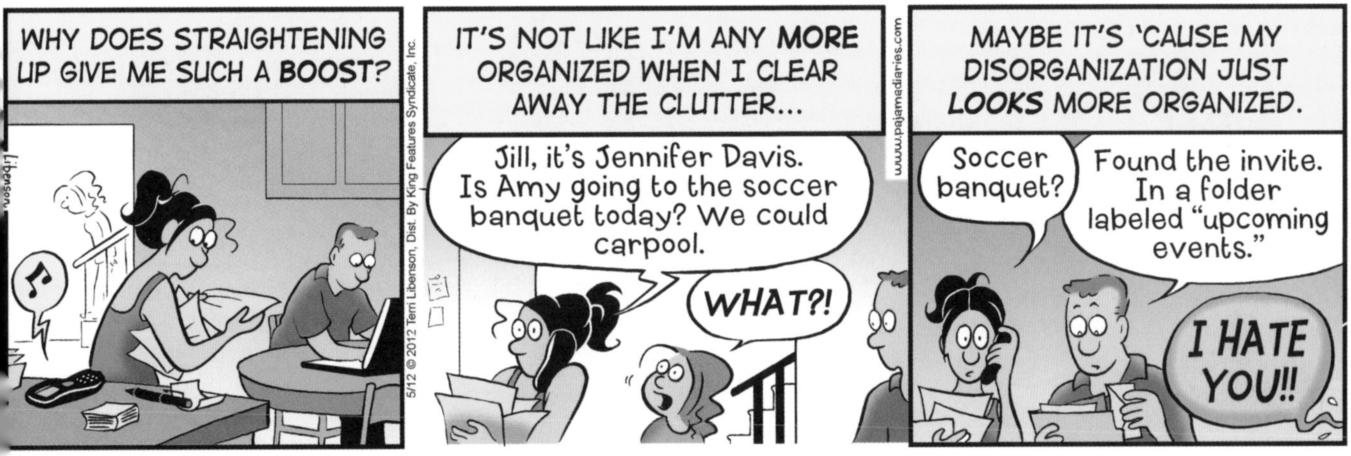
WHY DOES STRAIGHTENING UP GIVE ME SUCH A **BOOST**?
Libenson
5/12 © 2012 Terri Libenson, Dist. By King Features Syndicate, Inc.
IT'S NOT LIKE I'M ANY **MORE** ORGANIZED WHEN I CLEAR AWAY THE CLUTTER...
Jill, it's Jennifer Davis. Is Amy going to the soccer banquet today? We could carpool.
WHAT?!
www.pajamadiaries.com
MAYBE IT'S 'CAUSE MY DISORGANIZATION JUST ***LOOKS*** MORE ORGANIZED.
Soccer banquet?
Found the invite. In a folder labeled "upcoming events."
I HATE YOU!!

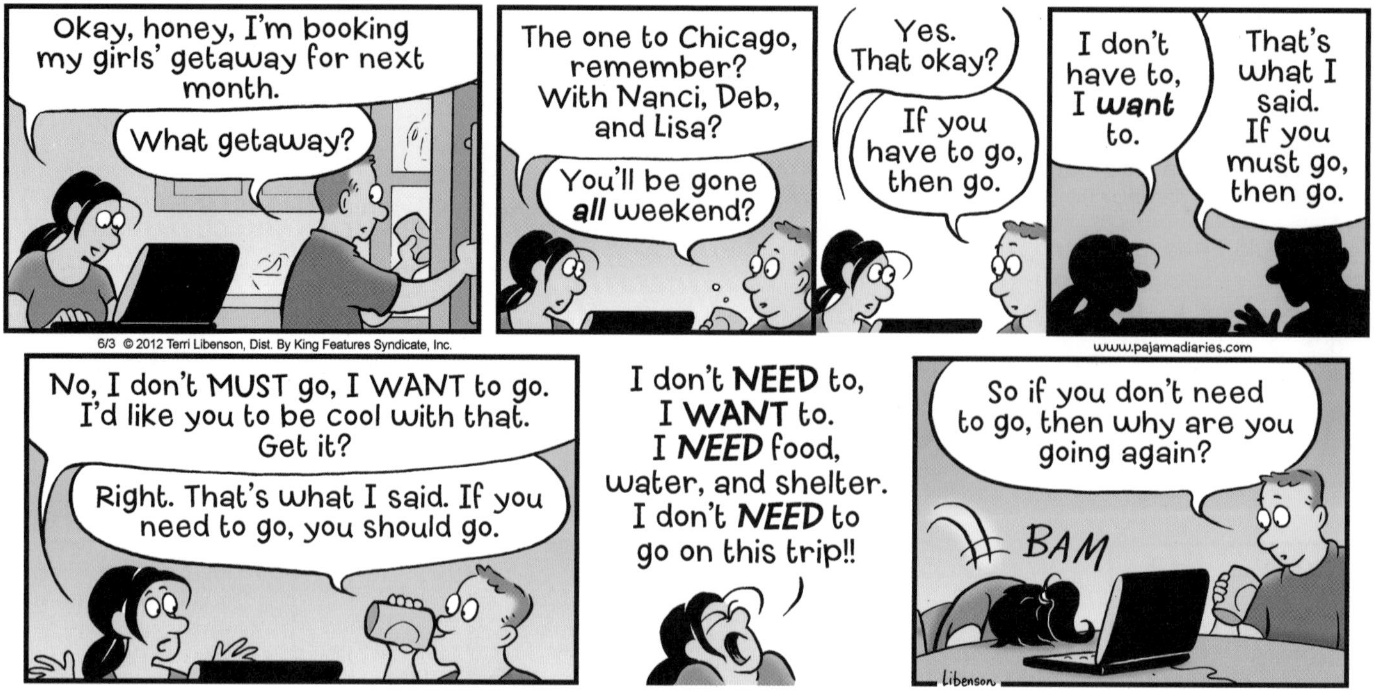
Okay, honey, I'm booking my girls' getaway for next month.
What getaway?
The one to Chicago, remember? With Nanci, Deb, and Lisa?
You'll be gone **all** weekend?
Yes. That okay?
If you have to go, then go.
I don't have to, I ***want*** to.
That's what I said. If you must go, then go.
6/3 © 2012 Terri Libenson, Dist. By King Features Syndicate, Inc.
www.pajamadiaries.com
No, I don't MUST go, I WANT to go. I'd like you to be cool with that. Get it?
Right. That's what I said. If you need to go, you should go.
I don't **NEED** to, I **WANT** to. I **NEED** food, water, and shelter. I don't **NEED** to go on this trip!!
So if you don't need to go, then why are you going again?
BAM
Libenson

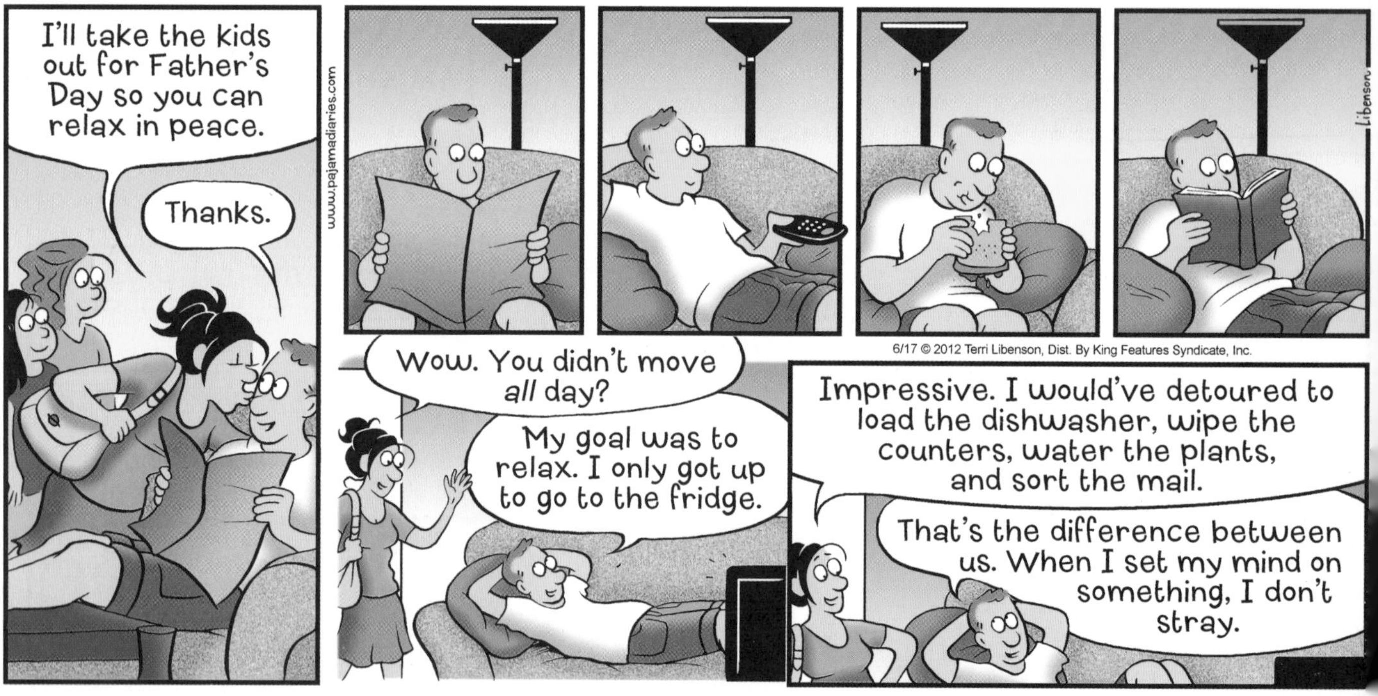
I'll take the kids out for Father's Day so you can relax in peace.
Thanks.
www.pajamadiaries.com
Libenson
6/17 © 2012 Terri Libenson, Dist. By King Features Syndicate, Inc.
Wow. You didn't move *all* day?
My goal was to relax. I only got up to go to the fridge.
Impressive. I would've detoured to load the dishwasher, wipe the counters, water the plants, and sort the mail.
That's the difference between us. When I set my mind on something, I don't stray.

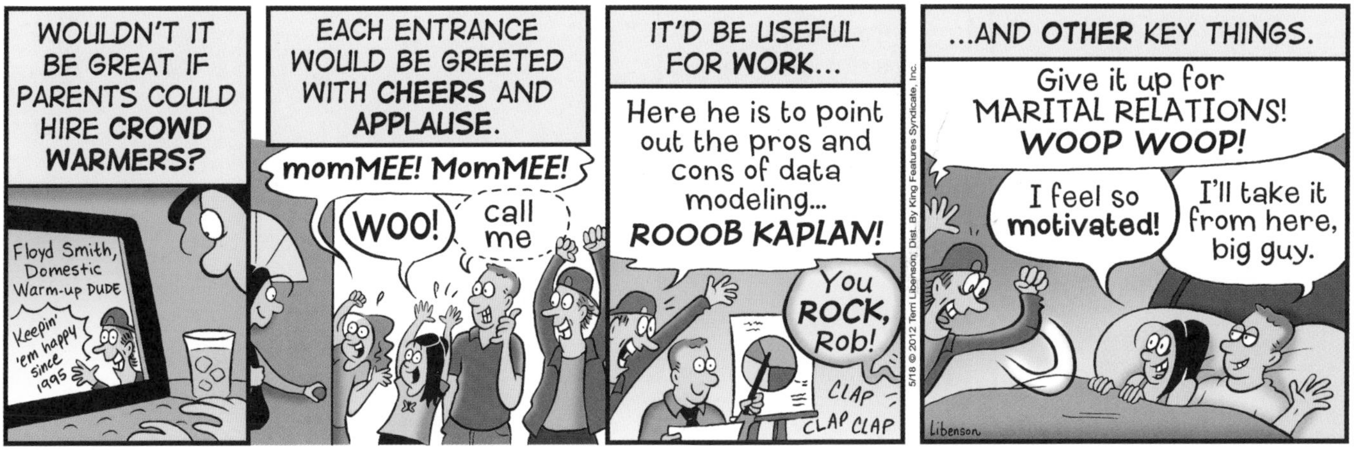
WOULDN'T IT BE GREAT IF PARENTS COULD HIRE CROWD WARMERS?
Floyd Smith, Domestic Warm-up DUDE
Keepin' 'em happy since 1995
EACH ENTRANCE WOULD BE GREETED WITH CHEERS AND APPLAUSE.
momMEE! MomMEE!
WOO!
call me
IT'D BE USEFUL FOR WORK...
Here he is to point out the pros and cons of data modeling... ROOOB KAPLAN!
You ROCK, Rob!
CLAP CLAP CLAP
5/18 © 2012 Terri Libenson, Dist. By King Features Syndicate, Inc.
...AND OTHER KEY THINGS.
Give it up for MARITAL RELATIONS! WOOP WOOP!
I feel so motivated!
I'll take it from here, big guy.
Libenson

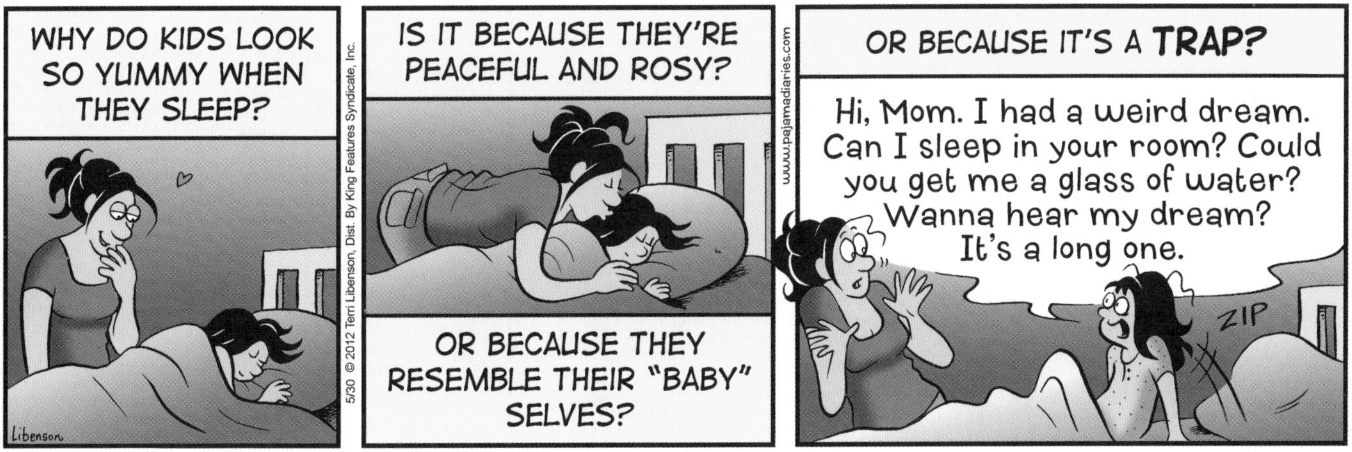
WHY DO KIDS LOOK SO YUMMY WHEN THEY SLEEP?
Libenson
5/30 © 2012 Terri Libenson, Dist. By King Features Syndicate, Inc.
IS IT BECAUSE THEY'RE PEACEFUL AND ROSY?
OR BECAUSE THEY RESEMBLE THEIR "BABY" SELVES?
www.pajamadiaries.com
OR BECAUSE IT'S A TRAP?
Hi, Mom. I had a weird dream. Can I sleep in your room? Could you get me a glass of water? Wanna hear my dream? It's a long one.
ZIP

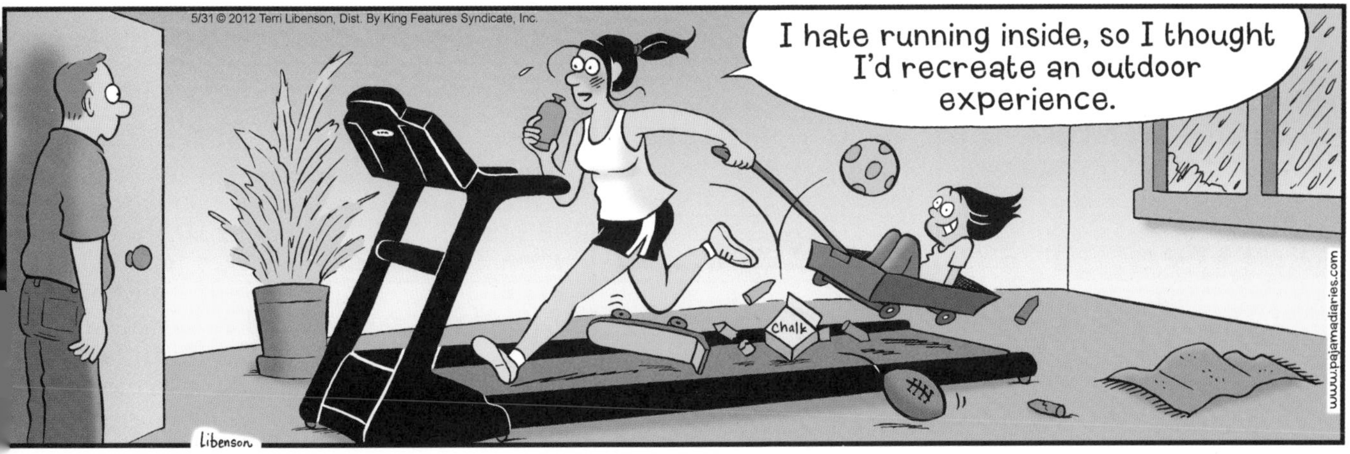
5/31 © 2012 Terri Libenson, Dist. By King Features Syndicate, Inc.
I hate running inside, so I thought I'd recreate an outdoor experience.
Chalk
www.pajamadiaries.com
Libenson

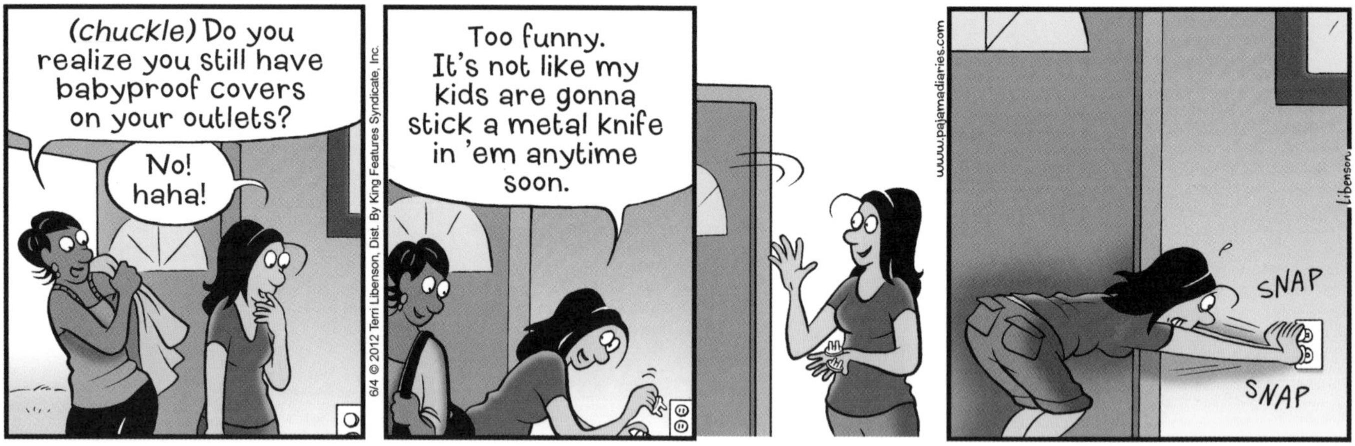
(chuckle) Do you realize you still have babyproof covers on your outlets?
No! haha!
6/4 © 2012 Terri Libenson, Dist. By King Features Syndicate, Inc.
Too funny. It's not like my kids are gonna stick a metal knife in 'em anytime soon.
www.pajamadiaries.com
SNAP
SNAP
Libenson

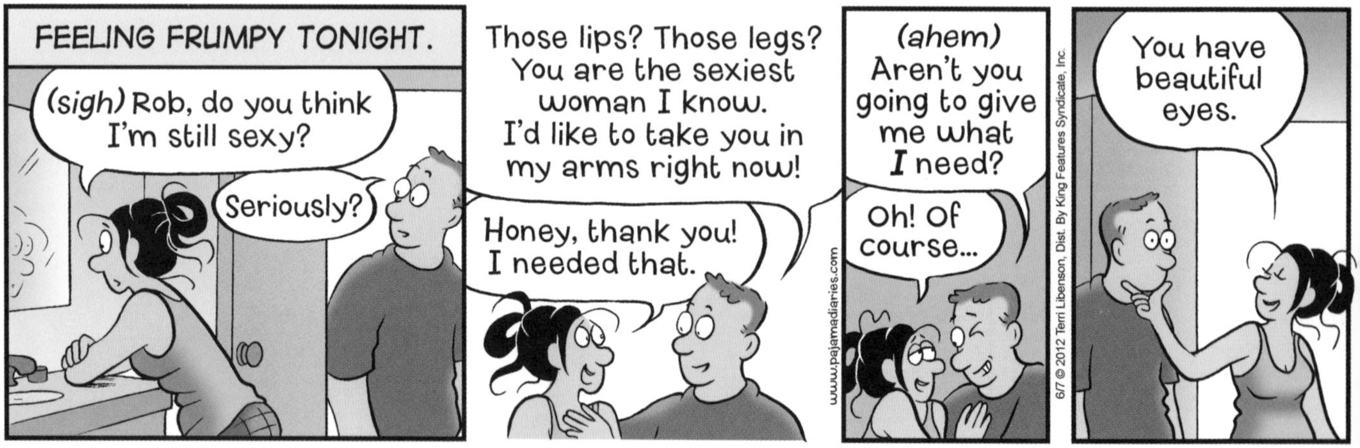
FEELING FRUMPY TONIGHT.
(sigh) Rob, do you think I'm still sexy?
Seriously?
Those lips? Those legs? You are the sexiest woman I know. I'd like to take you in my arms right now!
Honey, thank you! I needed that.
www.pajamadiaries.com
(ahem) Aren't you going to give me what I need?
Oh! Of course...
6/7 © 2012 Terri Libenson, Dist. By King Features Syndicate, Inc.
You have beautiful eyes.

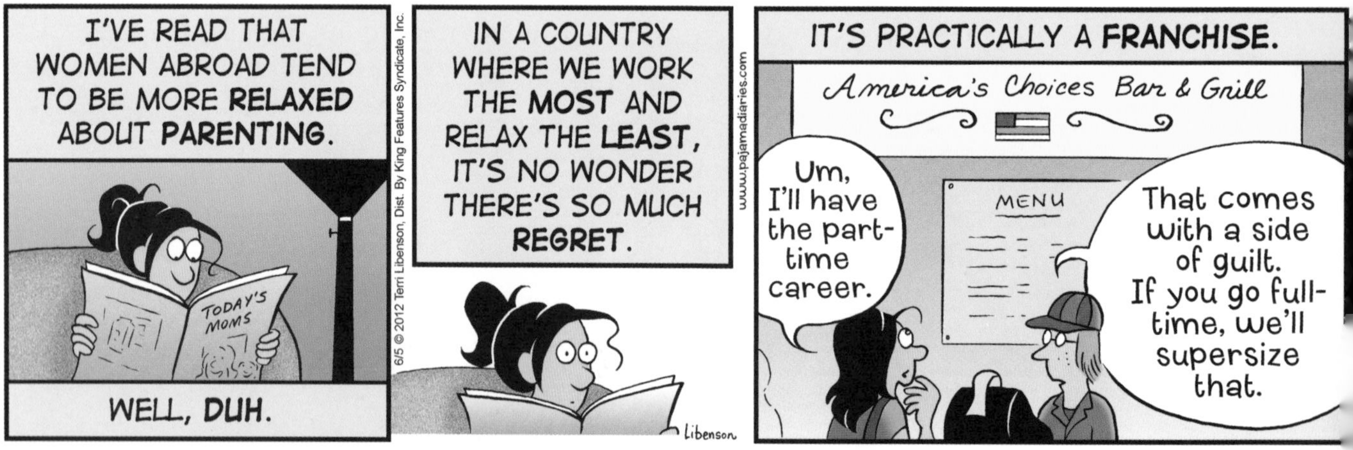
I'VE READ THAT WOMEN ABROAD TEND TO BE MORE RELAXED ABOUT PARENTING.
TODAY'S MOMS
WELL, DUH.
6/5 © 2012 Terri Libenson, Dist. By King Features Syndicate, Inc.
IN A COUNTRY WHERE WE WORK THE MOST AND RELAX THE LEAST, IT'S NO WONDER THERE'S SO MUCH REGRET.
Libenson
www.pajamadiaries.com
IT'S PRACTICALLY A FRANCHISE.
America's Choices Bar & Grill
MENU
Um, I'll have the part-time career.
That comes with a side of guilt. If you go full-time, we'll supersize that.

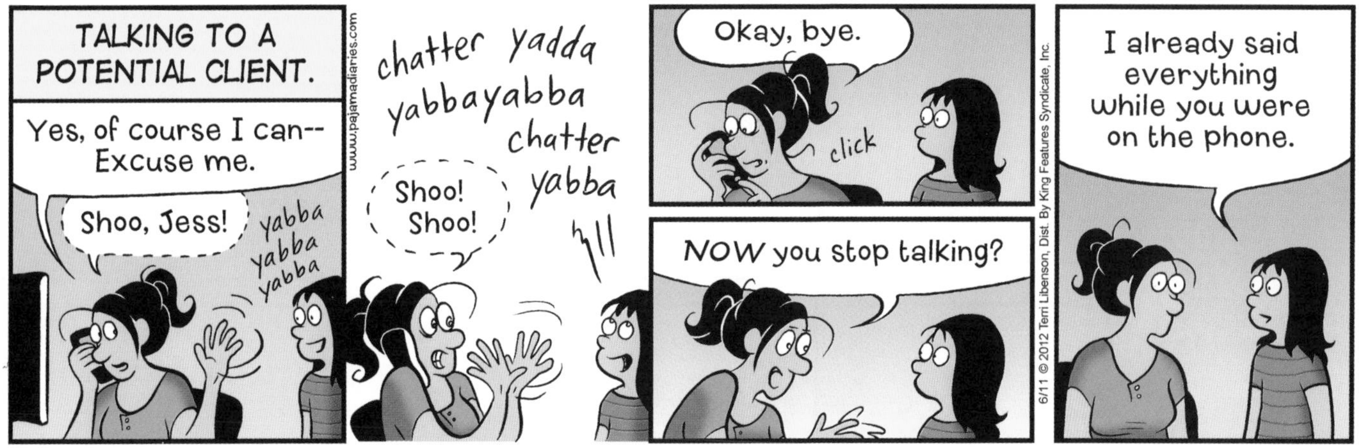
TALKING TO A POTENTIAL CLIENT.
Yes, of course I can-- Excuse me.
Shoo, Jess!
yabba yabba yabba
www.pajamadiaries.com
chatter yadda yabbayabba chatter yabba
Shoo! Shoo!
Okay, bye.
click
NOW you stop talking?
6/11 © 2012 Terri Libenson, Dist. By King Features Syndicate, Inc.
I already said everything while you were on the phone.

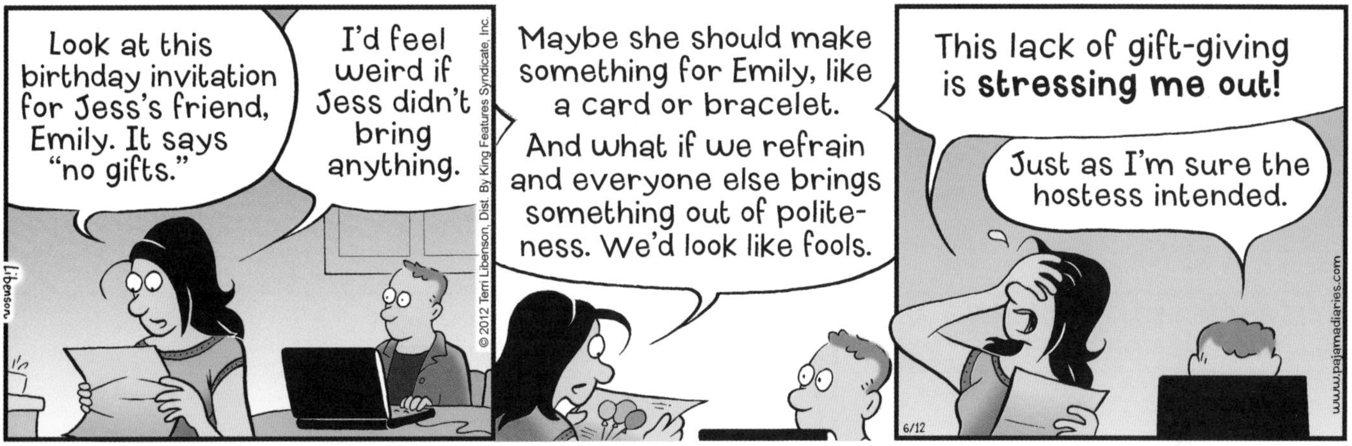
Look at this birthday invitation for Jess's friend, Emily. It says "no gifts."
I'd feel weird if Jess didn't bring anything.
Libenson
© 2012 Terri Libenson, Dist. By King Features Syndicate, Inc.
Maybe she should make something for Emily, like a card or bracelet.
And what if we refrain and everyone else brings something out of politeness. We'd look like fools.
This lack of gift-giving is **stressing me out!**
Just as I'm sure the hostess intended.
6/12
www.pajamadiaries.com

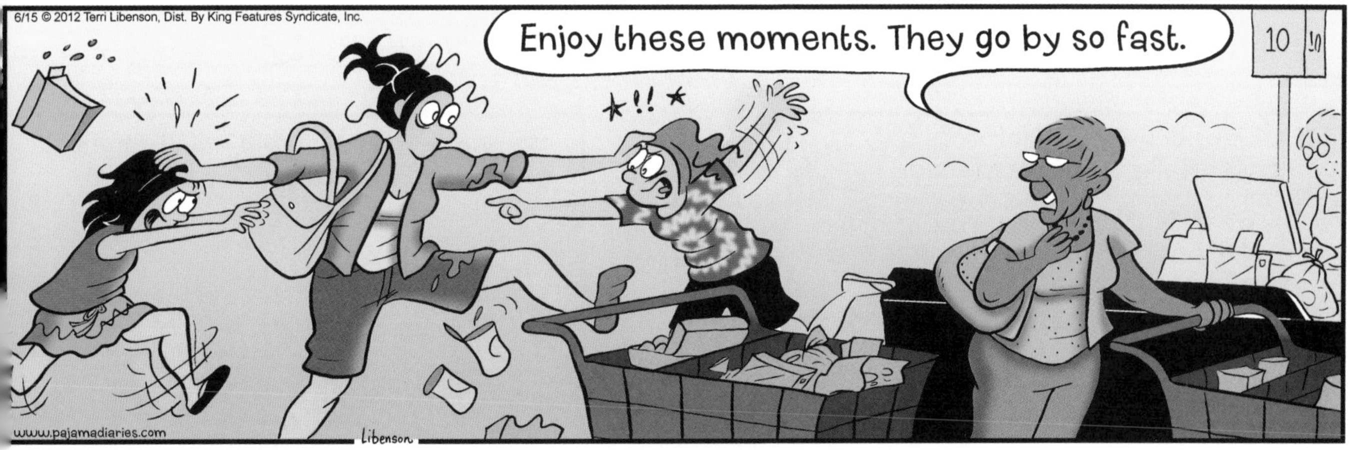
6/15 © 2012 Terri Libenson, Dist. By King Features Syndicate, Inc.
Enjoy these moments. They go by so fast.
10
www.pajamadiaries.com
Libenson

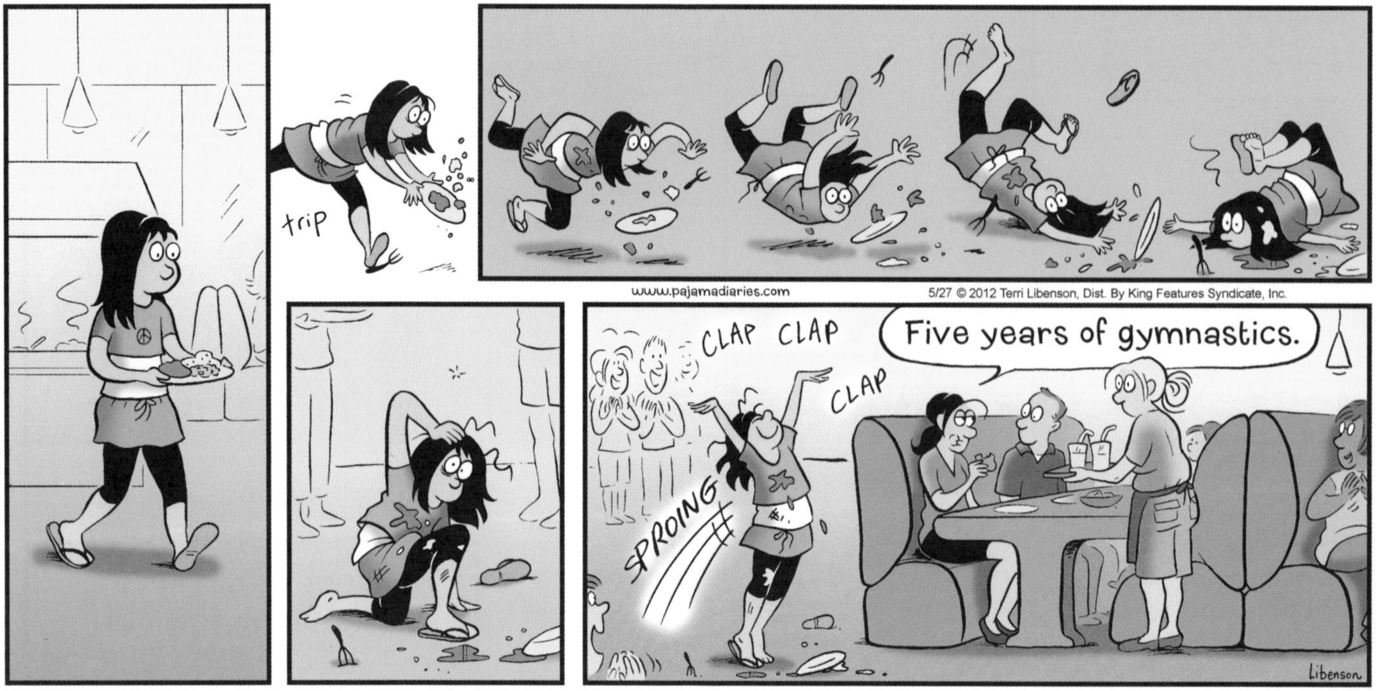
trip
www.pajamadiaries.com
5/27 © 2012 Terri Libenson, Dist. By King Features Syndicate, Inc.
CLAP CLAP
CLAP
SPROING
Five years of gymnastics.
Libenson

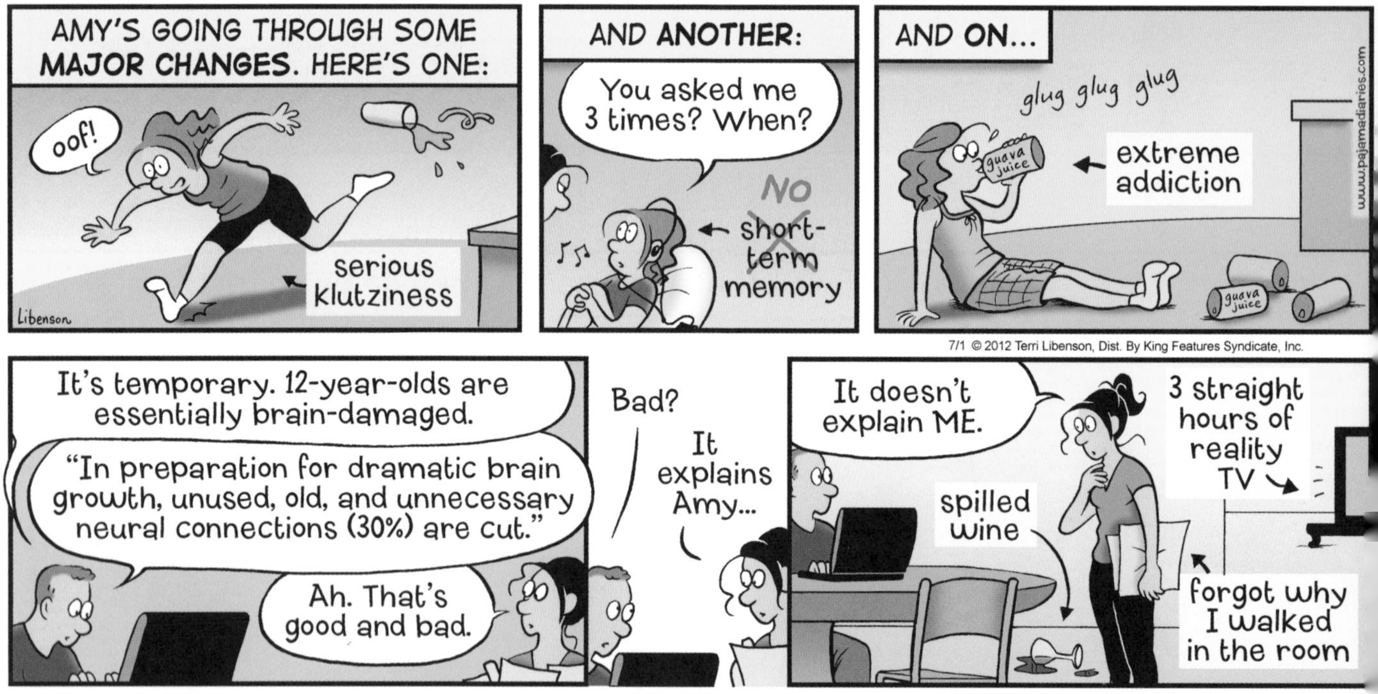
AMY'S GOING THROUGH SOME MAJOR CHANGES. HERE'S ONE:
oof!
serious klutziness
Libenson
AND ANOTHER:
You asked me 3 times? When?
~~short-~~ NO term memory
AND ON...
glug glug glug
guava juice
extreme addiction
guava juice
www.pajamadiaries.com
7/1 © 2012 Terri Libenson, Dist. By King Features Syndicate, Inc.
It's temporary. 12-year-olds are essentially brain-damaged.
"In preparation for dramatic brain growth, unused, old, and unnecessary neural connections (30%) are cut."
Ah. That's good and bad.
Bad?
It explains Amy...
It doesn't explain ME.
3 straight hours of reality TV
spilled wine
forgot why I walked in the room

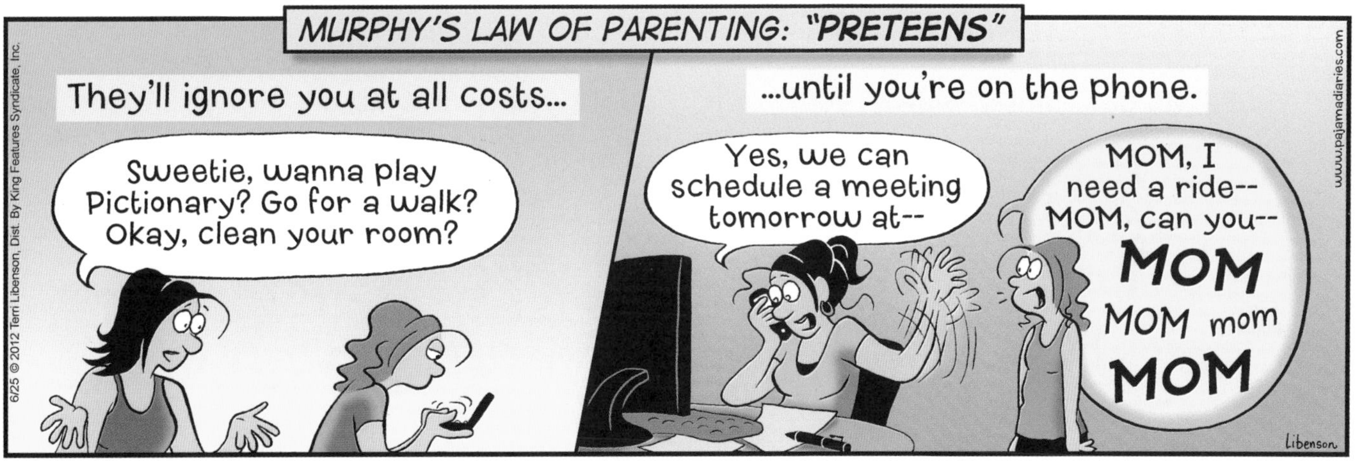
MURPHY'S LAW OF PARENTING: "PRETEENS"
They'll ignore you at all costs...
Sweetie, wanna play Pictionary? Go for a walk? Okay, clean your room?
...until you're on the phone.
Yes, we can schedule a meeting tomorrow at--
MOM, I need a ride-- MOM, can you-- MOM MOM mom MOM
6/25 © 2012 Terri Libenson, Dist. By King Features Syndicate, Inc.
www.pajamadiaries.com
Libenson

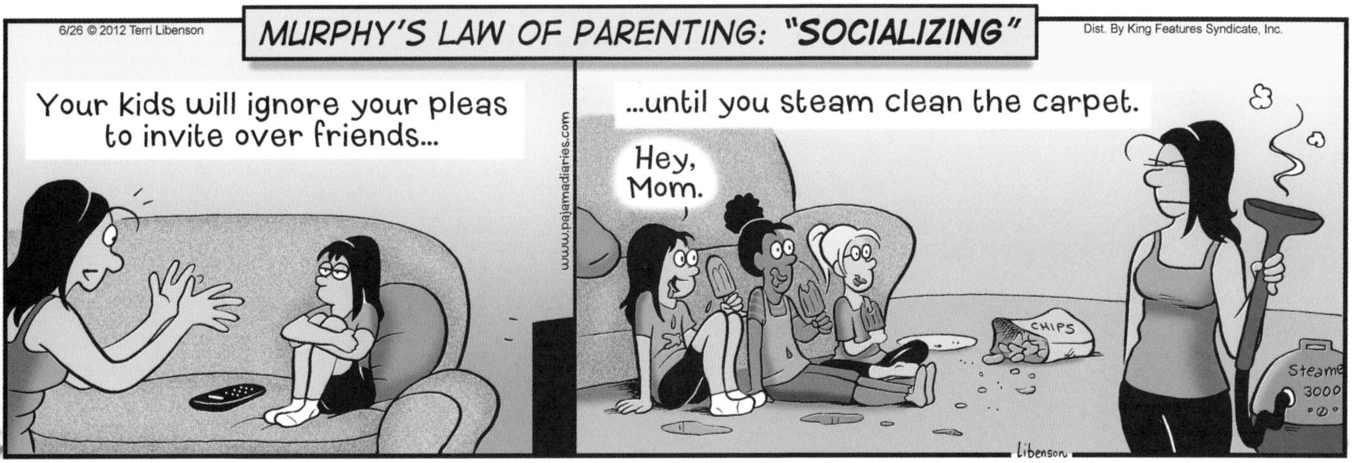
6/26 © 2012 Terri Libenson
MURPHY'S LAW OF PARENTING: "SOCIALIZING"
Dist. By King Features Syndicate, Inc.
Your kids will ignore your pleas to invite over friends...
www.pajamadiaries.com
...until you steam clean the carpet.
Hey, Mom.
CHIPS
Steame 3000
Libenson

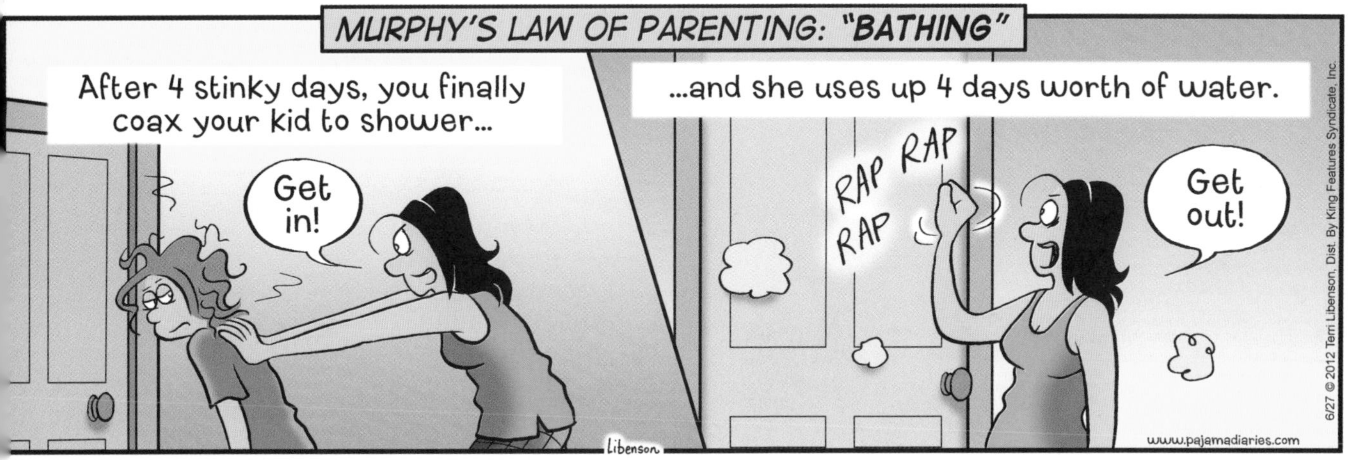
MURPHY'S LAW OF PARENTING: "BATHING"
After 4 stinky days, you finally coax your kid to shower...
Get in!
...and she uses up 4 days worth of water.
RAP RAP RAP
Get out!
6/27 © 2012 Terri Libenson, Dist. By King Features Syndicate, Inc.
www.pajamadiaries.com
Libenson

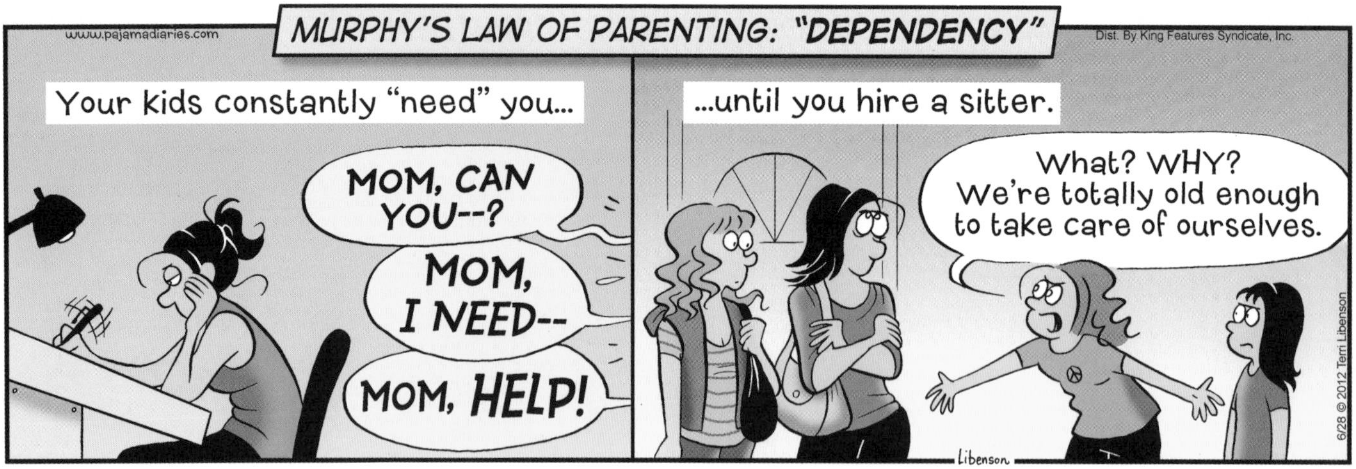
MURPHY'S LAW OF PARENTING: "DEPENDENCY"
www.pajamadiaries.com
Dist. By King Features Syndicate, Inc.
Your kids constantly "need" you...
MOM, CAN YOU--?
MOM, I NEED--
MOM, HELP!
...until you hire a sitter.
What? WHY? We're totally old enough to take care of ourselves.
Libenson
6/28 © 2012 Terri Libenson

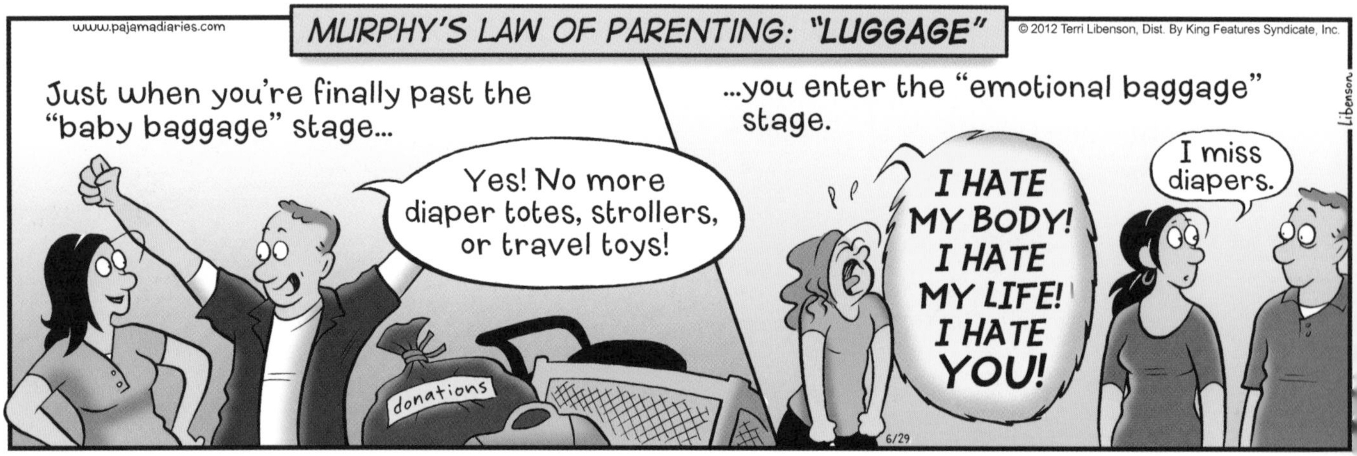
MURPHY'S LAW OF PARENTING: "LUGGAGE"
www.pajamadiaries.com
© 2012 Terri Libenson, Dist. By King Features Syndicate, Inc.
Just when you're finally past the "baby baggage" stage...
Yes! No more diaper totes, strollers, or travel toys!
donations
...you enter the "emotional baggage" stage.
I HATE MY BODY! I HATE MY LIFE! I HATE YOU!
I miss diapers.
Libenson
6/29

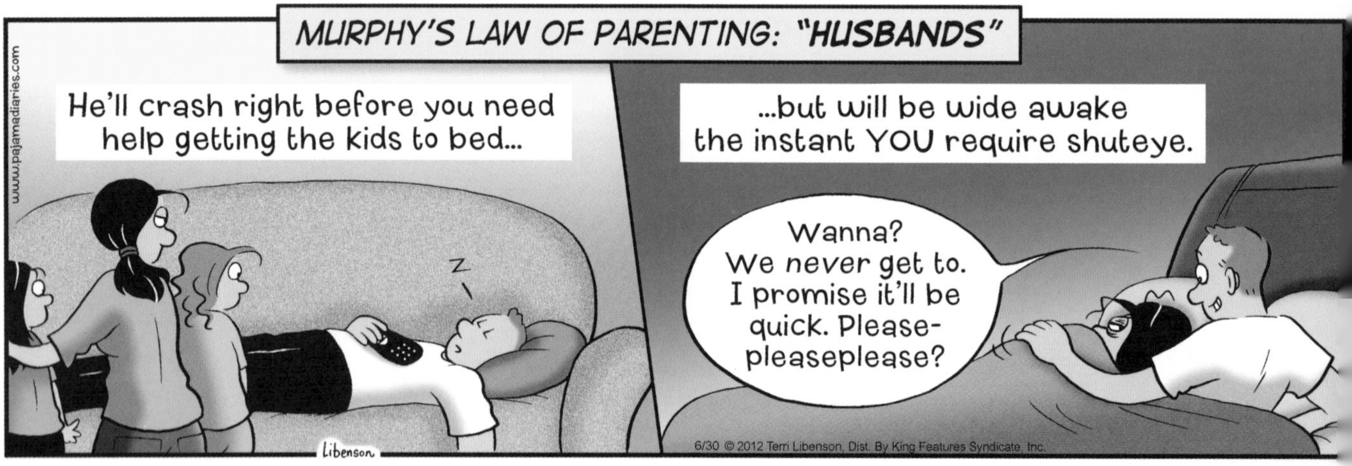
MURPHY'S LAW OF PARENTING: "HUSBANDS"
www.pajamadiaries.com
He'll crash right before you need help getting the kids to bed...
Z
...but will be wide awake the instant YOU require shuteye.
Wanna? We *never* get to. I promise it'll be quick. Please-pleaseplease?
Libenson
6/30 © 2012 Terri Libenson, Dist. By King Features Syndicate, Inc.

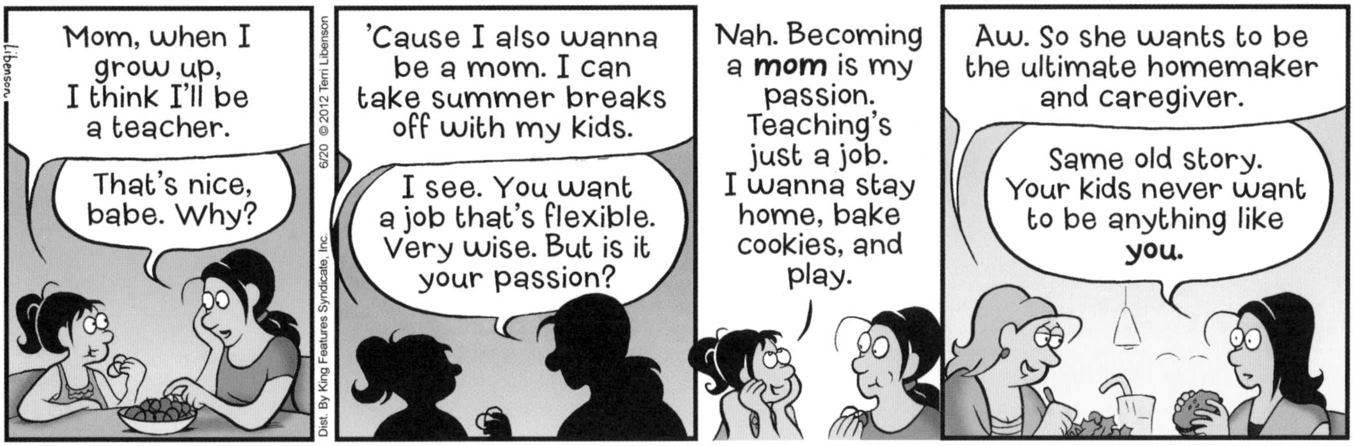
Mom, when I grow up, I think I'll be a teacher.
That's nice, babe. Why?
6/20 © 2012 Terri Libenson
Dist. By King Features Syndicate, Inc.
'Cause I also wanna be a mom. I can take summer breaks off with my kids.
I see. You want a job that's flexible. Very wise. But is it your passion?
Nah. Becoming a **mom** is my passion. Teaching's just a job. I wanna stay home, bake cookies, and play.
Aw. So she wants to be the ultimate homemaker and caregiver.
Same old story. Your kids never want to be anything like **you.**

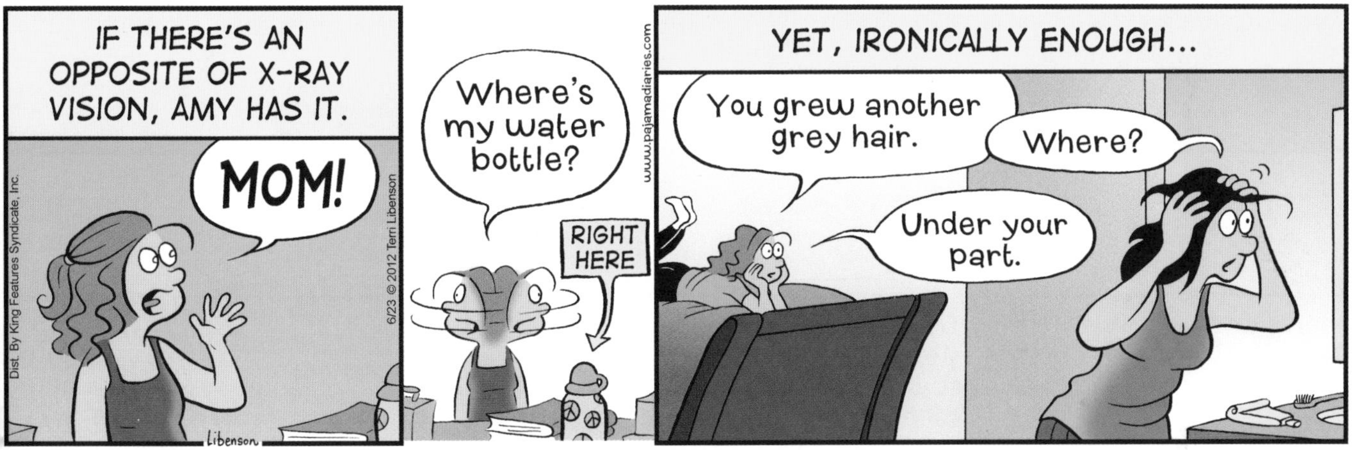
IF THERE'S AN OPPOSITE OF X-RAY VISION, AMY HAS IT.
MOM!
Libenson
Dist. By King Features Syndicate, Inc.
6/23 © 2012 Terri Libenson
Where's my water bottle?
RIGHT HERE
www.pajamadiaries.com
YET, IRONICALLY ENOUGH...
You grew another grey hair.
Where?
Under your part.

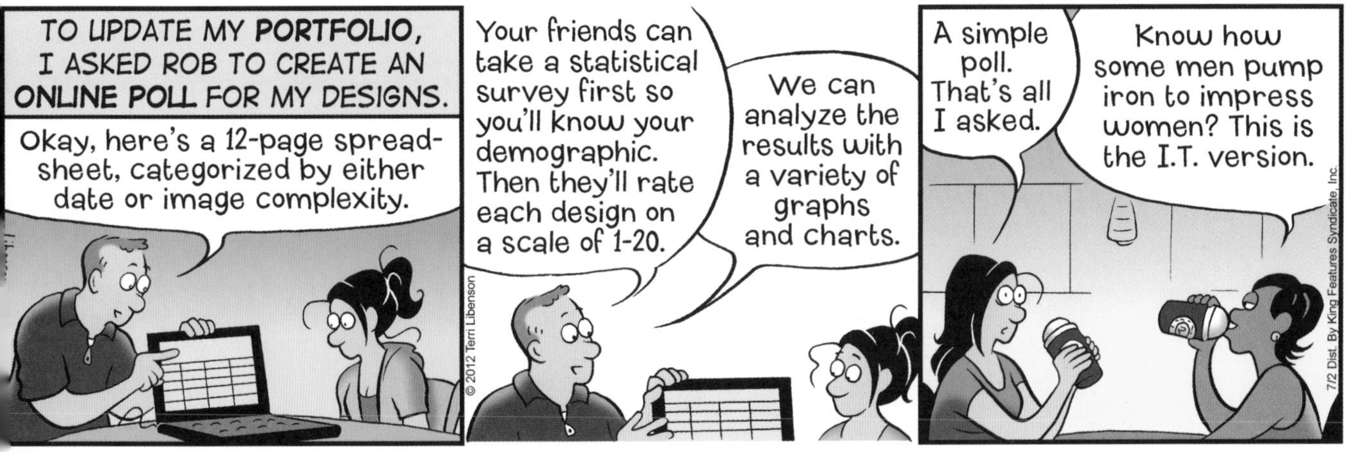
TO UPDATE MY **PORTFOLIO**, I ASKED ROB TO CREATE AN **ONLINE POLL** FOR MY DESIGNS.
Okay, here's a 12-page spread-sheet, categorized by either date or image complexity.
Your friends can take a statistical survey first so you'll know your demographic. Then they'll rate each design on a scale of 1-20.
© 2012 Terri Libenson
We can analyze the results with a variety of graphs and charts.
A simple poll. That's all I asked.
Know how some men pump iron to impress women? This is the I.T. version.
7/2 Dist. By King Features Syndicate, Inc.

The **head bone**'s connected to the **neck bone**...
The **neck bone**'s connected to the **shoulder bone**...
The **shoulder bone**'s connected to the **arm bone**...
The **arm bone**'s connected to the **laundry bone**...
The **laundry bone**'s connected to the **hip bone**...
7/22
Libenson
© 2012 Terri Libenson, Dist. By King Features Syndicate, Inc.
There's no laundry bone, Mom.
Really? It feels like such a part of me.
www.pajamadiaries.com

Mom, can you take us to see "Stampede 2" at the movies?
Hmm. Lemme do some research to make sure it's not too violent.
www.pajamadiaries.com
newspaper critic
online parent review
friend's opinion
Libenson
Okay, all clean.
YES!!
© 2012 Terri Libenson, Dist. By King Features Syndicate, Inc.
preview
BANGBANG
POW
OOF!!

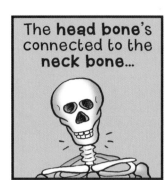

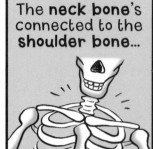

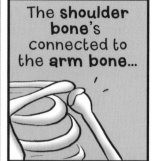

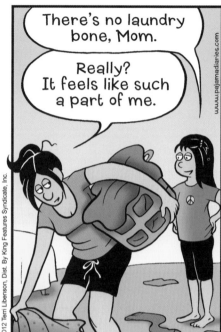

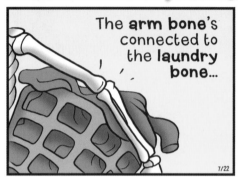

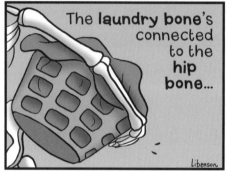

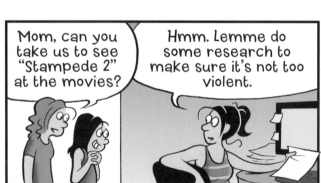

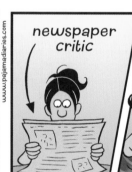

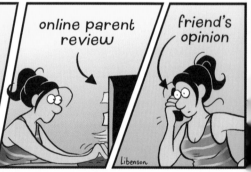

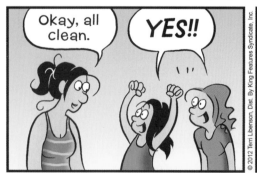

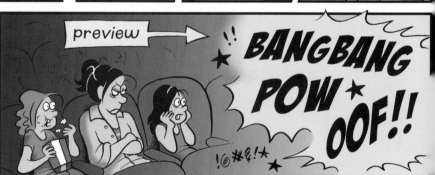

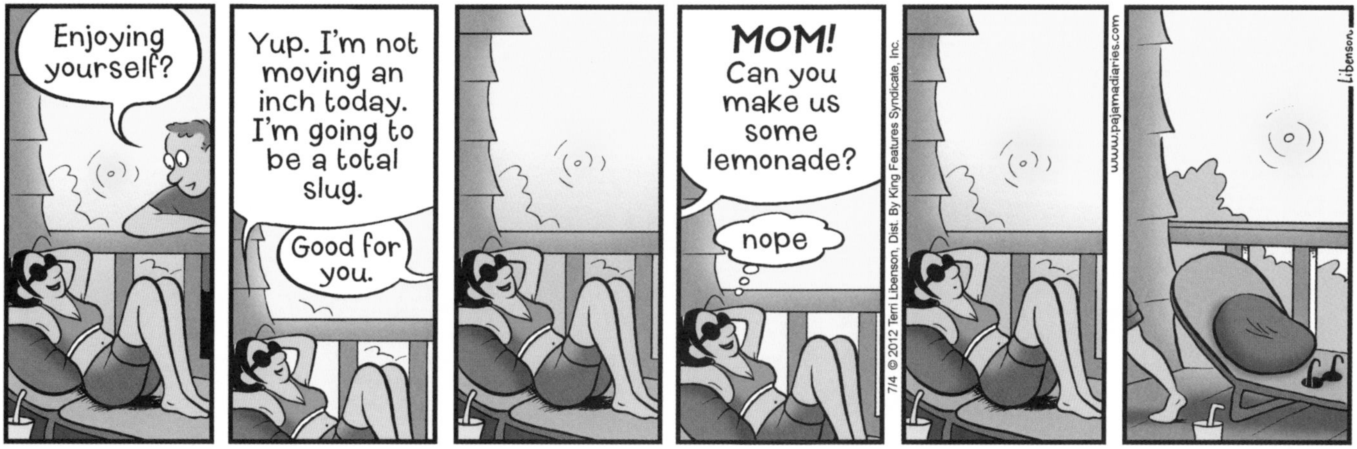
Enjoying yourself?
Yup. I'm not moving an inch today. I'm going to be a total slug.
Good for you.
MOM! Can you make us some lemonade?
nope
7/4 © 2012 Terri Libenson, Dist. By King Features Syndicate, Inc.
www.pajamadiaries.com
Libenson

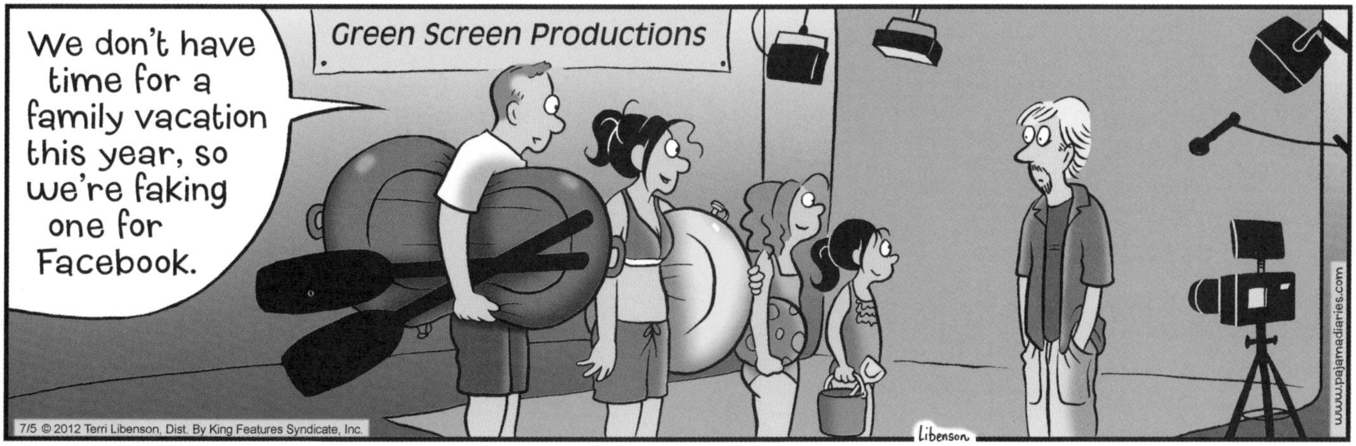
We don't have time for a family vacation this year, so we're faking one for Facebook.
Green Screen Productions
7/5 © 2012 Terri Libenson, Dist. By King Features Syndicate, Inc.
Libenson
www.pajamadiaries.com

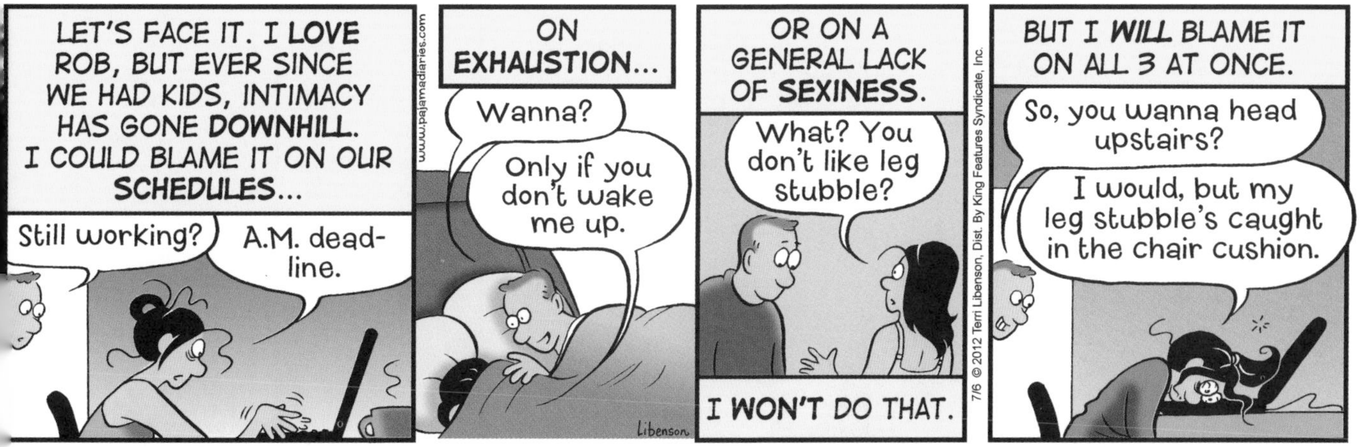
LET'S FACE IT. I LOVE ROB, BUT EVER SINCE WE HAD KIDS, INTIMACY HAS GONE DOWNHILL. I COULD BLAME IT ON OUR SCHEDULES...
Still working?
A.M. deadline.
www.pajamadiaries.com
ON EXHAUSTION...
Wanna?
Only if you don't wake me up.
Libenson
OR ON A GENERAL LACK OF SEXINESS.
What? You don't like leg stubble?
I WON'T DO THAT.
7/6 © 2012 Terri Libenson, Dist. By King Features Syndicate, Inc.
BUT I WILL BLAME IT ON ALL 3 AT ONCE.
So, you wanna head upstairs?
I would, but my leg stubble's caught in the chair cushion.

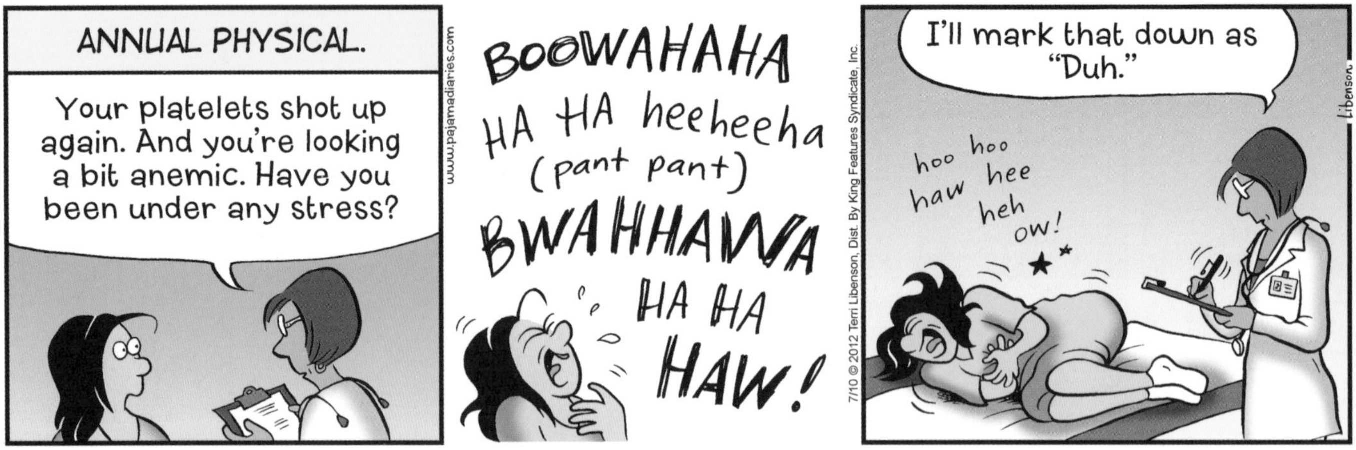
ANNUAL PHYSICAL.
Your platelets shot up again. And you're looking a bit anemic. Have you been under any stress?
www.pajamadiaries.com
BOOWAHAHA
HA HA heeheeha
(pant pant)
BWAHHAWA
HA HA
HAW!
7/10 © 2012 Terri Libenson, Dist. By King Features Syndicate, Inc.
I'll mark that down as "Duh."
hoo hoo
haw hee
heh
ow!
Libenson

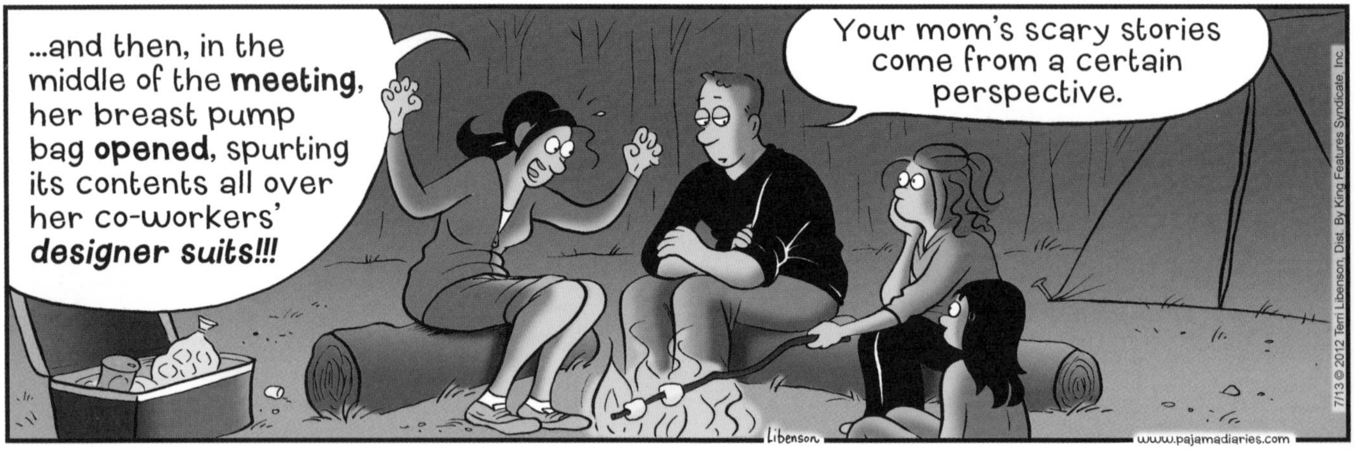
...and then, in the middle of the **meeting**, her breast pump bag **opened**, spurting its contents all over her co-workers' ***designer suits!!!***
Your mom's scary stories come from a certain perspective.
7/13 © 2012 Terri Libenson, Dist. By King Features Syndicate, Inc.
Libenson
www.pajamadiaries.com

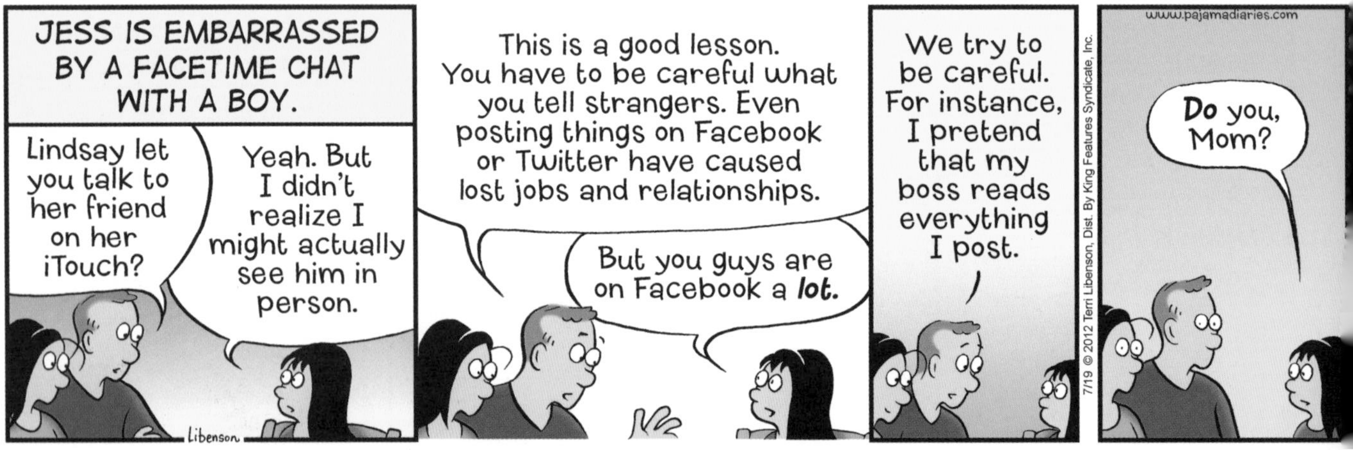
JESS IS EMBARRASSED BY A FACETIME CHAT WITH A BOY.
Lindsay let you talk to her friend on her iTouch?
Yeah. But I didn't realize I might actually see him in person.
Libenson
This is a good lesson. You have to be careful what you tell strangers. Even posting things on Facebook or Twitter have caused lost jobs and relationships.
But you guys are on Facebook a ***lot***.
We try to be careful. For instance, I pretend that my boss reads everything I post.
7/19 © 2012 Terri Libenson, Dist. By King Features Syndicate, Inc.
www.pajamadiaries.com
Do you, Mom?

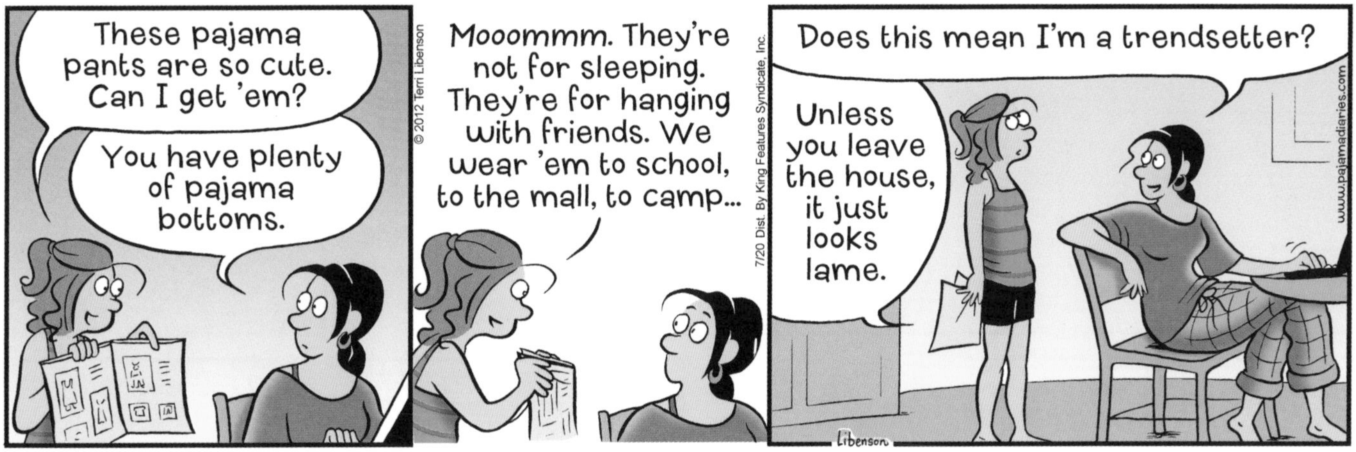
These pajama pants are so cute. Can I get 'em?
You have plenty of pajama bottoms.
© 2012 Terri Libenson
Mooommm. They're not for sleeping. They're for hanging with friends. We wear 'em to school, to the mall, to camp...
7/20 Dist. By King Features Syndicate, Inc.
Does this mean I'm a trendsetter?
Unless you leave the house, it just looks lame.
www.pajamadiaries.com
Libenson

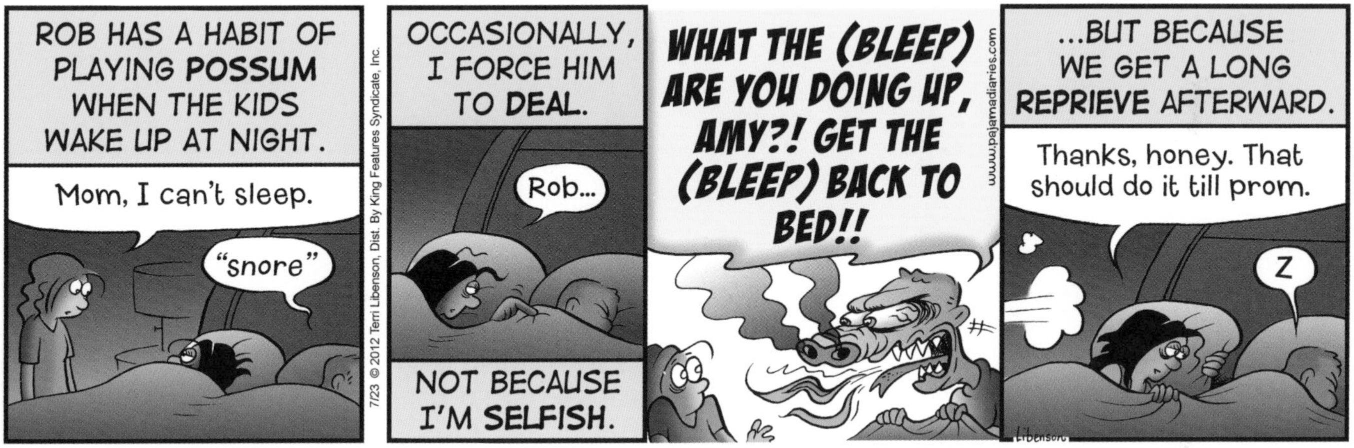
ROB HAS A HABIT OF PLAYING POSSUM WHEN THE KIDS WAKE UP AT NIGHT.
Mom, I can't sleep.
"snore"
7/23 © 2012 Terri Libenson, Dist. By King Features Syndicate, Inc.
OCCASIONALLY, I FORCE HIM TO DEAL.
Rob...
NOT BECAUSE I'M SELFISH.
WHAT THE (BLEEP) ARE YOU DOING UP, AMY?! GET THE (BLEEP) BACK TO BED!!
www.pajamadiaries.com
...BUT BECAUSE WE GET A LONG REPRIEVE AFTERWARD.
Thanks, honey. That should do it till prom.
Z
Libenson

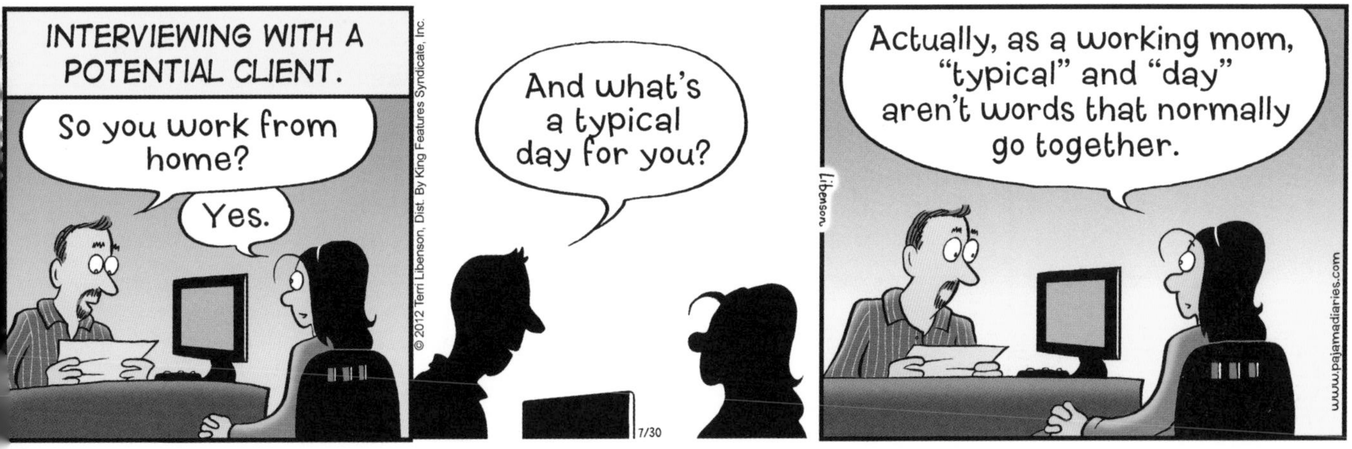
INTERVIEWING WITH A POTENTIAL CLIENT.
So you work from home?
Yes.
© 2012 Terri Libenson, Dist. By King Features Syndicate, Inc.
And what's a typical day for you?
7/30
Libenson
Actually, as a working mom, "typical" and "day" aren't words that normally go together.
www.pajamadiaries.com

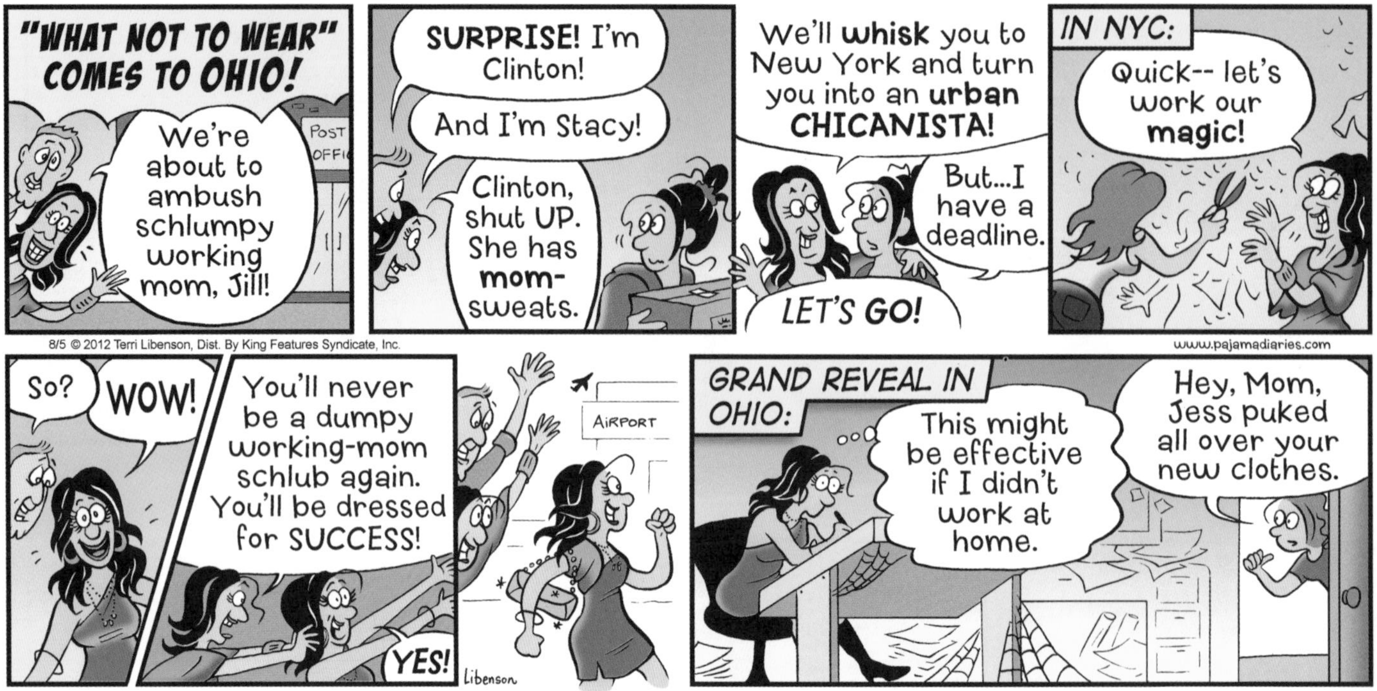

"WHAT NOT TO WEAR" COMES TO OHIO!
We're about to ambush schlumpy working mom, Jill!
POST OFFIC
SURPRISE! I'm Clinton!
And I'm Stacy!
Clinton, shut UP. She has mom-sweats.
We'll whisk you to New York and turn you into an urban CHICANISTA!
But...I have a deadline.
LET'S GO!
IN NYC:
Quick-- let's work our magic!
8/5 © 2012 Terri Libenson, Dist. By King Features Syndicate, Inc.
www.pajamadiaries.com
So?
WOW!
You'll never be a dumpy working-mom schlub again. You'll be dressed for SUCCESS!
YES!
AIRPORT
Libenson
GRAND REVEAL IN OHIO:
This might be effective if I didn't work at home.
Hey, Mom, Jess puked all over your new clothes.

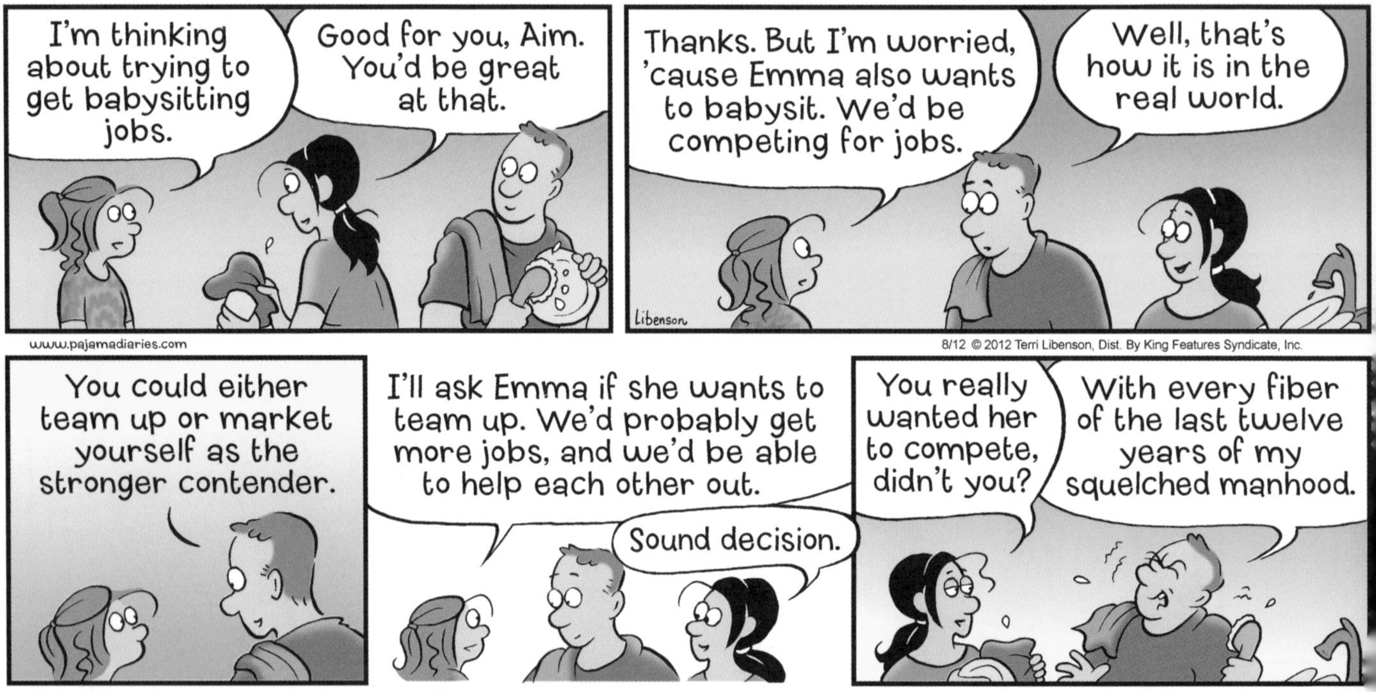

I'm thinking about trying to get babysitting jobs.
Good for you, Aim. You'd be great at that.
Thanks. But I'm worried, 'cause Emma also wants to babysit. We'd be competing for jobs.
Well, that's how it is in the real world.
Libenson
www.pajamadiaries.com
8/12 © 2012 Terri Libenson, Dist. By King Features Syndicate, Inc.
You could either team up or market yourself as the stronger contender.
I'll ask Emma if she wants to team up. We'd probably get more jobs, and we'd be able to help each other out.
Sound decision.
You really wanted her to compete, didn't you?
With every fiber of the last twelve years of my squelched manhood.

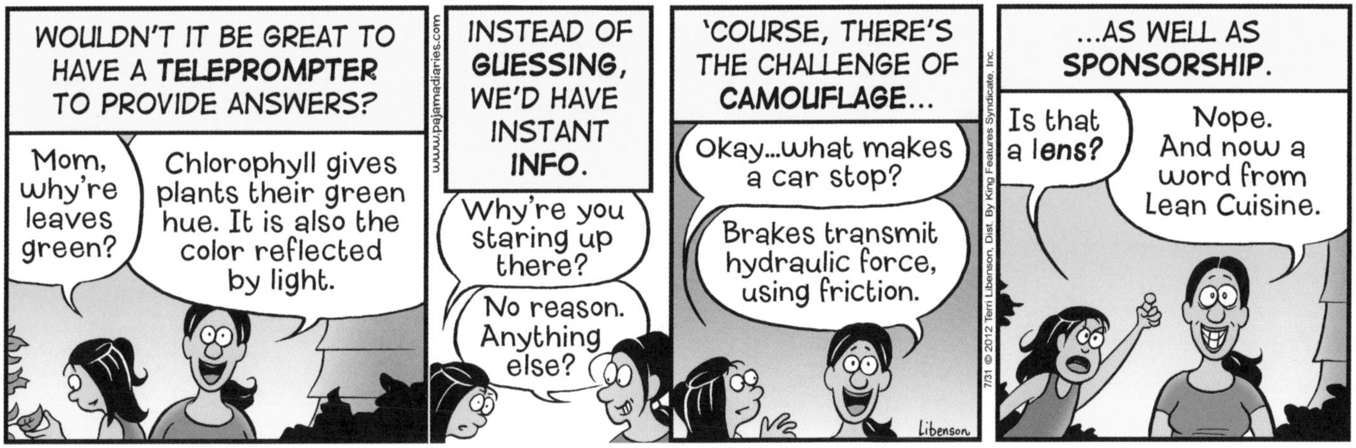
WOULDN'T IT BE GREAT TO HAVE A **TELEPROMPTER** TO PROVIDE ANSWERS?
Mom, why're leaves green?
Chlorophyll gives plants their green hue. It is also the color reflected by light.
www.pajamadiaries.com
INSTEAD OF **GUESSING**, WE'D HAVE INSTANT **INFO**.
Why're you staring up there?
No reason. Anything else?
'COURSE, THERE'S THE CHALLENGE OF **CAMOUFLAGE**...
Okay...what makes a car stop?
Brakes transmit hydraulic force, using friction.
Libenson
7/31 © 2012 Terri Libenson, Dist. By King Features Syndicate, Inc.
...AS WELL AS **SPONSORSHIP**.
Is that a l**ens?**
Nope. And now a word from Lean Cuisine.

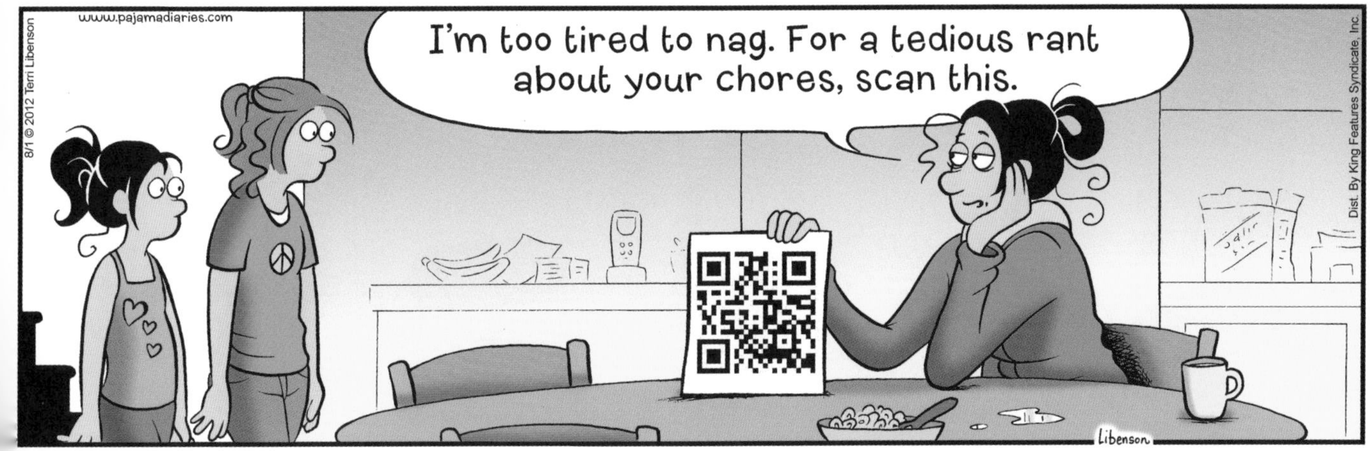
www.pajamadiaries.com
8/1 © 2012 Terri Libenson
I'm too tired to nag. For a tedious rant about your chores, scan this.
Libenson
Dist. By King Features Syndicate, Inc.

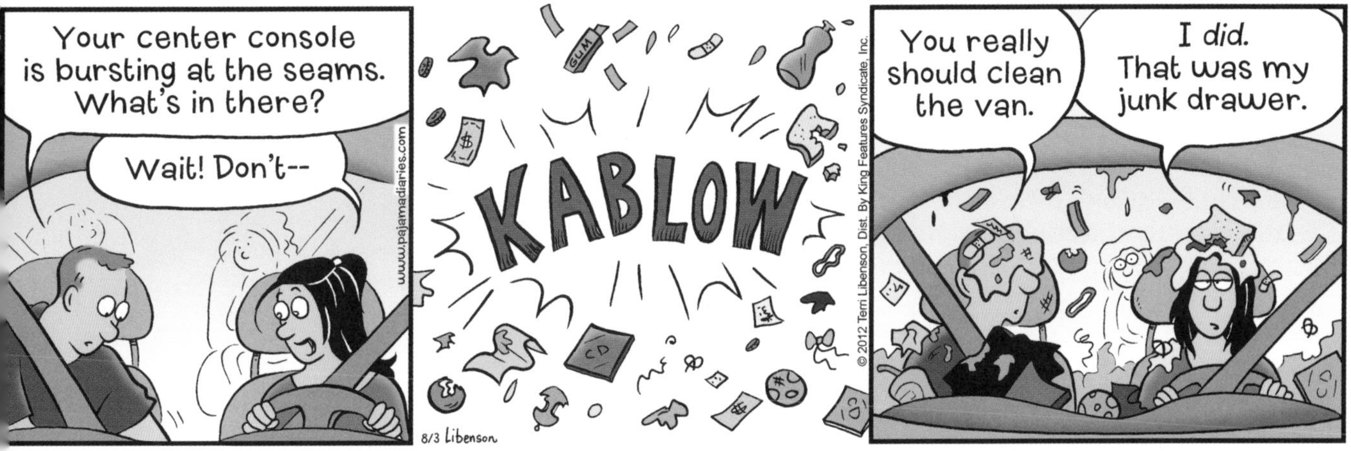
Your center console is bursting at the seams. What's in there?
Wait! Don't--
www.pajamadiaries.com
KABLOW
GUM
CD
8/3 Libenson
© 2012 Terri Libenson, Dist. By King Features Syndicate, Inc.
You really should clean the van.
I *did*. That was my junk drawer.

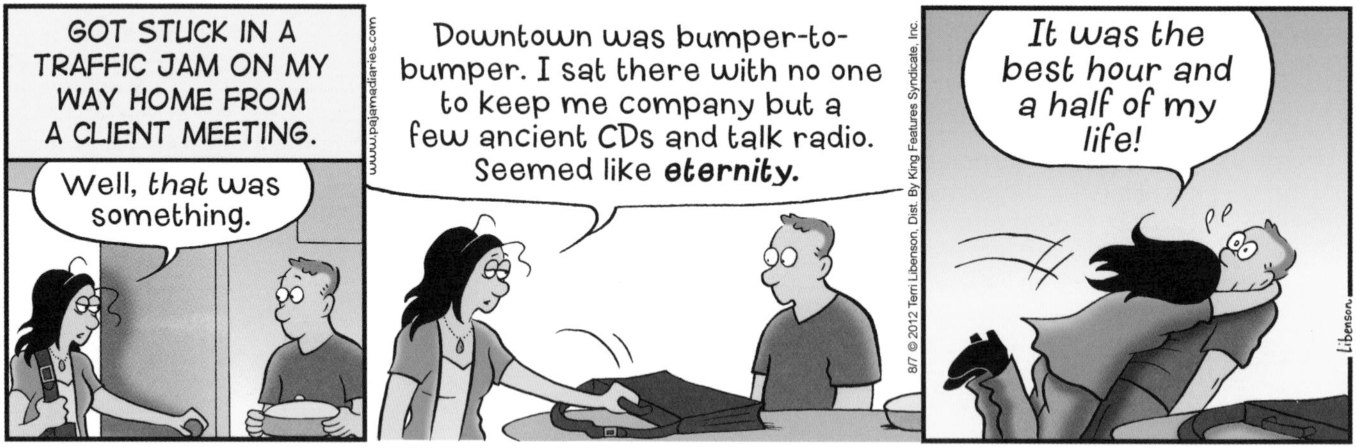
GOT STUCK IN A TRAFFIC JAM ON MY WAY HOME FROM A CLIENT MEETING.
Well, *that* was something.
www.pajamadiaries.com
Downtown was bumper-to-bumper. I sat there with no one to keep me company but a few ancient CDs and talk radio. Seemed like **eternity.**
8/7 © 2012 Terri Libenson, Dist. By King Features Syndicate, Inc.
It was the best hour and a half of my life!
Libenson

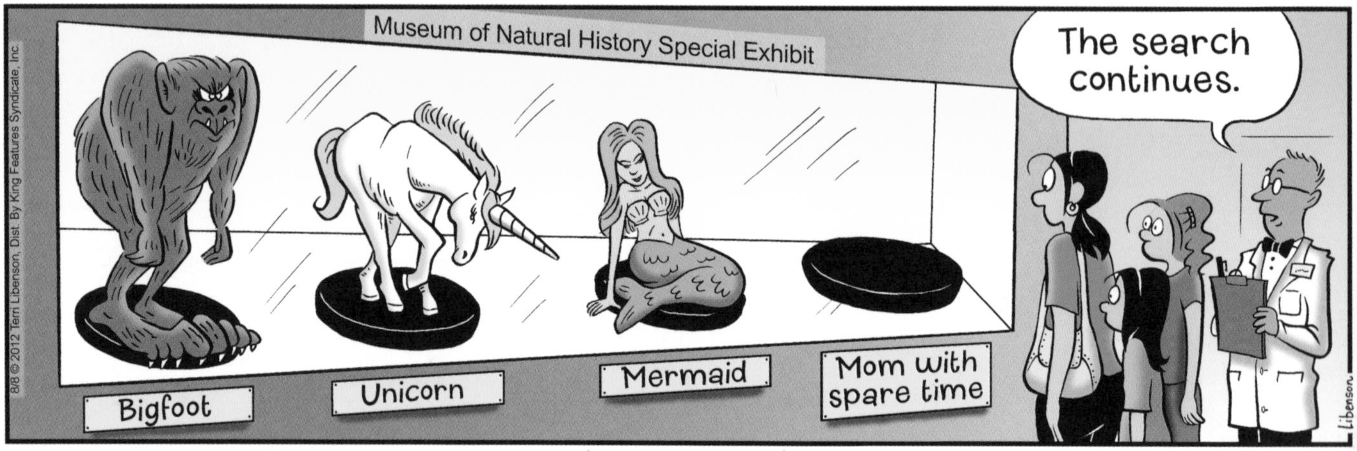
8/8 © 2012 Terri Libenson, Dist. By King Features Syndicate, Inc.
Museum of Natural History Special Exhibit
Bigfoot
Unicorn
Mermaid
Mom with spare time
The search continues.
Libenson

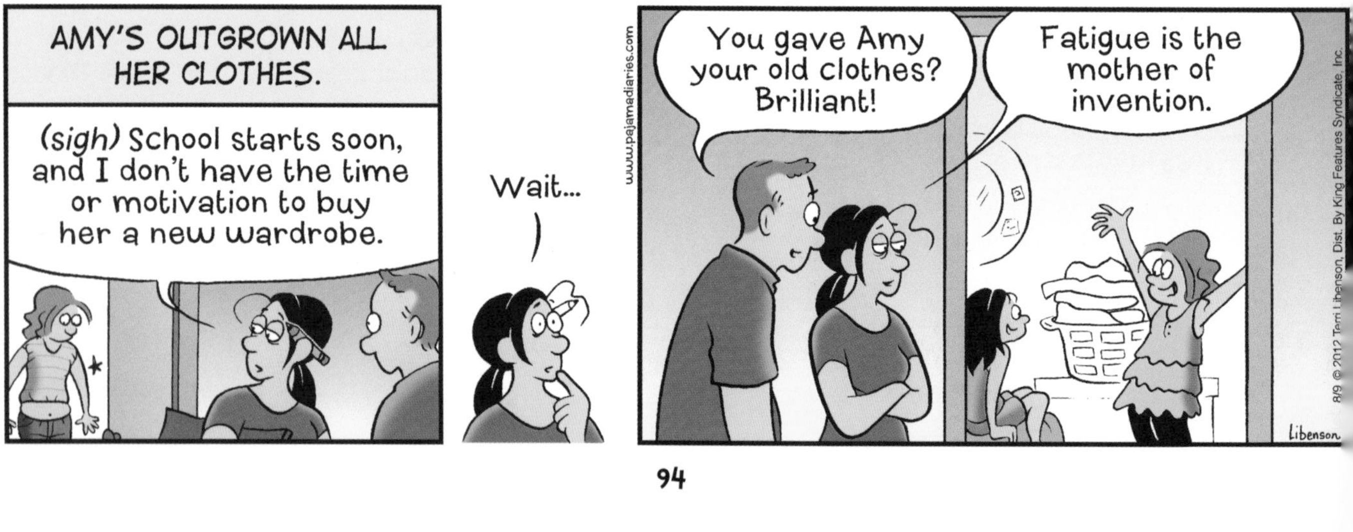
AMY'S OUTGROWN ALL HER CLOTHES.
(sigh) School starts soon, and I don't have the time or motivation to buy her a new wardrobe.
Wait...
www.pajamadiaries.com
You gave Amy your old clothes? Brilliant!
Fatigue is the mother of invention.
8/9 © 2012 Terri Libenson, Dist. By King Features Syndicate, Inc.
Libenson

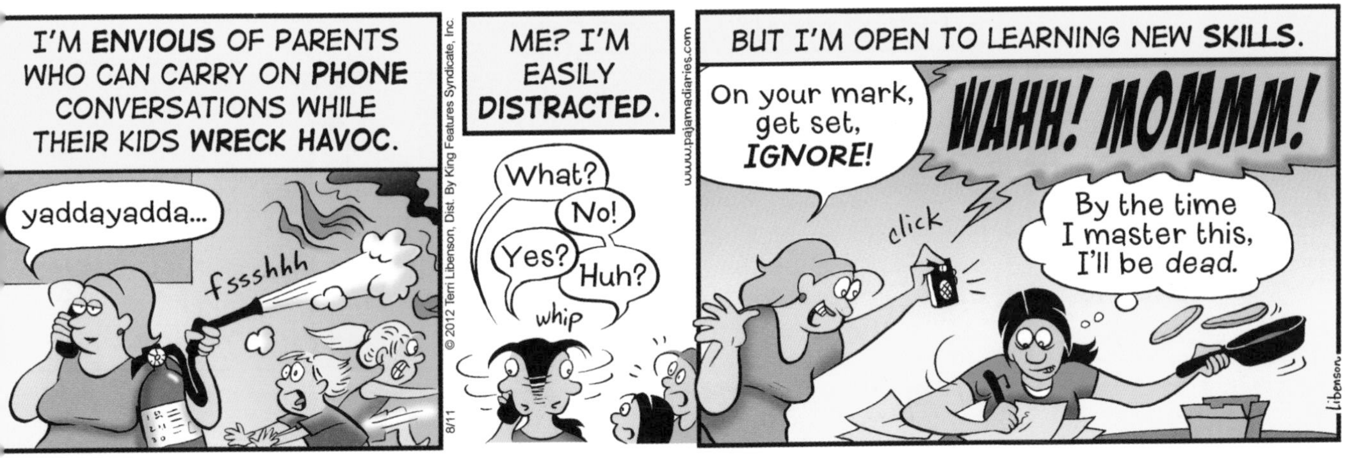
I'M ENVIOUS OF PARENTS WHO CAN CARRY ON PHONE CONVERSATIONS WHILE THEIR KIDS WRECK HAVOC.
yaddayadda...
fssshhh
8/11
© 2012 Terri Libenson, Dist. By King Features Syndicate, Inc.
ME? I'M EASILY DISTRACTED.
What?
No!
Yes?
Huh?
whip
www.pajamadiaries.com
BUT I'M OPEN TO LEARNING NEW SKILLS.
On your mark, get set, IGNORE!
WAHH! MOMMM!
click
By the time I master this, I'll be dead.
Libenson
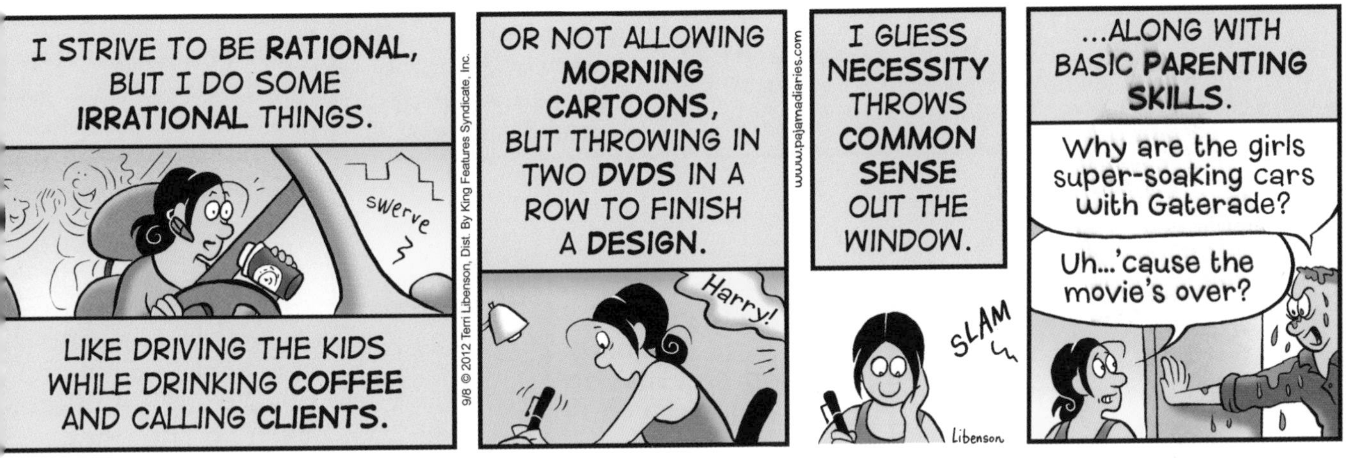
I STRIVE TO BE RATIONAL, BUT I DO SOME IRRATIONAL THINGS.
swerve
LIKE DRIVING THE KIDS WHILE DRINKING COFFEE AND CALLING CLIENTS.
9/8 © 2012 Terri Libenson, Dist. By King Features Syndicate, Inc.
OR NOT ALLOWING MORNING CARTOONS, BUT THROWING IN TWO DVDS IN A ROW TO FINISH A DESIGN.
Harry!
www.pajamadiaries.com
I GUESS NECESSITY THROWS COMMON SENSE OUT THE WINDOW.
SLAM
Libenson
...ALONG WITH BASIC PARENTING SKILLS.
Why are the girls super-soaking cars with Gaterade?
Uh...'cause the movie's over?
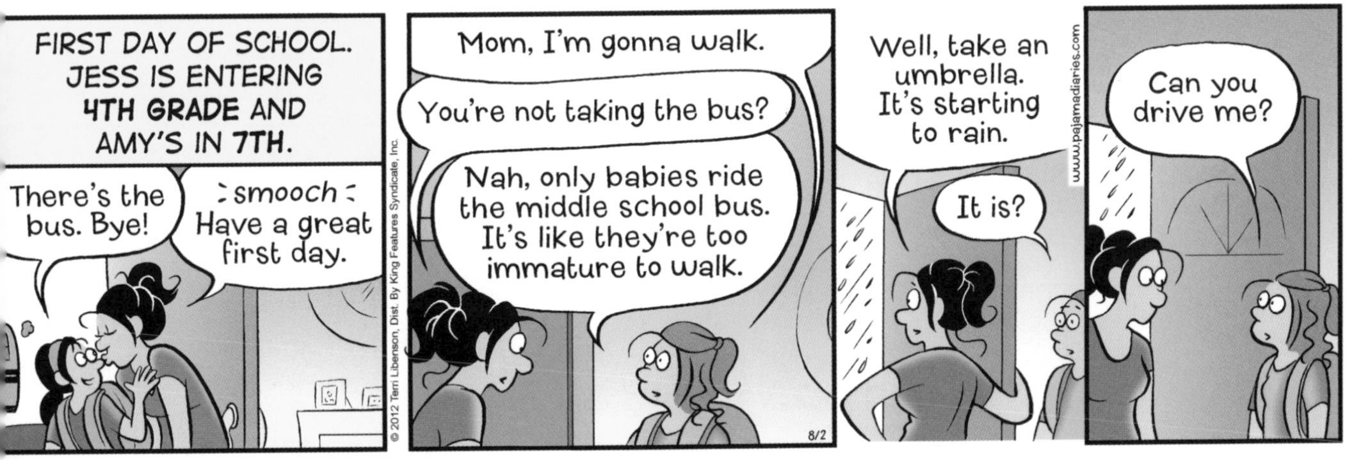
FIRST DAY OF SCHOOL. JESS IS ENTERING 4TH GRADE AND AMY'S IN 7TH.
There's the bus. Bye!
smooch
Have a great first day.
© 2012 Terri Libenson, Dist. By King Features Syndicate, Inc.
Mom, I'm gonna walk.
You're not taking the bus?
Nah, only babies ride the middle school bus. It's like they're too immature to walk.
8/2
Well, take an umbrella. It's starting to rain.
It is?
www.pajamadiaries.com
Can you drive me?

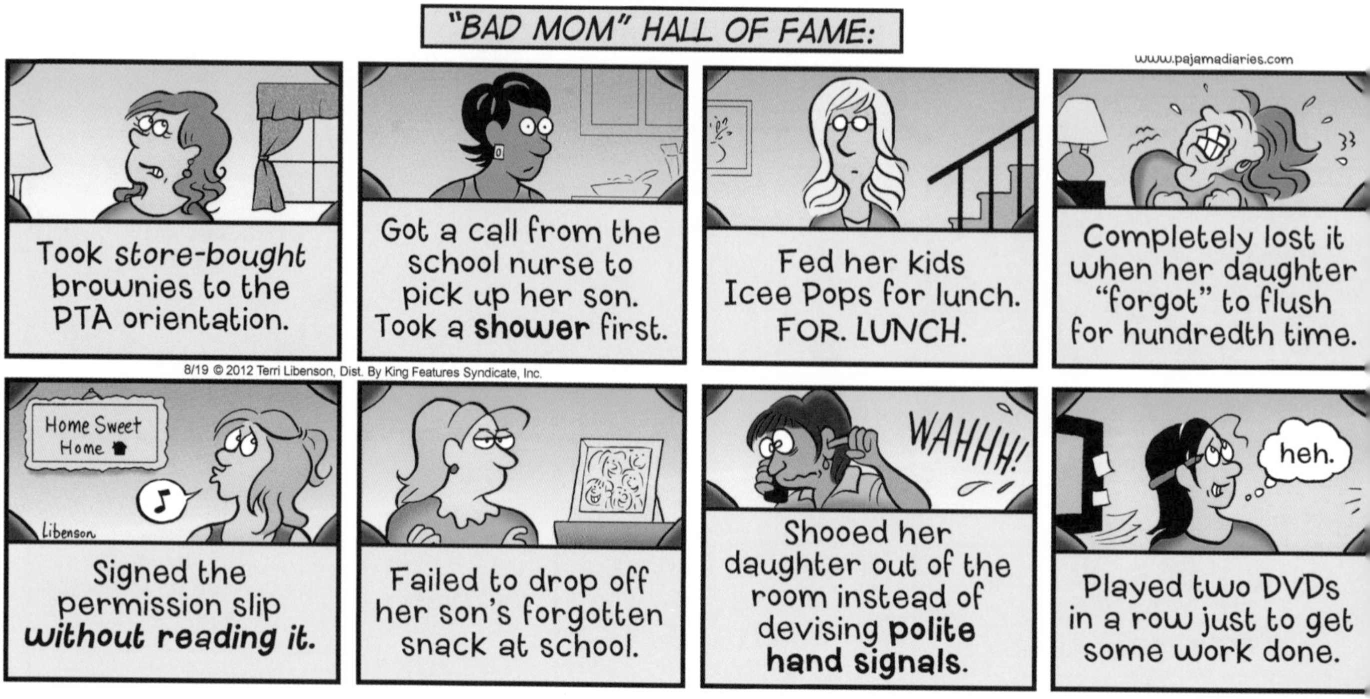
"BAD MOM" HALL OF FAME:
www.pajamadiaries.com
Took store-bought brownies to the PTA orientation.
Got a call from the school nurse to pick up her son. Took a **shower** first.
Fed her kids Icee Pops for lunch. FOR. LUNCH.
Completely lost it when her daughter "forgot" to flush for hundredth time.
Home Sweet Home
Libenson
Signed the permission slip ***without reading it.***
Failed to drop off her son's forgotten snack at school.
WAHHH!
Shooed her daughter out of the room instead of devising **polite hand signals.**
heh.
Played two DVDs in a row just to get some work done.

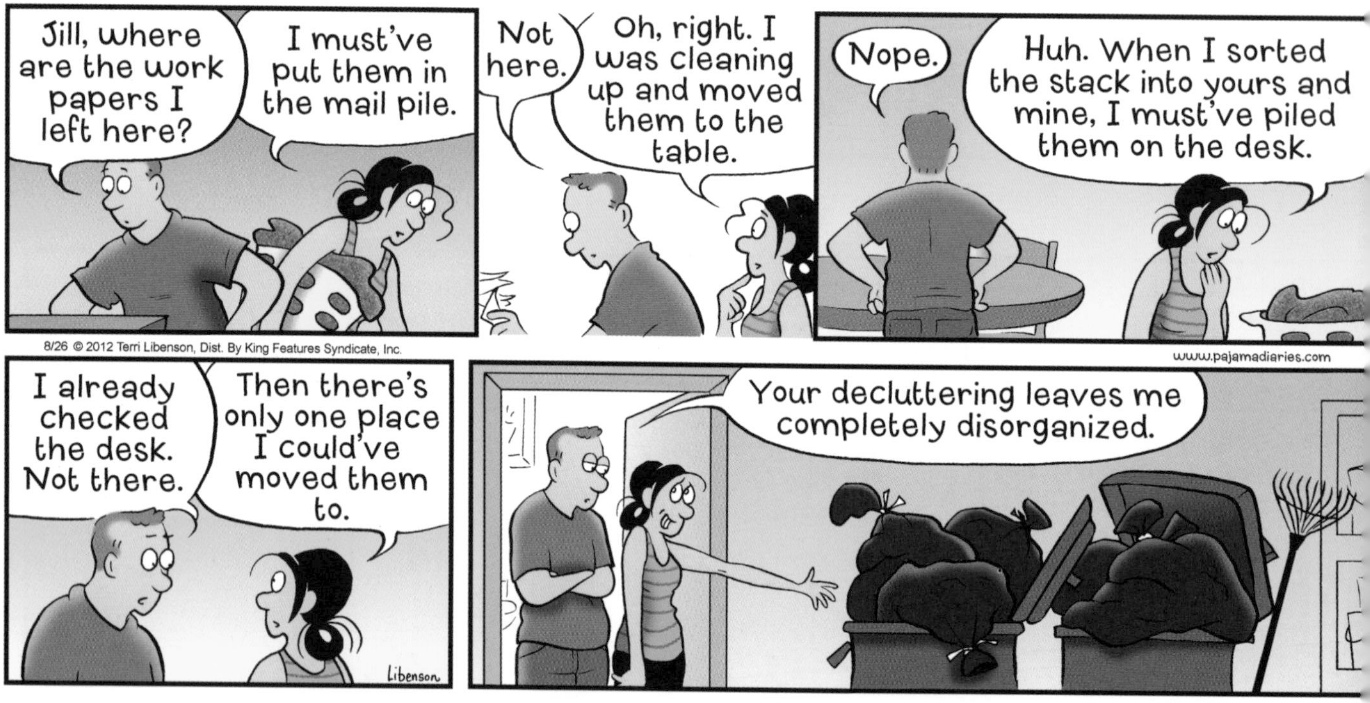
Jill, where are the work papers I left here?
I must've put them in the mail pile.
Not here.
Oh, right. I was cleaning up and moved them to the table.
Nope.
Huh. When I sorted the stack into yours and mine, I must've piled them on the desk.
www.pajamadiaries.com
I already checked the desk. Not there.
Then there's only one place I could've moved them to.
Libenson
Your decluttering leaves me completely disorganized.

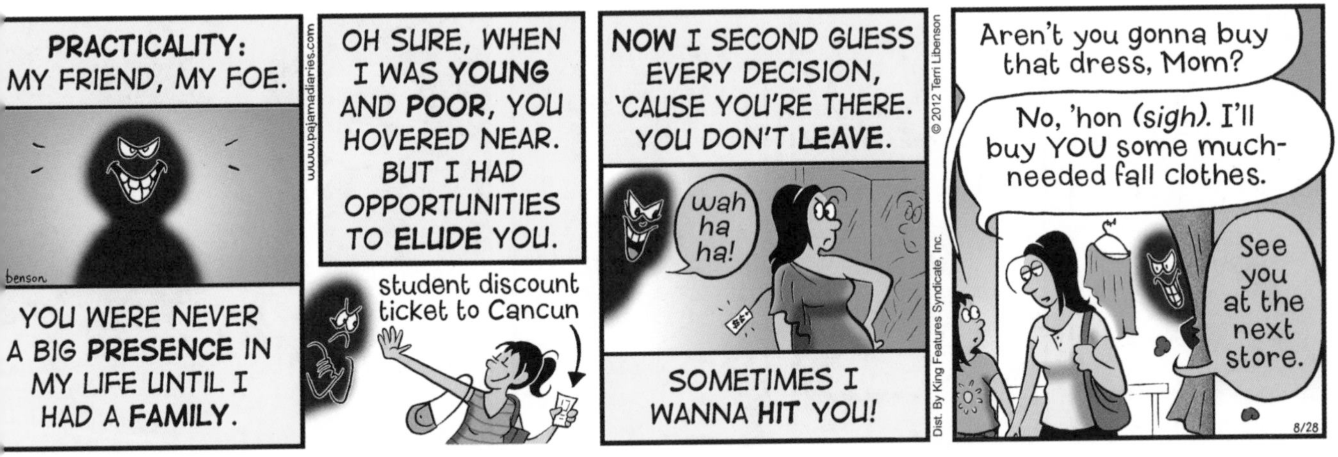
PRACTICALITY: MY FRIEND, MY FOE.
YOU WERE NEVER A BIG PRESENCE IN MY LIFE UNTIL I HAD A FAMILY.
benson
www.pajamadiaries.com
OH SURE, WHEN I WAS YOUNG AND POOR, YOU HOVERED NEAR. BUT I HAD OPPORTUNITIES TO ELUDE YOU.
student discount ticket to Cancun
NOW I SECOND GUESS EVERY DECISION, 'CAUSE YOU'RE THERE. YOU DON'T LEAVE.
wah ha ha!
SOMETIMES I WANNA HIT YOU!
© 2012 Terri Libenson
Dist. By King Features Syndicate, Inc.
Aren't you gonna buy that dress, Mom?
No, 'hon (sigh). I'll buy YOU some much-needed fall clothes.
See you at the next store.
8/28

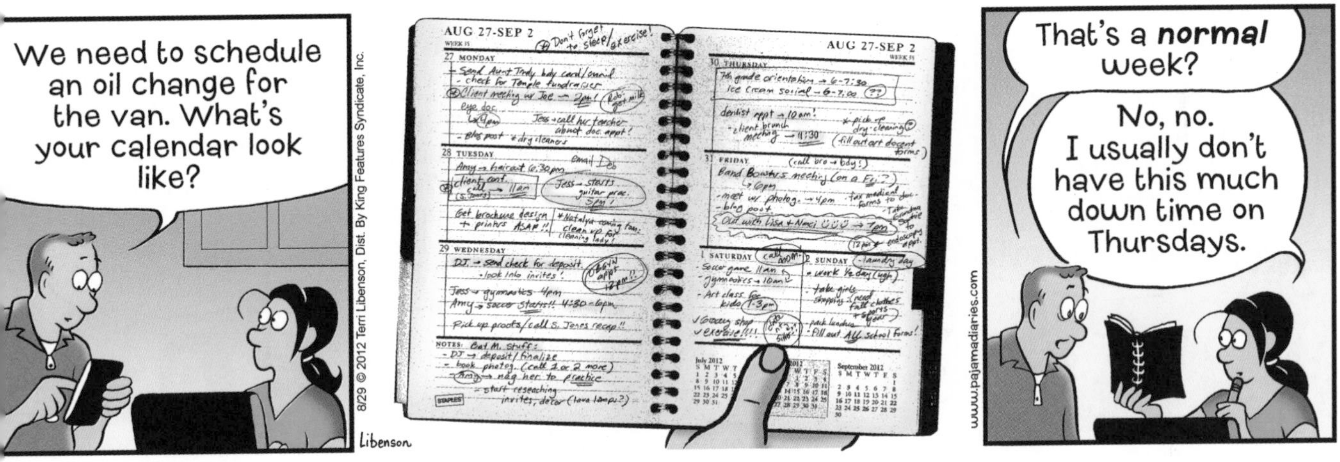
We need to schedule an oil change for the van. What's your calendar look like?
8/29 © 2012 Terri Libenson, Dist. By King Features Syndicate, Inc.
Libenson
AUG 27-SEP 2
AUG 27-SEP 2
That's a normal week?
No, no. I usually don't have this much down time on Thursdays.
www.pajamadiaries.com

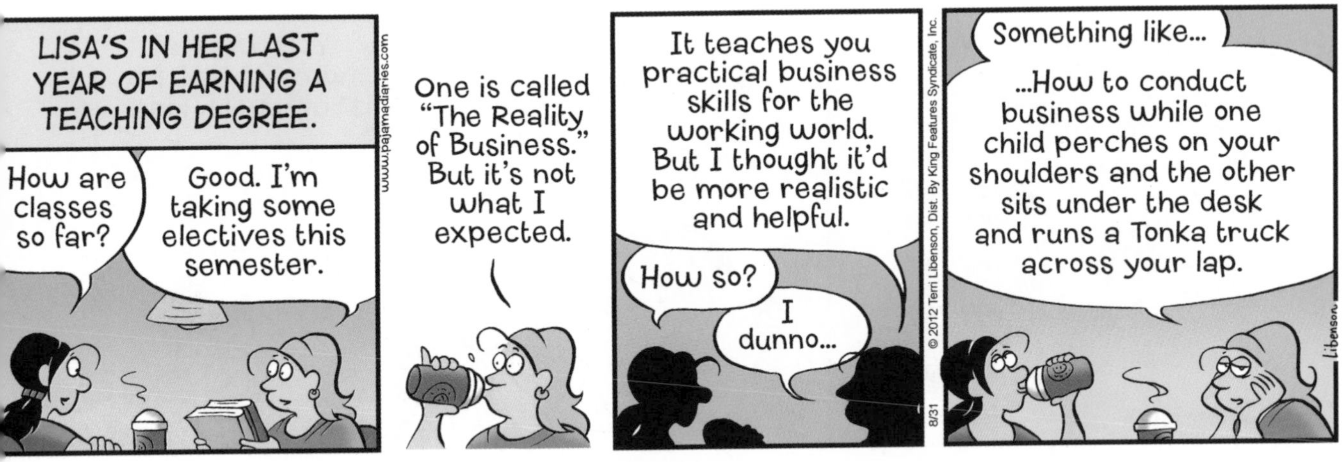
LISA'S IN HER LAST YEAR OF EARNING A TEACHING DEGREE.
How are classes so far?
Good. I'm taking some electives this semester.
www.pajamadiaries.com
One is called "The Reality of Business." But it's not what I expected.
It teaches you practical business skills for the working world. But I thought it'd be more realistic and helpful.
How so?
I dunno...
8/31 © 2012 Terri Libenson, Dist. By King Features Syndicate, Inc.
Something like...
...How to conduct business while one child perches on your shoulders and the other sits under the desk and runs a Tonka truck across your lap.
Libenson

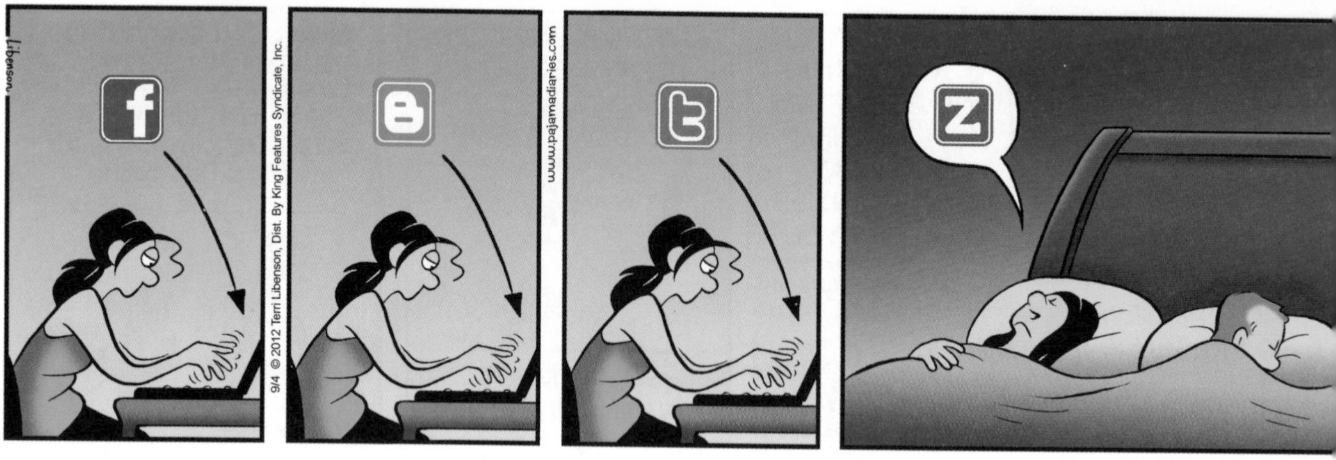
Libenson
9/4 © 2012 Terri Libenson, Dist. By King Features Syndicate, Inc.
www.pajamadiaries.com
Z

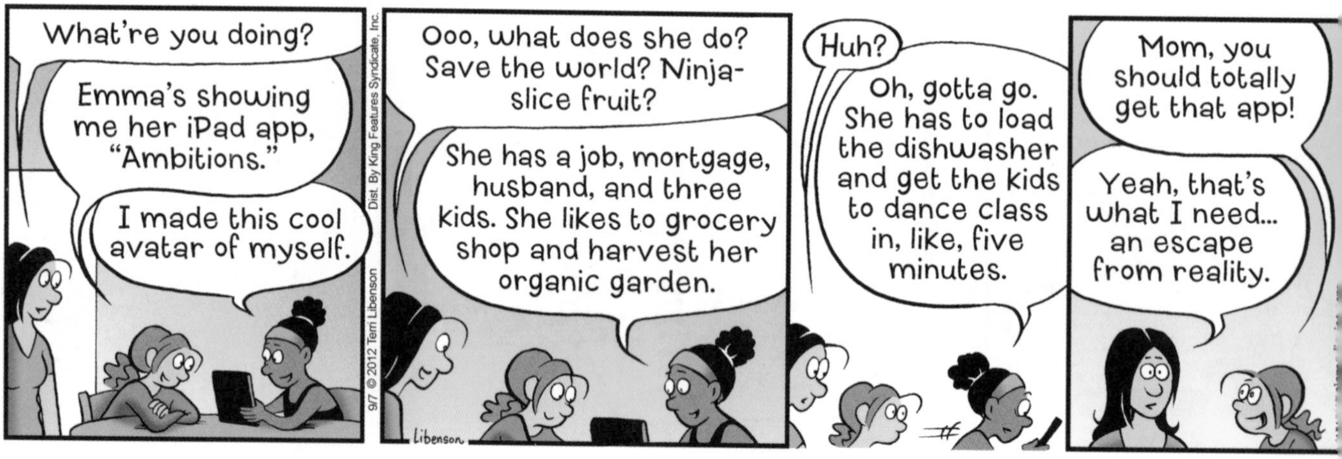
What're you doing?
Emma's showing me her iPad app, "Ambitions."
I made this cool avatar of myself.
9/7 © 2012 Terri Libenson Dist. By King Features Syndicate, Inc.
Ooo, what does she do? Save the world? Ninja-slice fruit?
She has a job, mortgage, husband, and three kids. She likes to grocery shop and harvest her organic garden.
Libenson
Huh?
Oh, gotta go. She has to load the dishwasher and get the kids to dance class in, like, five minutes.
Mom, you should totally get that app!
Yeah, that's what I need... an escape from reality.

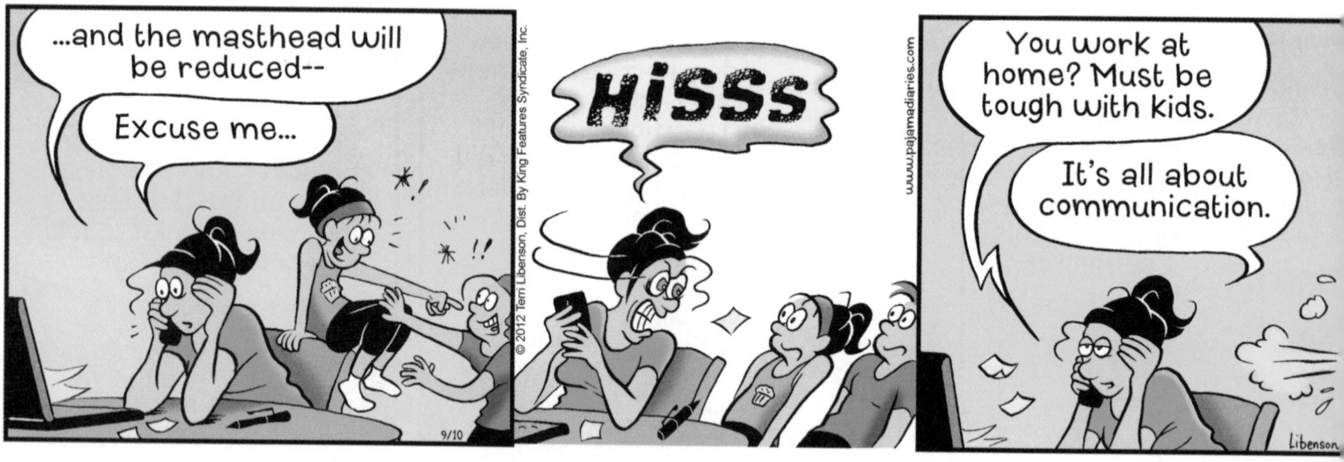
...and the masthead will be reduced--
Excuse me...
9/10
© 2012 Terri Libenson, Dist. By King Features Syndicate, Inc.
HISSS
www.pajamadiaries.com
You work at home? Must be tough with kids.
It's all about communication.
Libenson

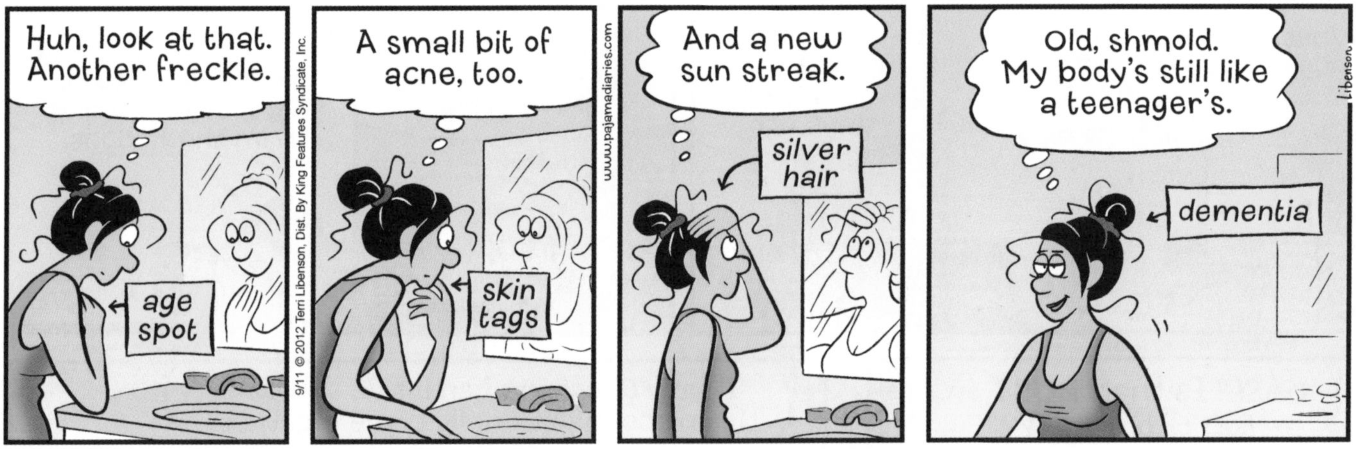
Huh, look at that. Another freckle.
age spot
9/11 © 2012 Terri Libenson, Dist. By King Features Syndicate, Inc.
A small bit of acne, too.
skin tags
www.pajamadiaries.com
And a new sun streak.
silver hair
Old, shmold. My body's still like a teenager's.
dementia
Libenson

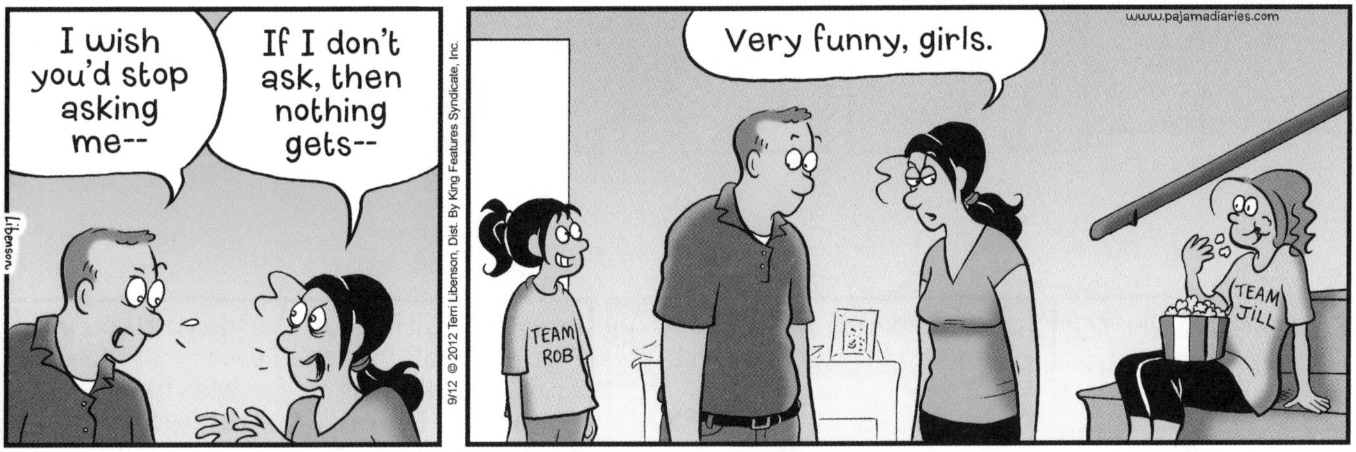
I wish you'd stop asking me--
If I don't ask, then nothing gets--
Libenson
9/12 © 2012 Terri Libenson, Dist. By King Features Syndicate, Inc.
www.pajamadiaries.com
Very funny, girls.
TEAM ROB
TEAM JILL

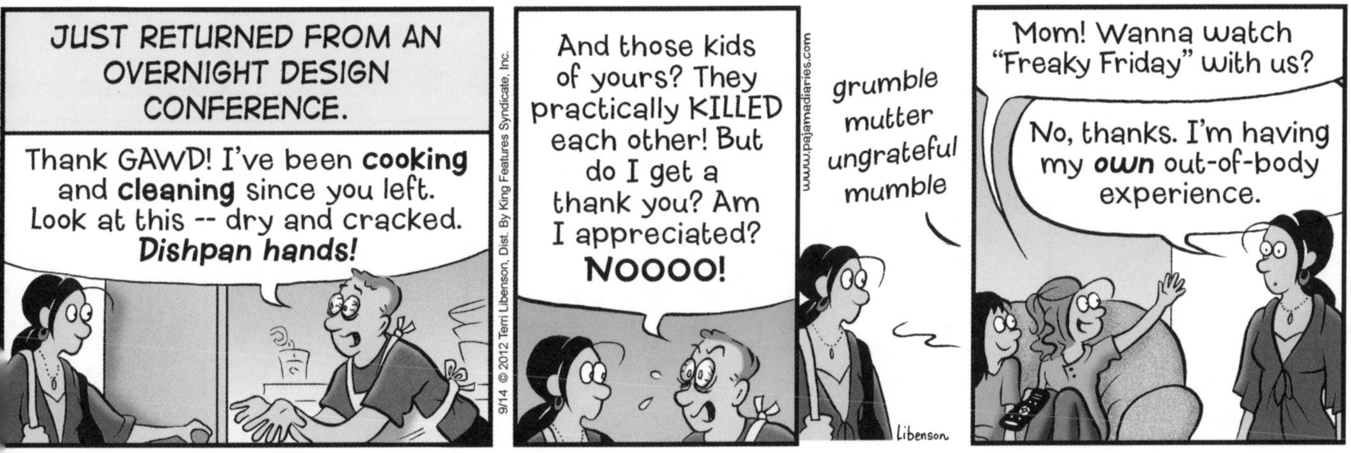
JUST RETURNED FROM AN OVERNIGHT DESIGN CONFERENCE.
Thank GAWD! I've been **cooking** and **cleaning** since you left. Look at this -- dry and cracked. ***Dishpan hands!***
9/14 © 2012 Terri Libenson, Dist. By King Features Syndicate, Inc.
And those kids of yours? They practically KILLED each other! But do I get a thank you? Am I appreciated? **NOOOO!**
www.pajamadiaries.com
grumble mutter ungrateful mumble
Libenson
Mom! Wanna watch "Freaky Friday" with us?
No, thanks. I'm having my ***own*** out-of-body experience.

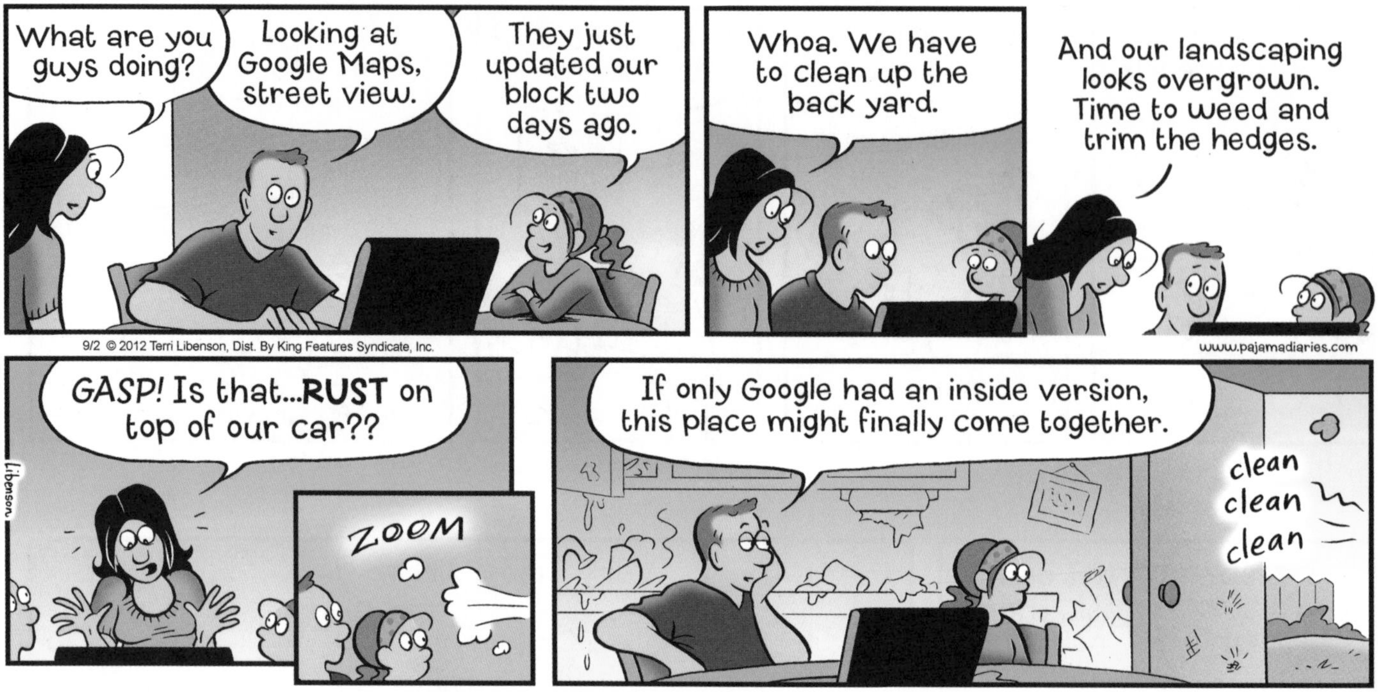
What are you guys doing?
Looking at Google Maps, street view.
They just updated our block two days ago.
Whoa. We have to clean up the back yard.
And our landscaping looks overgrown. Time to weed and trim the hedges.
GASP! Is that...RUST on top of our car??
ZOOM
If only Google had an inside version, this place might finally come together.
clean
clean
clean
Libenson

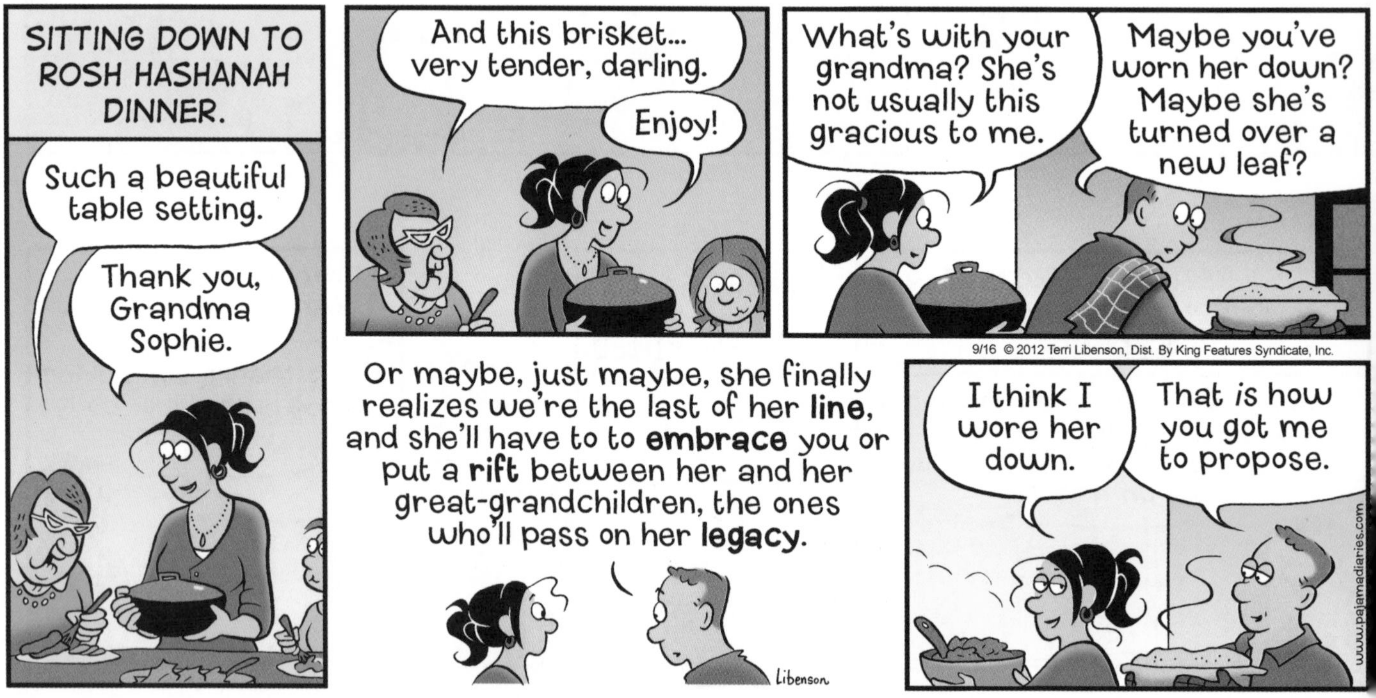
SITTING DOWN TO ROSH HASHANAH DINNER.
Such a beautiful table setting.
Thank you, Grandma Sophie.
And this brisket... very tender, darling.
Enjoy!
What's with your grandma? She's not usually this gracious to me.
Maybe you've worn her down? Maybe she's turned over a new leaf?
Or maybe, just maybe, she finally realizes we're the last of her **line**, and she'll have to to **embrace** you or put a **rift** between her and her great-grandchildren, the ones who'll pass on her **legacy**.
Libenson
I think I wore her down.
That *is* how you got me to propose.
www.pajamadiaries.com

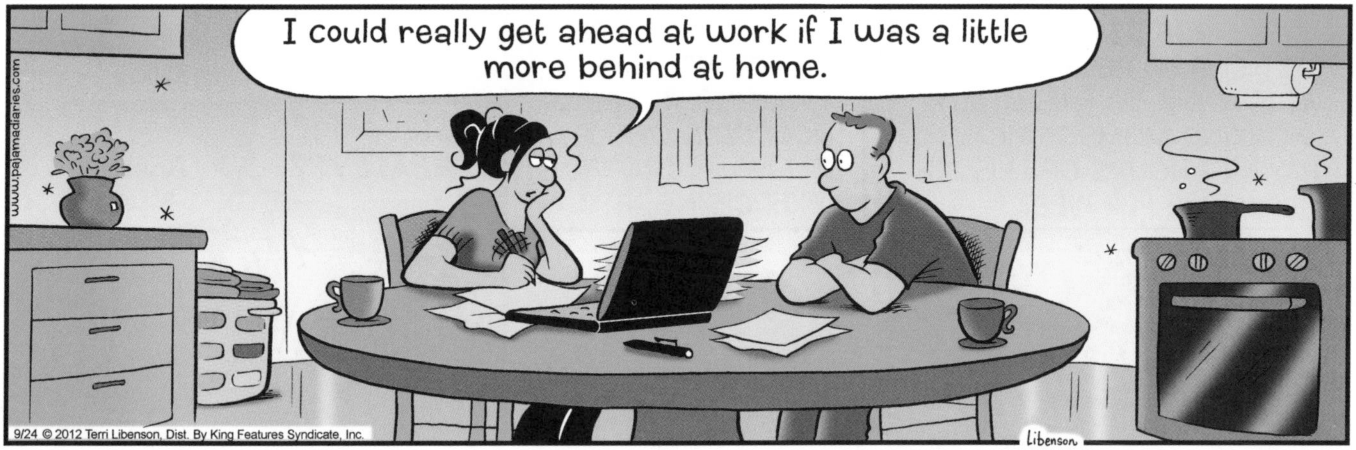
I could really get ahead at work if I was a little more behind at home.
www.pajamadiaries.com
9/24 © 2012 Terri Libenson, Dist. By King Features Syndicate, Inc.
Libenson

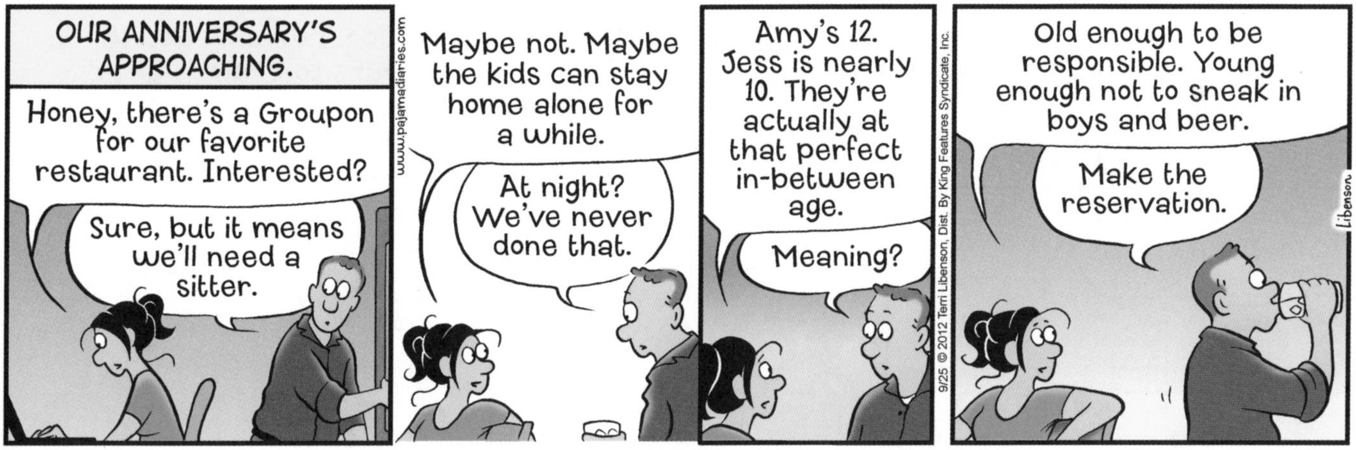
OUR ANNIVERSARY'S APPROACHING.
Honey, there's a Groupon for our favorite restaurant. Interested?
Sure, but it means we'll need a sitter.
Maybe not. Maybe the kids can stay home alone for a while.
At night? We've never done that.
Amy's 12. Jess is nearly 10. They're actually at that perfect in-between age.
Meaning?
Old enough to be responsible. Young enough not to sneak in boys and beer.
Make the reservation.
www.pajamadiaries.com
9/25 © 2012 Terri Libenson, Dist. By King Features Syndicate, Inc.
Libenson

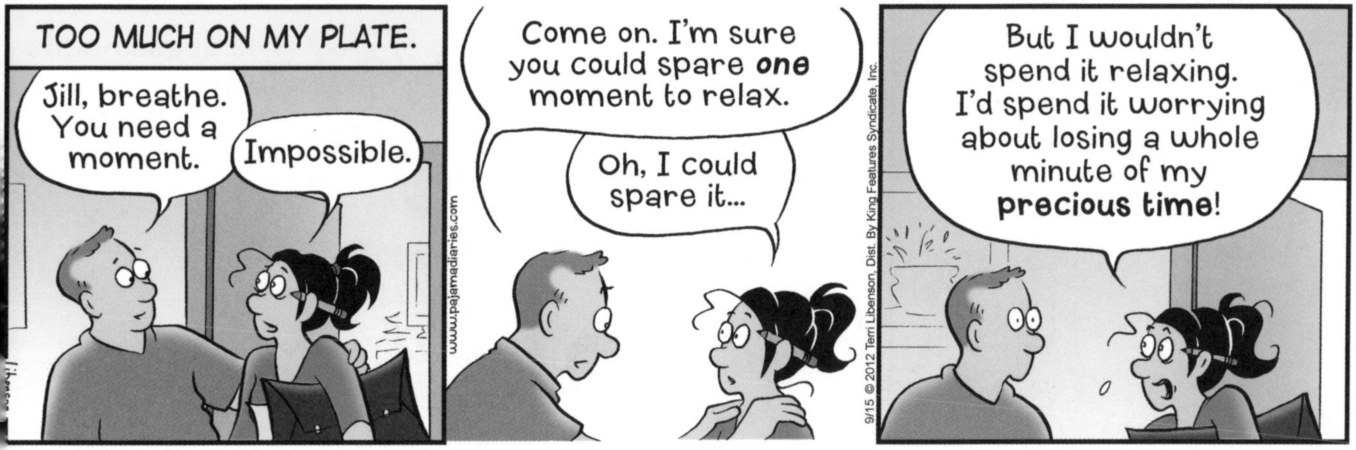
TOO MUCH ON MY PLATE.
Jill, breathe. You need a moment.
Impossible.
Come on. I'm sure you could spare **one** moment to relax.
Oh, I could spare it...
But I wouldn't spend it relaxing. I'd spend it worrying about losing a whole minute of my **precious time**!
www.pajamadiaries.com
9/15 © 2012 Terri Libenson, Dist. By King Features Syndicate, Inc.

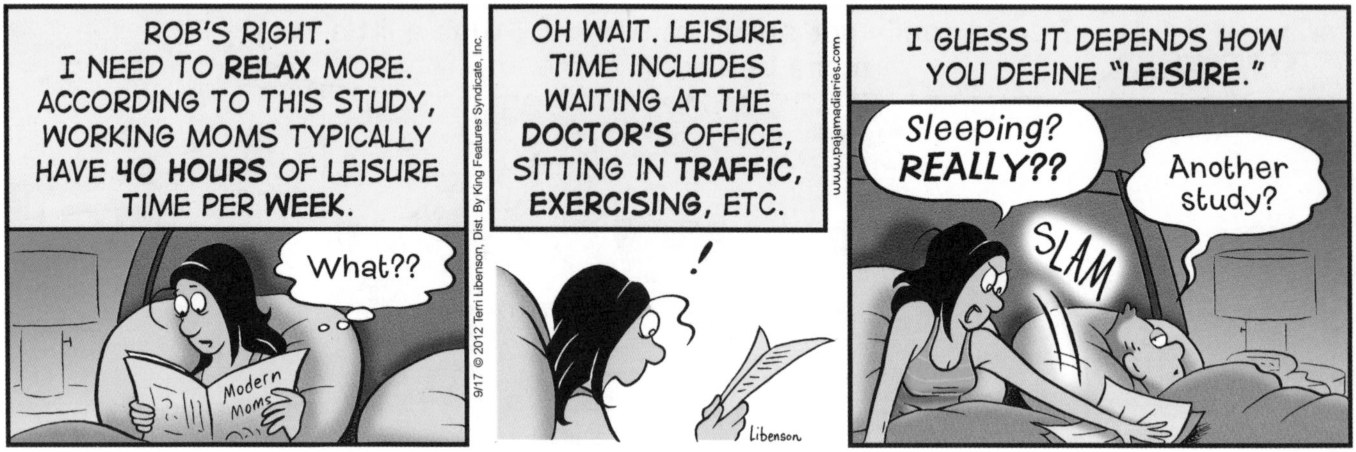
ROB'S RIGHT. I NEED TO RELAX MORE. ACCORDING TO THIS STUDY, WORKING MOMS TYPICALLY HAVE 40 HOURS OF LEISURE TIME PER WEEK.
What??
Modern Moms
9/17 © 2012 Terri Libenson, Dist. By King Features Syndicate, Inc.
OH WAIT. LEISURE TIME INCLUDES WAITING AT THE DOCTOR'S OFFICE, SITTING IN TRAFFIC, EXERCISING, ETC.
!
Libenson
www.pajamadiaries.com
I GUESS IT DEPENDS HOW YOU DEFINE "LEISURE."
Sleeping? REALLY??
Another study?
SLAM

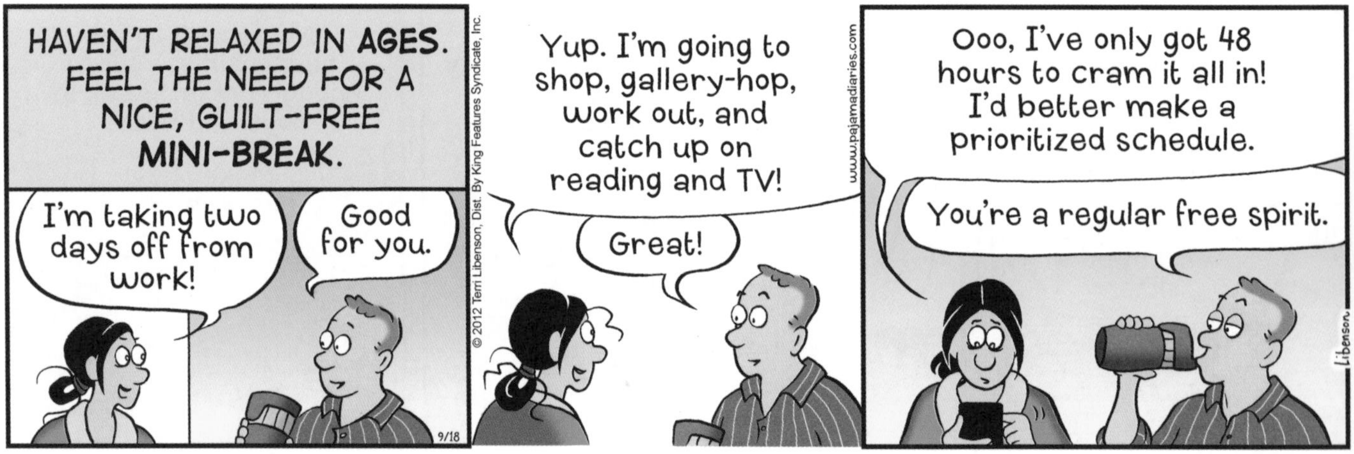
HAVEN'T RELAXED IN AGES. FEEL THE NEED FOR A NICE, GUILT-FREE MINI-BREAK.
I'm taking two days off from work!
Good for you.
9/18
© 2012 Terri Libenson, Dist. By King Features Syndicate, Inc.
Yup. I'm going to shop, gallery-hop, work out, and catch up on reading and TV!
Great!
www.pajamadiaries.com
Ooo, I've only got 48 hours to cram it all in! I'd better make a prioritized schedule.
You're a regular free spirit.
Libenson

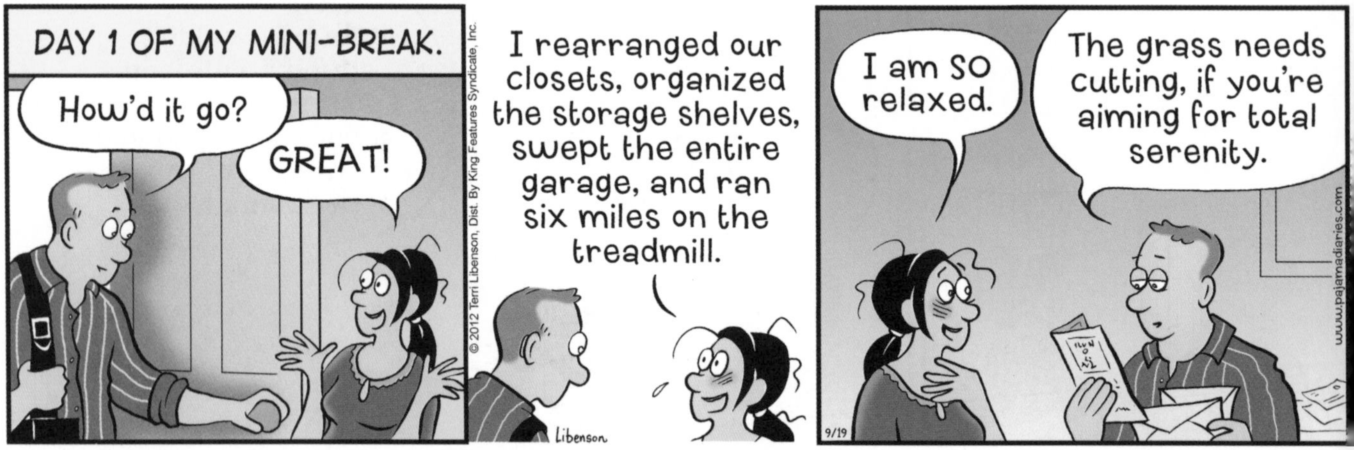
DAY 1 OF MY MINI-BREAK.
How'd it go?
GREAT!
© 2012 Terri Libenson, Dist. By King Features Syndicate, Inc.
I rearranged our closets, organized the storage shelves, swept the entire garage, and ran six miles on the treadmill.
Libenson
I am SO relaxed.
The grass needs cutting, if you're aiming for total serenity.
www.pajamadiaries.com
9/19

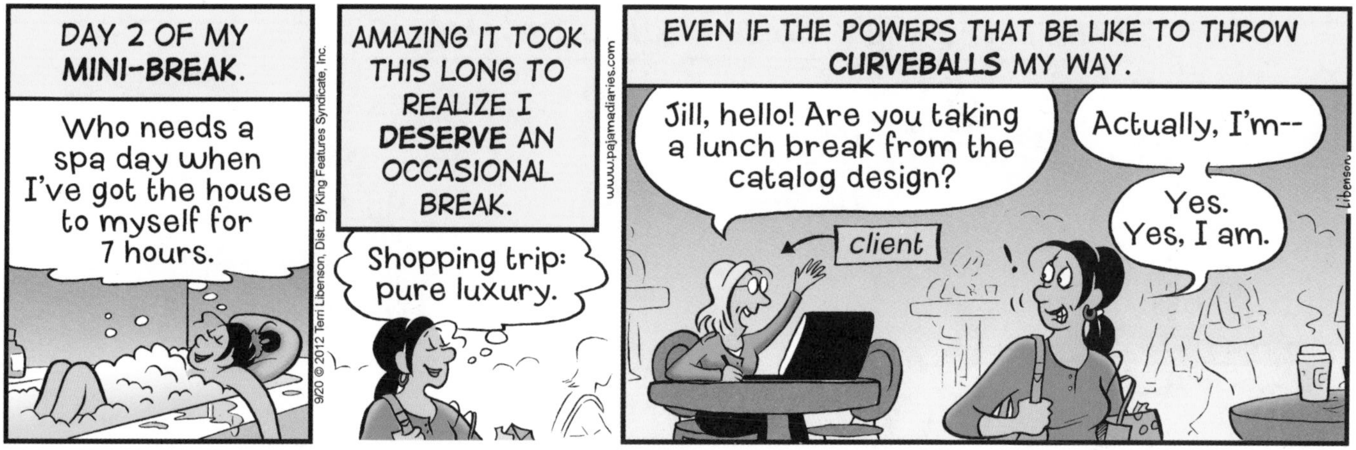
DAY 2 OF MY **MINI-BREAK**.
Who needs a spa day when I've got the house to myself for 7 hours.
9/20 © 2012 Terri Libenson, Dist. By King Features Syndicate, Inc.
AMAZING IT TOOK THIS LONG TO REALIZE I **DESERVE** AN OCCASIONAL BREAK.
Shopping trip: pure luxury.
www.pajamadiaries.com
EVEN IF THE POWERS THAT BE LIKE TO THROW **CURVEBALLS** MY WAY.
Jill, hello! Are you taking a lunch break from the catalog design?
client
Actually, I'm--
Yes. Yes, I am.
Libenson

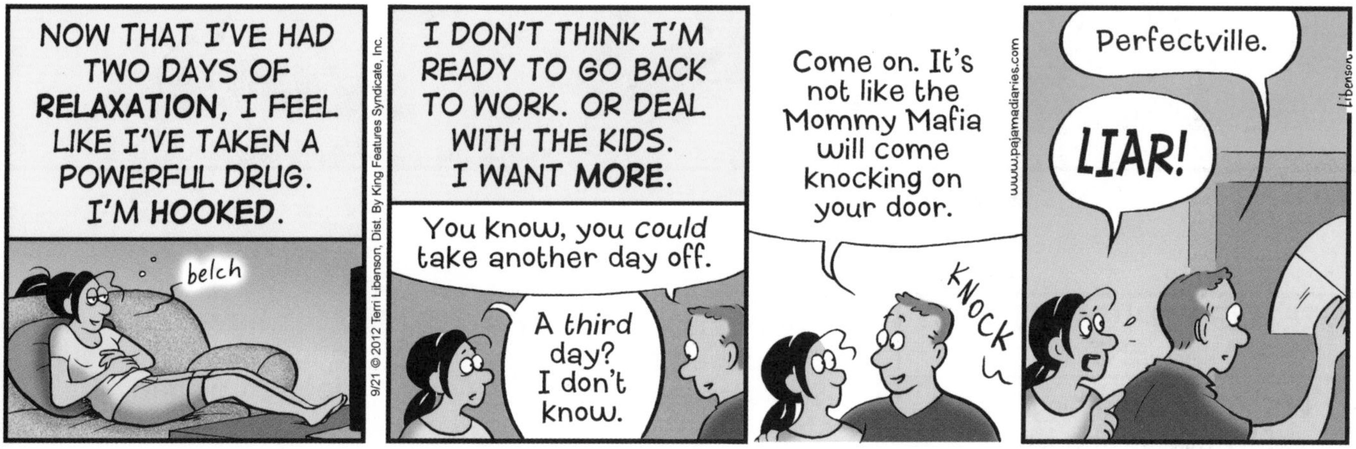
NOW THAT I'VE HAD TWO DAYS OF **RELAXATION**, I FEEL LIKE I'VE TAKEN A POWERFUL DRUG. I'M **HOOKED**.
belch
9/21 © 2012 Terri Libenson, Dist. By King Features Syndicate, Inc.
I DON'T THINK I'M READY TO GO BACK TO WORK. OR DEAL WITH THE KIDS. I WANT **MORE**.
You know, you *could* take another day off.
A *third* day? I don't know.
Come on. It's not like the Mommy Mafia will come knocking on your door.
KNOCK
www.pajamadiaries.com
Perfectville.
LIAR!
Libenson

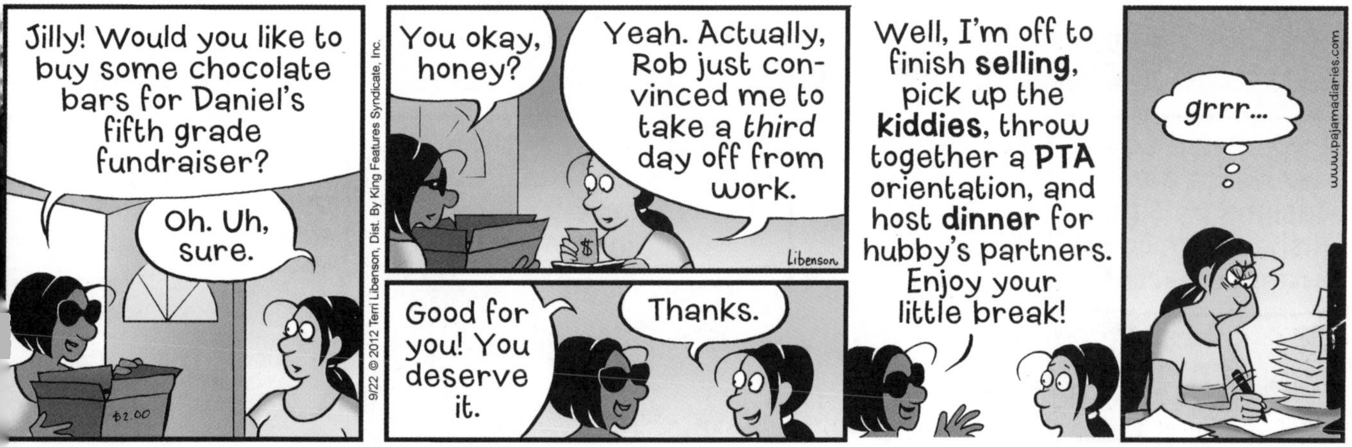
Jilly! Would you like to buy some chocolate bars for Daniel's fifth grade fundraiser?
Oh. Uh, sure.
9/22 © 2012 Terri Libenson, Dist. By King Features Syndicate, Inc.
You okay, honey?
Yeah. Actually, Rob just convinced me to take a *third* day off from work.
Libenson
Good for you! You deserve it.
Thanks.
Well, I'm off to finish **selling**, pick up the **kiddies**, throw together a **PTA** orientation, and host **dinner** for hubby's partners. Enjoy your little break!
grrr...
www.pajamadiaries.com

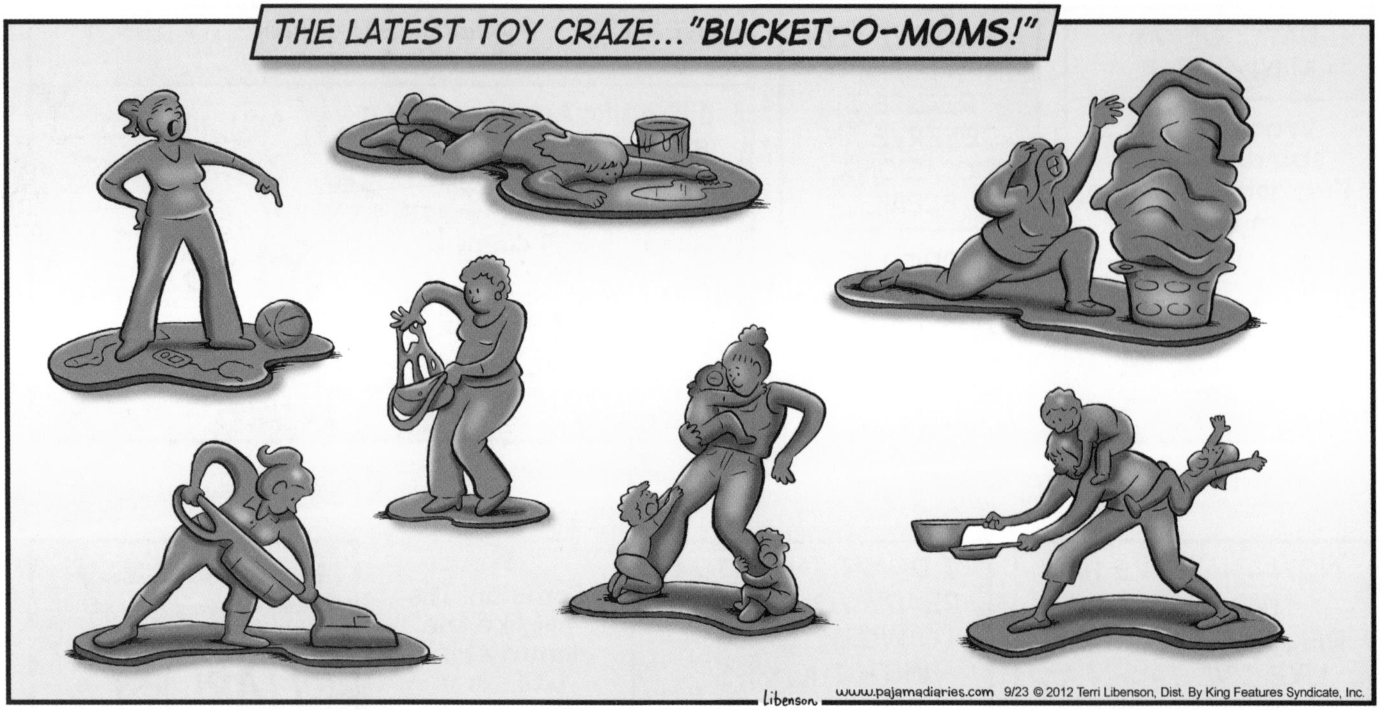
THE LATEST TOY CRAZE... "BUCKET-O-MOMS!"
Libenson
www.pajamadiaries.com 9/23 © 2012 Terri Libenson, Dist. By King Features Syndicate, Inc.

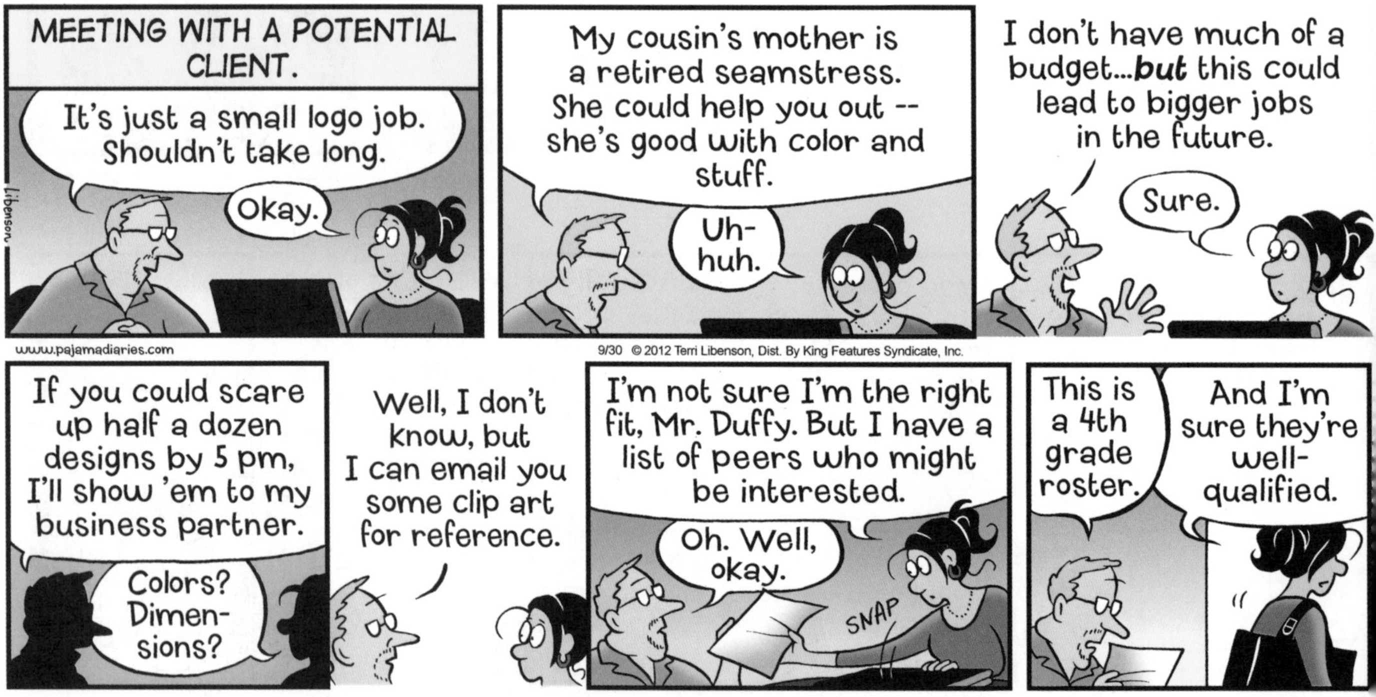
MEETING WITH A POTENTIAL CLIENT.
It's just a small logo job. Shouldn't take long.
Okay.
Libenson
My cousin's mother is a retired seamstress. She could help you out -- she's good with color and stuff.
Uh-huh.
I don't have much of a budget...**but** this could lead to bigger jobs in the future.
Sure.
www.pajamadiaries.com
9/30 © 2012 Terri Libenson, Dist. By King Features Syndicate, Inc.
If you could scare up half a dozen designs by 5 pm, I'll show 'em to my business partner.
Colors? Dimensions?
Well, I don't know, but I can email you some clip art for reference.
I'm not sure I'm the right fit, Mr. Duffy. But I have a list of peers who might be interested.
Oh. Well, okay.
SNAP
This is a 4th grade roster.
And I'm sure they're well-qualified.

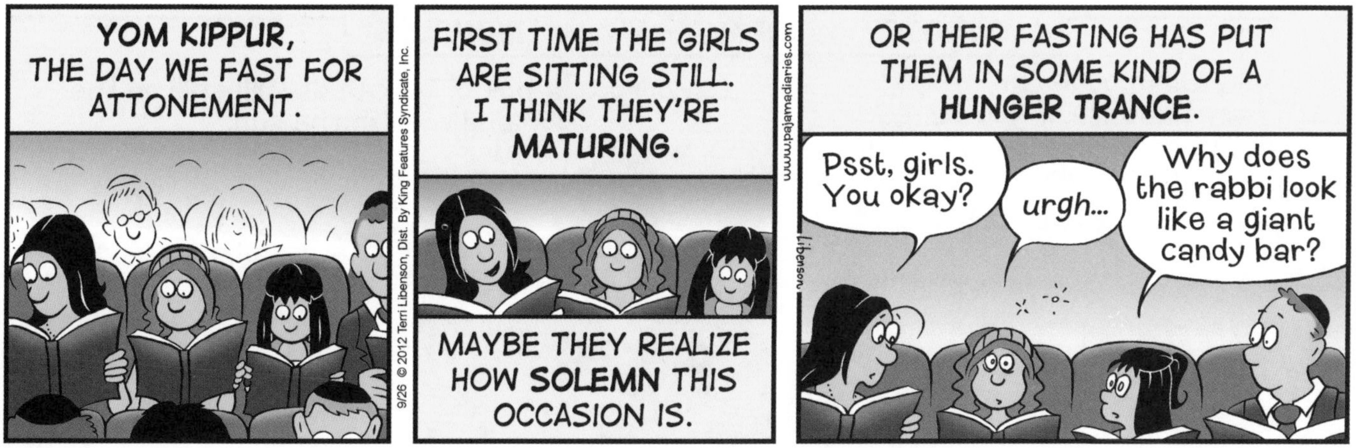
YOM KIPPUR, THE DAY WE FAST FOR ATTONEMENT.
9/26 © 2012 Terri Libenson, Dist. By King Features Syndicate, Inc.
FIRST TIME THE GIRLS ARE SITTING STILL. I THINK THEY'RE MATURING.
MAYBE THEY REALIZE HOW SOLEMN THIS OCCASION IS.
www.pajamadiaries.com
OR THEIR FASTING HAS PUT THEM IN SOME KIND OF A HUNGER TRANCE.
Psst, girls. You okay?
urgh...
Why does the rabbi look like a giant candy bar?
Libenson

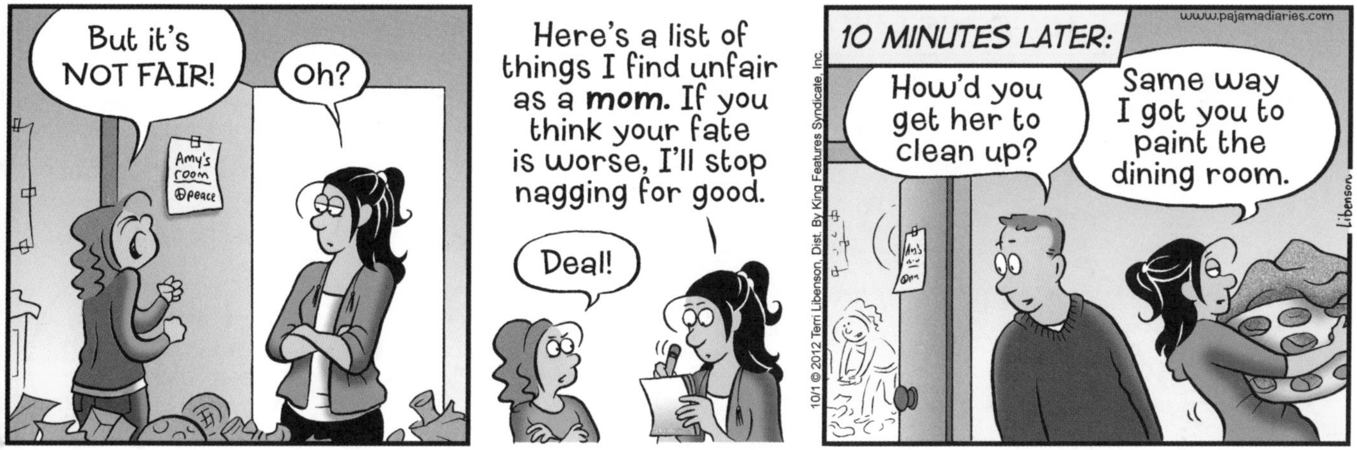
But it's NOT FAIR!
Oh?
Amy's room
peace
Here's a list of things I find unfair as a mom. If you think your fate is worse, I'll stop nagging for good.
Deal!
10/1 © 2012 Terri Libenson, Dist. By King Features Syndicate, Inc.
10 MINUTES LATER:
www.pajamadiaries.com
How'd you get her to clean up?
Same way I got you to paint the dining room.
Libenson

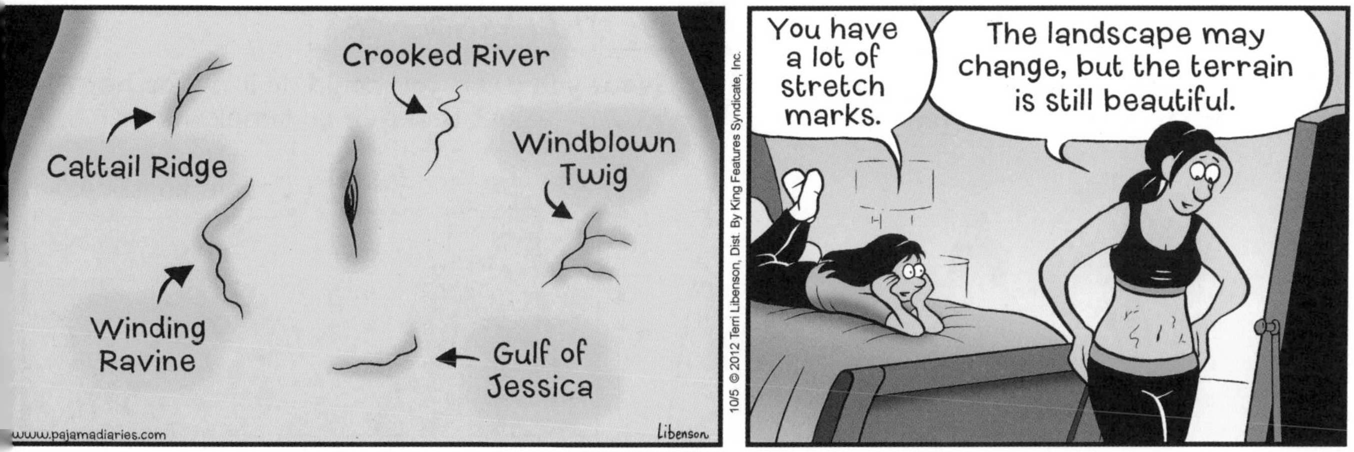
Crooked River
Cattail Ridge
Windblown Twig
Winding Ravine
Gulf of Jessica
www.pajamadiaries.com
Libenson
10/5 © 2012 Terri Libenson, Dist. By King Features Syndicate, Inc.
You have a lot of stretch marks.
The landscape may change, but the terrain is still beautiful.

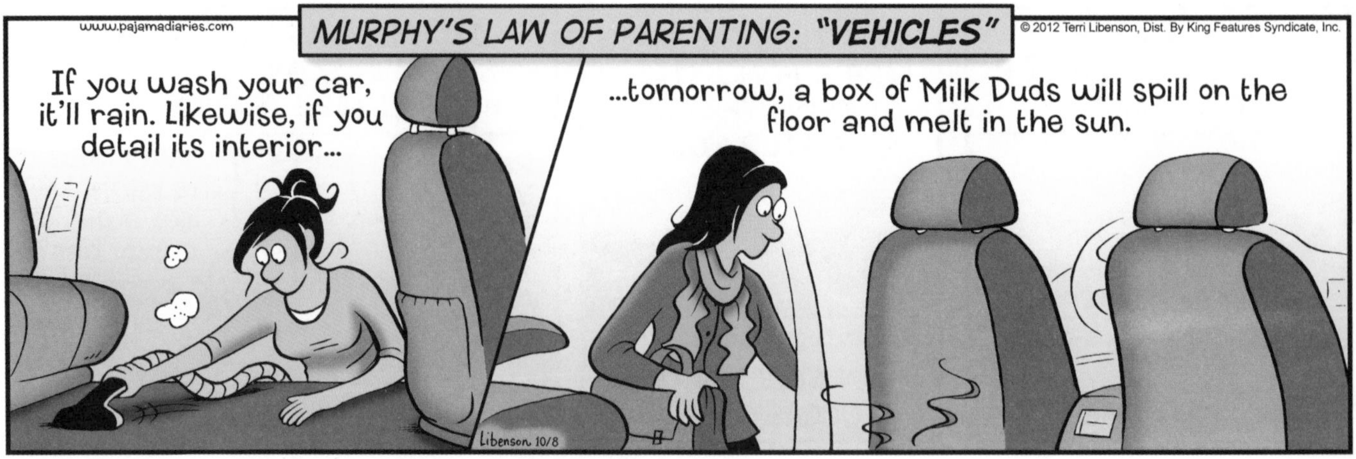
www.pajamadiaries.com
MURPHY'S LAW OF PARENTING: "VEHICLES"
© 2012 Terri Libenson, Dist. By King Features Syndicate, Inc.
If you wash your car, it'll rain. Likewise, if you detail its interior...
Libenson 10/8
...tomorrow, a box of Milk Duds will spill on the floor and melt in the sun.

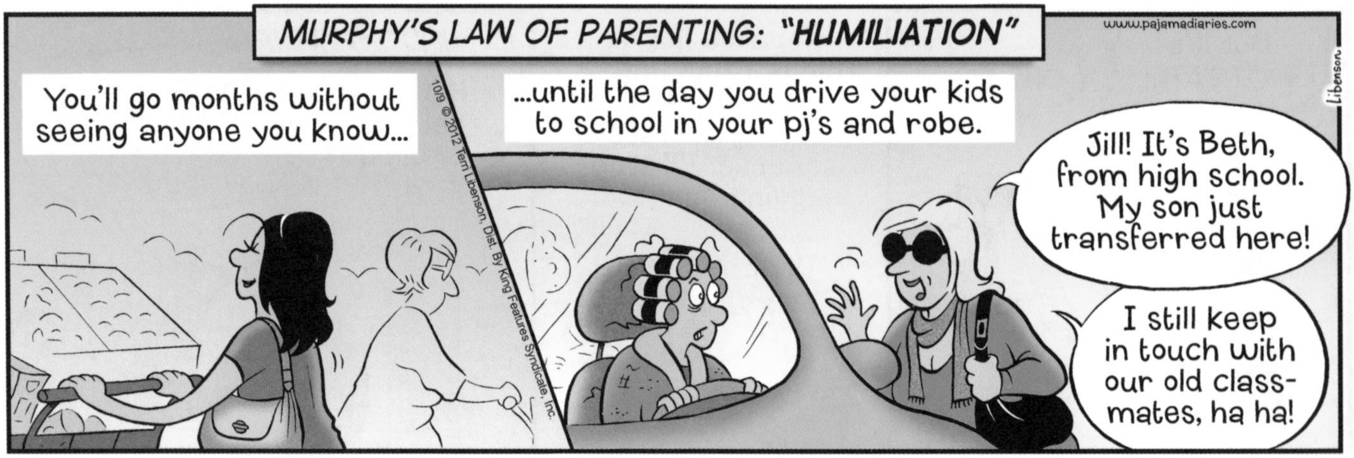
MURPHY'S LAW OF PARENTING: "HUMILIATION"
www.pajamadiaries.com
You'll go months without seeing anyone you know...
10/9 © 2012 Terri Libenson, Dist. By King Features Syndicate, Inc.
...until the day you drive your kids to school in your pj's and robe.
Jill! It's Beth, from high school. My son just transferred here!
I still keep in touch with our old class-mates, ha ha!
Libenson

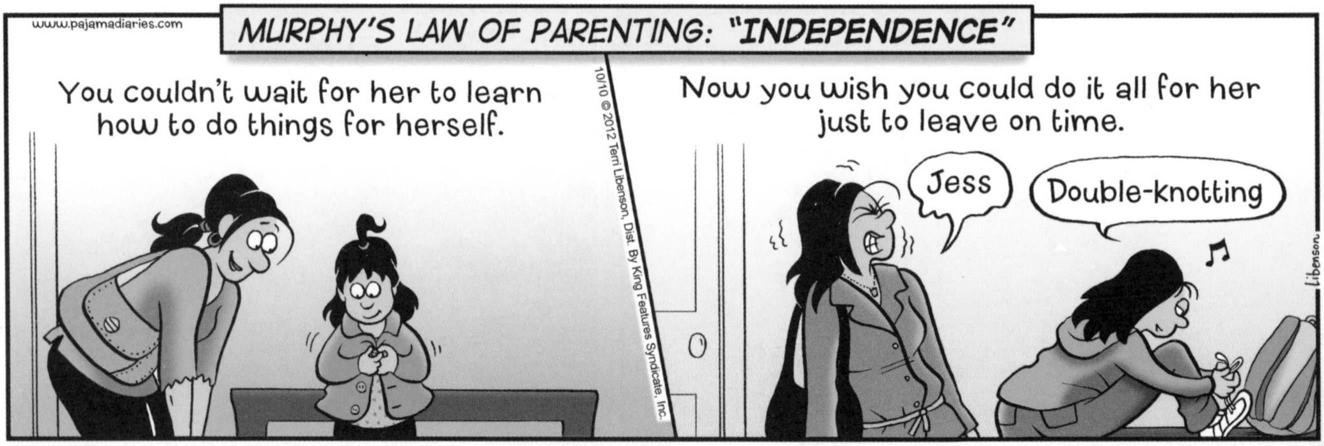
www.pajamadiaries.com
MURPHY'S LAW OF PARENTING: "INDEPENDENCE"
You couldn't wait for her to learn how to do things for herself.
10/10 © 2012 Terri Libenson, Dist. By King Features Syndicate, Inc.
Now you wish you could do it all for her just to leave on time.
Jess
Double-knotting
Libenson

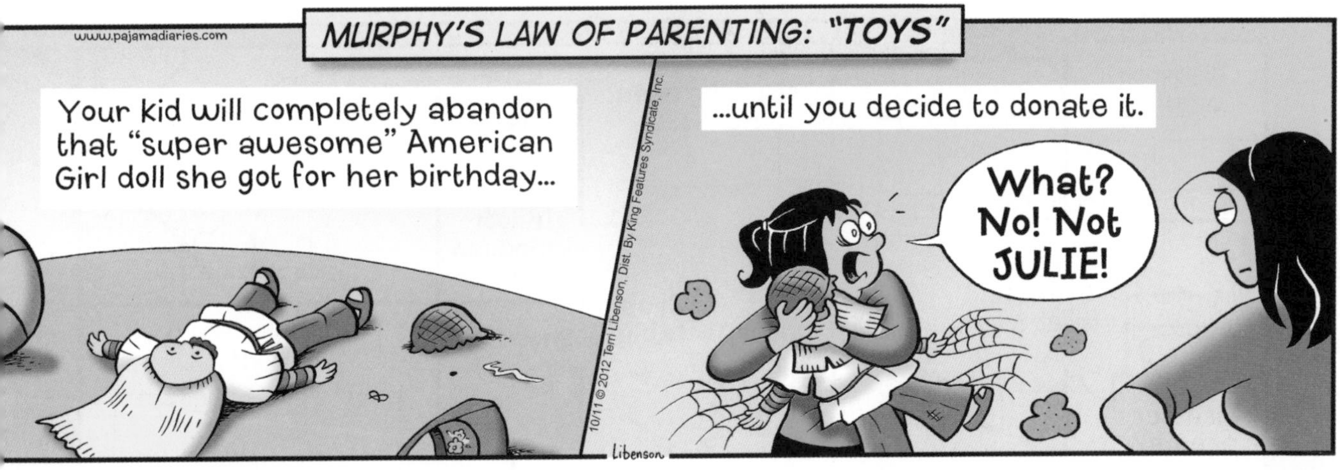
MURPHY'S LAW OF PARENTING: "TOYS"
www.pajamadiaries.com
Your kid will completely abandon that "super awesome" American Girl doll she got for her birthday...
10/11 © 2012 Terri Libenson, Dist. By King Features Syndicate, Inc.
Libenson
...until you decide to donate it.
What? No! Not JULIE!

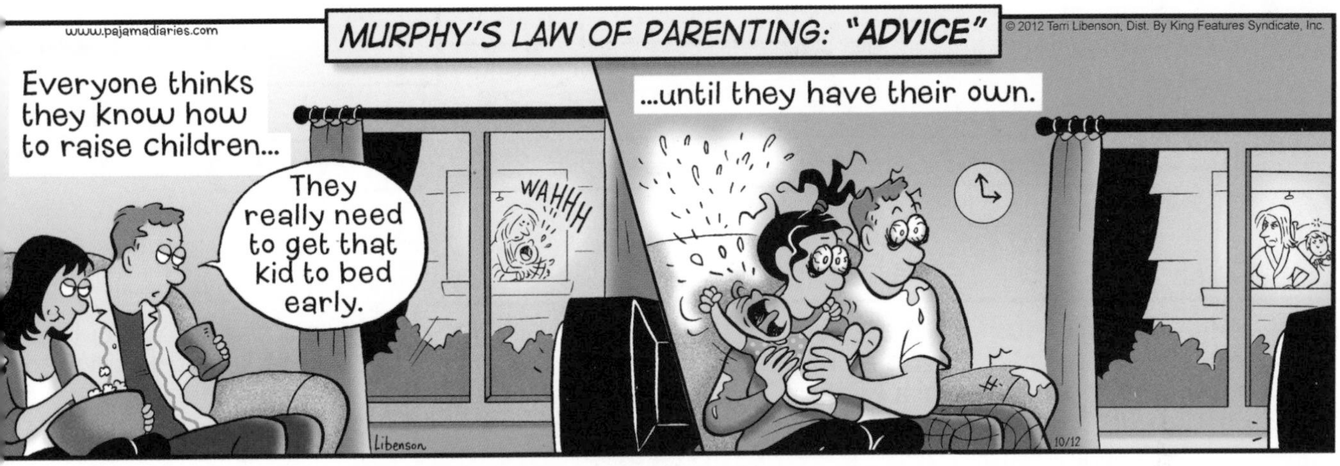
MURPHY'S LAW OF PARENTING: "ADVICE"
www.pajamadiaries.com
© 2012 Terri Libenson, Dist. By King Features Syndicate, Inc.
Everyone thinks they know how to raise children...
They really need to get that kid to bed early.
WAHHH
Libenson
...until they have their own.
10/12

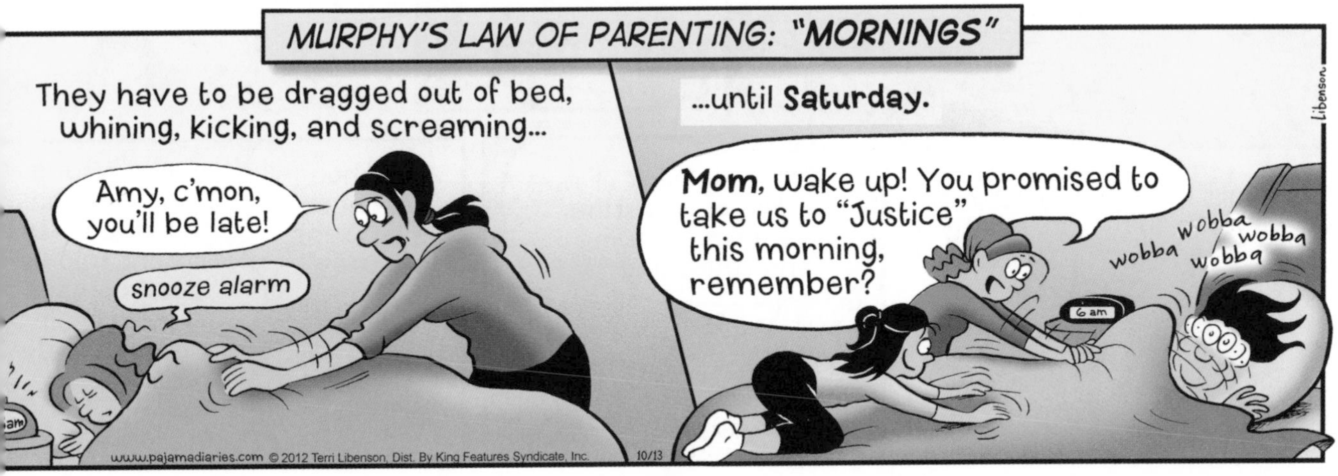
MURPHY'S LAW OF PARENTING: "MORNINGS"
They have to be dragged out of bed, whining, kicking, and screaming...
Amy, c'mon, you'll be late!
snooze alarm
www.pajamadiaries.com © 2012 Terri Libenson, Dist. By King Features Syndicate, Inc.
10/13
...until Saturday.
Libenson
Mom, wake up! You promised to take us to "Justice" this morning, remember?
6 am
wobba wobba wobba wobba

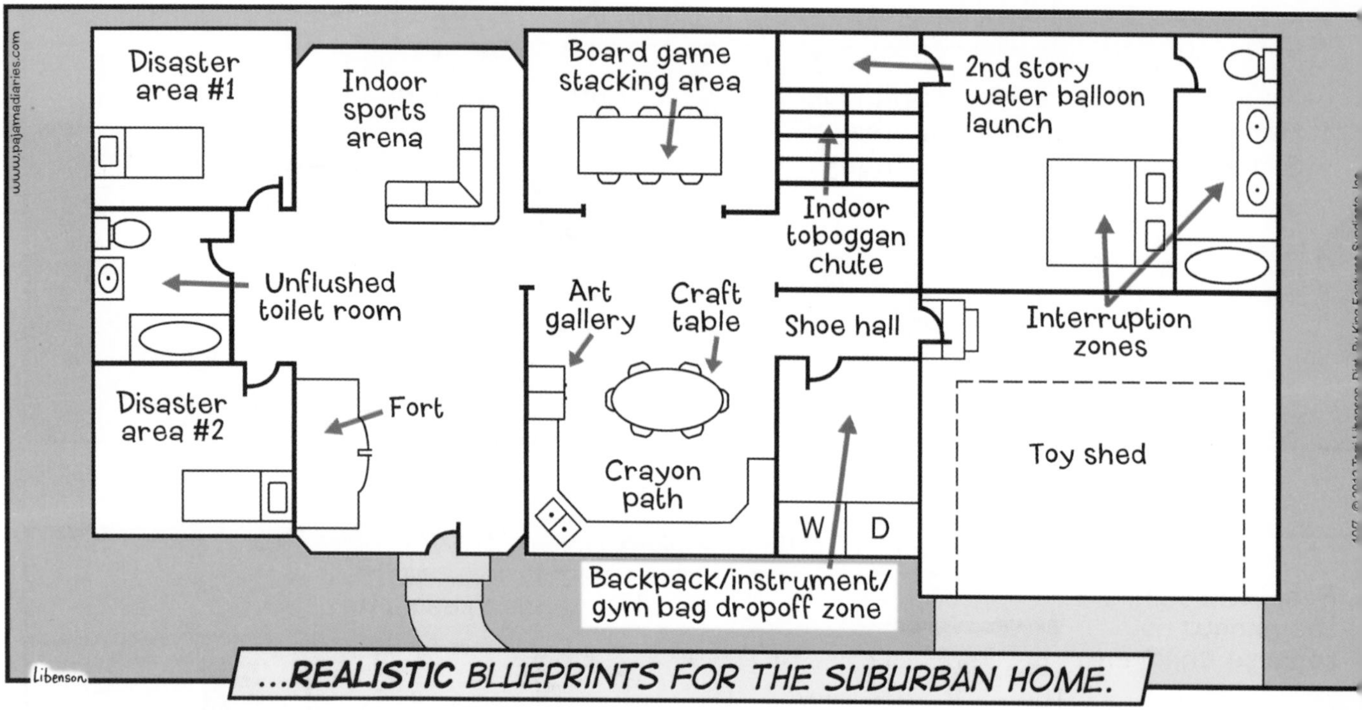
www.pajamadiaries.com
Disaster area #1
Indoor sports arena
Board game stacking area
2nd story water balloon launch
Indoor toboggan chute
Unflushed toilet room
Art gallery
Craft table
Shoe hall
Interruption zones
Disaster area #2
Fort
Crayon path
Toy shed
W
D
Backpack/instrument/gym bag dropoff zone
Libenson
...REALISTIC BLUEPRINTS FOR THE SUBURBAN HOME.

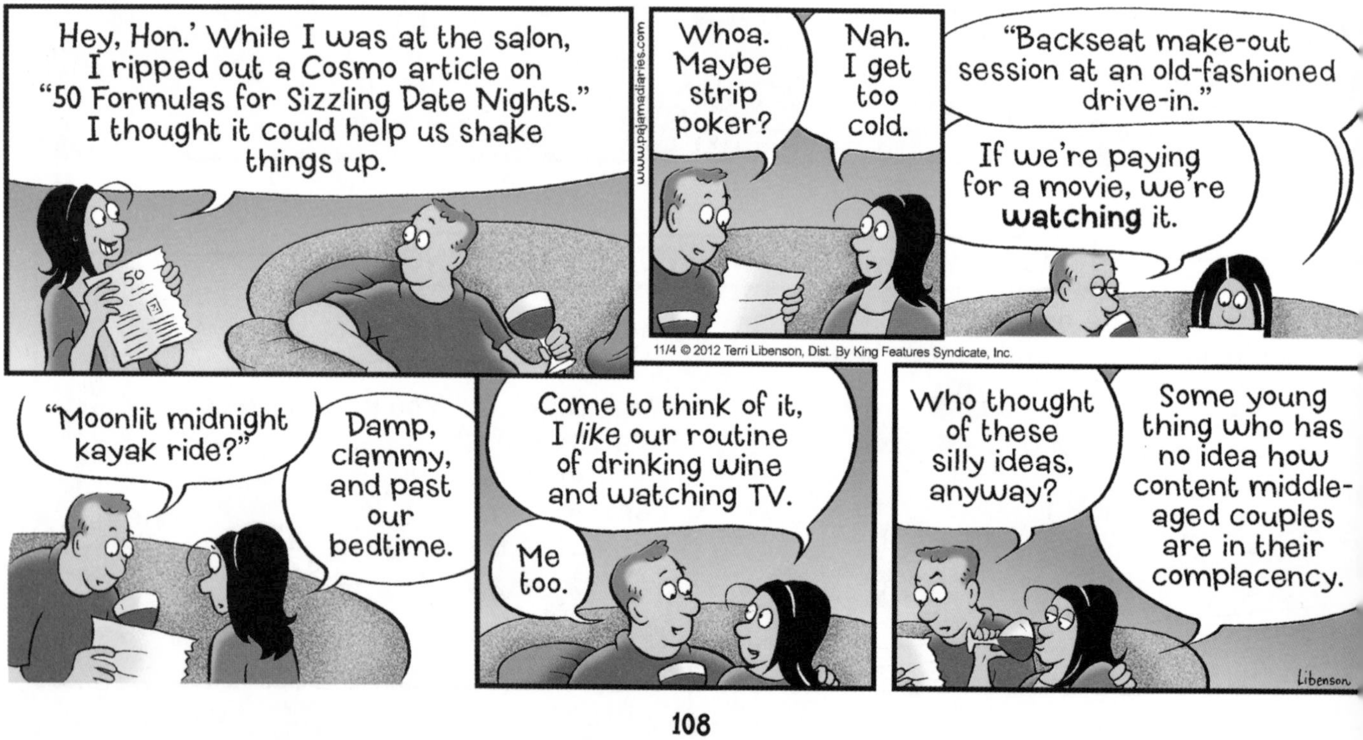
Hey, Hon.' While I was at the salon, I ripped out a Cosmo article on "50 Formulas for Sizzling Date Nights." I thought it could help us shake things up.
50
www.pajamadiaries.com
Whoa. Maybe strip poker?
Nah. I get too cold.
"Backseat make-out session at an old-fashioned drive-in."
If we're paying for a movie, we're **watching** it.
11/4 © 2012 Terri Libenson, Dist. By King Features Syndicate, Inc.
"Moonlit midnight kayak ride?"
Damp, clammy, and past our bedtime.
Come to think of it, I *like* our routine of drinking wine and watching TV.
Me too.
Who thought of these silly ideas, anyway?
Some young thing who has no idea how content middle-aged couples are in their complacency.
Libenson

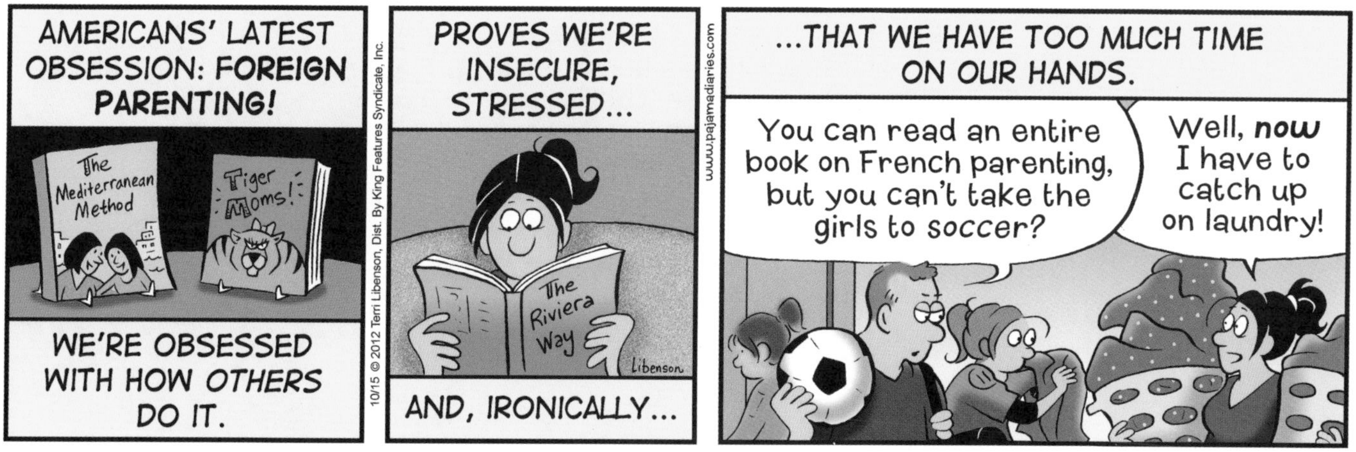
AMERICANS' LATEST OBSESSION: FOREIGN PARENTING!
The Mediterranean Method
Tiger Moms!
WE'RE OBSESSED WITH HOW OTHERS DO IT.
PROVES WE'RE INSECURE, STRESSED...
The Riviera Way
AND, IRONICALLY...
...THAT WE HAVE TOO MUCH TIME ON OUR HANDS.
You can read an entire book on French parenting, but you can't take the girls to soccer?
Well, now I have to catch up on laundry!
10/15 © 2012 Terri Libenson, Dist. By King Features Syndicate, Inc.
www.pajamadiaries.com
Libenson

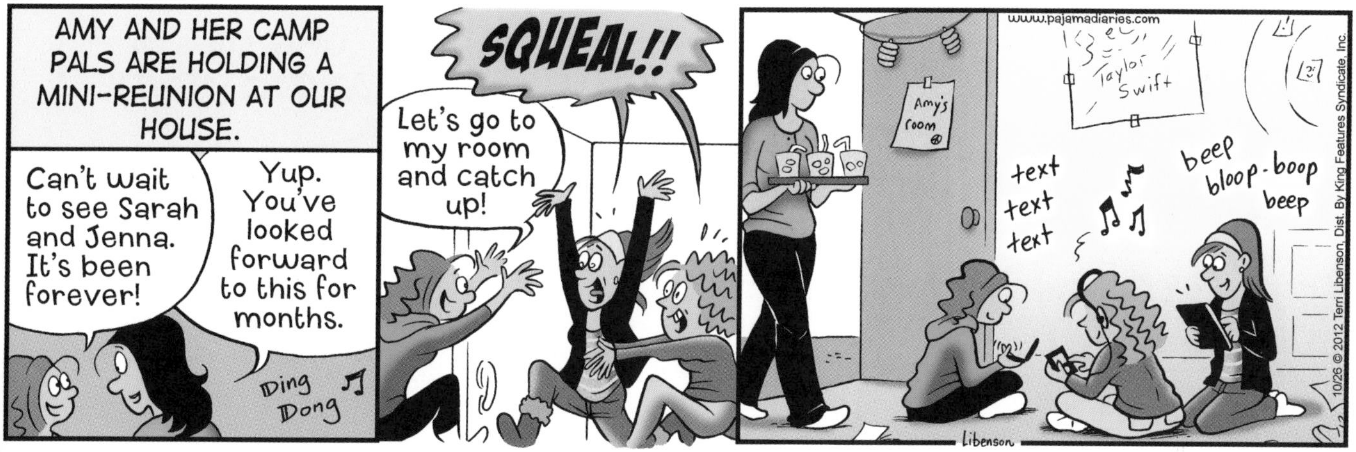
AMY AND HER CAMP PALS ARE HOLDING A MINI-REUNION AT OUR HOUSE.
Can't wait to see Sarah and Jenna. It's been forever!
Yup. You've looked forward to this for months.
Ding Dong
SQUEAL!!
Let's go to my room and catch up!
Amy's room
Taylor Swift
text text text
beep bloop-boop beep
www.pajamadiaries.com
10/26 © 2012 Terri Libenson, Dist. By King Features Syndicate, Inc.
Libenson

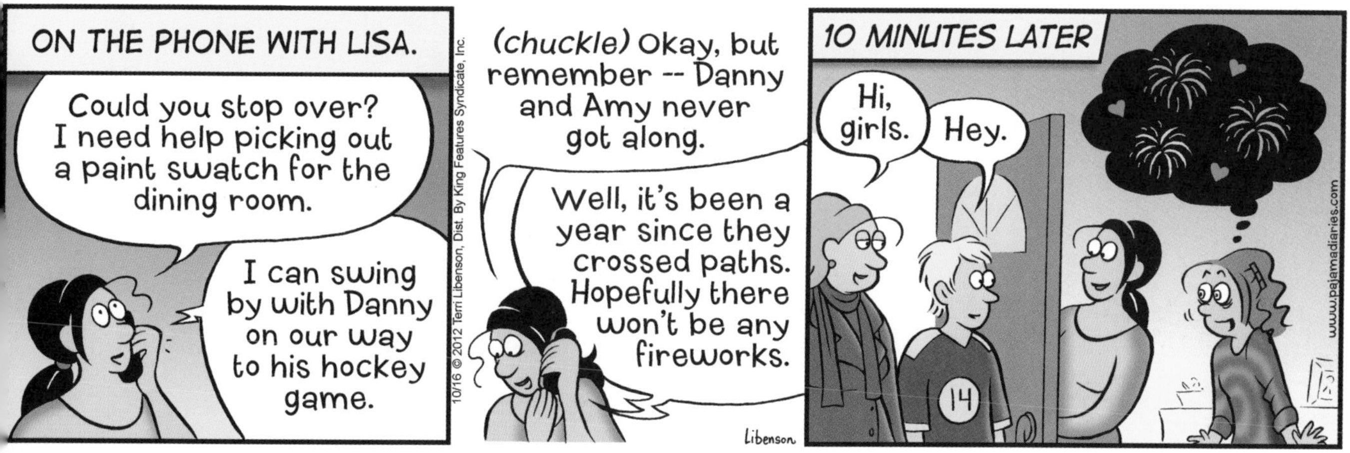
ON THE PHONE WITH LISA.
Could you stop over? I need help picking out a paint swatch for the dining room.
I can swing by with Danny on our way to his hockey game.
(chuckle) Okay, but remember -- Danny and Amy never got along.
Well, it's been a year since they crossed paths. Hopefully there won't be any fireworks.
10 MINUTES LATER
Hi, girls.
Hey.
14
10/16 © 2012 Terri Libenson, Dist. By King Features Syndicate, Inc.
www.pajamadiaries.com
Libenson

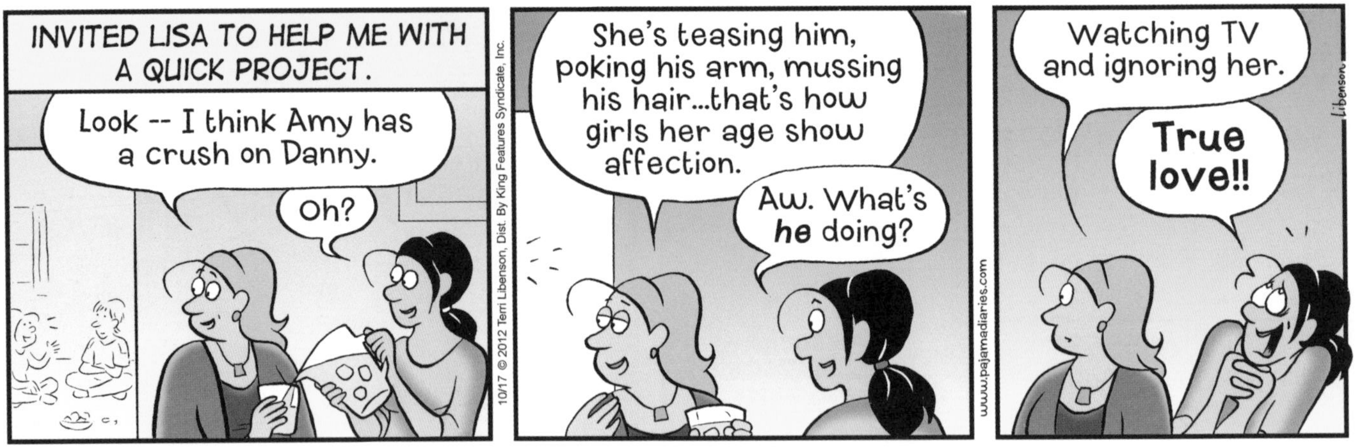
INVITED LISA TO HELP ME WITH A QUICK PROJECT.
Look -- I think Amy has a crush on Danny.
Oh?
10/17 © 2012 Terri Libenson, Dist. By King Features Syndicate, Inc.
She's teasing him, poking his arm, mussing his hair...that's how girls her age show affection.
Aw. What's **he** doing?
www.pajamadiaries.com
Watching TV and ignoring her.
True love!!
Libenson

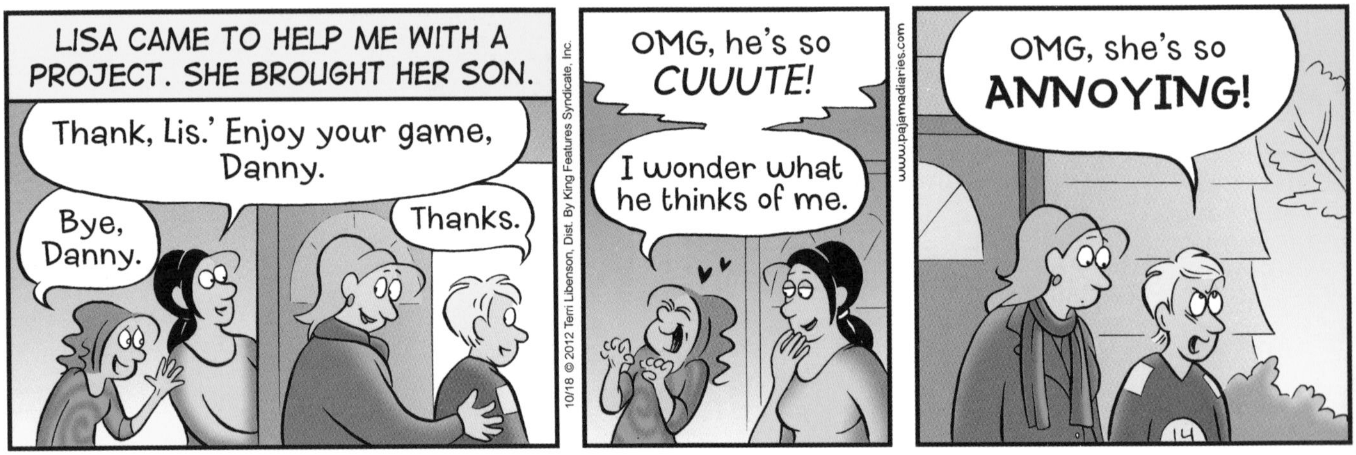
LISA CAME TO HELP ME WITH A PROJECT. SHE BROUGHT HER SON.
Thank, Lis.' Enjoy your game, Danny.
Bye, Danny.
Thanks.
10/18 © 2012 Terri Libenson, Dist. By King Features Syndicate, Inc.
OMG, he's so *CUUUTE!*
I wonder what he thinks of me.
www.pajamadiaries.com
OMG, she's so **ANNOYING!**
14

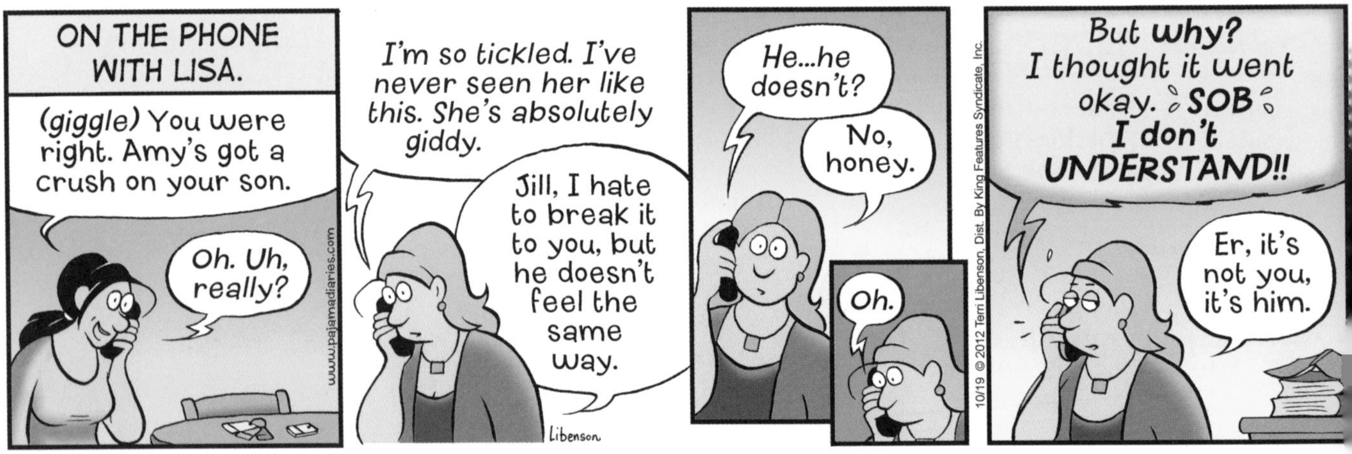
ON THE PHONE WITH LISA.
(giggle) You were right. Amy's got a crush on your son.
Oh. Uh, really?
www.pajamadiaries.com
I'm so tickled. I've never seen her like this. She's absolutely giddy.
Jill, I hate to break it to you, but he doesn't feel the same way.
Libenson
He...he doesn't?
No, honey.
Oh.
10/19 © 2012 Terri Libenson, Dist. By King Features Syndicate, Inc.
*But **why?** I thought it went okay.* ***SOB*** ***I don't UNDERSTAND!!***
Er, it's not you, it's him.

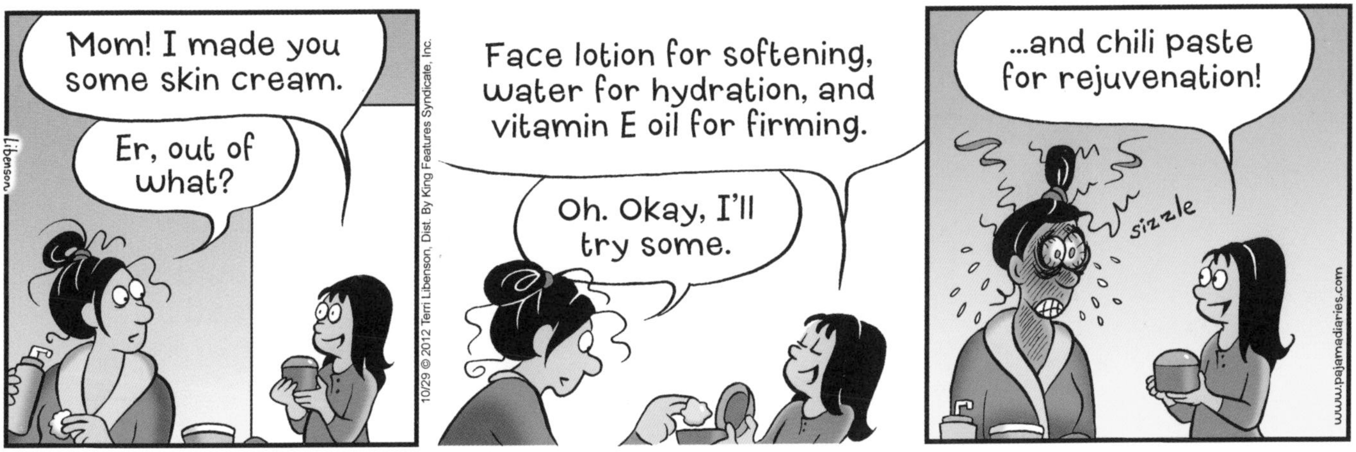
Libenson
Mom! I made you some skin cream.
Er, out of what?
10/29 © 2012 Terri Libenson, Dist. By King Features Syndicate, Inc.
Face lotion for softening, water for hydration, and vitamin E oil for firming.
Oh. Okay, I'll try some.
...and chili paste for rejuvenation!
sizzle
www.pajamadiaries.com

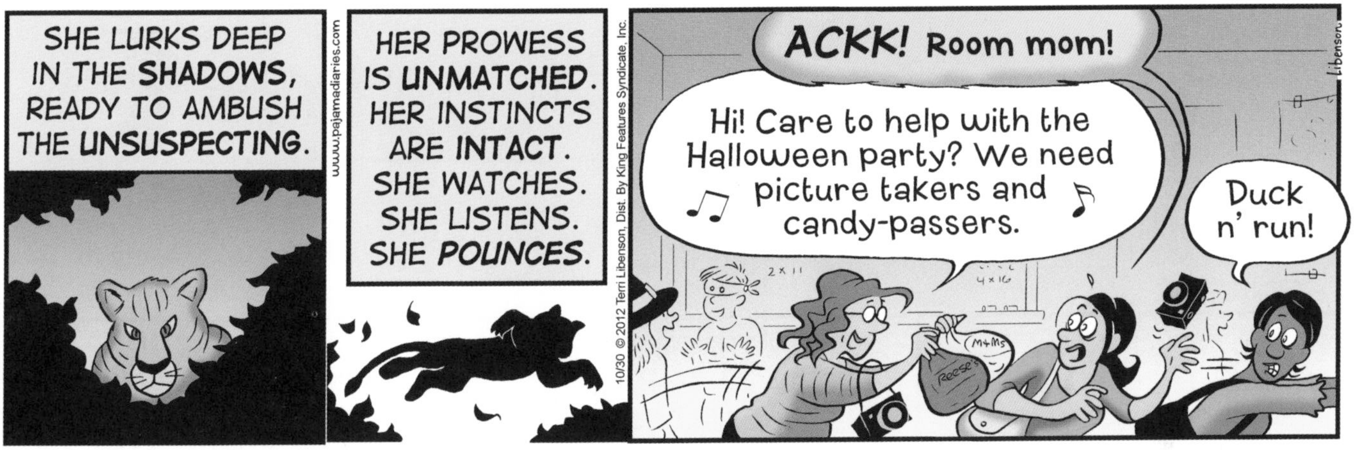
SHE LURKS DEEP IN THE **SHADOWS**, READY TO AMBUSH THE **UNSUSPECTING**.
www.pajamadiaries.com
HER PROWESS IS **UNMATCHED**. HER INSTINCTS ARE **INTACT**. SHE WATCHES. SHE LISTENS. SHE ***POUNCES***.
10/30 © 2012 Terri Libenson, Dist. By King Features Syndicate, Inc.
ACKK! Room mom!
Hi! Care to help with the Halloween party? We need picture takers and candy-passers.
Duck n' run!
Libenson

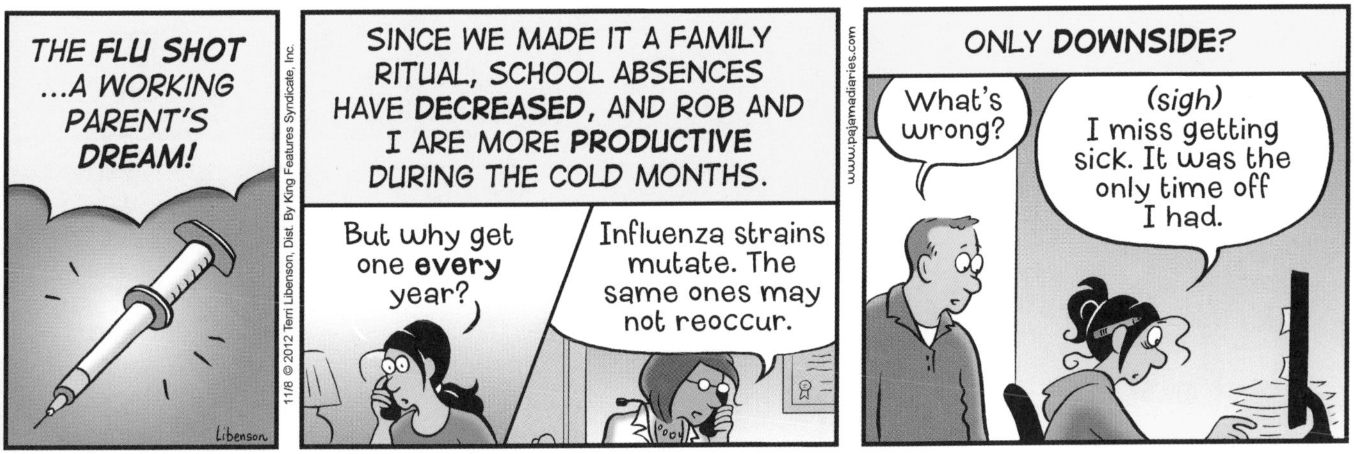
*THE **FLU SHOT** ...A WORKING PARENT'S **DREAM!***
Libenson
11/8 © 2012 Terri Libenson, Dist. By King Features Syndicate, Inc.
SINCE WE MADE IT A FAMILY RITUAL, SCHOOL ABSENCES HAVE **DECREASED**, AND ROB AND I ARE MORE **PRODUCTIVE** DURING THE COLD MONTHS.
But why get one **every** year?
Influenza strains mutate. The same ones may not reoccur.
www.pajamadiaries.com
ONLY **DOWNSIDE?**
What's wrong?
(sigh) I miss getting sick. It was the only time off I had.

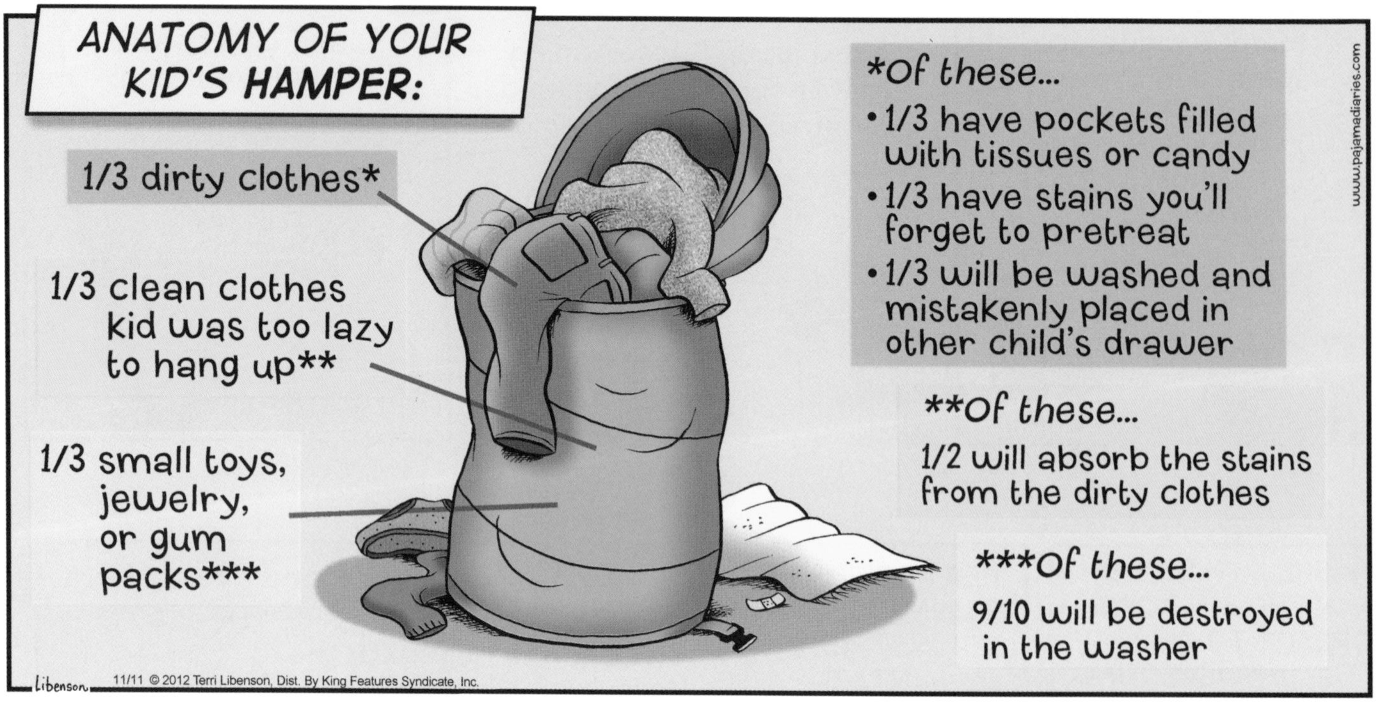
ANATOMY OF YOUR KID'S HAMPER:
1/3 dirty clothes*
1/3 clean clothes kid was too lazy to hang up**
1/3 small toys, jewelry, or gum packs***
*Of these...
• 1/3 have pockets filled with tissues or candy
• 1/3 have stains you'll forget to pretreat
• 1/3 will be washed and mistakenly placed in other child's drawer
**Of these...
1/2 will absorb the stains from the dirty clothes
***Of these...
9/10 will be destroyed in the washer
www.pajamadiaries.com
Libenson
11/11 © 2012 Terri Libenson, Dist. By King Features Syndicate, Inc.

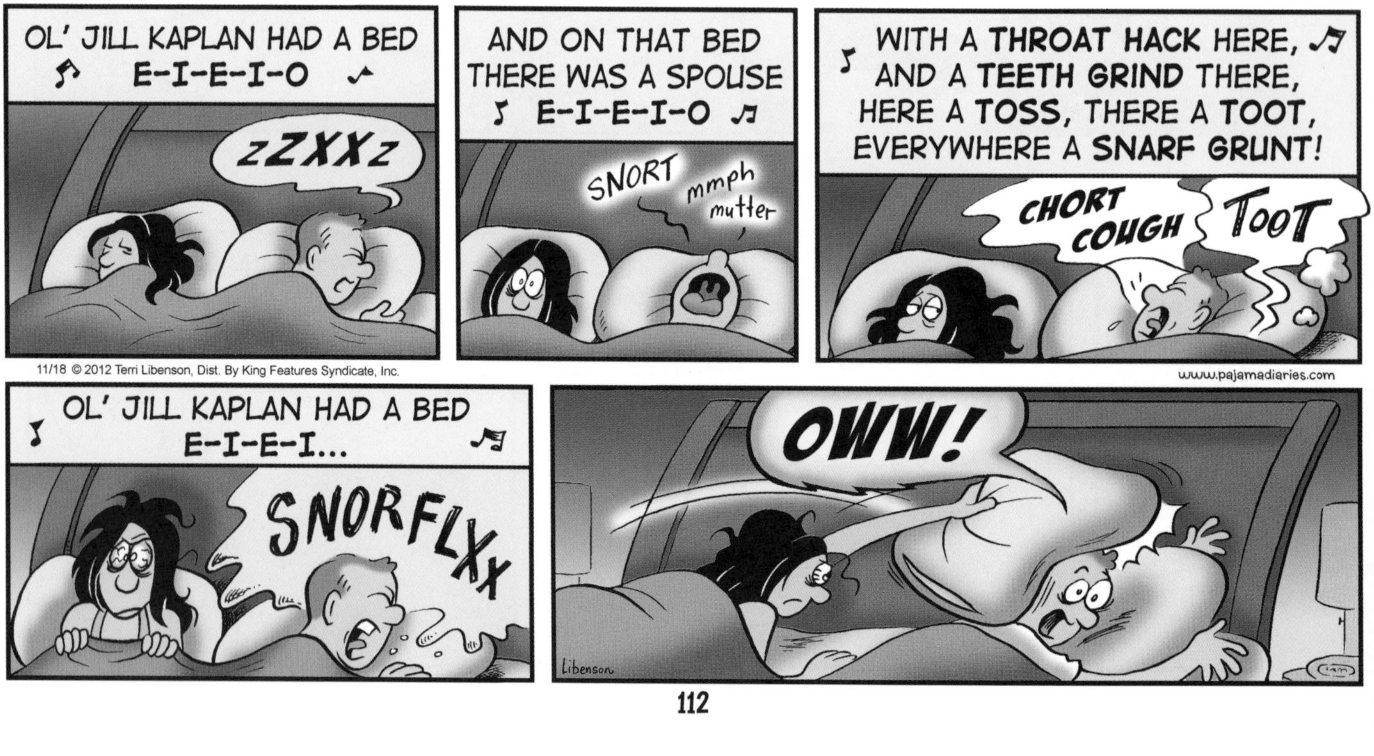
OL' JILL KAPLAN HAD A BED E-I-E-I-O
zZXXz
AND ON THAT BED THERE WAS A SPOUSE E-I-E-I-O
SNORT
mmph mutter
WITH A **THROAT HACK** HERE, AND A **TEETH GRIND** THERE, HERE A **TOSS**, THERE A **TOOT**, EVERYWHERE A **SNARF GRUNT**!
CHORT COUGH
TOOT
11/18 © 2012 Terri Libenson, Dist. By King Features Syndicate, Inc.
www.pajamadiaries.com
OL' JILL KAPLAN HAD A BED E-I-E-I...
SNORFLXX
OWW!
Libenson

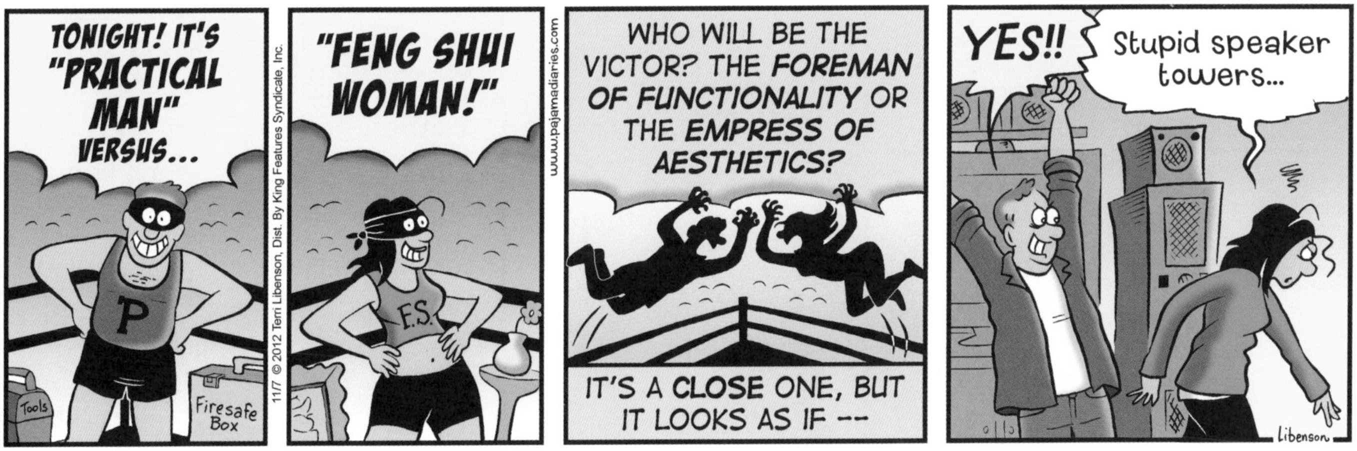
TONIGHT! IT'S "PRACTICAL MAN" VERSUS...
Tools
Firesafe Box
11/7 © 2012 Terri Libenson, Dist. By King Features Syndicate, Inc.
"FENG SHUI WOMAN!"
www.pajamadiaries.com
WHO WILL BE THE VICTOR? THE FOREMAN OF FUNCTIONALITY OR THE EMPRESS OF AESTHETICS?
IT'S A CLOSE ONE, BUT IT LOOKS AS IF --
YES!!
Stupid speaker towers...
Libenson

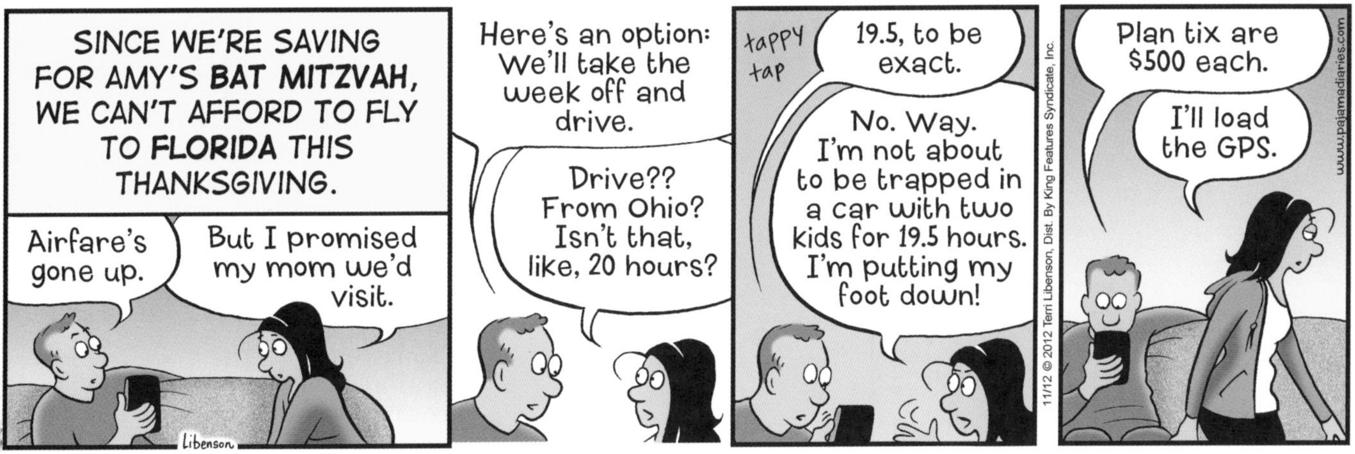
SINCE WE'RE SAVING FOR AMY'S BAT MITZVAH, WE CAN'T AFFORD TO FLY TO FLORIDA THIS THANKSGIVING.
Airfare's gone up.
But I promised my mom we'd visit.
Libenson
Here's an option: We'll take the week off and drive.
Drive?? From Ohio? Isn't that, like, 20 hours?
tappy tap
19.5, to be exact.
No. Way. I'm not about to be trapped in a car with two kids for 19.5 hours. I'm putting my foot down!
11/12 © 2012 Terri Libenson, Dist. By King Features Syndicate, Inc.
Plan tix are $500 each.
I'll load the GPS.
www.pajamadiaries.com

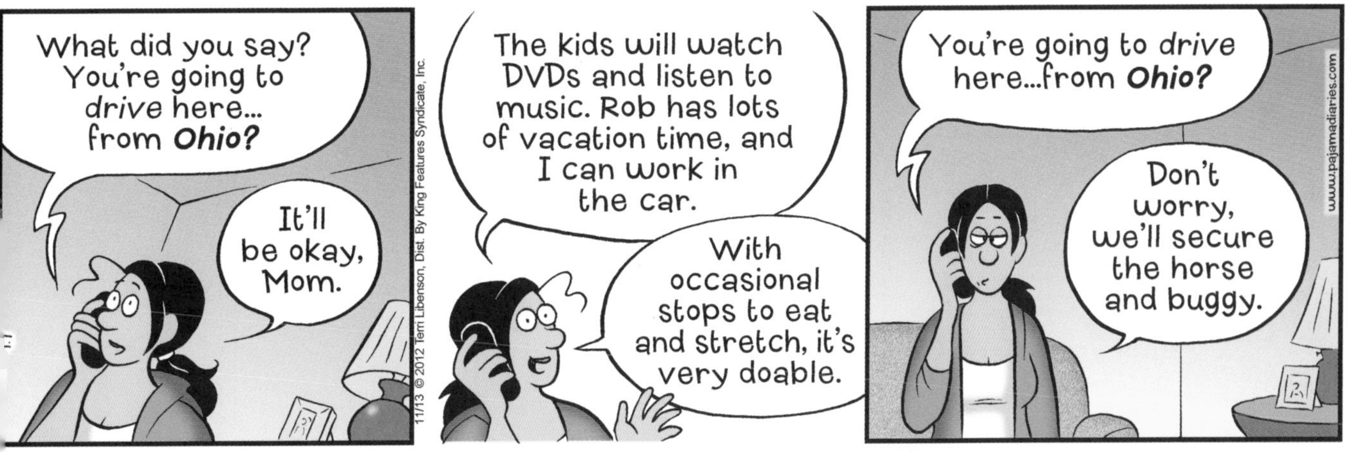
What did you say? You're going to drive here... from Ohio?
It'll be okay, Mom.
11/13 © 2012 Terri Libenson, Dist. By King Features Syndicate, Inc.
The kids will watch DVDs and listen to music. Rob has lots of vacation time, and I can work in the car.
With occasional stops to eat and stretch, it's very doable.
You're going to drive here...from Ohio?
Don't worry, we'll secure the horse and buggy.
www.pajamadiaries.com

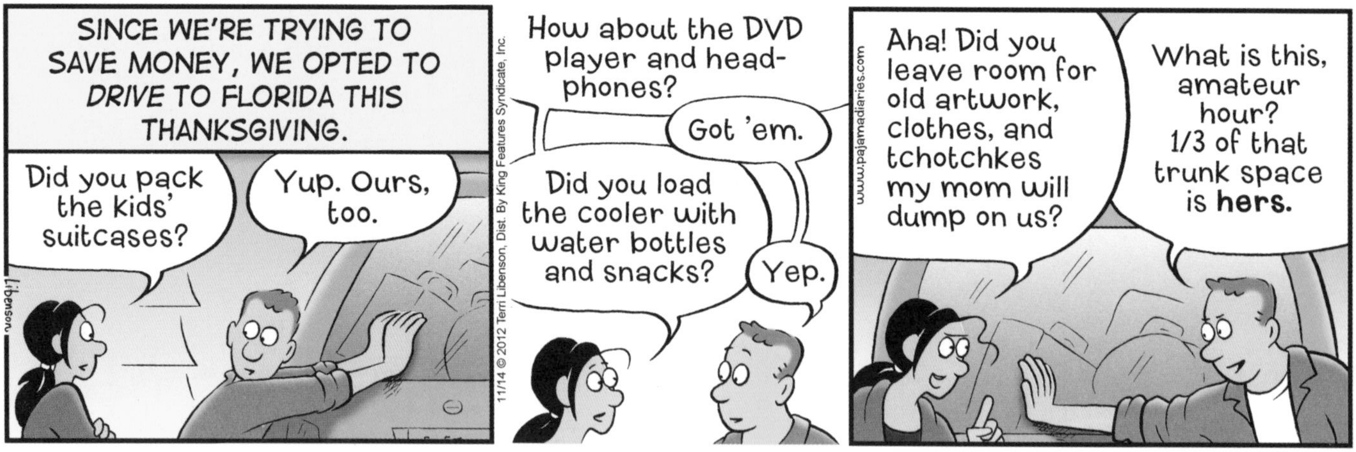
SINCE WE'RE TRYING TO SAVE MONEY, WE OPTED TO *DRIVE* TO FLORIDA THIS THANKSGIVING.
Did you pack the kids' suitcases?
Yup. Ours, too.
Libenson
11/14 © 2012 Terri Libenson, Dist. By King Features Syndicate, Inc.
How about the DVD player and headphones?
Got 'em.
Did you load the cooler with water bottles and snacks?
Yep.
www.pajamadiaries.com
Aha! Did you leave room for old artwork, clothes, and tchotchkes my mom will dump on us?
What is this, amateur hour? 1/3 of that trunk space is **hers.**

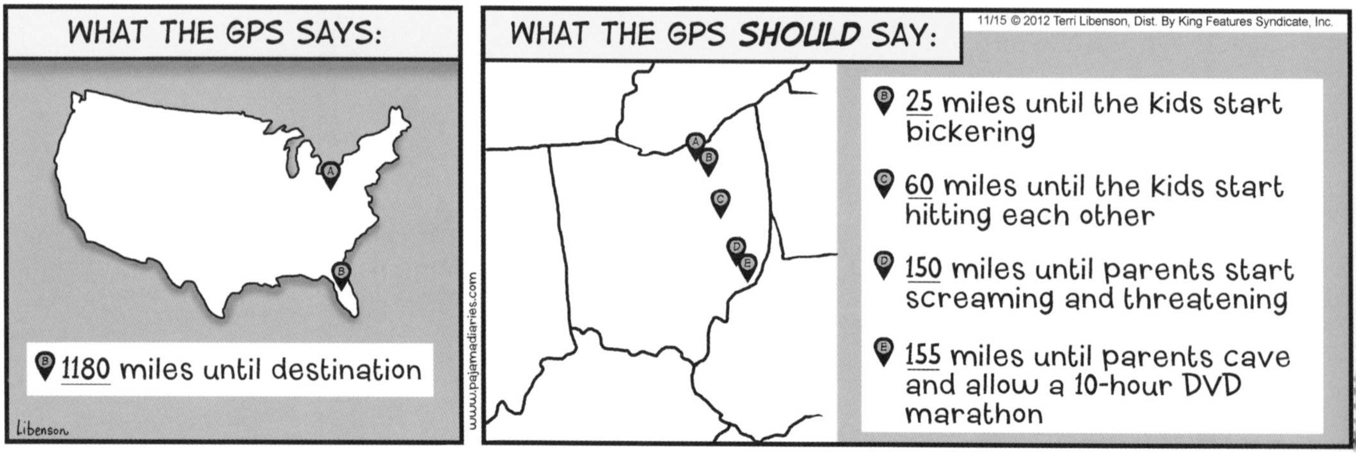
WHAT THE GPS SAYS:
1180 miles until destination
Libenson
www.pajamadiaries.com
WHAT THE GPS *SHOULD* SAY:
11/15 © 2012 Terri Libenson, Dist. By King Features Syndicate, Inc.
25 miles until the kids start bickering
60 miles until the kids start hitting each other
150 miles until parents start screaming and threatening
155 miles until parents cave and allow a 10-hour DVD marathon

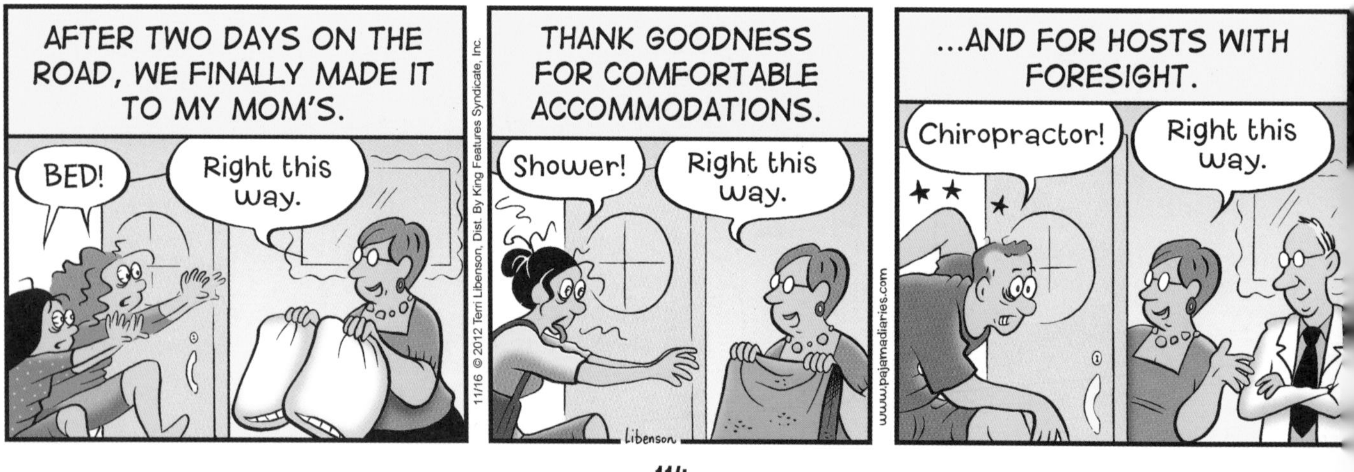
AFTER TWO DAYS ON THE ROAD, WE FINALLY MADE IT TO MY MOM'S.
BED!
Right this way.
11/16 © 2012 Terri Libenson, Dist. By King Features Syndicate, Inc.
THANK GOODNESS FOR COMFORTABLE ACCOMMODATIONS.
Shower!
Right this way.
Libenson
www.pajamadiaries.com
...AND FOR HOSTS WITH FORESIGHT.
Chiropractor!
Right this way.

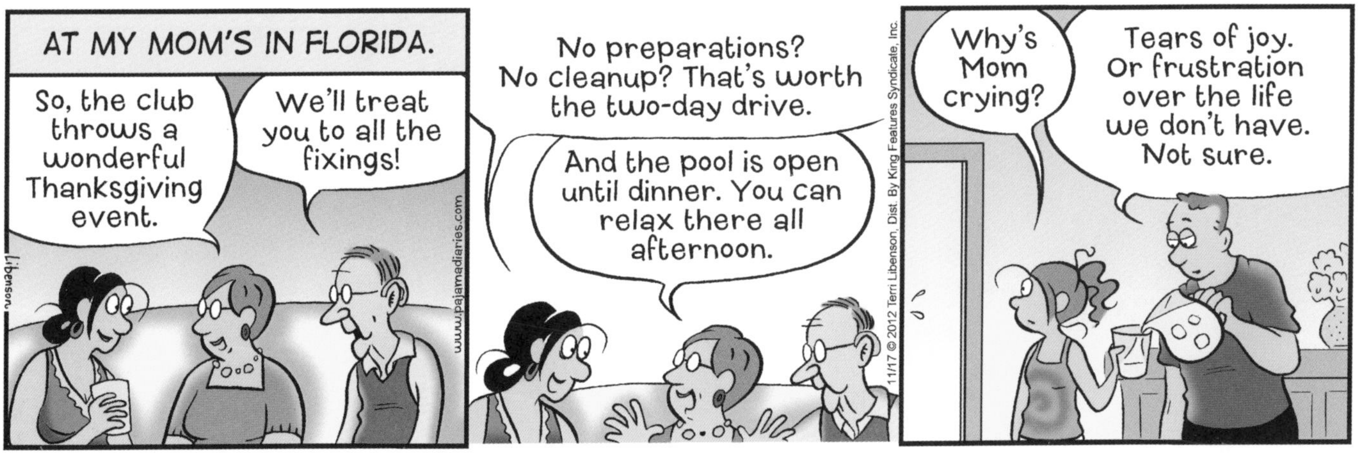
AT MY MOM'S IN FLORIDA.
So, the club throws a wonderful Thanksgiving event.
We'll treat you to all the fixings!
Libenson
www.pajamadiaries.com
No preparations? No cleanup? That's worth the two-day drive.
And the pool is open until dinner. You can relax there all afternoon.
11/17 © 2012 Terri Libenson, Dist. By King Features Syndicate, Inc.
Why's Mom crying?
Tears of joy. Or frustration over the life we don't have. Not sure.

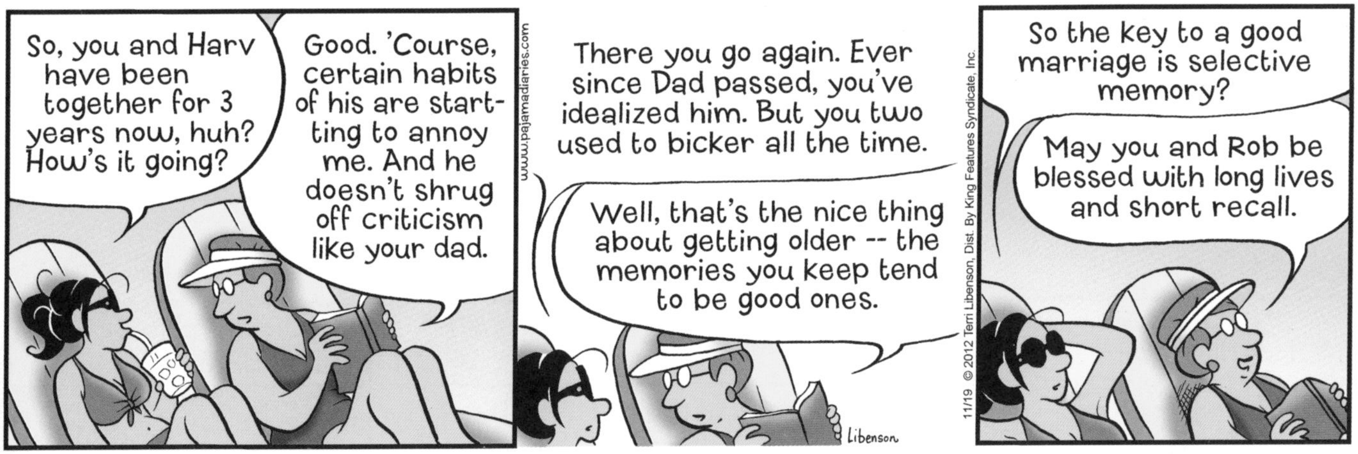
So, you and Harv have been together for 3 years now, huh? How's it going?
Good. 'Course, certain habits of his are start-ting to annoy me. And he doesn't shrug off criticism like your dad.
www.pajamadiaries.com
There you go again. Ever since Dad passed, you've idealized him. But you two used to bicker all the time.
Well, that's the nice thing about getting older -- the memories you keep tend to be good ones.
Libenson
11/19 © 2012 Terri Libenson, Dist. By King Features Syndicate, Inc.
So the key to a good marriage is selective memory?
May you and Rob be blessed with long lives and short recall.

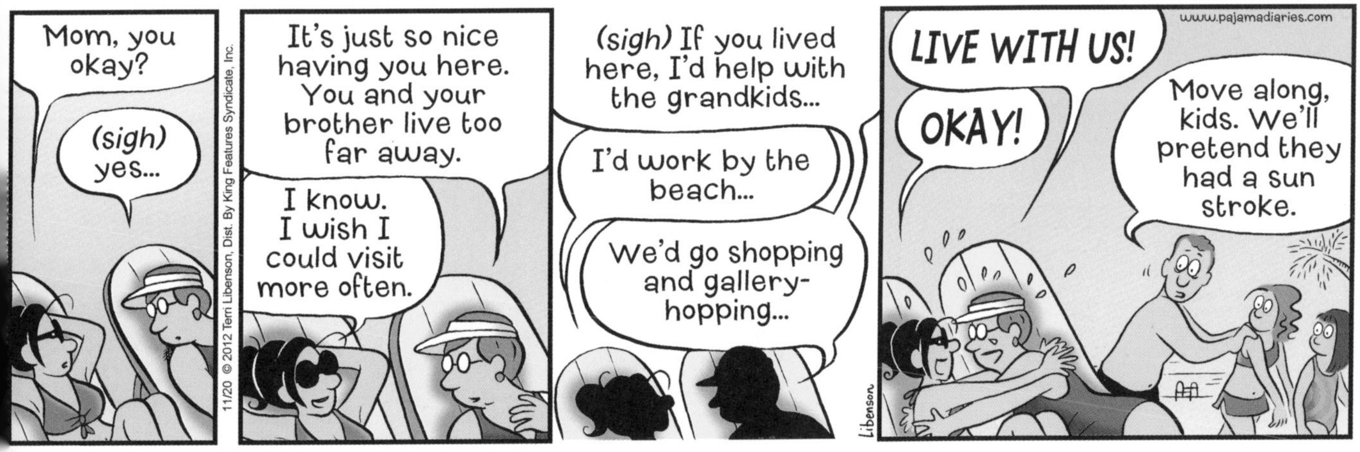
Mom, you okay?
(sigh) yes...
11/20 © 2012 Terri Libenson, Dist. By King Features Syndicate, Inc.
It's just so nice having you here. You and your brother live too far away.
I know. I wish I could visit more often.
(sigh) If you lived here, I'd help with the grandkids...
I'd work by the beach...
We'd go shopping and gallery-hopping...
Libenson
www.pajamadiaries.com
LIVE WITH US!
OKAY!
Move along, kids. We'll pretend they had a sun stroke.

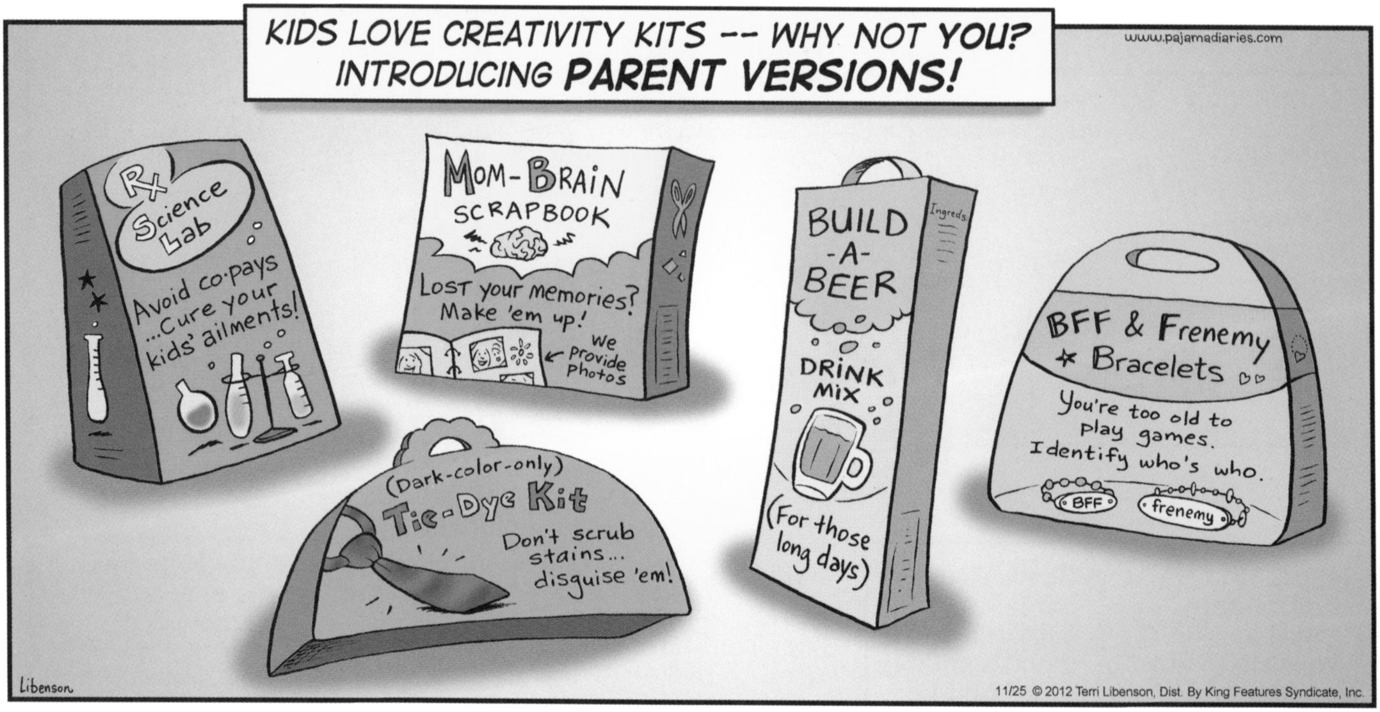
KIDS LOVE CREATIVITY KITS -- WHY NOT YOU? INTRODUCING PARENT VERSIONS!
www.pajamadiaries.com
Rx Science Lab
Avoid co-pays ...Cure your kids' ailments!
MOM-BRAIN SCRAPBOOK
Lost your memories? Make 'em up!
we provide photos
BUILD -A- BEER
Ingreds.
DRINK MIX
(For those long days)
BFF & Frenemy Bracelets
You're too old to play games. Identify who's who.
BFF
frenemy
(Dark-color-only) Tie-Dye Kit
Don't scrub stains... disguise 'em!
Libenson
11/25 © 2012 Terri Libenson, Dist. By King Features Syndicate, Inc.

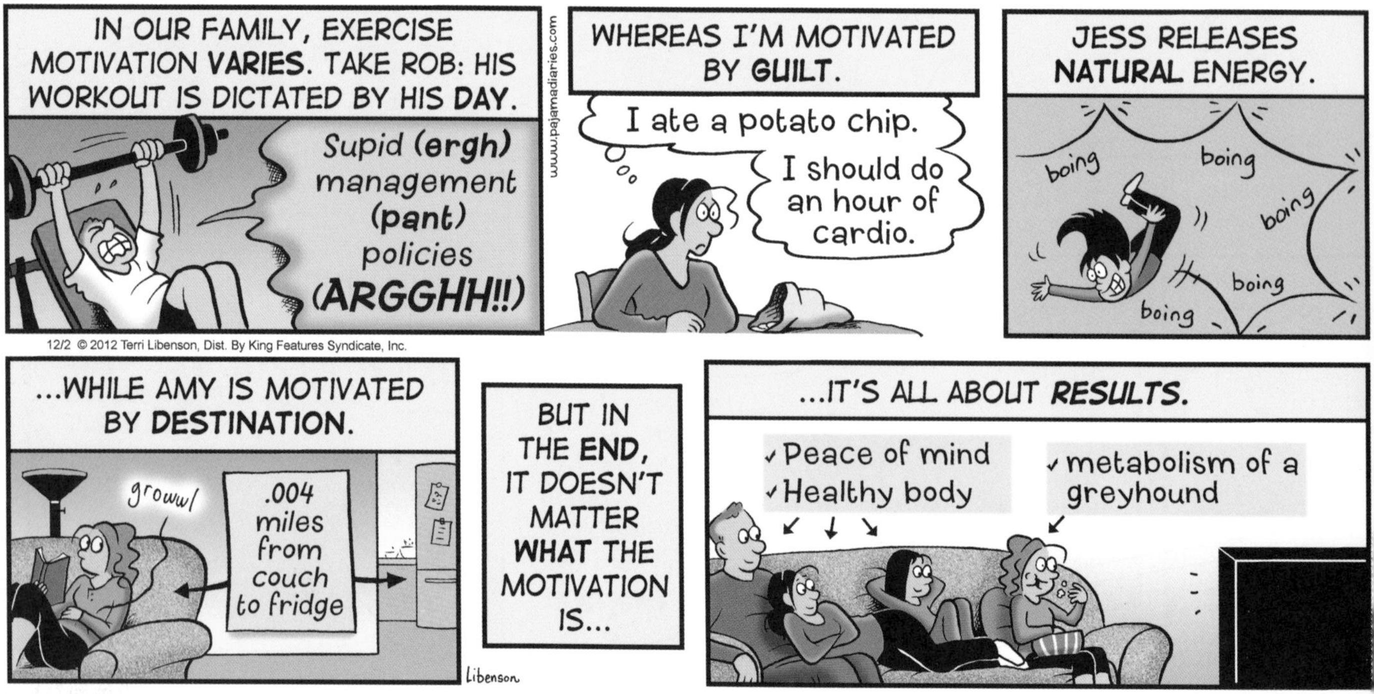
IN OUR FAMILY, EXERCISE MOTIVATION VARIES. TAKE ROB: HIS WORKOUT IS DICTATED BY HIS DAY.
Supid (ergh) management (pant) policies (ARGGHH!!)
www.pajamadiaries.com
WHEREAS I'M MOTIVATED BY GUILT.
I ate a potato chip.
I should do an hour of cardio.
JESS RELEASES NATURAL ENERGY.
boing
boing
boing
boing
boing
12/2 © 2012 Terri Libenson, Dist. By King Features Syndicate, Inc.
...WHILE AMY IS MOTIVATED BY DESTINATION.
growl
.004 miles from couch to fridge
BUT IN THE END, IT DOESN'T MATTER WHAT THE MOTIVATION IS...
...IT'S ALL ABOUT RESULTS.
Peace of mind
Healthy body
metabolism of a greyhound
Libenson

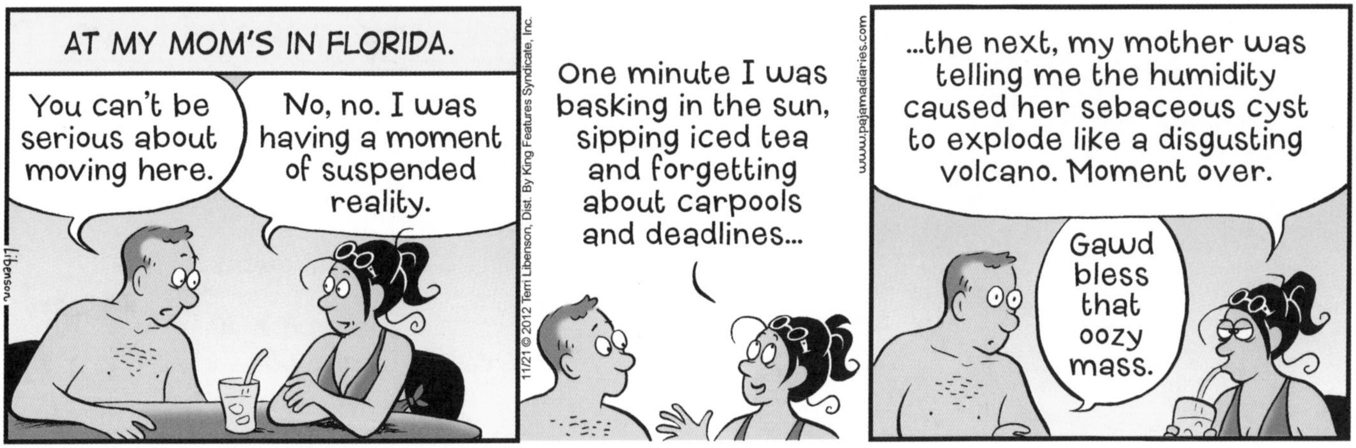
AT MY MOM'S IN FLORIDA.
You can't be serious about moving here.
No, no. I was having a moment of suspended reality.
Libenson
11/21 © 2012 Terri Libenson, Dist. By King Features Syndicate, Inc.
One minute I was basking in the sun, sipping iced tea and forgetting about carpools and deadlines...
www.pajamadiaries.com
...the next, my mother was telling me the humidity caused her sebaceous cyst to explode like a disgusting volcano. Moment over.
Gawd bless that oozy mass.

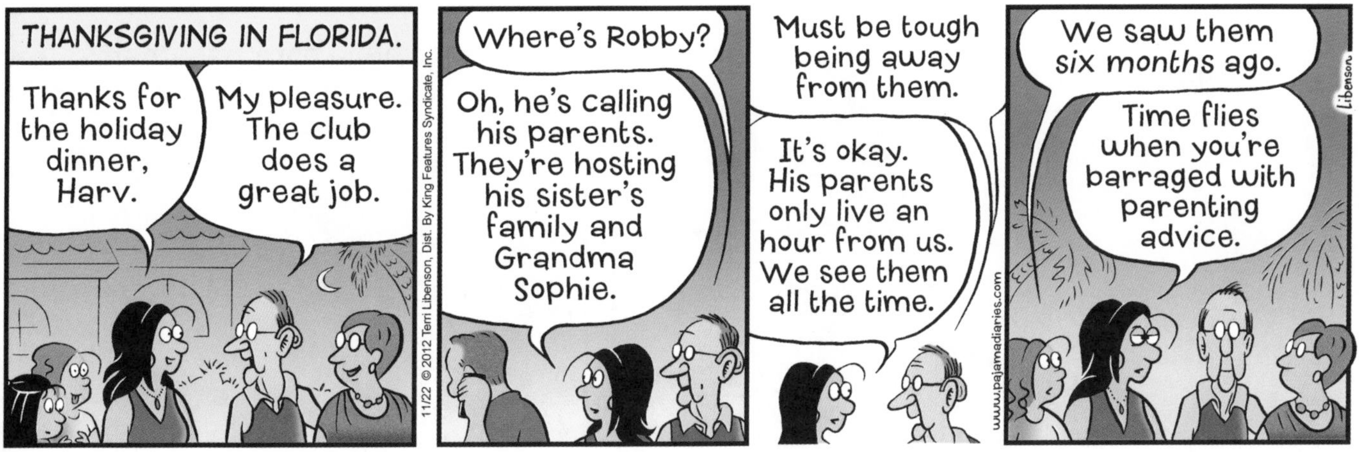
THANKSGIVING IN FLORIDA.
Thanks for the holiday dinner, Harv.
My pleasure. The club does a great job.
11/22 © 2012 Terri Libenson, Dist. By King Features Syndicate, Inc.
Where's Robby?
Oh, he's calling his parents. They're hosting his sister's family and Grandma Sophie.
Must be tough being away from them.
It's okay. His parents only live an hour from us. We see them all the time.
www.pajamadiaries.com
We saw them *six months* ago.
Time flies when you're barraged with parenting advice.
Libenson

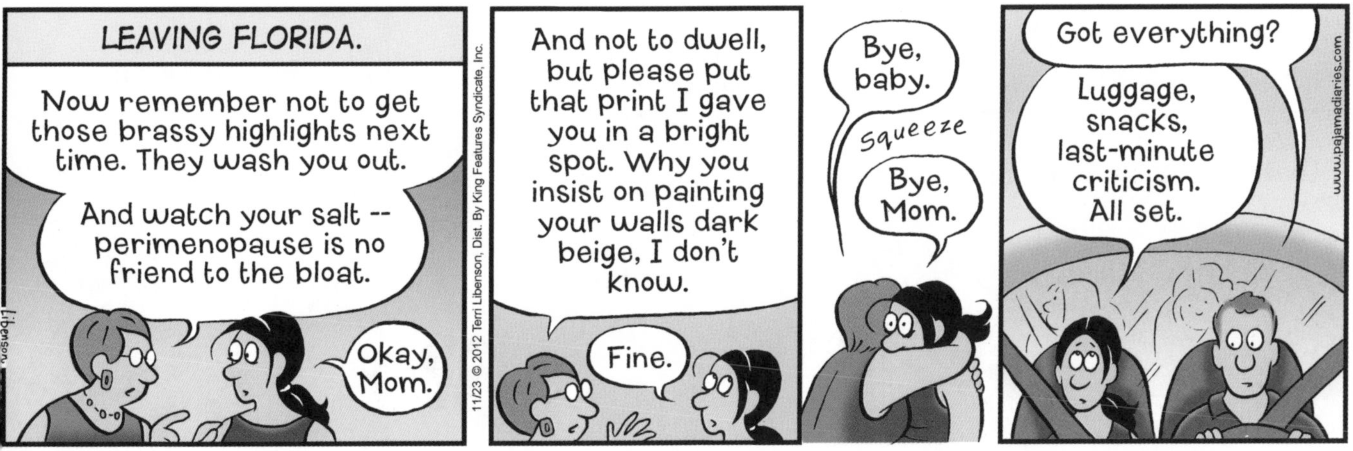
LEAVING FLORIDA.
Now remember not to get those brassy highlights next time. They wash you out.
And watch your salt -- perimenopause is no friend to the bloat.
Okay, Mom.
Libenson
11/23 © 2012 Terri Libenson, Dist. By King Features Syndicate, Inc.
And not to dwell, but please put that print I gave you in a bright spot. Why you insist on painting your walls dark beige, I don't know.
Fine.
Bye, baby.
squeeze
Bye, Mom.
Got everything?
Luggage, snacks, last-minute criticism. All set.
www.pajamadiaries.com

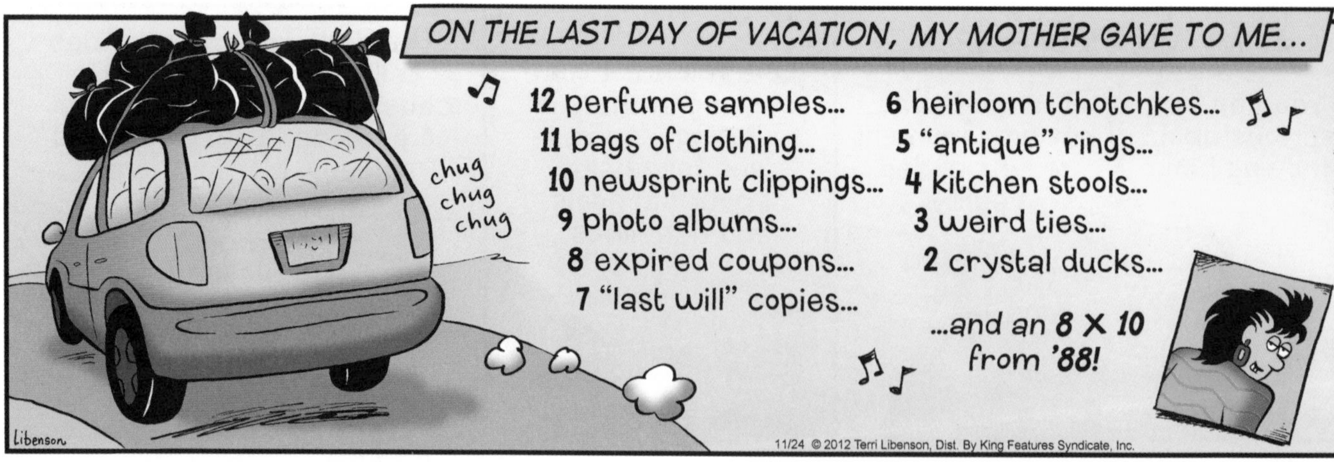
ON THE LAST DAY OF VACATION, MY MOTHER GAVE TO ME...
chug chug chug
12 perfume samples...
11 bags of clothing...
10 newsprint clippings...
9 photo albums...
8 expired coupons...
7 "last will" copies...
6 heirloom tchotchkes...
5 "antique" rings...
4 kitchen stools...
3 weird ties...
2 crystal ducks...
...and an 8 X 10 from '88!
Libenson
11/24 © 2012 Terri Libenson, Dist. By King Features Syndicate, Inc.
www.pajamadiaries.com

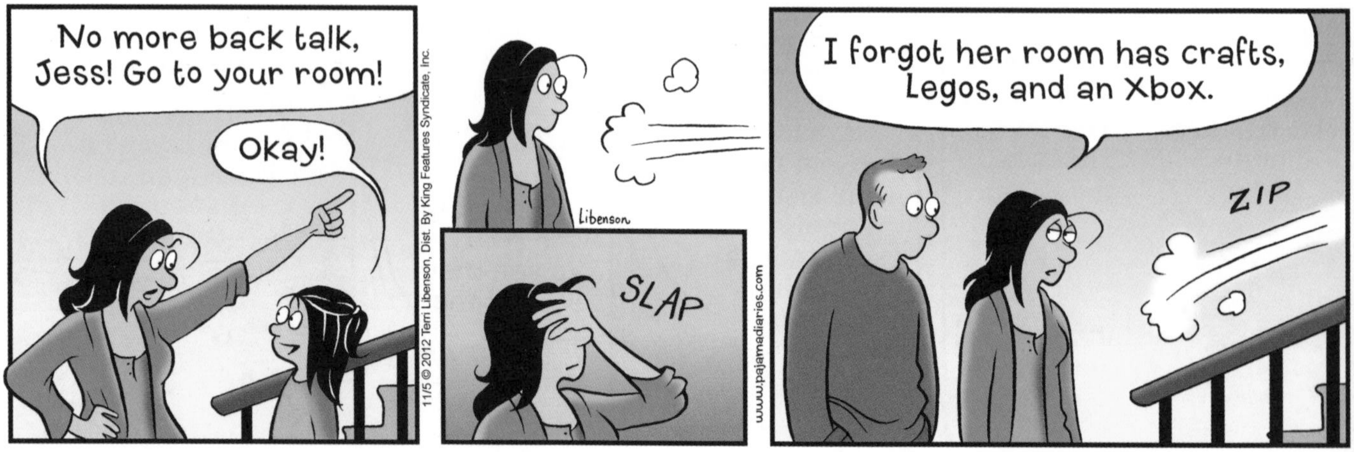
No more back talk, Jess! Go to your room!
Okay!
11/5 © 2012 Terri Libenson, Dist. By King Features Syndicate, Inc.
Libenson
SLAP
www.pajamadiaries.com
I forgot her room has crafts, Legos, and an Xbox.
ZIP

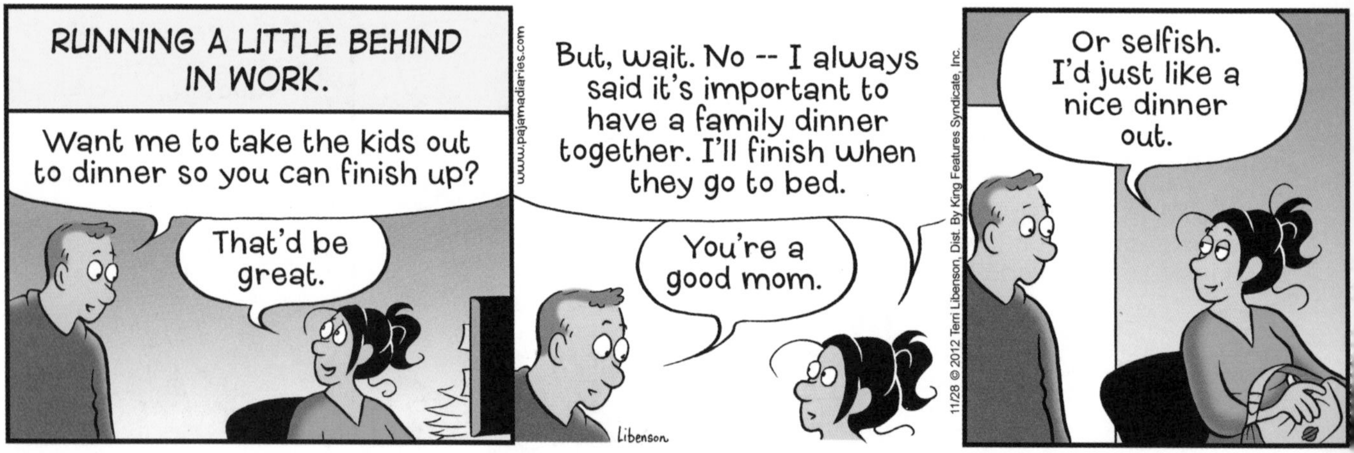
RUNNING A LITTLE BEHIND IN WORK.
Want me to take the kids out to dinner so you can finish up?
That'd be great.
www.pajamadiaries.com
But, wait. No -- I always said it's important to have a family dinner together. I'll finish when they go to bed.
You're a good mom.
Libenson
11/28 © 2012 Terri Libenson, Dist. By King Features Syndicate, Inc.
Or selfish. I'd just like a nice dinner out.

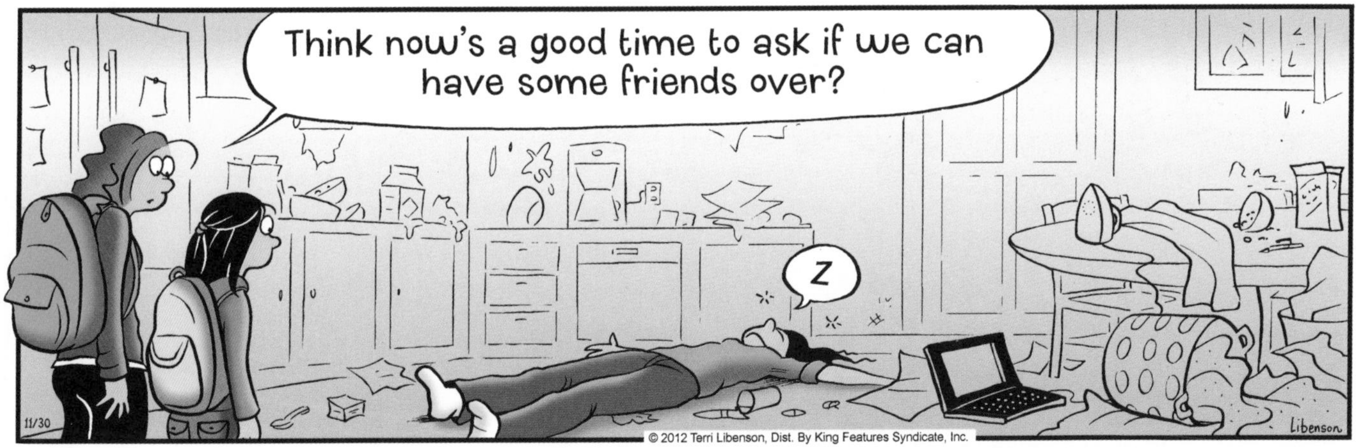
Think now's a good time to ask if we can have some friends over?
Z
11/30
Libenson
© 2012 Terri Libenson, Dist. By King Features Syndicate, Inc.

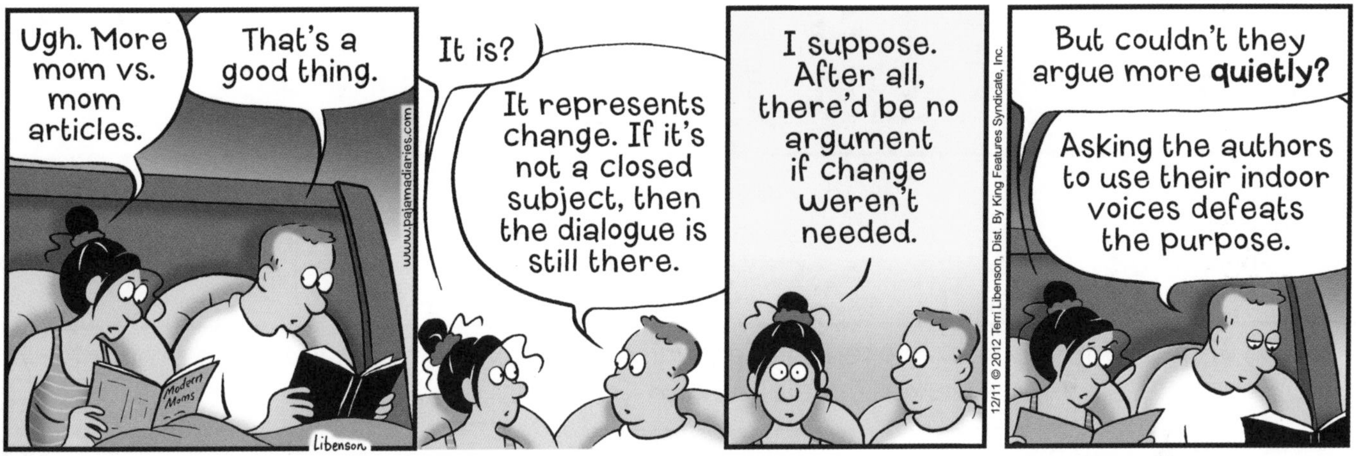
Ugh. More mom vs. mom articles.
That's a good thing.
Modern Moms
Libenson
www.pajamadiaries.com
It is?
It represents change. If it's not a closed subject, then the dialogue is still there.
I suppose. After all, there'd be no argument if change weren't needed.
12/11 © 2012 Terri Libenson, Dist. By King Features Syndicate, Inc.
But couldn't they argue more **quietly?**
Asking the authors to use their indoor voices defeats the purpose.

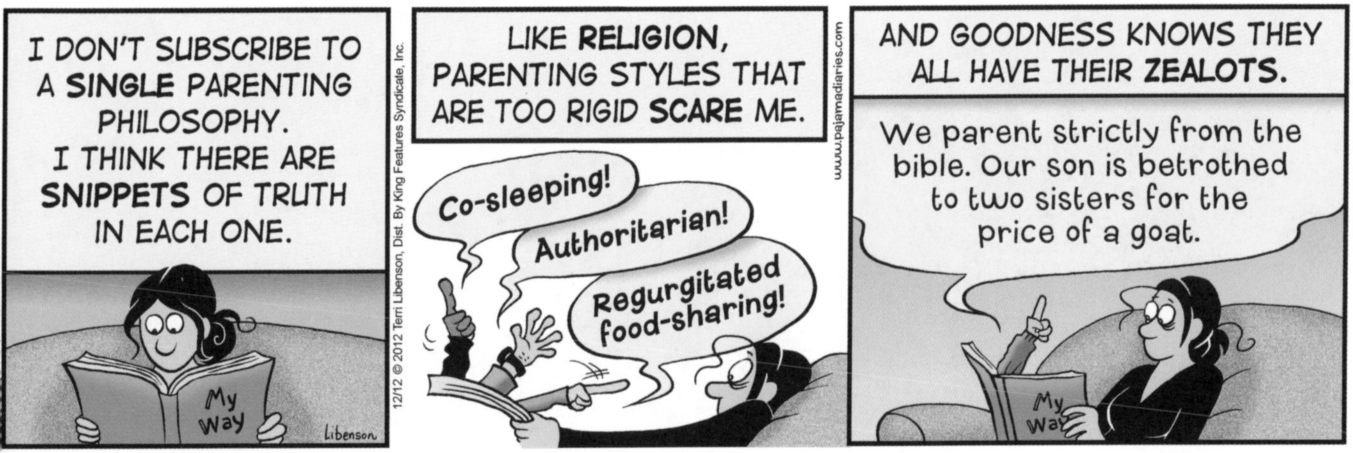
I DON'T SUBSCRIBE TO A **SINGLE** PARENTING PHILOSOPHY. I THINK THERE ARE **SNIPPETS** OF TRUTH IN EACH ONE.
My Way
Libenson
12/12 © 2012 Terri Libenson, Dist. By King Features Syndicate, Inc.
LIKE **RELIGION**, PARENTING STYLES THAT ARE TOO RIGID **SCARE** ME.
Co-sleeping!
Authoritarian!
Regurgitated food-sharing!
www.pajamadiaries.com
AND GOODNESS KNOWS THEY ALL HAVE THEIR **ZEALOTS**.
We parent strictly from the bible. Our son is betrothed to two sisters for the price of a goat.

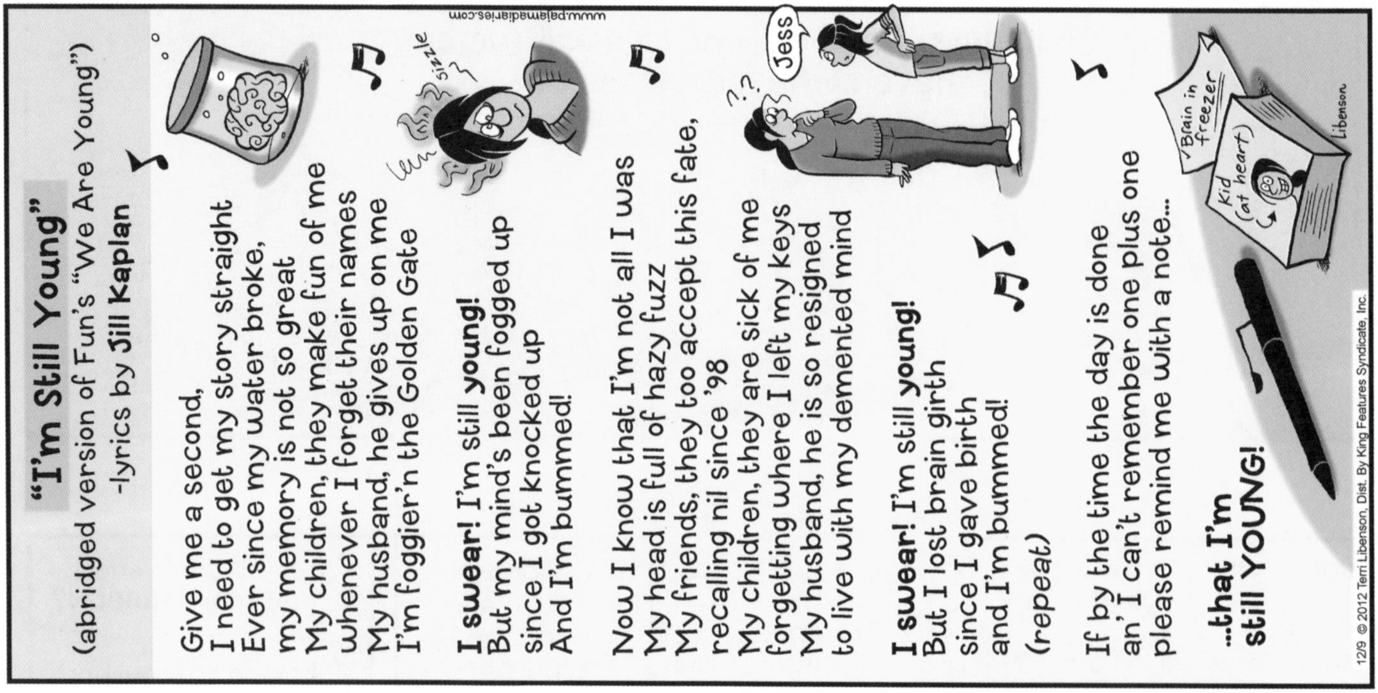
"I'm Still Young"
(abridged version of Fun's "We Are Young")
-lyrics by Jill Kaplan
Give me a second,
I need to get my story straight
Ever since my water broke,
my memory is not so great
My children, they make fun of me
whenever I forget their names
My husband, he gives up on me
I'm foggier'n the Golden Gate
sizzle
I swear! I'm still young!
But my mind's been fogged up
since I got knocked up
And I'm bummed!
Now I know that I'm not all I was
My head is full of hazy fuzz
My friends, they too accept this fate,
recalling nil since '98
My children, they are sick of me
forgetting where I left my keys
My husband, he is so resigned
to live with my demented mind
?.?
Jess
I swear! I'm still young!
But I lost brain girth
since I gave birth
and I'm bummed!
(repeat)
If by the time the day is done
an' I can't remember one plus one
please remind me with a note...
...that I'm still YOUNG!
Brain in freezer
Kid (at heart)
Libenson
www.pajamadiaries.com
12/9 © 2012 Terri Libenson, Dist. By King Features Syndicate, Inc.

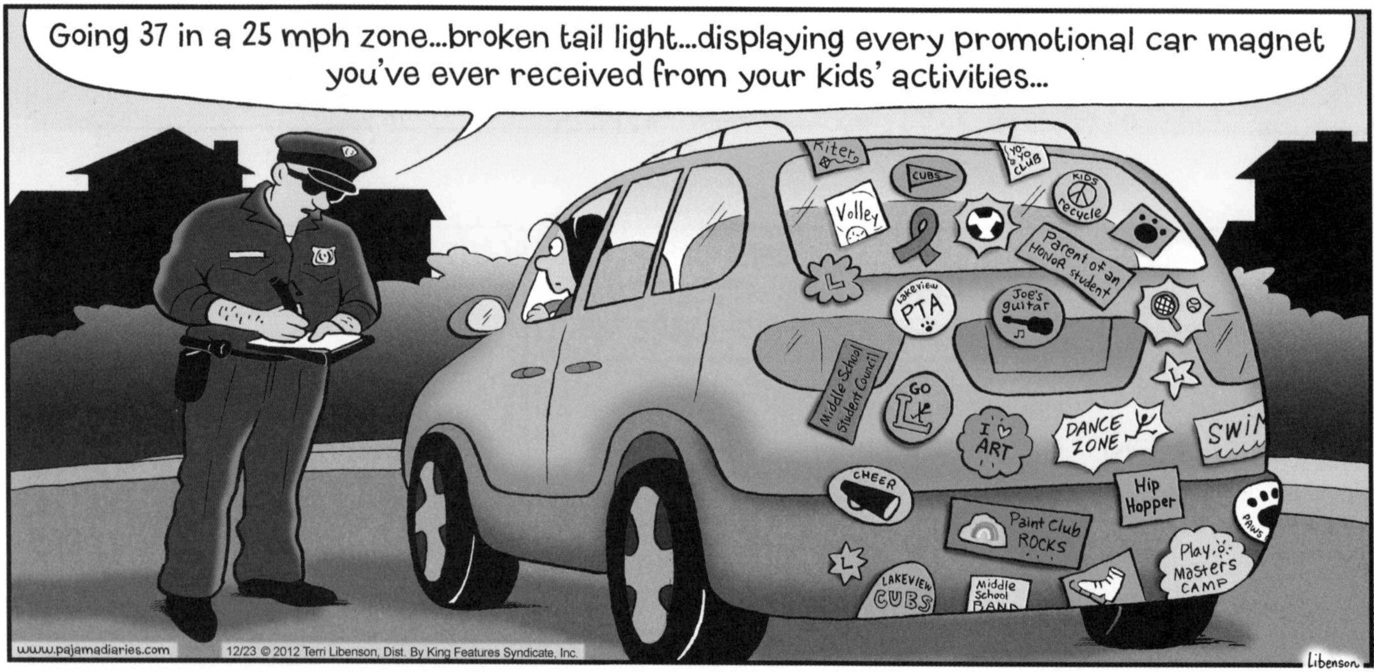
Going 37 in a 25 mph zone...broken tail light...displaying every promotional car magnet you've ever received from your kids' activities...
Kiter
CUBS
YO-YO CLUB
KIDS recycle
Volley
Parent of an HONOR student
Lakeview PTA
Joe's guitar
Middle School Student Council
GO L
I ♡ ART
DANCE ZONE
SWIM
CHEER
Hip Hopper
Paint Club ROCKS
PAWS
Play Masters CAMP
LAKEVIEW CUBS
Middle School BAND
www.pajamadiaries.com
12/23 © 2012 Terri Libenson, Dist. By King Features Syndicate, Inc.
Libenson

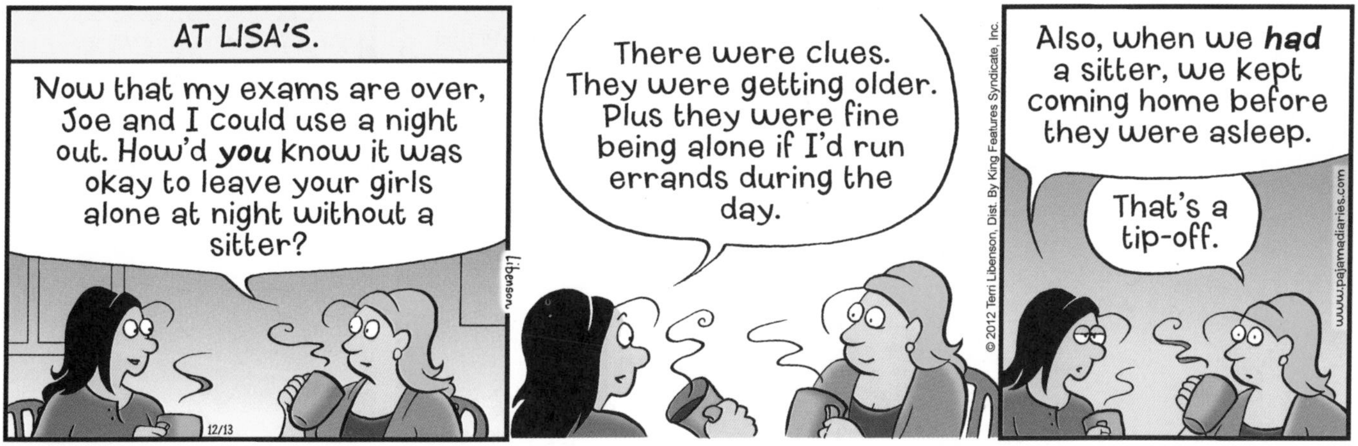
AT LISA'S.
Now that my exams are over, Joe and I could use a night out. How'd **you** know it was okay to leave your girls alone at night without a sitter?
Libenson
12/13
There were clues. They were getting older. Plus they were fine being alone if I'd run errands during the day.
© 2012 Terri Libenson, Dist. By King Features Syndicate, Inc.
Also, when we **had** a sitter, we kept coming home before they were asleep.
That's a tip-off.
www.pajamadiaries.com

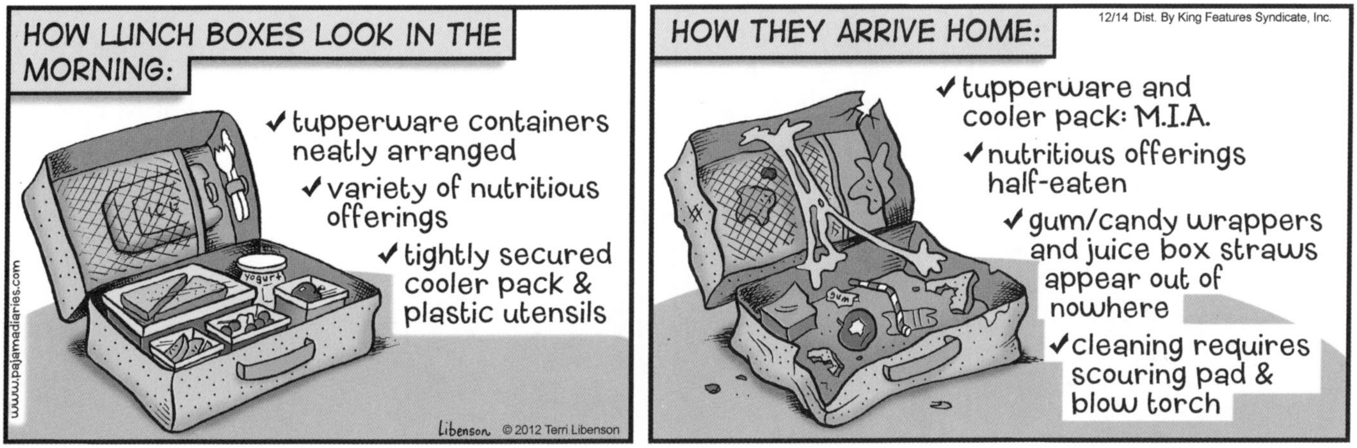
HOW LUNCH BOXES LOOK IN THE MORNING:
✓tupperware containers neatly arranged
✓variety of nutritious offerings
✓tightly secured cooler pack & plastic utensils
yogurt
www.pajamadiaries.com
Libenson © 2012 Terri Libenson
HOW THEY ARRIVE HOME:
12/14 Dist. By King Features Syndicate, Inc.
✓tupperware and cooler pack: M.I.A.
✓nutritious offerings half-eaten
✓gum/candy wrappers and juice box straws appear out of nowhere
✓cleaning requires scouring pad & blow torch
gum

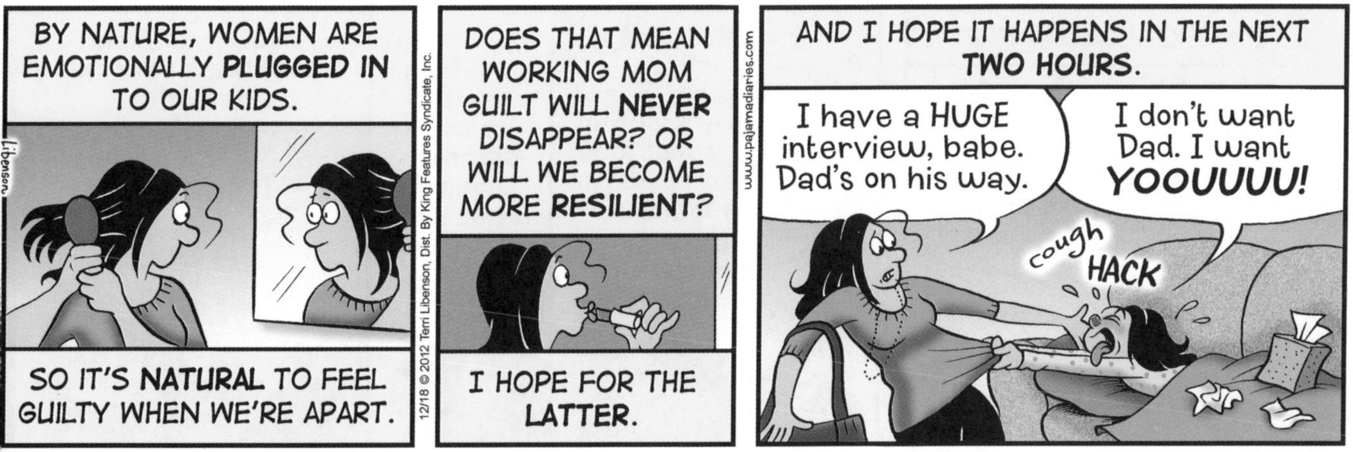
BY NATURE, WOMEN ARE EMOTIONALLY **PLUGGED IN** TO OUR KIDS.
Libenson
SO IT'S **NATURAL** TO FEEL GUILTY WHEN WE'RE APART.
12/18 © 2012 Terri Libenson, Dist. By King Features Syndicate, Inc.
DOES THAT MEAN WORKING MOM GUILT WILL **NEVER** DISAPPEAR? OR WILL WE BECOME MORE **RESILIENT**?
I HOPE FOR THE **LATTER**.
www.pajamadiaries.com
AND I HOPE IT HAPPENS IN THE NEXT **TWO HOURS**.
I have a HUGE interview, babe. Dad's on his way.
I don't want Dad. I want **YOOUUUU!**
cough
HACK

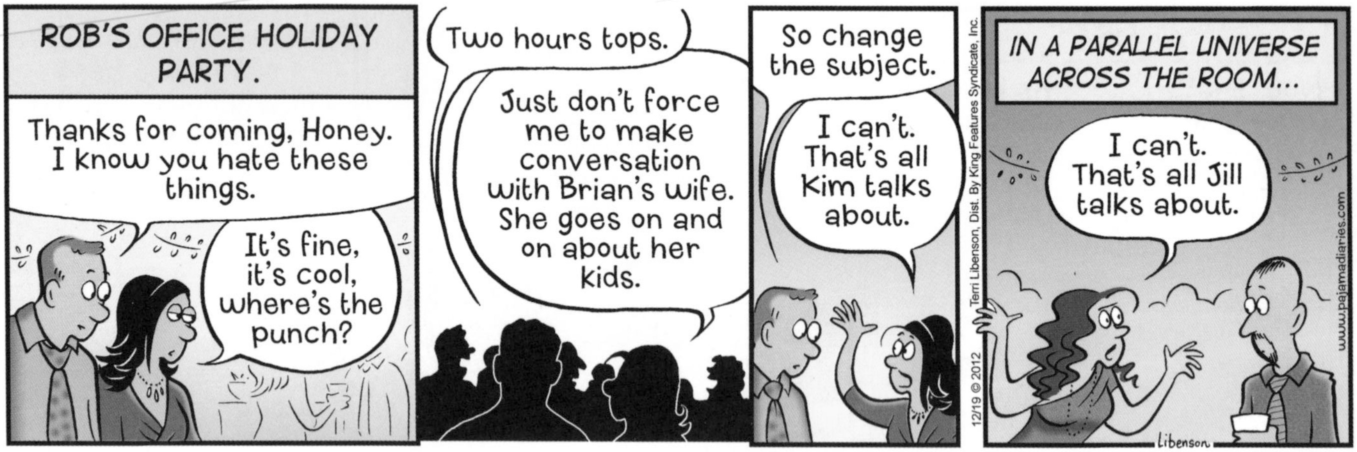
ROB'S OFFICE HOLIDAY PARTY.
Thanks for coming, Honey. I know you hate these things.
It's fine, it's cool, where's the punch?
Two hours tops.
Just don't force me to make conversation with Brian's wife. She goes on and on about her kids.
So change the subject.
I can't. That's all Kim talks about.
12/19 © 2012 Terri Libenson, Dist. By King Features Syndicate, Inc.
IN A PARALLEL UNIVERSE ACROSS THE ROOM...
I can't. That's all Jill talks about.
www.pajamadiaries.com
Libenson

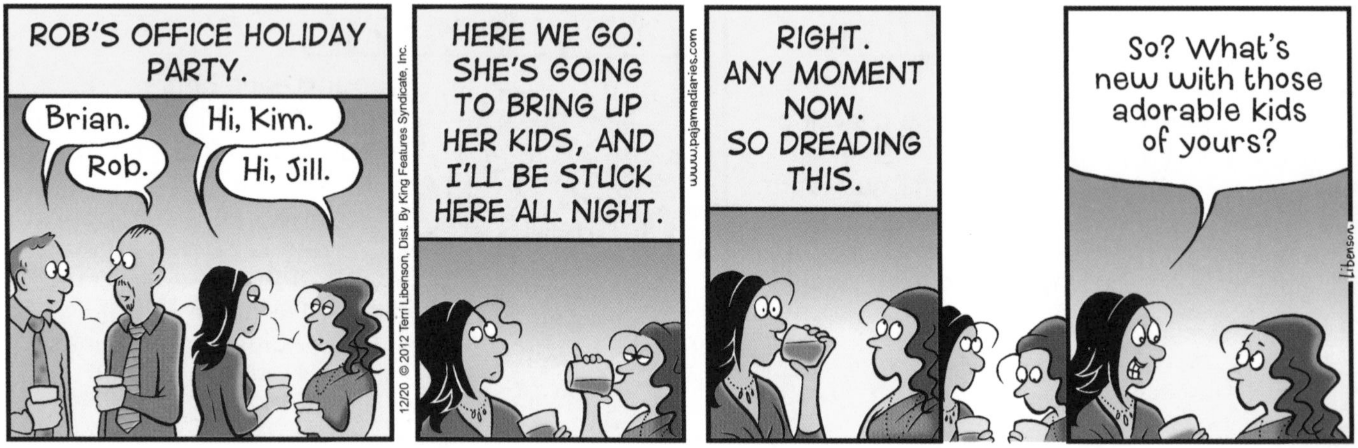
ROB'S OFFICE HOLIDAY PARTY.
Brian.
Rob.
Hi, Kim.
Hi, Jill.
12/20 © 2012 Terri Libenson, Dist. By King Features Syndicate, Inc.
HERE WE GO. SHE'S GOING TO BRING UP HER KIDS, AND I'LL BE STUCK HERE ALL NIGHT.
www.pajamadiaries.com
RIGHT. ANY MOMENT NOW. SO DREADING THIS.
So? What's new with those adorable kids of yours?
Libenson

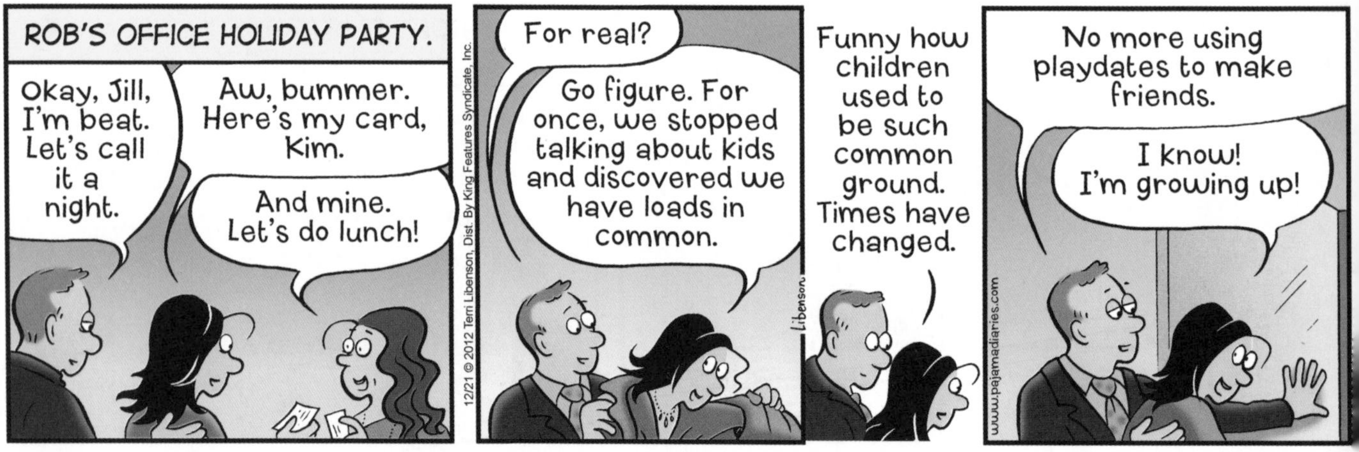
ROB'S OFFICE HOLIDAY PARTY.
Okay, Jill, I'm beat. Let's call it a night.
Aw, bummer. Here's my card, Kim.
And mine. Let's do lunch!
12/21 © 2012 Terri Libenson, Dist. By King Features Syndicate, Inc.
For real?
Go figure. For once, we stopped talking about kids and discovered we have loads in common.
Libenson
Funny how children used to be such common ground. Times have changed.
No more using playdates to make friends.
I know! I'm growing up!
www.pajamadiaries.com

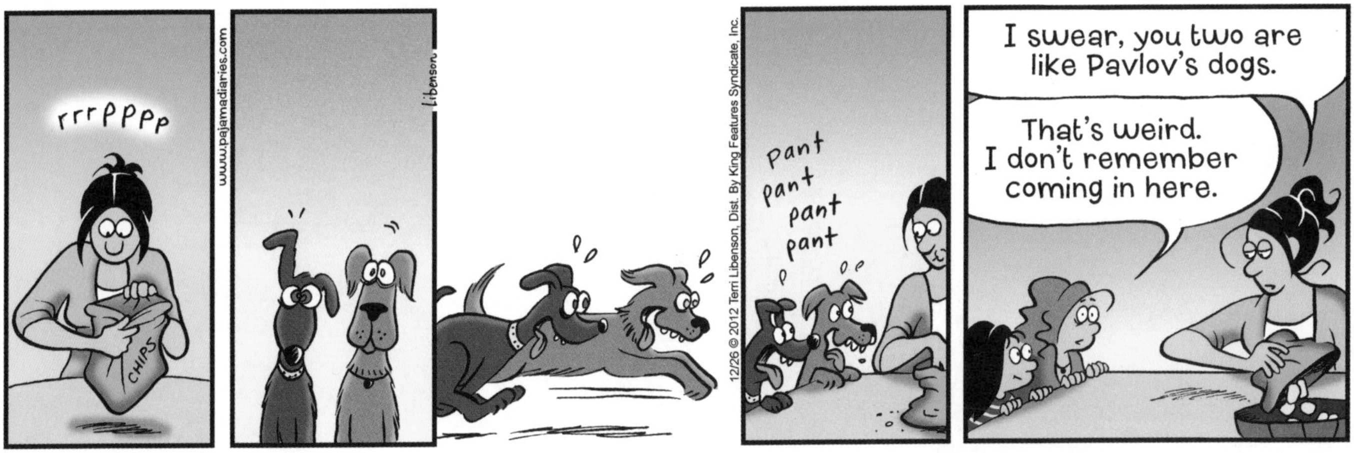
rrrPPPP
www.pajamadiaries.com
Libenson
CHIPS
12/26 © 2012 Terri Libenson, Dist. By King Features Syndicate, Inc.
pant pant pant pant
I swear, you two are like Pavlov's dogs.
That's weird. I don't remember coming in here.

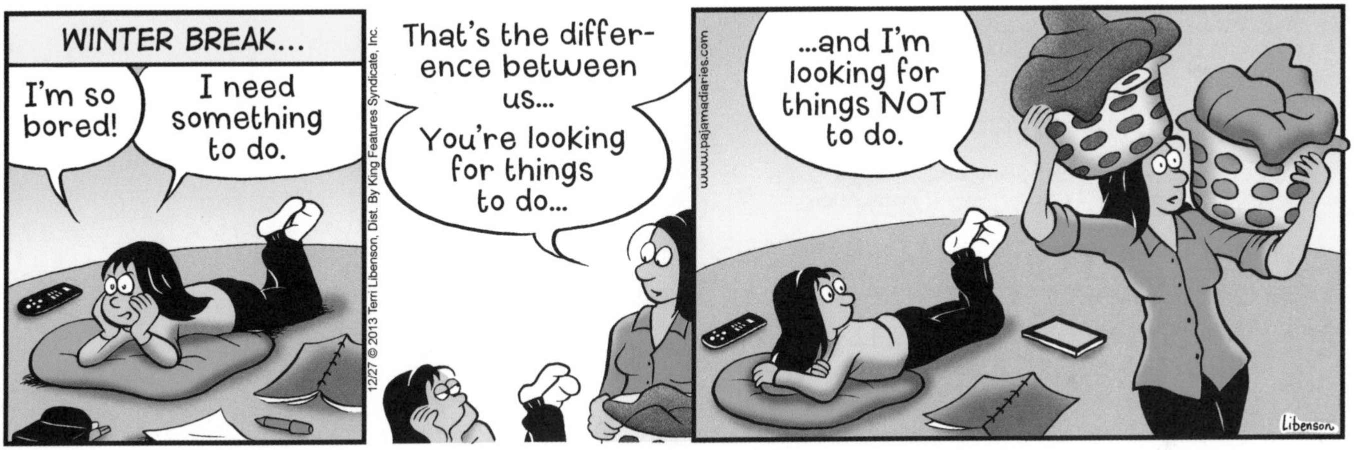
WINTER BREAK...
I'm so bored!
I need something to do.
12/27 © 2013 Terri Libenson, Dist. By King Features Syndicate, Inc.
That's the differ-ence between us...
You're looking for things to do...
www.pajamadiaries.com
...and I'm looking for things NOT to do.
Libenson

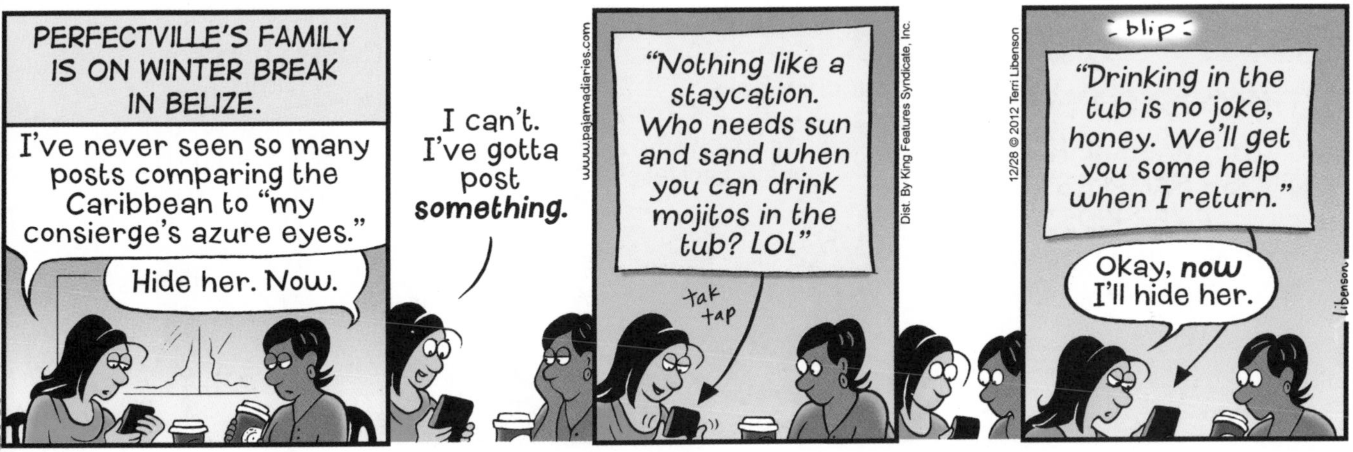
PERFECTVILLE'S FAMILY IS ON WINTER BREAK IN BELIZE.
I've never seen so many posts comparing the Caribbean to "my consierge's azure eyes."
Hide her. Now.
I can't. I've gotta post **something.**
www.pajamadiaries.com
"Nothing like a staycation. Who needs sun and sand when you can drink mojitos in the tub? LOL"
tak tap
Dist. By King Features Syndicate, Inc.
12/28 © 2012 Terri Libenson
blip
"Drinking in the tub is no joke, honey. We'll get you some help when I return."
Okay, **now** I'll hide her.
Libenson

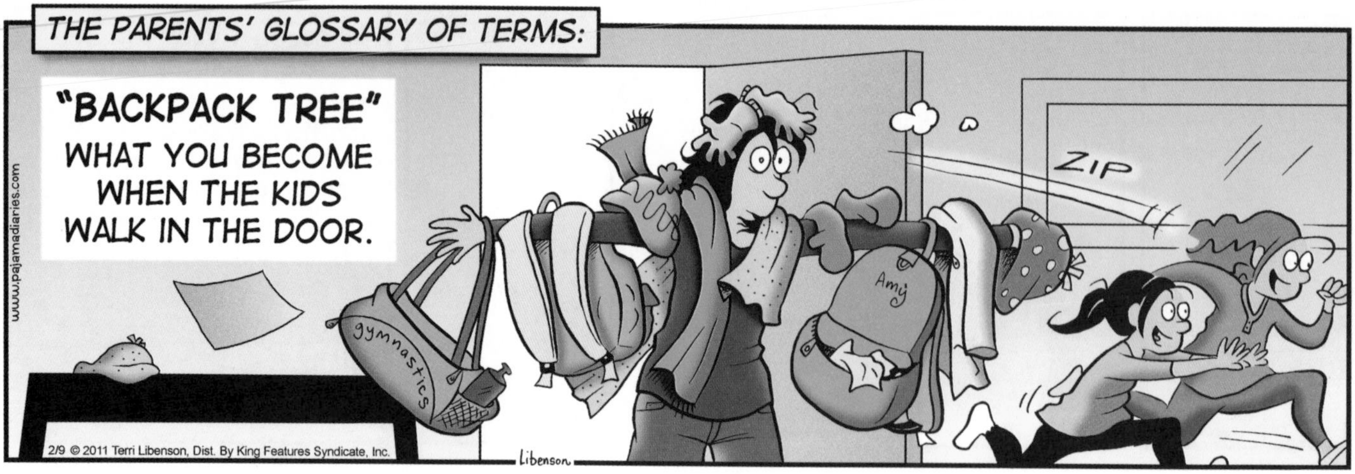
THE PARENTS' GLOSSARY OF TERMS:
"BACKPACK TREE"
WHAT YOU BECOME WHEN THE KIDS WALK IN THE DOOR.
ZIP
gymnastics
Amy
www.pajamadiaries.com
2/9 © 2011 Terri Libenson, Dist. By King Features Syndicate, Inc.
Libenson

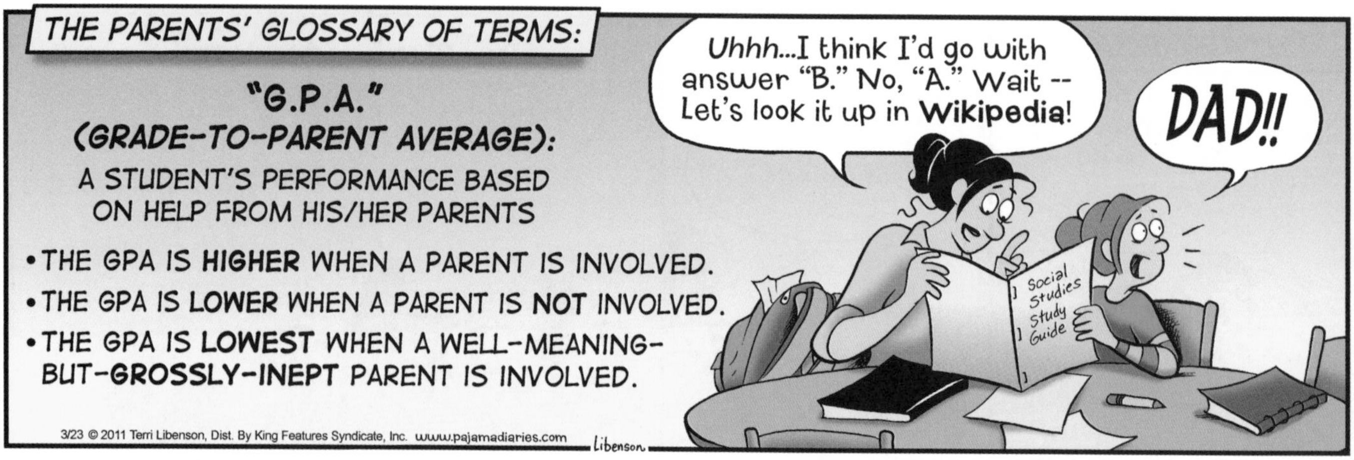
THE PARENTS' GLOSSARY OF TERMS:
"G.P.A."
(GRADE-TO-PARENT AVERAGE):
A STUDENT'S PERFORMANCE BASED ON HELP FROM HIS/HER PARENTS
• THE GPA IS HIGHER WHEN A PARENT IS INVOLVED.
• THE GPA IS LOWER WHEN A PARENT IS NOT INVOLVED.
• THE GPA IS LOWEST WHEN A WELL-MEANING-BUT-GROSSLY-INEPT PARENT IS INVOLVED.
Uhhh...I think I'd go with answer "B." No, "A." Wait -- Let's look it up in Wikipedia!
DAD!!
Social Studies Study Guide
3/23 © 2011 Terri Libenson, Dist. By King Features Syndicate, Inc. www.pajamadiaries.com
Libenson

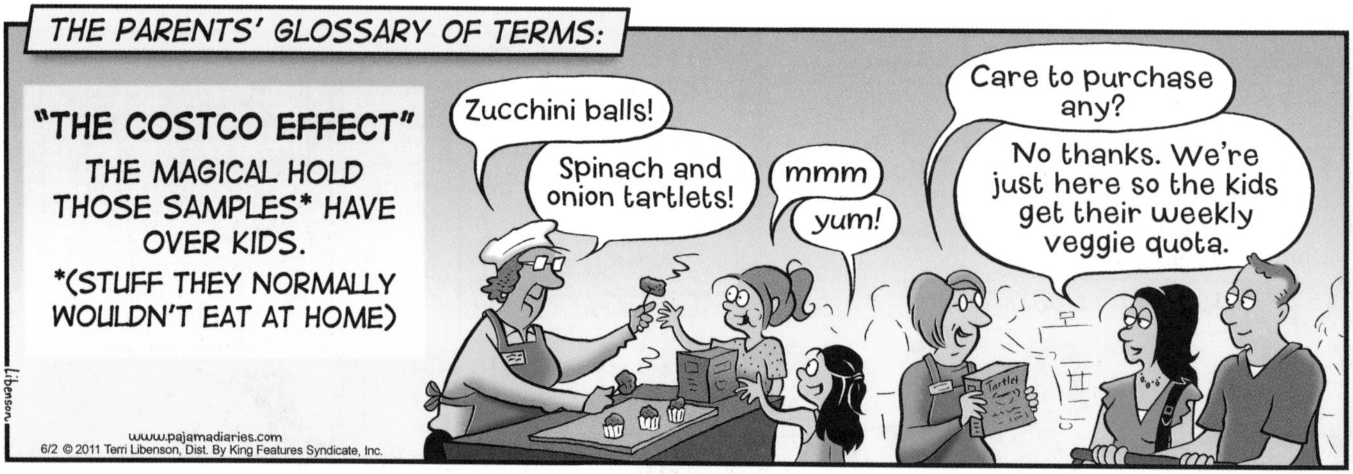
THE PARENTS' GLOSSARY OF TERMS:
"THE COSTCO EFFECT"
THE MAGICAL HOLD THOSE SAMPLES* HAVE OVER KIDS.
*(STUFF THEY NORMALLY WOULDN'T EAT AT HOME)
Zucchini balls!
Spinach and onion tartlets!
mmm
yum!
Care to purchase any?
No thanks. We're just here so the kids get their weekly veggie quota.
Tartlet
Libenson
www.pajamadiaries.com
6/2 © 2011 Terri Libenson, Dist. By King Features Syndicate, Inc.

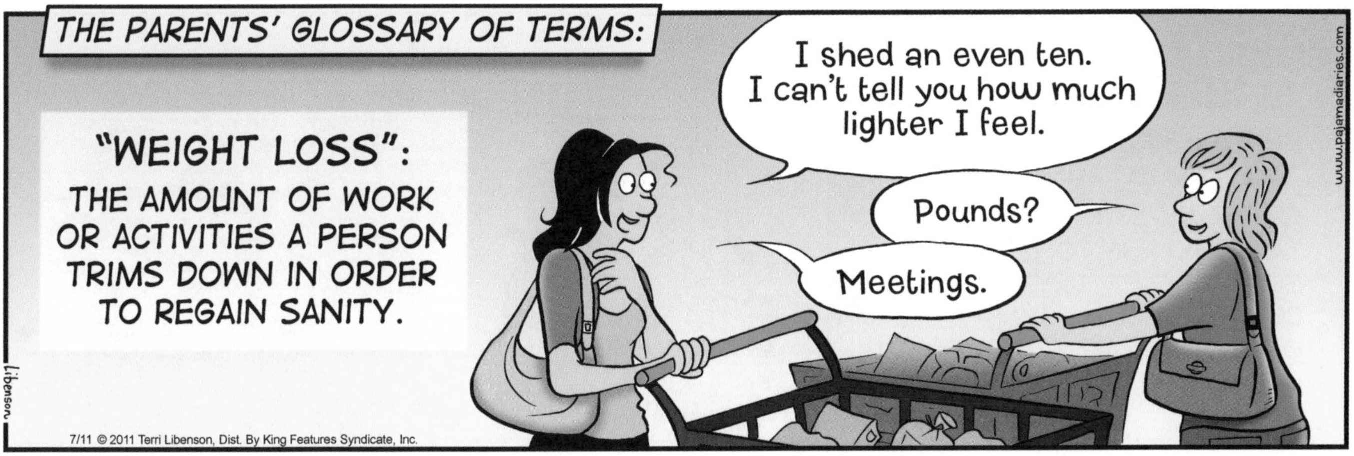
THE PARENTS' GLOSSARY OF TERMS:
"WEIGHT LOSS":
THE AMOUNT OF WORK OR ACTIVITIES A PERSON TRIMS DOWN IN ORDER TO REGAIN SANITY.
I shed an even ten. I can't tell you how much lighter I feel.
Pounds?
Meetings.
www.pajamadiaries.com
Libenson
7/11 © 2011 Terri Libenson, Dist. By King Features Syndicate, Inc.

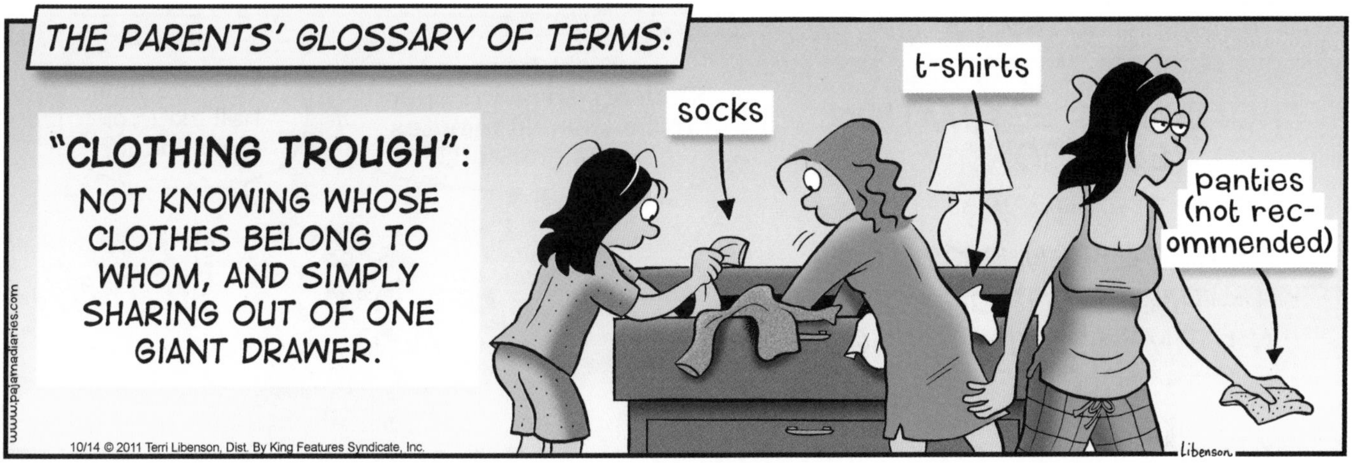
THE PARENTS' GLOSSARY OF TERMS:
"CLOTHING TROUGH":
NOT KNOWING WHOSE CLOTHES BELONG TO WHOM, AND SIMPLY SHARING OUT OF ONE GIANT DRAWER.
socks
t-shirts
panties (not recommended)
www.pajamadiaries.com
10/14 © 2011 Terri Libenson, Dist. By King Features Syndicate, Inc.
Libenson

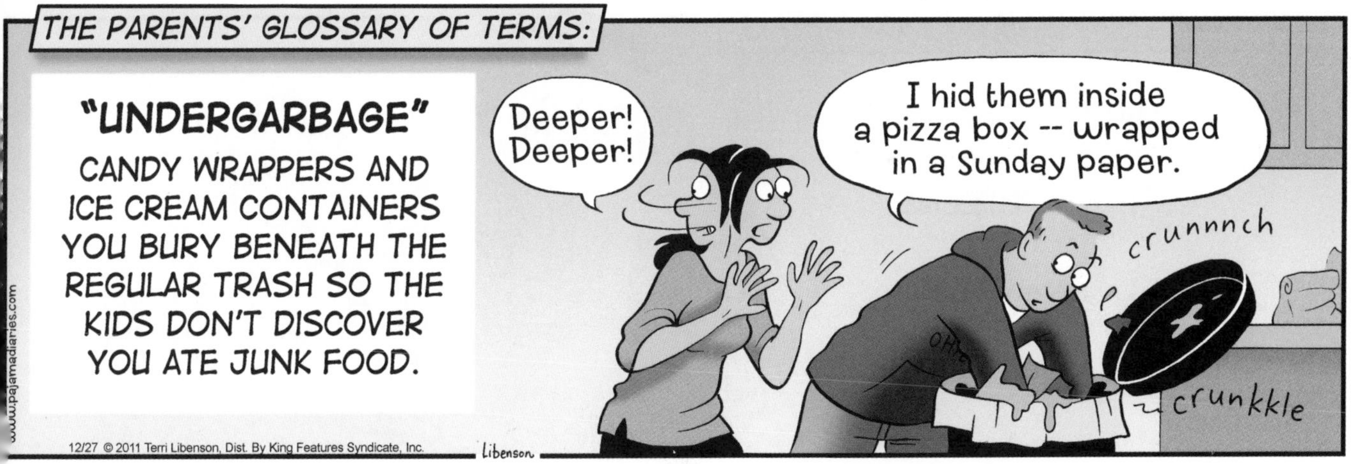
THE PARENTS' GLOSSARY OF TERMS:
"UNDERGARBAGE"
CANDY WRAPPERS AND ICE CREAM CONTAINERS YOU BURY BENEATH THE REGULAR TRASH SO THE KIDS DON'T DISCOVER YOU ATE JUNK FOOD.
Deeper! Deeper!
I hid them inside a pizza box -- wrapped in a Sunday paper.
crunnnch
crunkkle
www.pajamadiaries.com
12/27 © 2011 Terri Libenson, Dist. By King Features Syndicate, Inc.
Libenson

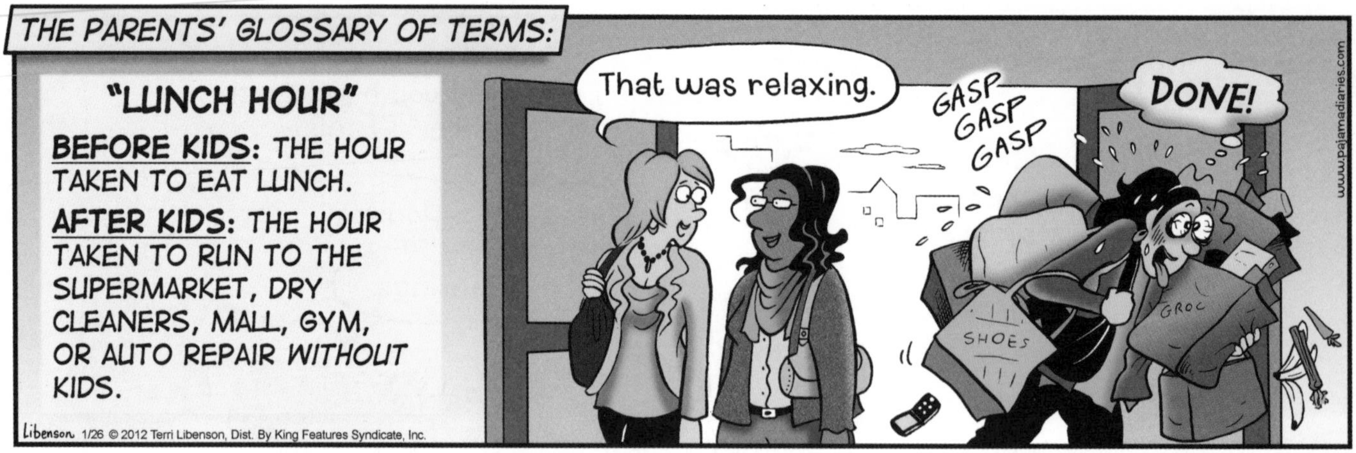
THE PARENTS' GLOSSARY OF TERMS:
"LUNCH HOUR"
BEFORE KIDS: THE HOUR TAKEN TO EAT LUNCH.
AFTER KIDS: THE HOUR TAKEN TO RUN TO THE SUPERMARKET, DRY CLEANERS, MALL, GYM, OR AUTO REPAIR WITHOUT KIDS.
That was relaxing.
GASP GASP GASP
DONE!
SHOES
GROC
www.pajamadiaries.com
Libenson 1/26 © 2012 Terri Libenson, Dist. By King Features Syndicate, Inc.

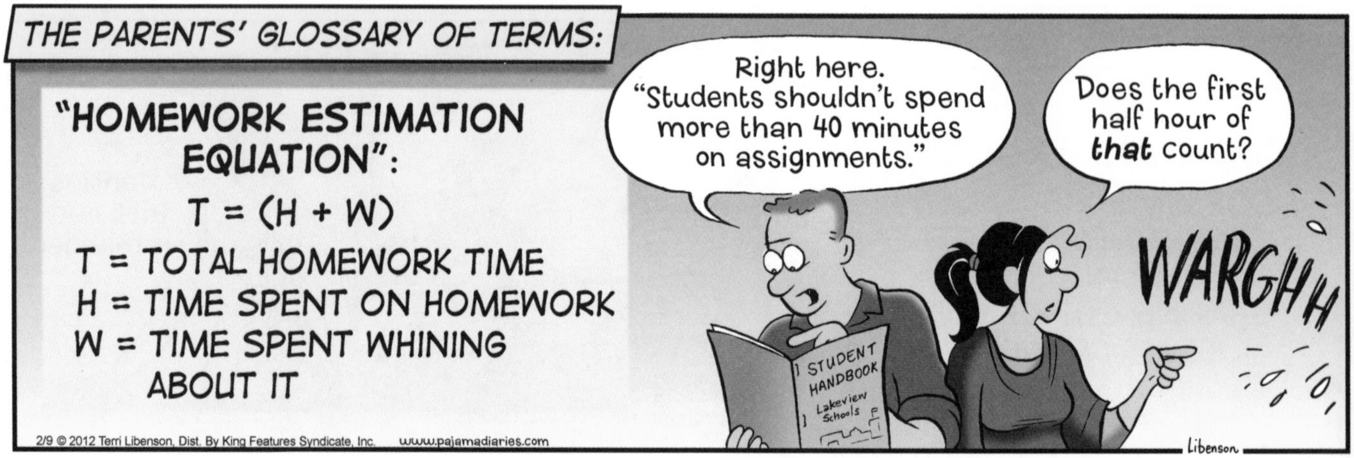
THE PARENTS' GLOSSARY OF TERMS:
"HOMEWORK ESTIMATION EQUATION":
T = (H + W)
T = TOTAL HOMEWORK TIME
H = TIME SPENT ON HOMEWORK
W = TIME SPENT WHINING ABOUT IT
Right here. "Students shouldn't spend more than 40 minutes on assignments."
Does the first half hour of that count?
WARGHH
STUDENT HANDBOOK Lakeview Schools
2/9 © 2012 Terri Libenson, Dist. By King Features Syndicate, Inc. www.pajamadiaries.com
Libenson

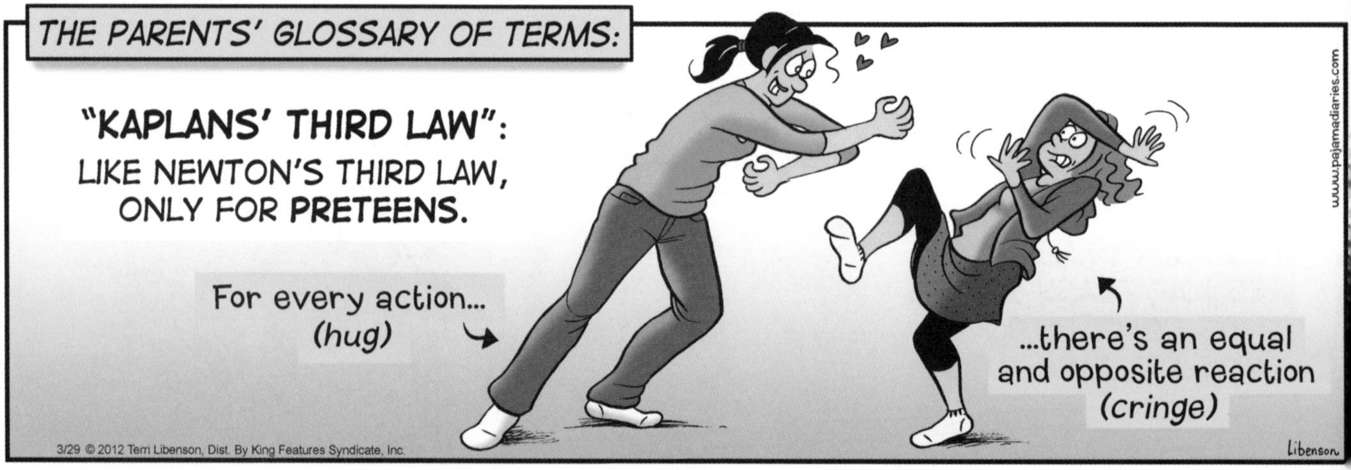
THE PARENTS' GLOSSARY OF TERMS:
"KAPLANS' THIRD LAW":
LIKE NEWTON'S THIRD LAW, ONLY FOR PRETEENS.
For every action... (hug)
...there's an equal and opposite reaction (cringe)
www.pajamadiaries.com
3/29 © 2012 Terri Libenson, Dist. By King Features Syndicate, Inc.
Libenson

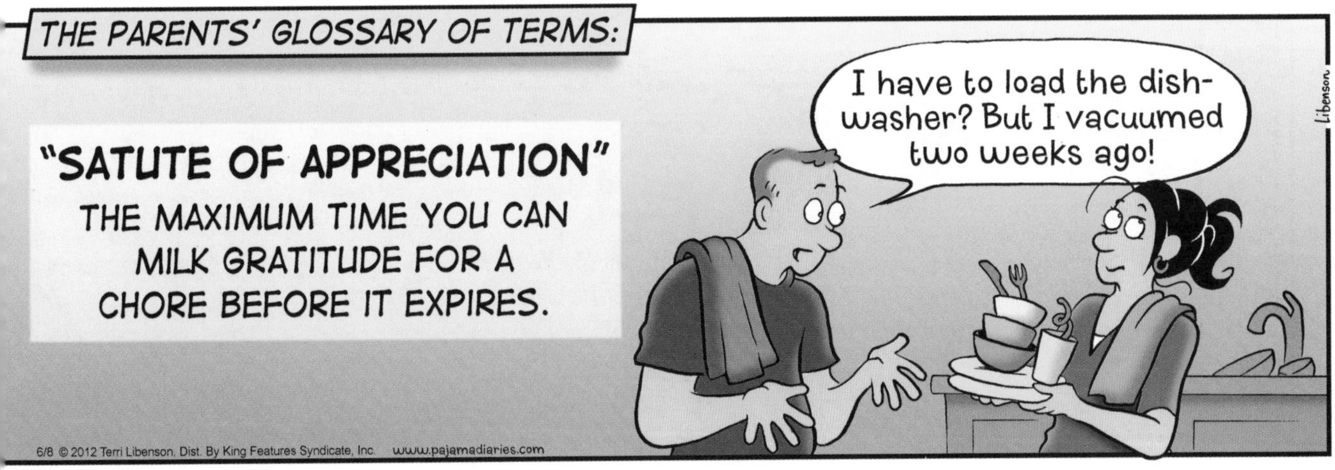
THE PARENTS' GLOSSARY OF TERMS:
"SATUTE OF APPRECIATION"
THE MAXIMUM TIME YOU CAN MILK GRATITUDE FOR A CHORE BEFORE IT EXPIRES.
I have to load the dish-washer? But I vacuumed two weeks ago!
Libenson
6/8 © 2012 Terri Libenson, Dist. By King Features Syndicate, Inc. www.pajamadiaries.com

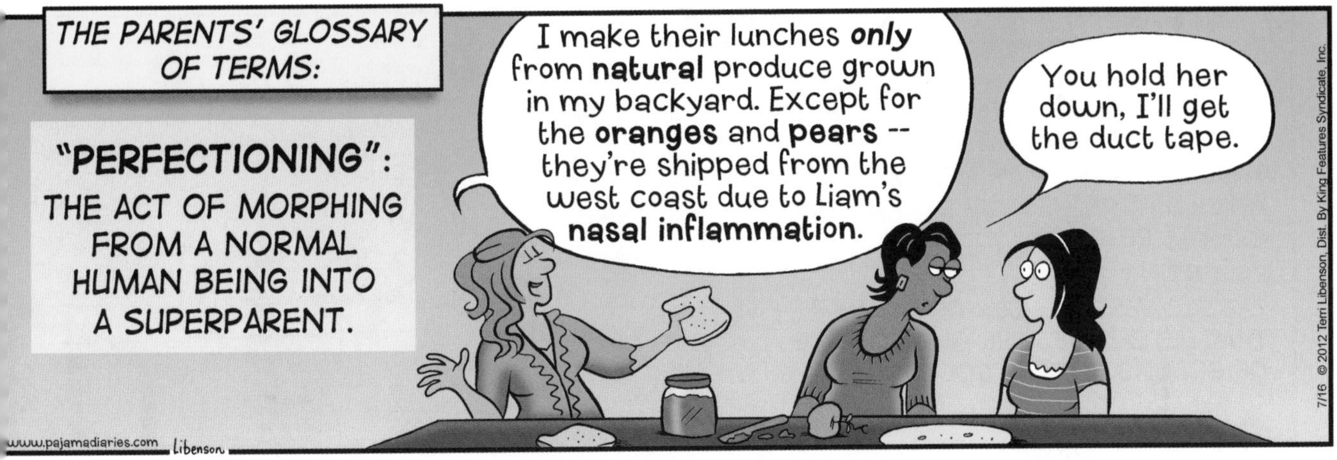
THE PARENTS' GLOSSARY OF TERMS:
"PERFECTIONING":
THE ACT OF MORPHING FROM A NORMAL HUMAN BEING INTO A SUPERPARENT.
I make their lunches only from natural produce grown in my backyard. Except for the oranges and pears -- they're shipped from the west coast due to Liam's nasal inflammation.
You hold her down, I'll get the duct tape.
7/16 © 2012 Terri Libenson, Dist. By King Features Syndicate, Inc.
www.pajamadiaries.com Libenson

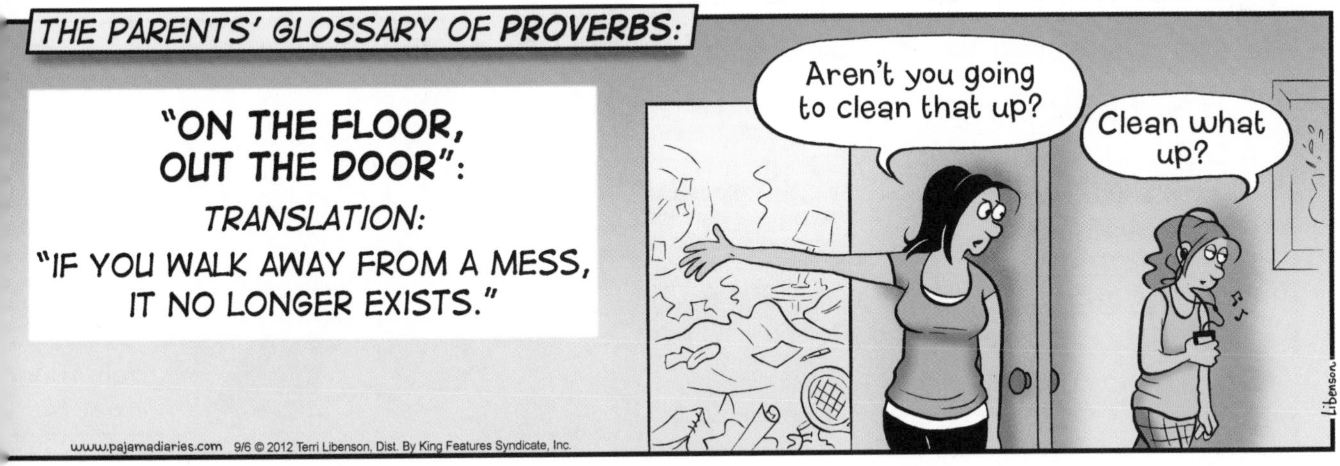
THE PARENTS' GLOSSARY OF PROVERBS:
"ON THE FLOOR, OUT THE DOOR":
TRANSLATION:
"IF YOU WALK AWAY FROM A MESS, IT NO LONGER EXISTS."
Aren't you going to clean that up?
Clean what up?
Libenson
www.pajamadiaries.com 9/6 © 2012 Terri Libenson, Dist. By King Features Syndicate, Inc.

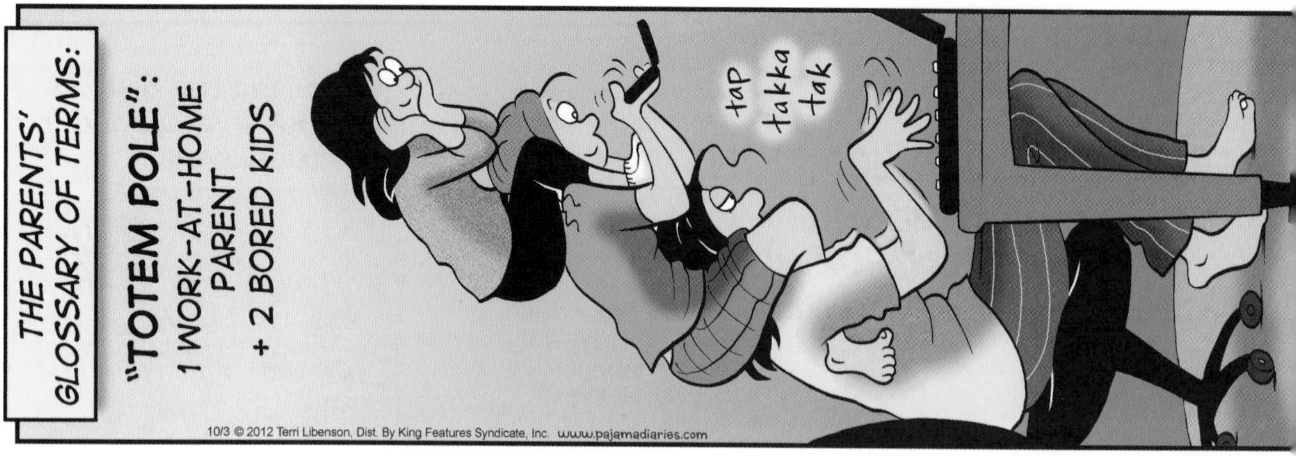
THE PARENTS' GLOSSARY OF TERMS:
"TOTEM POLE":
1 WORK-AT-HOME PARENT
+ 2 BORED KIDS
tap takka tak
10/3 © 2012 Terri Libenson, Dist. By King Features Syndicate, Inc. www.pajamadiaries.com

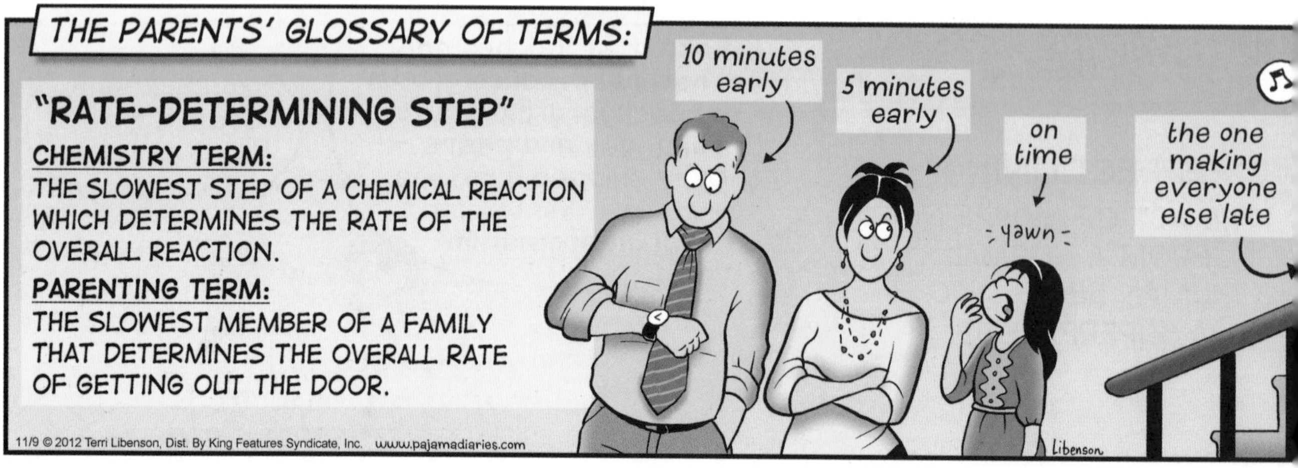
THE PARENTS' GLOSSARY OF TERMS:
"RATE-DETERMINING STEP"
CHEMISTRY TERM:
THE SLOWEST STEP OF A CHEMICAL REACTION WHICH DETERMINES THE RATE OF THE OVERALL REACTION.
PARENTING TERM:
THE SLOWEST MEMBER OF A FAMILY THAT DETERMINES THE OVERALL RATE OF GETTING OUT THE DOOR.
10 minutes early
5 minutes early
on time
:yawn:
the one making everyone else late
Libenson
11/9 © 2012 Terri Libenson, Dist. By King Features Syndicate, Inc. www.pajamadiaries.com

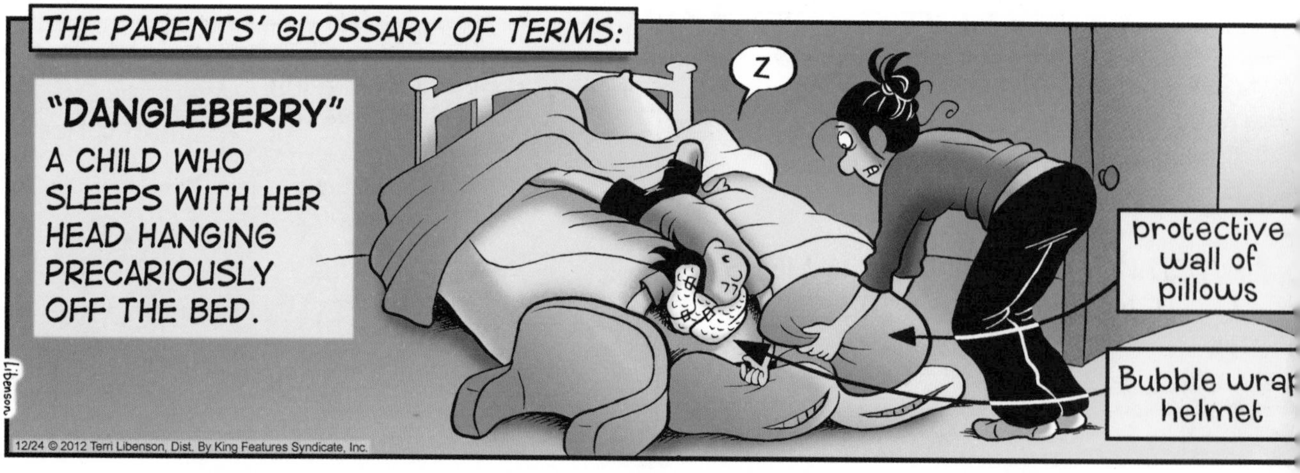
THE PARENTS' GLOSSARY OF TERMS:
"DANGLEBERRY"
A CHILD WHO SLEEPS WITH HER HEAD HANGING PRECARIOUSLY OFF THE BED.
Z
protective wall of pillows
Bubble wrap helmet
Libenson
12/24 © 2012 Terri Libenson, Dist. By King Features Syndicate, Inc.